A MONOGRAPH IN
THE COMPUTER SOCIETY PRESS SERIES

JSP & JSD: THE JACKSON APPROACH
TO SOFTWARE DEVELOPMENT

John R. Cameron

IEEE CATALOG NUMBER EHO206-3
LIBRARY OF CONGRESS NUMBER 83-81873
IEEE COMPUTER SOCIETY ORDER NUMBER 516
ISBN NUMBER O-8186-8516-6

**COMPUTER
SOCIETY
PRESS**

IEEE COMPUTER SOCIETY

THE INSTITUTE OF ELECTRICAL AND ELECTRONICS ENGINEERS, INC.

Published by IEEE Computer Society Press
1109 Spring Street
Suite 300
Silver Spring, MD 20910

IEEE Catalog Number EHO206-3
Library of Congress Number 83-81873
IEEE Computer Society Order Number 516
ISBN 0-8186-8516-6 (casebound)
ISBN 0-8186-4516-4 (microfiche)

Order from: IEEE Computer Society   IEEE Service Center
Post Office Box 80452   445 Hoes Lane
Worldway Postal Center   Piscataway, NJ 08854
Los Angeles, CA 90080

 The Institute of Electrical and Electronics Engineers, Inc.

Acknowledgements

I learned most of the important ideas in this book from Michael Jackson. Some of them are his own. In the case of others he has been responsible for understanding their significance in the more practical world of software development. In 1977, when I joined Michael Jackson Systems Limited (MJSL), JSP was fully developed and some of the framework of JSD was in place. The subsequent development of JSD has been (and still is) a cooperative effort.

Most of the examples came to us from our customers as "challenge" problems. I developed solutions and eventually used them as part of MJSL course material. Other people in MJSL also worked on the material reproduced here, including Andrew Farncombe, John Clough, and Ashley McNeile. Gene Lowrimore supplied the solution to the problem of Integration Using Simpson's Rule.

Thanks are due to many people at Bell Laboratories, particularly to Dave Bergland, in whose department I spent a mini-sabbatical writing this book, and to Pamela Zave, who read an early draft of the book and made many valuable suggestions. Jack Holm, Tom Emerson, and Rich Thompson also made helpful comments.

International Computers Limited kindly gave permission to reprint an article from their technical journal, "Structured Programming in Interrupt-Driven Routines".

At a crucial stage in writing the text my wife Denise joined me rather than beat me and copy edited the draft manuscript.

Finally, I would like to thank the many people who have attended our courses and through their comments and criticisms have helped in the development of our ideas. Particularly I think those who went back from the courses, persuaded their colleagues, cajoled their managers and made the methods work in practice. To mention names is unfair to many others, but Hans Nageli, Dave Clenshaw, Bruce Oakley, and Jackie Kathirasoo have all, at various times and in various ways, been a great help. If JSD stands the test of time, they will have made a significant contribution to software engineering.

Table of Contents

PART ONE

INTRODUCTION

Chapter 1.1 Guide to This Tutorial Text

1.1.1 Aims of the Book

The aim of this book is to describe JSP and JSD, two closely related methods of developing, respectively, computer programs and computer-based systems.

JSP (an acronym for Jackson Structured Programming) is a method of program design. JSP was developed between 1972 and 1974 by Michael Jackson and has been fairly widely promulgated, particularly in Europe, where a number of large and important organisations use it as a standard.

JSD (an acronym for Jackson System Development) covers the complete technical development of a wide class of systems, from an initial statement of need through to their final implementation and subsequent maintenance. JSD is a superset of JSP. JSD was developed by Michael Jackson and the author from 1978 to 1981, when public courses were first presented. Several commercial organisations have started to use the method successfully to develop their systems. The framework and much of the detail of JSD are solidly defined, but there is room for refinement and further development in a number of important areas.

Some particular aims, in roughly decreasing order of importance are:

1. To illustrate the methods by a range of examples of reasonable size and complexity. None of the case studies in Parts Three and Five are published elsewhere, nor are any comparable JSP or JSD examples.

2. To give for some of the examples a blow-by-blow account of the developer's thinking as the solution is built up. In most cases a course solution has been reprinted directly in the text, followed by comments that give extra explanation and discussion of the solution.

3. To include (in Chapters 2.4 and 4.2) concise reference descriptions of the methods.

4. Generally to supplement the two main published descriptions, Jackson [1] and [2].

5. To outline the methodological arguments behind the methods. JSD is not based on stepwise refinement or top-down design, nor does a JSD development start either by building a functional specification or a data model. The reasons why not are fuel for the debate on development methods that is surely necessary if we are ever to move towards a consensus.

6. To try to correct some common misconceptions about JSP. (The following are the correct statements, not the misconceptions.)

    a. JSP is not particularly oriented towards batch programming or to COBOL.

    b. JSP data structures are imposed on data in the context of a particular problem and are not inherent in the data itself or the way it is stored. (See particularly Section 2.2.4.)

    c. The program structure must be developed very exactly and the allocation of operations enforces a check on the program structure.

    d. Program inversion is a technique of very wide application, particularly in the design of variable state subroutines. (See particularly Sections 2.3.3 and 2.4.2.)

7. To help make the study of method a little more respectable. There is a trend in computer science, accentuated by the insecurity of a new academic discipline, toward viewing anything nonmathematical as suspect. Salvation is sought through formality, and only through formality. However, accurate intuition is necessary for a successful formalisation in any discipline. Misdirected, a formalisation will be dull and useless (unless it has some intrinsic mathematical interest). The author believes that the direct, though informal, assault on the software problem by analysing methods of development is also valuable. The direct payoff is that a clear, well-defined method will make software cheaper, more reliable, and more maintainable. The indirect payoff is that there will be a clearer intuition about what needs to be formalised.

1.1.2 Who the Book Is For

The book is for everyone technically involved in developing software. It is for system analysts; system designers and programmers; for teachers of analysis, design, and programming; and for managers technically responsible for software development.

The book should be of special interest to two categories of people: the academic who wants to present a course on systematic methods of analysis and design, and the technical manager in an organisation who has been charged with investigating ways of improving software quality and productivity.

1.1.3 Contents and Organisation

The book has six parts: An introduction on method in software development in general, two parts on JSP, two on JSD, and a final part on the problems of introducing software methods into organisations. For each of JSP and JSD, the first of the two parts (Parts Two and Four) introduces and motivates the method, using small examples for illustration. The second of the two parts (Parts Three and Five) each describes the use of the method to solve some case studies.

The size of systems defeats our best intentions of illustrating the methods by realistic examples. For JSP, this possibility is approached by the problems in Part Three; for JSD, it cannot, at least not without devoting almost the whole of the book to one system. Nevertheless, the two case studies in Part Five have been chosen to give as good an idea as possible of the flavour of a JSD development, and they are from sufficiently separate application areas to give an idea of JSD's range.

The examples and case studies demand more than just passive attention. The reader will not be able to follow the discussion of the development of a solution, of the wrong paths and the reasonable alternatives, and of the consequences of different assumptions and decisions unless he has invested enough effort to come to grips with the detail of the problem. A discussion of a solution is like the annotations to a game of chess. You cannot expect to understand the annotations unless you play through the game.

These methods are meant to be used for real systems and not just in the classroom. Experience has shown that even after a technical problem in software development is solved, human problems remain. A profession that, more than most, has changed the working practices of others is often very reluctant to change its own. Part Six is a discussion of the nontechnical issues surrounding the adoption and use of JSP and JSD.

Many sections of the text are relatively self-contained. Here is some more specific advice on the chapters that may be omitted or read in a different order.

If you are interested in a general description of the methods, without getting involved too much with examples, you should read Chapter 1.3; Chapters 2.1 and 2.2; and Chapters 4.1, 4.2, and 4.5.

For more insight into JSP, read Chapters 2.3 and 2.4 lightly, and then read Chapters 2.5 and 2.6.

For more insight into JSD, read Chapter 4.3 lightly and Chapter 5.1.

Like many introductions, the rest of Part One may be read last instead of first.

Part Six may also be read independently.

If you are interested in the arguments behind the the JSP and JSD approach, read Chapters 1.2, 2.2, 2.5, and 4.5.

Chapter 1.2   Method in Software Development

1.2.1 Method and Methodology

Unfortunately, the words "method" and "methodology" are used interchangeably in computer science and software engineering. No distinction is made between "method", meaning "a process or procedure for attaining an object", and "methodology", meaning "the study or science of method". The cause (and to some extent the effect) of this lack of discrimination is the lack of work that has been done in the area of method and methodology in software development.

The limiting case of a method is a completely precise algorithm. One way to start programmers thinking about method is to get them to write a simple program, ask them how they did it, and then ask them to write a program to do what they have just done. The limiting case of a precise algorithm is unattainable, but it helps clarify the direction in which we are heading. A more realistic aim for a method of software development is to achieve a decomposition of the development task into a number of well-defined steps that the developer can take with some confidence that they are leading to a satisfactory solution. Anything less than this does not deserve to be called a method.

At each step of the method, a number of decisions will be made about the system or program that is being developed. A method will imply and indeed be characterised by the ordering and organisation of the decisions that make up the development.

We are interpreting the word "decision" in a wide sense. A decision may simply be an explicit statement of a fact about the subject matter of the system. The following are all examples of decisions:

to define a certain abstract data type,

to settle on a screen format,

to decide that no customer of the bank may have more than one checking account,

to decide that an account must be opened before any transactions are allowed,

to decide that data will be stored on an indexed sequential file,

to decide that the file will be updated on-line,

to specify a database organisation,

to write down a loop invariant,

to decide that a telephone user must replace the handset when he is given a busy tone before he can make another call,

to declare a local variable of a given type, and

to decompose a system function into three parts.

The entire development task consists of making decisions in this wide sense. A method organises the development by ordering and organising the decisions.

One principle of methodology is concerned with decision dependency: if decision Y depends on the outcome of decision X, then X should precede Y.

The principle supports, for example, the separation of specification decisions from implementation decisions. How a specification is fitted into a hardware/software environment obviously depends on what the specification is.

Often we are forced to make decisions prematurely and to accept the risk that this entails. We would argue that the natural decision order should still be respected. A specification should be written as if the implementation is not known, even though the hardware is already selected and the installation is already committed to a particular database management system. These implementation decisions are metaphorically put in a box that is not to be opened until the specification is finished.

Repeatability is another principle of methodology: two developers faced with similar situations ought to follow similar paths.

A methodologist refines a method by analysing situations in which there seems to be a choice of direction. He will try

(1) to show that one direction is superior to another and state the reasons in a general enough manner to become part of his method, or

(2) to show that the two directions are in fact equivalent, or

(3) to show that the two directions are really different and clarify the nature of the decision that must be made between them.

The principle of repeatability can be stated in another way. If a less talented developer (or a good developer having a bad day) is able to make poor decisions, and there is nothing in his approach that forces him to recognise that the decisions are bad, then his approach is not yet methodical enough.

We are not aiming for a total ordering of development decisions. Indeed, that would be rather distressing, for it would imply that two people could not work in parallel on the same software project. Having a group of people cooperating on a project implies a decision structure in which disjoint sets of decisions are independent one from another and can be made in parallel. Such independence cannot be imposed where it doesn't exist. A poor decomposition leads to integration or system testing problems and to the observation that, for some jobs, one programmer will take one month, but two programmers will take two months.

Expectations* of method in software development have been and are very low. People have not looked hard for methods because they did not really believe methods were possible. The difference between knowing a programming language well and being able to program well is widely understood; the idea that good programming practice can be stated more formally as a method is not.

1.2.2 Method and Language

Just as it is important to distinguish method from methodology, so also it is helpful to distinguish method from the notations and languages a method uses. Much of what is written about "methodology" is actually about notation or language and assumes something approximating to a hierarchical top-down approach to method.

Both JSP and JSD contain some formal notations and, therefore, at various points in the respective methods, the developer is told exactly what language to use to express something. At other places in the method, the developer is told "List operations from the programming language you are going to use" or "Express this requirement in the database query language if you are going to use one". In this way, the methods can be language-independent, in the sense that the steps that have to be followed are the same for any language, even though the results of following the steps using different languages will be different. This also means that the results of a method of specification can be precise, without implying the use of a single specification language.

The importance of the whole issue of programming languages is affected. Why do people say, for example, "What a crime it is that computers used in schools run BASIC only, rather than Pascal, and that children therefore learn to think about programming in such a poor

way"? Because, no doubt rightly, they see that without any guidance over programming method, the habits of thought likely to be formed by using BASIC are worse than those likely to be formed by using Pascal. However, Pascal, by itself, will not make a good programmer, any more than BASIC forces one to program badly. The Pascal programmer needs a method too; if his thought patterns are channelled by a good method, then using BASIC will not prove much of a handicap. The crime, if there is a crime, is that programming languages are taught without an accompanying method of using them.

We would argue that the issue of method takes precedence over the issue of language. One of the main factors in comparing languages is the ease with which they fit your accepted programming method. This is the underlying reason for preferring Pascal to BASIC, even though the method of using Pascal is not necessarily well defined.

This procedure is soon put to the test. Program inversion is an instance in JSP in which the correct use of the method is relatively awkward in most of the conventionally available languages, including Pascal. (Program inversion is introduced and illustrated in Section 2.3.3. Briefly, a coding convention full of ugly GOTOs has to be adopted, because the program has to be cast in a form with a suspend-and-resume mechanism, in which the resume points may be in the middle of iterations and selections.) There is a conflict, essentially between good design and ugly code as opposed to bad design and more elegant code. We argue in Sections 2.3.3, 2.4.2, and 3.3 that the coding or language issue is less important than the design issue and that method should dominate language in that a construct or expression that is methodologically sound should not be avoided because it is awkward to express in a particular language. The extra awkwardness of using BASIC rather than Pascal for JSP programming is probably about the same as the awkwardness of using Pascal to do program inversion. Both are unwelcome, but neither is that serious.

1.2.3 The Disadvantages of Stepwise Refinement

The charge against stepwise refinement is that although it is excellent for describing known solutions, it is inadequate for developing solutions that are not already known.

Textbook writers, among others, often blur the distinction between effective description and effective development and seem under the illusion that the terms are synonymous. Significantly, mathematical textbook authors are not under the equivalent illusion that their orderly description of definitions, lemmas, proofs, and counterexamples bears any relationship to the way the subject was originally developed.

---

*We don't mean here the expectations of the people buying a structured methodology. We mean the expectations of people searching for decompositions of the development task other than simply by decomposing the problem.

In Jackson (3) the small problem of printing, in order, the prime numbers less than 1000 is used to illustrate this distinction. Three possible refinements are given:

```
begin
        generate table of primes;
        print table of primes
end
or:
for n:=2 step 1 until 1000
        if n is prime then print n fi;
or:
begin
    n:=2;
    while n < =1000
            do
                print n;
                generate next prime n
            od
end
```

It is argued that if you know nothing at all about the problem all three refinements look plausible. The choice between them can only be made if the problem is more or less completely solved. The description of a known solution may proceed. The development of a new solution cannot, because the only basis for making the choice is, in effect, the invention of the complete solution.

The top-down developer actually does most of the development by experience and intuition in his head before he starts to write anything down. That's why the best take a long time to start writing.

Let us now consider the issue from a methodological point of view. The following statements refer to the first decision of the development. However, stepwise refinement is a recursive method* and the statements apply to every other decision as well, because every decision is the first decision in the development of some subsystem.

The structure of decision dependency in stepwise refinement is hierarchical; every subsequent decision depends on the first decision. Obviously, then, the first decision is very critical; if it is less than perfect everything else is affected. Yet in fact it is very error prone and demands considerable foresight and experience of the designer. A bad first decision may never be discovered if different people do the subsequent development. Even if it is detected, the discovery is liable to come after so many refinements that recovery will be practically impossible. Too many other decisions are affected.

The reader will not now be surprised to learn that JSP and JSD are based on composition and not on decomposition. In JSP data structures are drawn separately and then merged to form the skeleton of the program. Then executable operations and finally conditions are added to the skeleton. Even in developing one data structure, which is of course a hierarchical tree, the process is not necessarily top-down. The task is essentially to find a suitable connection of the root to the leaves, which are fairly well understood from the outset. JSD specifications are also developed by composition, by adding processes to a network and by elaborating existing processes in the network. More new processes may be added during the implementation phase, which involves the transformation rather than the refinement of the processes in the specification.

The steps of the method contribute to the finished program in the same way as successive colours are added in colour printing: at each step another aspect of the whole is considered, not another part of the whole. The distinction between approaches based on composition and approaches based on decomposition is perhaps the most fundamental the software methodologist has to make.

---

*To apply stepwise refinement to a problem, decompose the problem into parts and apply stepwise refinement to any part that is not trivially simple.

Chapter 1.3   JSP and JSD: Overview and Scope

1.3.1 Scope of JSP and JSD

JSP is a method of designing programs, or (almost synonymously) of developing algorithms, or (again synonymously) of formalising specifications. JSP can be applied to almost any non-mathematical programming. The slightly fuzzy limits of JSP's usefulness are explored in Chapter 2.5.

The starting point of a JSP development is a no doubt incomplete and imprecise specification of the problem in terms of inputs and outputs. The endpoint is essentially the completed program.

JSD addresses the technical aspects of almost the whole life cycle of systems whose subject matter is strongly sequential. Usually time is the important sequential dimension. The phrase "strongly sequential subject matter" then means that the system is concerned with objects and entities whose behaviour and state vary over time. An order-processing system is concerned with orders, stock, customers and suppliers, all of which have states that vary in time as they participate in events, either actively or passively. So do an account in a financial system, an aircraft in an air traffic control system, an employee in a payroll system, a telephone in a switching system and a resource in an operating system. In a system without a time-varying subject matter the main data, whether held in files, control blocks, tree structures or a database, is never updated.

Project selection and business justification are not part of JSD. The starting point is an extremely rough specification, what is often called a statement of need. The first major phase is concerned with analysing the subject matter as a step towards building the specification. The final phase delivers the code, the JCL and the operator instructions of the finished system. Maintenance is addressed mainly by iterating over appropriate JSD phases. (See Section 4.4.5.) Certain specialised techniques, for example physical database design, are fitted at the appropriate place in the JSD framework. The management of projects is affected by JSD but is not specifically addressed.

1.3.2 Relationship between JSP and JSD

Both methods start by describing the subject matter of the program or system in question. The description is in terms of sequential processes that collectively are called "the model".

The essential difference between JSP and JSD is in the nature of their subject matter. For JSP, the subject matter is on a smaller scale and consists of input and output data streams. The model consists of the data structure diagrams (see Chapter 2.1) that describe these data streams. Because the problem is relatively small-scale, the basic JSP assumption is that the several data structures can be composed into a single process structure. The cases for which the composition is not possible are classified as "structure clashes", and prescriptions are given for dealing with each type.

JSP breaks down for larger problems because of two reasons: there are too many structure clashes for the method to work and the input and output data streams are not already defined for large problems.

For JSD, the subject matter is on a much larger scale, and at least for applications systems, consists entirely of noncomputer objects and events. The model in JSD consists of a set of disconnected processes that describe the time-ordered behaviour of the entities of interest. The basic JSD assumption throughout the specification phase is that processes should be kept separate unless there is some sequential relationship that will be lost unless they are combined.

A JSP specification (effectively the program itself) is completed by elaborating the single process resulting from composition of the data structures. In JSD the specification is completed by adding many new processes as well as elaborating the processes that make up the model.

In both cases the specification is executable, and no implementation phase is absolutely necessary. For the smaller problems addressed by JSP, this is more or less true. For the larger problems addressed by JSD, a direct implementation of the specification would be unacceptably inefficient. An implementation phase is necessary to transform the specification into a more efficient form. As we will see, the transformations we have in mind are in principle mechanisable, though the choice of transformation is almost certainly not.

JSD is an extension of JSP in that the same ideas are applied to a larger class of problems. Everything in JSP appears somewhere in JSD. However, JSD is not exactly a front end to JSP in that it does not tackle, say, requirements and design, leaving a programming phase to JSP. In applying the same set of ideas to systems, the systems development life cycle is rearranged. The traditional development life cycle (approximately requirements, design, and programming) differs in a number of important respects from the JSD life cycle of model, function, and implementation. JSP permeates the whole of JSD, not just the final phase.

Sometimes in a JSD development, particularly in the function phase, a subproblem is separated, to which JSP is directly applicable.

The differences in the life cycles will become clearer as JSD is described in Part Four. There is also some discussion of the implications of the different life cycles in Chapter 6.2.

In neither JSP nor JSD do we think of the system as a function from inputs to outputs. Instead the model is

the fundamental structure of the system (because it preserves in the software the sequential structure of the subject matter) on to which functions are superimposed. In JSD especially we can view the model processes simply as the domain of the fun

In neither JSP nor JSD do we think of the system as a function from inputs to outputs. Instead the model is the fundamental structure of the system (because it preserves in the software the sequential structure of the subject matter) on to which functions are superimposed. In JSD especially we can view the model processes simply as the domain of the functions that produce the outputs. In this we are generalising certain ideas from simulation systems, where the separation of model and function is already well accepted.

PART TWO

JSP PRINCIPLES
AND SMALL EXAMPLES

Chapter 2.0   Introduction to Part Two

Chapter 2.1 introduces the basic JSP method by an illustration of a very simple example, the Stores Movement Problem.

Chapter 2.2 discusses some of the ideas underlying the basic method.

Chapter 2.3 uses three versions of POP, an on-line conversational program, to illustrate the basic method and more advanced techniques of error processing, backtracking, and program inversion.

Chapter 2.4 contains the JSP Handbook, a succinct statement of JSP that is normally printed as a pocket-sized booklet. There is also some elaboration of the Handbook's detailed prescriptions. Note that backtracking and inversion are discussed in Section 2.4.2 as well as in Chapter 2.3.

Chapter 2.5 explores further the ideas behind JSP: the emphasis on static as opposed to dynamic aspects of programs and specifications, a comparison with a func-tional approach to programming, the limits of applicability of JSP, and the use of JSP with applicative languages.

Six reprints are at the end of Part Two. "Constructive Methods of Program Design" is an academically oriented description of JSP. "The Importance of Program Structure" and "Program Inversion and Its Consequences" are two sections of an introductory technical brochure. "Getting It Wrong" is a story, referred to in Chapter 2.2, that emphasises the importance of correct program structure. "On-line Program Dismemberment" describes the dismemberment of POP. This reprint is referred to in Section 2.4.2. "Integration Using Simpson's Rule" is referred to in Section 2.5.3 as an illustration of the application of JSP to mathematical problems. Two other references, Jackson [1] and Ingevladsson [1], are particularly worth mentioning. They are a source of backup material and further explanation of JSP.

EHO206-3/83/0000/0013$01.00 © 1983 IEEE   13

Chapter 2.1   The Basic JSP Method

2.1.1 JSP Outline

The basic JSP method has four steps. The first two build up the structure of the program, that is, they specify the pattern of sequence, selection, and iteration components that define the possible paths of control flow. The last two complete the program, at the same time checking that the program structure is correct for the problem. This checking of the program structure is very important. It has not been well understood, yet it is central to the method. In outline, the four steps are these:

(1) Draw structure diagrams to describe each of the data streams input to or output from the program.

(2) Merge these data structure diagrams into a single structure diagram, the program structure diagram.

(3) Make a suitable list of executable operations from the programming language to be used. Allocate the operations one by one into the program structure. Any difficulty here shows that the program structure is not correct.

(4) Convert the program from the diagrammatic representation into a textual form and add conditions to iteration and selection components.

You will notice that this explanation of JSP is proceeding in a top-down manner. JSP was not developed in this way, but now that it is well understood, a top-down approach to description and explanation is perfectly appropriate.

2.1.2 The Method in More Detail

You may prefer to look at the Stores Movement Problem example (Section 2.1.3) before reading this section, or you may skip this section entirely and refer to it as you go over the samples in the JSP part of the book. It consists of a miscellany of comments on, explanation of, and more detailed prescription of each of the four steps of the method.

Data Structures. One data structure is drawn for each serial data stream in the problem. A data structure (in the JSP sense) is a structure diagram. Structure diagrams are tree structures built by composing the three basic constructs of structured programming with the use of the notation described below. (Structure text is an equivalent formal pseudocode sometimes used in step four of JSP.)

Structure Diagram	Structure Text	
| | ```
A seq
  B;
  C;
  D;
A end
``` | Sequence: A consists of one B, followed by one C, followed by one D. A is a sequence of B, C and D. |
| | ```
A iter
  B;
A end
``` | Iteration: A consists of zero or more whole Bs. A is an iteration of B. |
| | ```
A select
  B;
A alt
  C;
A alt
  D;
A end
``` | Selection: A consists of either one B, or one C, or one D. A is a selection of B, C or D. |

Normally we use iteration in data structure diagrams (and thus also later in the structure text). For inherently recursive problems, structure diagrams containing recursive components are needed. An example is given in Chapter 3.3.

The top-level component, or root, of a data structure is the name of the complete data stream. The elementary components of the structure are records of the data stream, that is, the units that are accessed in a single I/O operation.

You have to solve a few problems using JSP to appreciate the flavour of this, the most difficult and time-consuming step of the whole method. A data structure must capture all the relationships between data components which are relevant to and which have meaning for the particular problem. If a particular group of data items is important, then that group must appear in the data structure; and if a pair of records is relevant, then a pair must appear; if a distinction is relevant between whole sets of components, then the distinction must be made at that level in the data structure. Otherwise there will be some operation that cannot be allocated properly at the third step of the method. JSP beginners find it hard to draw data structures for even simple problems that will survive the later checkpoints in the method, and even experienced JSP programmers take several attempts to get a structure right.

Portions of this Chapter are excerpted from previously unpublished Michael Jackson Systems Limited (MJSL) internal documents with permission from MJSL.
```

JSP tightens the iteration that is probably inevitable in software development. Instead of discovering an error during testing, a JSP programmer determines that something is wrong at one of the checkpoints in the second or third step. When he is able to pass these checkpoints, his confidence is very high that the design is correct.

Programmers new to JSP can find it unnerving that they have so much to do before they reach the reassuring familiarity of the coding pad or terminal. If they persevere, though, they soon realise that a difficulty concerning a data structure reflects a real difficulty that must be resolved sooner or later and that the data structures are a context for resolving the difficulty that is free of many extraneous details of the problem.

Program Structure. To merge the data structures, first define correspondences between components of different data structures. Two components correspond if

there is the same number of each component in any one program instance;

there is some functional relationship between the components; and

the functional relationship is a one-to-one relationship between pairs of instances of the components, the pairs occurring in the same order.

Corresponding components must form a single component in the program structure. The program structure is a supertree of the data structures in the sense that it contains each of the data structures.

If the data structures are wrong, then probably it will not be possible to define enough correspondences to merge the structures into a supertree. This is an important checkpoint in the method, second only in importance to the ease of allocating operations in the third step. In practice, a programmer will often attempt one of the data structures, next try one of the others, and then redraw the first, bearing in mind the components that seemed important in the second structure. He knows that he has to view the two files in a compatible enough way for their structures to be composed. (Sometimes, there is something about the problem that makes this impossible, in which case the problem needs more than one program structure. These situations are called "structure clashes", and they will be discussed later.)

Any data structure can be recovered from the program structure by deleting irrelevant components and applying some simple rules to remove or collapse over-elaborate parts of what remains. Verifying that the program structure is a supertree of the data structures is one of the checkpoints in the method, but it is not an important one. In practice, the composition of data structures is easy, if it can be done at all, and mistakes are seldom made.

Listing and Allocating Operations. The use of JSP with non-procedural languages is briefly discussed in Chapter 2.5. In this discussion of the latter two steps of the method, we assume a procedural language. The operations to be listed are the executable operations of the programming language that is to be used. JSP is not a programming language; it is a method for developing programs. Thus although any example of the use of JSP will necessarily use some language or other, JSP itself is language-independent.

The listed operations are assignment operations and I/O operations. No operations concerned with flow of control are included. The program structure already specifies the flow of control in the program.

A shorthand form of the operation can be used. Often, a simple sequence of operations may be included as a single element in the list. However, there must be no control structures other than a simple sequence hidden in an operation, unless a bottom-up component (see below) has previously been defined.

The list of operations is made by working backwards from the output to the input. First, list the I/O operations on the output streams; next the operations that set up the output records; then, the operations that do the calculations to set up the values that must appear in the output records; and so on until you reach the input I/O operations that supply the values used in the calculations.

An operation is allocated into the program structure by asking two questions.

(1) How often must this operation be executed? Once per *X*.

Here the "*X*" stands for the name of a program component in the program structure. The answer can be of the form "once per *X* and once per *Y* and once per *Z*" where *X* and *Y* and *Z* are all components of the program structure.

(2) Where, in the sequence of components that are already part of *X*, should the operation be placed?

When an operation is added to the structure, the diagram ought still to satisfy the syntactic rules. To ensure this is so, extra components have to be added when operations are allocated to components that are not already sequences. Examples of this are given later. The extra components have no significance, except that they keep the diagrams legal.

Operations become the elementary components in a diagram. Normally, when all operations have been allocated, they will be the only elementary components. The skeleton of the program structure is fleshed out into a program.

The question "how often must this operation be executed" is crucial to the JSP method. There must be a component (or components) in the program structure with which the operation is naturally associated. If there is any difficulty in naming the appropriate component, even any hesitation, then the program structure is not correct. This is the most important checkpoint in the basic JSP method. When experienced JSP programmers draw data structures, they are trying to name and express the relationships between components relevant to the problem. Looking ahead to the later steps of the method, they have to find the components to which operations can be allocated. Usually, the operation that causes the difficulty will give a clue about what is wrong with the program structure and the sort of change that must be made.

The read operation is allocated according to a special rule, normally a single read-ahead scheme, to ease the recognition (parsing) problem, that is, the evaluation of the conditions on selections and iterations. The single read-ahead rule is not the only read allocation rule. Sometimes a multiple read-ahead scheme is adopted to solve a more difficult recognition problem. Sometimes the different read operations in, say, a database environment, or the mutual I/O constraints between two data streams as in, say, on-line conversational problems, force the adoption of some variant of the rule. This point is elaborated in Chapter 2.4.

Some operations in the list will be added not for the purpose of calculating output but purely to help in evaluating conditions. Chapter 2.4 has some comments on the restrictions JSP places on the use of local variables.

The programming language can be enhanced by some bottom-up design. Bottom-up components are conceptually an extension of the program language. They must be defined as clearly and precisely as any other operation in the language. They should be used for components that are of general utility in the problem area and should not be used simply to take advantage of accidental commonality. Clear-cut examples are matrix-handling routines for a language that doesn't have them, string-handling routines, date-checking routines, and table-look-up and other table-handling routines. Bottom-up components define more complex data objects as well as more complex functional objects. The existence of a bottom-up component affects the necessary level of detail in a data structure.

Historical note. Early software developments were often based on successive definition of ever more powerful bottom-up components. For example, first you made an add component, next a multiplier; then, an exponentiation component; finally, components to evaluate integrals; and pretty soon you could do nuclear physics.

For a long time people thought you could follow a similar path through adder, multiplier, monthly pay calculator, and then payroll system. There is plenty of experimental evidence to show this is not true. The reason is that the subject matter of the computation in mathematical systems (at least of the sort referred to above) is functions and expressions and the like. These functions are defined in terms of other, more standard functions in a hierarchical manner. Therefore, it is no surprise that a hierarchical mode of development through successively more powerful, though less standard, functions should prove successful. However, the world of the payroll system is not hierarchical, and so a purely hierarchical view of the system and its development is not appropriate. When JSD is described in Part Four, we shall see that the world of the payroll system can best be described in terms of a set of disconnected sequential processes.

Conditions and Program Text. The effect of the single read-ahead rule is to make a record available at all times in the program for the evaluation of conditions. If there is no recognition problem that needs more than one record read ahead, writing these conditions is all that remains to complete the program. If there is such a recognition difficulty, then we will have to use either multiple read-ahead or the backtracking technique. These are described later in Chapters 2.3 and 2.4.

In this step, a textual form of the program is written for the first time. Structure text, a formalised pseudocode, can be used as an intermediate step between the program structure with operations allocated and the final code. It is valuable when there is a significant backtracking problem or if the program is to be inverted, if a low-level language is being used, or if the programmer is a beginner. Otherwise the program can be coded directly in a high-level language. Inversion is described in Section 2.3.3. Comments are also made on inversion in Chapters 2.4 and 3.3.

Commercial programmers are often surprised, when they first transcribe a structure diagram with operations allocated into structure text, at how close to a finished program they were. They take some time to get used to the idea that JSP diagramming is really programming. Of course many diagrams in manuals and methodologies are imprecise and ill-defined. People won't be persuaded that coding should be delayed in favour of design if the only design tools supplied are badly defined. They will still think, quite reasonably, that the real (i.e. precise) work doesn't begin until coding, and the sooner they get on with that, the better.

Each input record has three fields: MOVEMENTID, MOVEMENTTYPE, and MOVEMENTQTY. For this trivial example, we assume that there are no input errors.

Implementation. Structure text (pseudo-code) has the advantage of clearly delineating the boundary between design/specification and implementation. It is likely to be omitted in those cases for which the obvious and direct implementation is in a high-level language.

Implementation issues may include separate compilation of program components, optimisations of the kind discussed in Jackson[1], program inversion, program dismemberment (Chapter 2.4), exploitation of commonality, and so on.

2.1.3 The Stores Movement Problem

The Stores Movement Problem is a trivial problem, but it can be used to illustrate the basic JSP method. First, read the problem statement and the JSP solution that follows. If you are conscientious, you might try the problem before reading the solution.

Specification of the Stores Movement Problem. The Stores section in a factory issues and receives parts. Each issue and each receipt is recorded on a punch card. The card contains the part number, the movement type ("I" for issue, "R" for receipt), and the quantity. The cards have already been written to a data set and sorted into ascending sequence by part number. The data set is called SMF (Sorted Movements File).

The program to be designed has to produce a simple summary report, SUMMY, showing the net movement of each part. The format of the summary is:

STORES MOVEMENTS SUMMARY

A1736	NET MOVEMENT	−450
A1932	NET MOVEMENT	+35
...		
...		
Y4640	NET MOVEMENT	+1845

END OF SUMMARY

In this illustration of the report format, the net movement of part A1736 is −450 units. That is, 450 more units of part A1736 have been issued than received in the period covered by the report. Each net movement line has a similar meaning.

No attention is to be paid to page breaks. There is only one heading line and one footing line, exactly as shown above, even if the report occupies more than one page.

STORES MOVEMENT PROBLEM — Solution

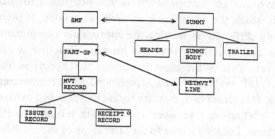

Data Structures With Correspondences

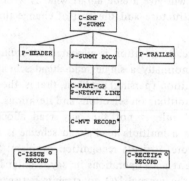

The Program Structure

Operations list

1. open output SUMMY
2. close SUMMY
3. write HEADER
4. write NETMVT LINE
5. write TRAILER

These are the operations which directly produce the output SUMMY file. Now we must list the operations which set up the output records.

6. move "STORES MOVEMENT SUMMARY" to HEADER
7. move PARTGPID to NETMVTLINEID
8. move PARTGPNETMVT to NETMVTLINEQTY
9. move "END OF SUMMARY" to TRAILER

So far so good. Now we have to think about the variables PARTGPID and PARTGPNETMVT. For PARTGPID,

10. move MOVEMENTID to PARTGPID

and then for PARTGPNETMVT

11. move zero to PARTGPNETMVT
12. add MOVEMENTQTY to PARTGPNETMVT
13. subtract MOVEMENTQTY from PARTGPNETMVT

These operations use MOVEMENTID and MOVEMENTQTY, variables accessible directly from the input MOVEMENT RECORD to set up the local variables PARTGPID and PARTGPNETMVT. That's fine but we haven't yet got any operations to access the input MOVEMENT RECORD. We need the operations

14. open input SMF
15. close SMF
16. read SMF

And that completes the operations list.

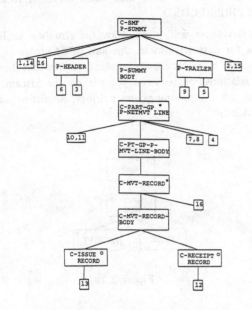

Program Structure With All Operations Allocated.

FINAL STRUCTURE TEXT FOR THE STORES MOVEMENT PROBLEM

```
C-SMF-P-SUMMY  seq
  open output SUMMY; open input SMF; read SMF;
  P-HEADER seq
    move 'STORES MOVEMENT SUMMARY' to HEADER;
    write HEADER;
  P-HEADER end
  P-SUMMY-BODY iter   until eof-SMF
    C-PART-GP-P-NETMVT-LINE seq
      move MOVEMENTID to PARTGPID;
      move zero to PARTGPNETMVT;
      C-PT-GP-P-MVT-LINE-BODY iter   while (not eof-SMF) and
                                           (MOVEMENTID = PARTGPID)
        C-MVT-RECORD seq
          C-MVT-RECORD-BODY  select (MOVEMENTTYPE = 'I')
            subtract MOVEMENTQTY from PARTGPNETMVT;
          C-MVT-RECORD-BODY  alt  (MOVEMENTTYPE = 'R')
            add MOVEMENTQTY to PARTGPNETMVT;
          C-MVT-RECORD-BODY end
          read SMF;
        C-MVT-RECORD end
      C-PT-GP-P-MVT-LINE-BODY end
      move PARTGPID to NETMVTLINEID;
      move PARTGPNETMVT to NETMVTLINEQTY;
      write NETMVTLINE;
    C-PART-GP-P-NETMVT-LINE end
  P-SUMMY-BODY end
  P-TRAILER seq
    move 'END OF SUMMARY' to TRAILER;
    write TRAILER;
  P-TRAILER end
  close SUMMY; close SMF;
C-SMF-P-SUMMY end
```

POSSIBLE COBOL CODING FOR STORES MOVEMENTS PROBLEM

```
ID DIVISION.
...
DATA DIVISION.
...
WORKING-STORAGE SECTION.
...
    02  SMF-EOF  PIC X VALUE SPACE.
      88  SMF-ENDFILE-MARKER VALUE 'E'.
...
PROCEDURE DIVISION.
C-SMF-P-SUMMY-SEQ.
    OPEN OUTPUT SUMMY, INPUT SMF.
    READ SMF AT END MOVE 'E' TO SMF-EOF.
    MOVE 'STORES MOVEMENTS SUMMARY' TO SUMMYHEAD.
    WRITE SUMMYHEAD AFTER ADVANCING TO-HEAD-OF-PAGE.
    PERFORM C-PARTGROUP-P-NETMVTLINE UNTIL SMF-ENDFILE-MARKER.
    MOVE 'END OF SUMMARY' TO SUMMYFOOT.
    WRITE SUMMYFOOT AFTER ADVANCING 1 LINES.
    CLOSE SUMMY, SMF.
C-SMF-P-SUMMY-END.  EXIT PROGRAM.
C-PARTGROUP-P-NETMVTLINE-SEQ.
    MOVE MOVEMENTID TO PARTGROUPID.
    MOVE ZERO TO PARTGROUPNETMVT.
    PERFORM C-MOVEMENT UNTIL ((SMF-ENDFILE-MARKER) OR
                         (MOVEMENTID NOT EQUAL TO PARTGROUPID)).
    MOVE PARTGROUPID TO NETMVTLINEID.
    MOVE PARTGROUPNETMVT TO NETMVTLINEQTY.
    WRITE NETMVTLINE AFTER ADVANCING 1 LINES.
C-PARTGROUP-P-NETMVTLINE-END. NOTE END OF PARTGROUP.
C-MOVEMENT-SEQ.
    IF MOVEMENTTYPE EQUAL TO 'I'
      SUBTRACT MOVEMENTQTY FROM PARTGROUPNETMVT
    ELSE ADD MOVEMENTQTY TO PARTGROUPNETMVT.
    READ SMF AT END MOVE 'E' TO SMF-EOF.
C-MOVEMENT-END.  NOTE END OF MOVEMENT.
```

POSSIBLE PL/I CODING FOR STORES MOVEMENTS PROBLEM

```
CSMF:  PROC OPTIONS(MAIN);
       DCL ... ;
       DCL SMF_EOF BIT(1) INIT('0'B);
       ON ENDFILE(SMF) SMF_EOF = '1'B;
       OPEN FILE(SMF);  OPEN FILE(SUMMY);
       READ FILE(SMF) INTO(MOVEMENT);
       SUMMYHEAD = 'STORES MOVEMENTS SUMMARY';
       WRITE FILE(SUMMY) FROM SUMMYHEAD;
       DO WHILE (SMF_EOF ¬= '1'B);
         PARTGROUPID = MOVEMENTID;
         PARTGROUPNETMVT = 0;
         DO WHILE ((SMF_EOF ¬= '1'B) & (MOVEMENTID = PARTGROUPID));
           IF MOVEMENTTYPE = 'I'
             THEN PARTGROUPNETMVT = PARTGROUPNETMVT - MOVEMENTQTY;
             ELSE PARTGROUPNETMVT = PARTGROUPNETMVT + MOVEMENTQTY;
           READ FILE(SMF) INTO(MOVEMENT);
         END;
         NETMVTLINEID = PARTGROUPID;
         NETMVTLINEQTY = PARTGROUPNETMVT;
         WRITE FILE(SUMMY) FROM NETMVTLINE;
       END;
       SUMMYFOOT = 'END OF SUMMARY';
       WRITE FILE(SUMMY) FROM(SUMMYFOOT);
       CLOSE FILE(SUMMY); CLOSE FILE(SMF);
END CSMF;
```

POSSIBLE FORTRAN CODING FOR STORES MOVEMENT PROBLEM

```
C
C * STORES MOVEMENT PROBLEM.
C
      COMMON / READ / ITYPE, IPART, MVT, IFEOF
C
      CALL RFILE
      WRITE(6,9001)
```

continued...

```
C
C * P-SUMMY-BODY-ITR.
C
 1000  IF(IFEOF .EQ. 2) GOTO 6000
        JPART =     IPART
        ITOTMV=     0
C
C * C-PT-GP-P-MVT-LINE-BODY-ITR.
C
 2000  IF(IFEOF .EQ. 2 .OR. JPART .NE. IPART) GOTO 5000
        IF(ITYPE .EQ. 1HR) GOTO 3000
C
C * THIS IS AN ISSUE.
C
        ITOTMV=      ITOTMV - MVT
        GOTO 4000
C
C * THIS IS A RECEIPT.
C
 3000  ITOTMV=      ITOTMV + MVT
C
C * READ NEXT RECORD.
C
 4000  CALL RFILE
        GOTO 2000
C
C * END OF FILE OR PART NO CHANGE.
C
 5000  WRITE(6,9002) JPART, ITOTMV
        GOTO 1000
C
C * PROGRAM END.
C
 6000  WRITE(6,9003)
        STOP
 9001  FORMAT(1H1,23HSTORES MOVEMENT SUMMARY)
 9002  FORMAT(1X,A6,6X,12HNET MOVEMENT,2X,I6)
 9003  FORMAT(1X,14HEND OF SUMMARY)
        END
        SUBROUTINE RFILE
C
C * READS CARDS AND SETS EOF FLAG: 1=.NOT.EOF; 2=EOF
C
        COMMON / READ / ITYPE, IPART, MVT, IFEOF
        READ(5,9001,END=1000) ITYPE,IPART,MVT
        GOTO 9000
 1000  IFEOF =     2
 9000  RETURN
 9001  FORMAT(A1,A6,I5)
        END

        BLOCK DATA
C
C * INITIALISES VARIABLES HELD IN COMMON
C * INITIALISE IFEOF TO 1.
C
        COMMON / READ / ITYPE, IPART, MVT, IFEOF
C
        DATA IFEOF / 1 /
C
        END
/*
```

Note: The I/O scheme used in this FORTRAN coding assumes each variable will be held in one 36-bit word. Characters read in using "A" format will each occupy 6 bits. One word of storage therefore can hold up to 6 characters.

Comments on the Solution

The solution is deceptive in that two-thirds of the work is described in the first two diagrams of the solution. The crucial observation is that there must be a PARTGP component in the data structure of the SMF input stream. A PART-GP is the set of records that refers to one part, that is, the set of records (necessarily consecutive because of the sorting) with the same PART-NO. Without this component, there will be no correspondence with NETMVTLINE in the output structure, and therefore there will be no reasonable composition of the data structure trees. This component must be in the program structure, otherwise, we could not, for example, allocate the operations

10. move zero to PARTGPNETMVT

4. write NETMVTLINE

in the required trivial way. Both operations must be executed "once per PART".

There is no structure below the level of the record in either data structure diagram. The component ISSUE RECORD is a whole record, not just the issue field, even though it is this field that distinguishes it from the RECEIPT RECORD.

Beginners will often draw the structure in Figure 2.1a for data streams in this and other problems. This structure is almost always wrong; it implies that there are no relationships between records on the stream, that there are no groupings, no pairings, or distinctions of any kind.

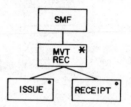

Figure 2.1a

The input data structure reflects the assumption that there are only two movement record types. If there could be a third error type, there would have to be a third part to the MOVEMENT RECORD selection.

The program structure contains within it the two data structures. The prefixes C- and P- in the names of program structure components mean CONSUME- and PRODUCE- and are used to distinguish input and output components. This is simply a naming convention, which you may or may not wish to adopt.

In the operations list, a COBOL-like language is assumed. Don't be put off by this. If you want, make a list in your preferred language, and allocate these operations to the structure.

During the allocation, extra components C-PART-GP-P-MVT-LINE-BODY and C-MVT-RECORD-BODY have been introduced to keep the diagram legal.

The program component names can be retained in the final program code as either labels or comments. This helps the comparison of different parts of the documentation. Often shortened versions of the names are used. (The C- P- can be tiresome.) Often sequence component names are dropped.

The final coding is included to show that the job is finished rather than as an example of elegant coding style.

Overall, the main lessons of this example are

(1) the PART-GP component in the input data structure, and

(2) a simple example of the use of the JSP steps to complete the solution.

Chapter 2.2   Ideas Underlying the Basic Method

2.2.1 Program Structure and Problem Structure

"The structure of a program should be based on the structure of the underlying problem."

The idea that the components recognisable in and relevant to a problem should map directly onto the components of the program is at the heart of JSP. Any object recognisably important in the problem must have a corresponding program component. In the Stores Movement Problem, the PART was the interesting example of such an object. PART therefore appeared in both the data structures, and consequently it appeared in the program structure.

The naming of the intermediate components of data structures is important because these names identify the objects of interest. JSP beginners find this tiresome but, with experience, it becomes a welcome discipline.

These program components have both a beginning and an end, to which functional components can be attached. In the "Getting It Wrong" story, whose main point is to show how intractable programs can be when their structure is wrong, the problem is the lack of a place in the program text corresponding to the beginning of a PART.

In JSP, the structure of the problem constrains the class of acceptable solutions to a very narrow range.

A difficulty in allocating an operation is a sign that some object that is of interest is not yet identified in the program structure. (Remember that at the gross level, JSP first builds a program structure and then finishes the program, at the same time checking to see that the program structure is correct.)

Correct program structure is also important because it makes the subsequent maintenance much easier. A variety of related specifications are related precisely because they refer to the same or nearly the same set of underlying objects. A program whose components map onto these objects will be easier to maintain because it will be obvious which parts of the program remain unchanged, which require change, and in what way. The section on program maintenance in the reprint, "The Importance of Program Structure", describes some simple maintenance on a problem very similar to the Stores Movement Problem.

This JSP idea of correctness is in this respect more stringent than is achieved by a proof of correctness. A program can be proved correct in the mathematical sense, yet it can still have a structure that does not match that of the problem.

Perhaps disadvantage of the recent advances in techniques of program proving is that a program proof has been made to seem a sufficient goal. The argument over whether program proving is attainable in practice has distracted attention from the question of whether it is a sufficient goal in the first place.

These issues are discussed further in Chapter 2.5, which also includes a more precise formulation of the scope of JSP and a comparison with a more functional view of programming.

2.2.2 Static and Dynamic

A program has both static properties that are concerned with its text and dynamic properties that are concerned with its execution. During development, JSP emphasises the static properties and encourages the programmer to think about the data and the program in a static way.

Most programmers are accustomed to thinking of their programs very dynamically. For them, this change of outlook can be difficult and is probably the biggest technical barrier they face in learning JSP.

An input data structure, for example, is a description of the complete input data stream. To draw a data structure, a programmer does not think about the execution properties of a program. He is deciding which static relationships between data components are important in the problem. The data structure will lead to a program structure, which is the framework of the program text, and only indirectly to a description of the program execution. In contrast, a flow chart is a description of a program's execution.

To explain the difference, the following analogy may be helpful. Compare the following two views of a train. In one, the train is moving slowly across a hillside far away from the on-looker and at right angles to his line of sight. The on-looker can see the locomotive at the

Portions of this Chapter are excerpted from previously unpublished Michael Jackson Systems Limited (MJSL) internal documents with permission from MJSL.

front of the train, the caboose at the back, and the arrangement of the various types of railcars in between. In the second, the on-looker is right beside (or even underneath) the track, and the train is thundering past. The on-looker can see only one railcar at a time. The latter is the traditional programmer's view of his input data. He thinks of one record at a time; he asks himself what needs to be done with the next record. His view of the data is very dynamic.

The first view is more like that of the JSP programmer. He views the whole data stream, describing in a data structure the groups, the pairings, and the other relationships between the records.

A comfortable understanding of the null component is a good test of whether a programmer is thinking in a static way. Dynamically, some record is always the next record, even if it is only the end-of-stream marker. You can only think of a null component, meaning nothing, if you can think statically of a gap between other components, a gap in which something may or may not be present.

The following exercise is a simple test of understanding of the null component.

Exercise. How are each of the following two data streams interpreted by the structures GA and CB in Figures 2.2a and 2.2b?

T5, T2, T2, T2, T3, eof.
T2, T2, T2, T4, eof.

A NOT T1 record is any record that is not type 1, but a null component means nothing, a gap.

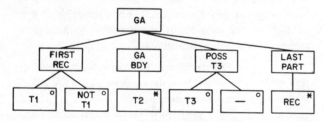

Figure 2.2a

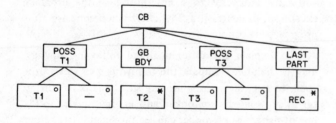

Figure 2.2b

Answer.

GA

    T5 is NOT T1 in FIRST REC
    3 T2s in GA BDY
    T3 in POSS T3
    no RECs in LAST PART

    T2 is NOT T1 in FIRST REC
    2 T2s in GA BDY
    POSS T3 is NULL
    T4 is 1 REC in LAST PART

CB

    POSS T1 is NULL
    no records in GB BDY
    POSS T3 is NULL
    5 RECs in LAST PART

    POSS T1 is NULL
    3 T2s in GB BDY
    POSS T3 is NULL
    T4 is 1 REC in LAST PART

A recognition difficulty is a condition that cannot be evaluated on the basis of one record read ahead. The static/dynamic distinction is particularly important in problems that involve recognition difficulties. There can be a real mental block over describing a group of records as a selection of a good group that contains no errors, and of a bad group that contains some errors, or over describing a table as a selection of a table in which you will find the element you are looking for and of a table in which you will not find the element. The description of data may be exactly appropriate. The inhibition is because, later, the selection cannot be evaluated on the basis of only a single record read ahead.

Approximately, the first three steps of the method are concerned with static issues, and the fourth step, which handles conditions and recognition difficulties, is concerned with dynamic properties.

If you look over someone's shoulder while he is allocating operations and see a diagram like Figure 2.2c, you will know that he is thinking dynamically and not allocating operations in the right way. He is thinking about how the program will execute. He is going round the diagram, selecting suitable operations from the list to add to the diagram. This can only be done by thinking about the execution of the program and by asking, "Having reached this point in the text, what should the program do?" We can tell he is doing this because all the operations allocated are in the top left of the diagram. He should be going down the list, allocating each operation in turn to the structure, asking the question, "How often should the operation be executed?" Then he would have (say) the first *n* operations allocated to

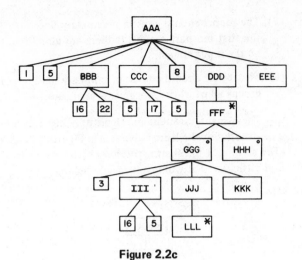

Figure 2.2c

whatever components of the structure they belonged. This is better for two reasons: it is easier and it embodies the check on the program structure. If you add operations by dynamically working round the program tree, you can add operations between components, not noticing that the component to which the operation really belongs is missing from the program structure.

A final point: by taking the static view, and using the diagrammatic notation, you work with a very concise and comprehensible picture of the whole program and its components.

2.2.3 Method

The aim of the methodologist is to achieve a decomposition of the development task for a class of problems. A decomposition of the development is different from a decomposition of a problem. JSP achieves a genuine decomposition of development.

Another methodological aim is to have checkpoints within the development that will ensure that whatever standards of quality have been set, they are indeed being achieved. JSP has such checkpoints. The most important is the allocation of operations, which is a check on the correctness of the program structure as well as being an integral part of the development of the program. The second most important checkpoint (see Section 2.1.2) is on the data structures: Can we find enough correspondences to merge them into a program structure.

A checkpoint is only useful if it is possible to fail. A checkpoint that you are bound to pass can have no value. Moreover, checkpoints that depend only on opinion and experience are, everything else being equal, less valuable than checkpoints that are objective.

In traditional program development, there is only one objective checkpoint, the first clean compile. There

may also be some subjective checkpoints, for example, if, during the development, there is a walkthrough on the design or on the code.

In JSP development there are a number of checkpoints that are objective in the sense that different reviewers will apply them to get the same results. (The reviewer may be the programmer himself.)

Don't go overboard about the idea of objective checkpoints. Subjective intelligence is always better than objective nonsense. It is easy to invent objective measures of a program that are nonsensical or which fail to capture exactly, or even nearly, the property for which you were aiming. The value of the JSP checkpoints is not just that they are objective, though that is a bonus, but that they add up to a reliable check on the correctness of the structure of the program.

The documentation of the program is produced as a by-product of the development. The data structures, program structure, list of operations, program structure with operations allocated, and the structure text make up the technical documentation of the program.

Data and program structures have the happy property that they are much easier to read than to write. The comprehension time for a structure diagram is very much less than the time taken to construct the diagram in the first place. This is not true of program code, certainly not of flow charts. In consequence, JSP programmers find it very much easier to explain their work and to review and help on other programs. More experienced programmers are better able to support novices. Programming can become, if you want it to be, a more public activity.

JSP is also a method of maintaining programs, provided that the programs were produced using JSP. Simply repeat the steps of development. For example, in the data structure step, ask what changes need to be made to the data structures. There are a number of examples of program maintenance scattered through Parts Two and Three. JSP can only be used to maintain non JSP programs if the change is such that it involves the rewriting of a whole program as subroutine.

2.2.4 Data Streams and Data Structures

A data stream is any serial stream of data records, where a record is the unit of I/O. Examples of data streams include

the stream of input messages from a keyboard;

the stream of records sent to a lineprinter;

the stream of characters analysed by a compiler;

the stream of records passing across a subroutine interface;

the stream of records read from a database;

the stream of records read from a table;

the stream of interrupts input to an interrupt handler;

the stream of characters, lines, or pages (as appropriate) read or written by an on-line text editor;

the stream of access requests input to and the stream of access responses output from an input-output procedure (an access method);

the stream of screens output from a program in a screen-based on-line environment; and

the stream of records read or written from a physically sequential medium like a magnetic tape.

A data stream is certainly not just the last of these. There is no implication that the records of a data stream have to be stored together on a serially accessible physical dataset.

The JSP meaning of data structure is different from the meaning of data structure exemplified by linked lists, binary trees, and stacks. To avoid confusion, some organisations have used the term "data usage diagram" for JSP data structures.

A data structure in the JSP sense is a structure diagram of the possible data stream instances that describes them in a way that is (one hopes) appropriate for the problem.

If copies of the same data streams were input to different programs, they would be described by different data structures. Different problems imply different data structures. A data stream in isolation; that is, a data stream not set in the context of a problem can have no data structure in the JSP sense.

Exercise. Draw data structures to describe the input to the Stores Movement Problem, as it would need to be described for each of the following problems.

(1) Copy the file to a line printer.

(2) List only the issue-type movement records.

(3) List only movement records with quantities greater than 100, both issue and receipt.

(4) Summarise the gross movement instead of the net movement.

(5) The report should consist of summary lines only for every other part, starting with the first. For simplicity, assume there is an even number of parts.

(6) The report should consist of summary lines only for part groups that have a net positive movement.

(7) The report should consist of summary lines only for the first ten part groups, if there are more than ten on the input stream.

(8) The report should consist of summary lines only for groups all of whose movements are issues.

These eight different problems have eight different data structures, which are illustrated in Figures 2.2d–2.2k. (The sixth and the eighth structures each have a recognition difficulty that will involve backtracking.)

Figure 2.2d

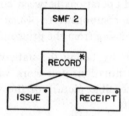

Figure 2.2e

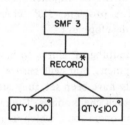

Figure 2.2f

Figure 2.2g

26

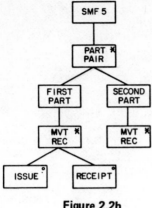

Figure 2.2h

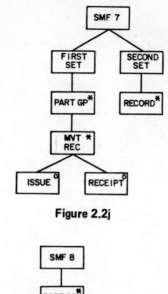

Figure 2.2j

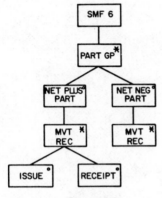

Figure 2.2i

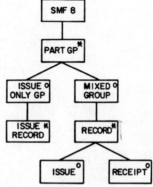

Figure 2.2k

When drawing a data structure, a programmer has to make a structure that is both true and true enough. The structure must be true in the sense that it does describe all the possible instances of the data stream. The structure must be true enough in the sense that it is sufficiently rich. It must describe enough components for the rest of the JSP steps to be completed successfully.

The structure in Figure 2.2d is always true, but it is hardly ever true enough.

27

Chapter 2.3   The Purchase Order Problem

2.3.1 Purchase Order Problem (Version One)

This chapter is a discussion of three closely related examples. They are not realistically large, but they can be used in courses that introduce and illustrate JSP topics.

Specification. In a simple purchasing application, entry of purchase order data is on-line. To enter an order, the terminal operator begins by entering the transaction code, PO. This causes the operating system to pass subsequent input to the purchase order program, POP. POP is the program to be designed.

The operator first enters the vendor-id prefixed by the message code VN. POP replies "ORDER-ID IS xxxxxx" and prompts.

After obtaining the ORDER-ID, the operator enters the items to be ordered. The first input message for an item is the product-id prefixed by the code PN. POP then replies by displaying the 30-character product description and prompts. At this point, the operator may cancel the item by entering only the message code CC, in which case the current item is ignored and the program responds only by prompting. Alternatively, the operator enters the quantity of the item to be ordered. This is done by entering the message code QY followed by an unsigned integer. After the quantity is entered, POP prompts for the next part of the dialogue. Note that, if the operator so wishes, the "QY nnn" message may be omitted, in which case the program assumes that only 1 of the required item is to be ordered. If this is the case, POP outputs the message "QUANTITY 1 ASSUMED FOR PRODUCT xxxxxx". The operator terminates the order by entering, as the last input message, either SV or DL. SV causes the order to be saved; DL causes it to be deleted. At termination, POP outputs either "ORDER SAVED" or "ORDER DELETED", as appropriate, and the conversation is terminated.

The operator can terminate the conversation at any time by hitting the REQUEST key and entering "CANCEL", but this is a facility of the operating system, not of POP.

POP accesses the order processing database as follows:

GETVEND   accesses the vendor section
GETPROD   accesses the product section

Both routines already exist and can be linked into POP after compilation. On invocation, each routine is passed either the vendor-id or product-id, as appropriate, and returns the required record from the database together with a code indicating whether the requested record was successfully located. This is returned with the value "Y" if located and "N" if not. Possible codings might be:

COBOL:

CALL "GETVEND" USING VEND-ID, VEND-REC, IFVENDEXI.
CALL "GETPROD" USING PROD-ID, PROD-REC, IFPRODEXI.

PL/I:

CALL GETVEND(VEND_ID, VEND_REC, IFVEND-EXI);
CALL GETPROD(PROD_ID, PROD_REC, IFPROD-EXI);

Each new order is allocated an identifier by POP. These are generated automatically by calling a supplied routine called "NXTORDID". It must be noted that this routine assumes the appropriate vendor record is in main storage. If it is not, operation of NXTORDID is unspecified.

POP is run under a multiprogramming operating system which handles multiple terminals and swapping in and out of main storage automatically. This enables the designers of POP the luxury of being able to assume that POP is to run on a dedicated processor. Output to the terminal is by means of a special DISPLAY verb. Input is solicited from the terminal by using the verb ACCEPT. The effect of an ACCEPT is to cause the left-arrow prompt to appear in column 1 of the current line on the terminal screen. Keyed-in data is "sent" when the operator presses the "ENTER" key. "Rolling and scrolling" of characters displayed on the screen is handled automatically by the screen-driver software in the operating system.

Order data is saved by writing LOG messages to a log file which is batch-processed later. This file is mounted by the computer operator at the start of each shift and is open to be written to by any version of POP servicing any terminal.

Portions of this Chapter are excerpted from previously unpublished Michael Jackson Systems Limited (MJSL) internal documents with permission from MJSL.

An order is SAVED if each item is LOGged. For an order to be LOGged, one record per item ordered must be written to the LOG file. This record contains ORDER-ID, PROD-ID, and QTY. At the end of each order, there should be an order trailer containing ORDER-ID "****". If this trailer is missing, the program which processes the LOG file ignores any LOGged items, thus effectively deleting the entire order.

The purchase order terminal operators have very strict instructions to enter data in the sequence implied in this program specification, and they know that any departure from laid-down procedures will have unspecified effects.

You are required to design POP on the assumption that the operators will key in the data correctly. The problem of errors will be addressed in the second version of POP.

Specification. Comments/Solution Hints. The problem description is not very well organised, and many of the details are at first confusing. We cannot reasonably restrict ourselves to elegant specifications if we are to be of use to practising programmers.

This is an on-line problem with a data stream input from the terminal and a data stream output to the terminal. As in many on-line problems, these data streams are the most important, in that they contribute most to the program structure. The unit of I/O on the terminal data streams is a line. Therefore, the data structures of these streams have lines as their elementary components. Many on-line environments are screen based. Their basic unit of I/O on the terminal data streams is the screen; screens are the elementary components in their data structures. (We shall see in the case study in Chapter 3.2 that there is sometimes extra structure below the level of the screen.)

There is other input to the program from the database and from the NXTORDID subroutine and other output to the LOG file. In this problem, the database is treated only as a direct-access object and therefore will not contribute to the program structure. Nor will NXTORDID, which has only one input (per instance of POP). The LOG file is the only other data stream for which a data structure need be drawn. The system network diagram has TERM IN as input to POP and TERM OUT and LOG as output.

For all problems, but particularly for on-line problems, it is helpful to make one or two examples of the data streams we are trying to structure. Here is a sample conversation.

- PO

- VN ABC-CO
ORDER-ID IS 307/07

- PN S1138
ONE INCH STEEL SCREW
- QY 2

- PN S1139
TWO INCH STEEL SCREW
- PN SD124
QUANTITY 1 ASSUMED FOR S1139
STANDARD SCREW-DRIVER
- QY 1

- SV
ORDER SAVED

Here is another sample conversation.

- PO

- VN XYZ-CO
ORDER-ID IS 307/08
- PN S1139
TWO INCH STEEL SCREW
- CC
- PN SD127
LARGE SCREW-DRIVER
- QY 5

- PN SD124
STANDARD SCREW-DRIVER
- DL
QUANTITY 1 ASSUMED FOR SD124
ORDER DELETED

Each order is for a number of products. When the quantity line is omitted, there are two replies on TERM OUT, the "QUANTITY 1 ASSUMED . . ." message and the reply to whatever was entered instead of the QY input.

The PO input is consumed by the operating system and not passed on to POP as part of the TERM IN data stream. Similarly the REQUEST key and "CANCEL" option (not to be confused with CC) is a facility of the operating system and not the concern of POP.

Of course, these sample conversations and the accompanying comments are the results of particular interpretations of the written specification. You can regard the answers given here as coming from the user of the system. The questions of interpretation have arisen as we tried to clarify the contents of the data streams for which data structures must be drawn.

Now you should try to solve the problem using JSP. The first step is to draw data structures of the three data streams in the problem. Once you have these right and can compose them via correspondences, the rest should follow easily.

Solution

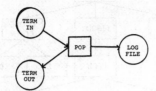

Data Structures

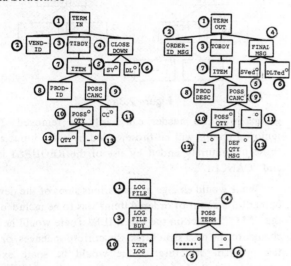

Program Structure

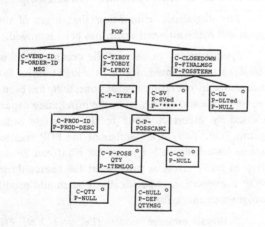

Operations List

1. OPEN TERM-OUT
2. CLOSE TERM-OUT
3. WRITE 'ORDER-ID IS ',ORDER-ID TO TERM-OUT
4. WRITE PROD-DESC TO TERM-OUT
5. WRITE 'QUANTITY 1 ASSUMED FOR PRODUCT ', PROD-ID TO TERM-OUT
6. WRITE 'ORDER SAVED' TO TERM-OUT
7. WRITE 'ORDER DELETED' TO TERM-OUT
8. CALL NXTORDID(ORDER-ID)
9. CALL GETPROD(PROD-ID, PROD-REC, IFPRODEXI)
10. OPEN TERM-IN
11. CLOSE TERM-IN
12. READ TERM-IN
13. WRITE ORDER-ID, PROD-ID, QTY TO LOGFILE
14. WRITE ORDER-ID, '****' TO LOGFILE
15. CALL GETVEND(VEND-ID, VEND-REC, IFVENDEXI)
16. QTY:=1
17. QTY:=PRODQTY IN TERM-IN-REC
18. PROD-ID:=PROD-CODE IN TERM-IN-REC
19. VEND-ID:=VEND-CODE IN TERM-IN-REC
20. OPEN LOGFILE
21. CLOSE LOGFILE

Program with allocated operations

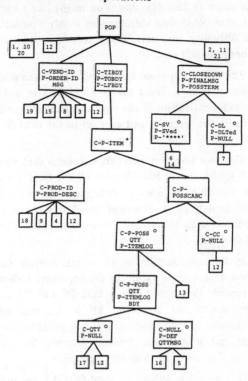

Structure Text

```
POP seq
    open TERM-OUT, open TERM-IN, open LOGFILE;
    read TERM-IN;
    C-VEND-ID-P-ORDER-IDMSG seq
        VEND-ID:=VEND-CODE in TERM-IN-REC;
        call GETVEND(VEND-ID, VEND-REC, IFVENDEXI);
        call NXTORDID(ORDER-ID);
        write 'ORDER-ID IS ', ORDER-ID to TERM-OUT;
        read TERM-IN;
    C-VEND-ID-P-ORDER-IDMSG end
    C-TIBDY-P-TOBDY-P-LFBDY itr while(not 'SV' and not 'DL')
        C-PROD-ID-P-PROD-DESC seq
            PROD-ID:=PROD-CODE in TERM-IN-REC;
            call GETPROD(PROD-ID, PROD-REC, IFPRODEXI);
            write PROD-DESC to TERM-OUT;
            read TERM-IN;
        C-PROD-ID-P-PROD-DESC end
        C-P-POSSCANC sel (not 'CC')
            C-P-POSSQTY-P-ITEMLOGBDY sel ('QY')
                QTY:=PRODQTY in TERM-IN-REC;
                read TERM-IN;
            C-P-POSSQTY-P-ITEMLOGBDY alt (else)
                QTY:=1;
                write 'QUANTITY 1 ASSUMED FOR PRODUCT ', PROD-ID
                                                to TERM-OUT;
            C-P-POSSQTY-P-ITEMLOGBDY end
            write ORDER-ID, PROD-ID, QTY to LOGFILE;
        C-P-POSSCANC alt (else)
            read TERM-IN;
        C-P-POSSCANC end
    C-TIBDY-P-TOBDY-P-LFBDY end
    C-CLOSEDOWN-P-FINALMSG-P-POSSTERM sel ('SV')
        write 'ORDER SAVED' to TERM-OUT,
        write ORDER-ID, '****' to LOGFILE;
    C-CLOSEDOWN-P-FINALMSG-P-POSSTERM alt (else)
        write 'ORDER DELETED' to TERM-OUT;
    C-CLOSEDOWN-P-FINALMSG-P-POSSTERM end
    close TERM-OUT, close TERM-IN, close LOGFILE;
POP end
```

Comments on the Solution. The data structure of
TERM IN is a sequence of the VN record, the main part
of the file, TIBDY, and the CLOSE DOWN message.
TIBDY consists of a number of ITEMs, each of which
has a PN record and possibly a second record to specify
the quantity or to cancel the product. Progress can't be

made with the JSP solution until the data structure looks more or less like this. You might like to experiment with other data structures to satisfy yourself that some difficulty with correspondences or with allocating an operation will arise.

The null component in the selection means nothing, as distinct from a record that is not a QTY record. This is an exact reflection of the user's view of the problem. He omits the quantity and goes on to the next item or to the CLOSE DOWN.

The two levels of two-part selections that describe POSS CANC in TERM IN and TERM OUT have the same meaning as does a three-part selection. POSS CANC is defined in this way to allow a direct correspondence with the record component ITEM LOG of the LOGFILE.

In the specification an SV or DL message can be entered at any time except at the beginning before the VN record. This hasn't meant that SV and DL appear everywhere in the structure. SV or DL may appear dynamically as the next record at any point in the data stream, but in our static structure diagram, they appear once, at the end of the high-level sequence.

One record is written to the LOGFILE per ordered item. The data structure describes the LOGFILE as perceived by this program (i.e. as written by this program). The physical LOGFILE no doubt contains all the logged orders, including whatever interleaving results from the simultaneous operation of different instances of POP on different terminals.

Figure 2.3a is an alternative structure for TERM IN. A level of sequence has been exchanged with a level of selection. This data structure reflects a slightly different view of the problem. We think of the whole item as being cancelled and of the whole non-cancelled item as producing the logged record. When two data structures both satisfy all the checkpoints built in to the JSP method, you should choose the one that best seems to reflect the problem. There is a recognition problem between the two types of ITEM in Figure 2.3a, but this should not be a factor in making the choice.

In the solution, the correspondences have been denoted by numbers close to the diagram. As is common in on-line problems, TERM IN is structurally identical to TERM OUT.

There is nothing remarkable in the rest of the solution. You may prefer to make a list of operations from your favoured language.

Presumably, another program of the system will sort the physical logfile of all the orders, bringing the "****" trailer to the head of each order group. Then, the order

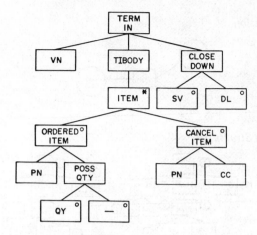

Figure 2.3a

groups with no header can easily be removed. The removed groups will be those ended by a DL input and those prematurely ended by use of the REQUEST key and "CANCEL".

What would change in the various steps of the development if a count of ordered items was to be included in the "****" trailer on the LOGFILE? There would be no change to the data structures, the correspondences, or to the program structure. There would be some extra operations in the operations list that would be allocated in an obvious way.

2.3.2 Purchase Order Problem (Version Two)

The unrealistic assumption that users of the program will make no input errors has been removed.

Specification. In spite of the computer and personnel departments' insistence on thorough training and rigid adherence to operating instructions, there has been much wasted time and confusion in the purchasing department caused by incorrect input to the purchase order program, POP. You, as a member of the POP maintenance team, have been called in to see what can be done to trap as many errors as possible at the source during the POP conversations. Specifically, you should modify the program to check for

* illegal message codes (i.e. *not* VN, PN, CC, QY, SV, or DL),
* nonexistent vendor–ids,
* nonexistent product–ids, and
* out-of-range order quantities (max/min quantities are specified in the product record in the database).

As in the original specification, the operator should be able to cancel an item at any time. Obviously, you should try to make any error diagnostics produced by the program sufficiently meaningful to enable the operator to realise what he or she has done wrong and to recover the errors.

The data structure of an input data stream must describe both good and error data. The full data structure can be developed most easily by elaborating a data structure that describes only good data. There are many ways of elaborating a data structure to include errors. The choice depends on the required interpretation of errors. As any user of a compiler knows, once one error is detected, the particular interpretation of this error will determine the subsequent interpretation of good as well as error data.

For on-line problems, errors are usually interpreted as spurious insertions on the input stream. Correct input is solicited from the screen. The user is kept at the same place in the program until he supplies good input (or some high-level quit).

The range of validity of JSP programs is defined by the input data structure. Elaborating a data structure extends the range of validity to include errors.

The two standard patterns for elaboration for errors of insertion are illustrated in Figure 2.3b. One pattern is the addition of an iteration component before a component in a sequence. In Figure 2.3b, GARB GP1 is added before T1 and GARB GB2, before T2. The other pattern, used where an iteration component already exists, is to add a selection component below the iteration, as in EFBDY in Figure 2.3b. This is both more economical and more general than adding new iterations before and after the existing one.

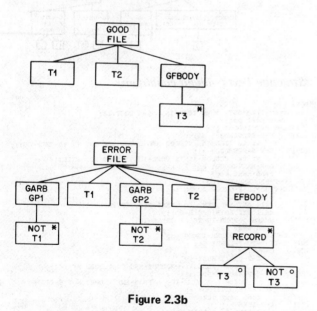

Figure 2.3b

All standard on-line error handling can be dealt with by elaborating good data structures with a combination of these two patterns.

You should now try to elaborate the good data structure of TERM IN using these patterns and so derive the full data structure for Version Two of the problem. If you can do this, the other steps should follow easily, at least up to the text and conditions step.

As a final hint, Figure 2.3c is another example of the standard insertion/on-line error elaboration.

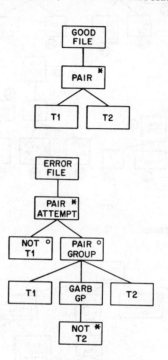

Figure 2.3c

Solution
Data Structures

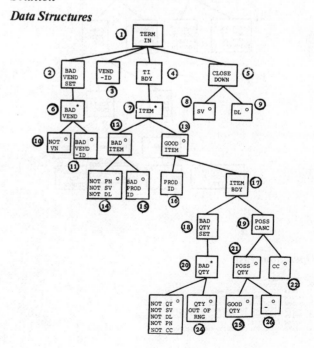

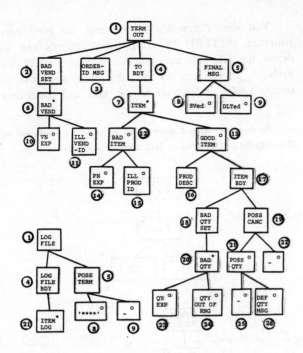

Program Structure

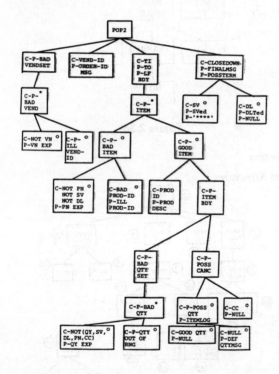

Operations List

```
1.  open TERM-OUT
2.  close TERM-OUT
3.  write 'ILLEGAL VENDOR-MSG CODE. USE VN'
4.  write 'VENDOR-ID '; VEND-ID; ' DOES NOT EXIST'
5.  write 'ORDER-ID IS '; ORDER-ID
6.  write 'ILLEGAL PRODUCT-MSG CODE. USE PN'
7.  write 'PRODUCT-ID '; PROD-ID; ' DOES NOT EXIST'
8.  write PROD-DESC
9.  write 'ILLEGAL QUANTITY-MSG CODE. USE QY'
```

Operations List (continued)

```
10. write 'INPUT QUANTITY OUT OF RANGE'
11. write 'QUANTITY 1 ASSUMED FOR PRODUCT '; stored-PROD-ID
12. write 'ORDER SAVED'
13. write 'ORDER DELETED'
14. store VEND-ID
15. store PROD-ID
16. store QTY
17. stored-QTY:=1
18. call GETVEND(VEND-ID, VEND-REC, IFVENDEXI)
19. call GETPROD(PROD-ID, PROD-REC, IFPRODEXI)
20. call NXTORDID(ORDER-ID)
21. open TERM-IN
22. close TERM-IN
23. read next msg
24. write ORDER-ID, stored-PROD-ID, stored-QTY to LOGFILE
25. write ORDER-ID,'****' to LOGFILE
26. open LOGFILE
27. close LOGFILE
```

Program with allocated operations

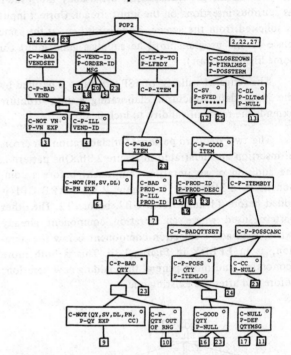

Structure Text (without conditions)

```
POP2 seq
         open TERM-OUT, open TERM-IN, open LOGFILE;
         read next msg;
(C1) C-P-BADVENDSET itr
(C2)     C-P-BADVENDBDY sel
                 write 'ILLEGAL VENDOR-MSG CODE. USE VN' (, to TERM-OUT);
(C3)     C-P-BADVENDBDY alt
                 write 'VENDOR-ID '; VEND-ID; ' DOES NOT EXIST';
         C-P-BADVENDBDY end
         read next msg;
     C-P-BADVENDSET end
     C-VEND-ID-P-ORDER-IDMSG seq
         store VEND-ID;
         call GETVEND(VEND-ID, VEND-REC, IFVENDEXI);
         call NXTORDID(ORDER-ID);
         write 'ORDER-ID IS '; ORDER-ID;
         read next msg;
     C-VEND-ID-P-ORDER-IDMSG end
(C4) C-TI-P-TO-P-LFBDY itr
(C5)     C-P-ITEM sel
                 C-P-BADITEMBDY sel
                         write 'ILLEGAL PRODUCT-MSG CODE. USE PN';
(C6)             C-P-BADITEMBDY alt
                         write 'PRODUCT-ID '; PROD-ID; ' DOES NOT EXIST';
                 C-P-BADITEMBDY end
                 read next msg;
(C7)     C-P-ITEM alt
                 C-PROD-ID-P-PROD-DESC seq
                     store PROD-ID;
                     call GETPROD(PROD-ID, PROD-REC, IFPRODEXI);
                     write PROD-DESC;
                     read next msg;
                 C-PROD-ID-P-PROD-DESC end
(C9)     C-P-BADQTYSET itr
(C10)        C-P-BADQTYBDY sel
                     write 'ILLEGAL QUANTITY-MSG CODE. USE QY';
```

34

```
(C11)           C-P-BADQTYBDY alt
                    write 'INPUT QUANTITY OUT OF RANGE';
                C-P-BADQTYBDY end
                read next msg;
            C-P-BADQTYSET end
(C12)       C-P-POSSCANC sel
(C13)           C-P-POSSQTY-P-ITEMLOGBDY sel
                    store QTY;
                    read next msg;
(C14)           C-P-POSSQTY-P-ITEMLOGBDY alt
                    stored-QTY:=1;
                    write 'QUANTITY 1 ASSUMED FOR PRODUCT '; stored-
                                                            PROD-ID;
                C-P-POSSQTY-P-ITEMLOGBDY end
                write ORDER-ID; stored-PROD-ID; stored-QTY to LOGFILE;
(C15)           C-P-POSSCANC alt
                    read next msg;
                C-P-POSSCANC end
            C-P-ITEM end
        C-TI-P-TO-P-LFBDY end
(C16)   C-CLOSEDOWN-P-FINALMSG-P-POSSTERM sel
            write 'ORDER SAVED';
            write ORDER-ID; '*****' to LOGFILE;
(C17)   C-CLOSEDOWN-P-FINALMSG-P-POSSTERM alt
            write 'ORDER DELETED';
        C-CLOSEDOWN-P-FINALMSG-P-POSSTERM end
        close TERM-OUT, close TERM-IN, close LOGFILE;
POP2 end
```

Condition evaluation

Careful consideration of the set of conditions to be evaluated (nos. 1 to 17) reveal that two recognition difficulties exist. In the C-P-BADVENDSET iteration (condition no. 1), we wish to iterate while there is another BADVEND. Although one of the conditions for a BADVEND is testable (msg-code NE "VN"), the other condition requires us to have interrogated the VENDOR database and examined the IFVENDEXI flag. The solution to this recognition difficulty is to treat it as a case of backtracking in iteration. That is, we POSIT [another BADVEND)/ADMIT(GOODVEND)], locate the QUITs, and consider any possible side-effects.

Since we have already decided that the first condition is testable, no changes are necessary until we get to the second part of the selection, which concerns non-existent VENDORs. If we insert a "CALL" to GET-VEND at the beginning of C-P-ILL-VEND-ID (which is shown in the program structure but not the text) and if we insert a "QUIT" if IFVENDEXI = "Y", the recognition difficulty will have been solved. Consideration of the side-effects reveals that GETVEND will be invoked twice (once in C-P-ILL-VEND-ID and once in C-VEND-ID-P-ORDER-IDMSG). This is a beneficent side-effect which can be resolved by deleting the invocation of GETVEND in C-VEND-ID-P-ORDER-IDMSG.

The selection condition on C-P-ITEM (condition no. 5) presents us with a very similar sort of recognition difficulty to that described above. Clearly, if the msg-code is incorrect, we have a BAD ITEM, and this condition is testable at the selection. However, as in the previous case, the second condition for a BAD ITEM (the ID not being found on the data base) is not, since we do not invoke GETPROD until C-PROD-ID-P-PROD-DESC. Again we have a problem which is resolvable by a simple piece of backtracking. This time it comes in the form of the selection variant where we substitute

POSIT/ADMIT for SEL/ALT in the standard way. We POSIT(BAD ITEM)/ADMIT(GOOD ITEM) and QUIT if the PROD-ID is present on the database. As in the previous case, the only side-effect is the beneficent extra and unnecessary CALL to GETPROD. This can be simply deleted.

All other conditions are straightforward and can be derived in the standard way.

The final version of the structure text with all recognition difficulties solved and side-effects handled is shown below.

Final structure text

```
POP2 seq
    open TERM-OUT, open TERM-IN, open LOGFILE;
    read nexr msg;
    C-P-BADVENDSET itr /* while (another BAD VENDor) */
        C-P-BADVENDBDY sel (not VN)
            write 'ILLEGAL VENDOR-MSG CODE. USE VN';
        C-P-BADVENDBDY alt (else)
            call GETVEND(VEND-ID, VEND-REC, IFVENDEXI);
        C-P-BADVENDSET quit (IFVENDEXI = 'Y')
            write 'VENDOR-ID '; VEND-ID; ' DOES NOT EXIST';
        C-P-BADVENDBDY end
        read next msg;
    C-P-BADVENDSET end
    C-VEND-ID-P-ORDER-IDMSG seq
        store VEND-ID;
        call NXTORDID(ORDER-ID);
        write 'ORDER-ID IS '; ORDER-ID;
        read next msg;
    C-VEND-ID-P-ORDER-IDMSG end
    C-TI-P-TO-P-LFBDY itr while (not SV and not DL)
        C-P-ITEM posit (BAD ITEM)
            C-P-BADITEMBDY sel (not PN)
                write 'ILLEGAL PRODUCT-MSG CODE. USE PN';
            C-P-BADITEMBDY alt (else)
                call GETPROD(PROD-ID, PROD-REC, IFPRODEXI);
            C-P-ITEM quit (IFPRODEXI = 'Y')
                write 'PRODUCT-ID '; PROD-ID; ' DOES NOT EXIST';
            C-P-BADITEMBDY end
            read next msg;
        C-P-ITEM admit (GOOD ITEM)
            C-PROD-ID-P-PROD-DESC seq
                store PROD-ID;
                write PROD-DESC;
                read next msg;
            C-PROD-ID-P-PROD-DESC end
            C-P-BADQTYSET itr while (not(QY,SV,DL,PN,CC) or
                                    (QY and not(MIN LE QTY LE MAX)))
                C-P-BADQTYBDY sel (not QY)
                    write 'ILLEGAL QUANTITY-MSG CODE. USE QY';
                C-P-BADQTYBDY alt (else)
                    write 'INPUT QUANTITY OUT OF RANGE';
                C-P-BADQTYBDY end
                read next msg;
            C-P-BADQTYSET end
            C-P-POSSCANC sel (not CC)
                C-P-POSSQTY-P-ITEMLOGBDY sel (QY)
                    store QTY;
                    read next msg;
                C-P-POSSQTY-P-ITEMLOGBDY alt (else)
                    stored-QTY:=1;
                    write 'QUANTITY 1 ASSUMED FOR PRODUCT ';
                                            stored-PROD-ID;
                C-P-POSSQTY-P-ITEMLOGBDY end
                write ORDER-ID; stored-PROD-ID; stored-QTY to LOGFILE;
            C-P-POSSCANC alt (else)
                read next msg;
            C-P-POSSCANC end
        C-P-ITEM end
    C-TI-P-TO-P-LFBDY end
    C-CLOSEDOWN-P-FINALMSG-P-POSSTERM sel (SV)
        write 'ORDER SAVED';
        write ORDER-ID; '****' to LOGFILE;
    C-CLOSEDOWN-P-FINALMSG-P-POSSTERM alt (else)
        write 'ORDER DELETED';
    C-CLOSEDOWN-P-FINALMSG-P-POSSTERM end
    close TERM-OUT, close TERm-IN, close LOGFILE;
POP2 end
```

Comments on the Solution. An iteration component has been inserted in the top level sequence before a good VEND-ID and in the GOOD ITEM sequence before POSS CANC. The component BAD ITEM has been added in a selection beneath the iterated component

ITEM. There are selections beneath these added components because different input cases are distinguished so that different diagnostics can be produced. If the single diagnostic "?" or even the three diagnostics "VENDOR?", "PRODUCT?", and "QUANTITY?", were used then, these extra selections would not be necessary.

Notice the close relationship between the meaning of the diagnostics and the additional components added when a good structure is elaborated. A well-chosen name in a data structure component should describe the component as it is to be interpreted by the program; so should a diagnostic, if the component is to be interpreted as error data.

A list of diagnostics in a program specification describes a list of (usually elementary) data structure components without saying anything about the relationships among the components. This is an example of what Michael Jackson calls the crime of arboricide (tree murder). Someone has cut the leaves off the tree and has listed the leaves in the specification. In any non-trivial case, this list is liable to be incomplete and to contain inconsistent sets of diagnostics; any program that can produce some of the set will never produce the others.

We will meet more examples of arboricide later, in other contexts.

Two Questions and Two Answers. Is any data stream of properly formatted records valid input for this program? No. The data stream must contain somewhere a good vendor record and sometime after that an SV or DL. Nothing may appear after the SV or DL.

At any point during the execution of the program, is there any input record for which the operation of the program is unspecified? No. Even though not all data streams are valid input, the operation of the program is specified for any properly formatted record. A DL entered before a good vendor record will be interpreted as a bad vendor record; a vendor record immediately following a good product record will be interpreted as a bad quantity record; nothing can come in after an SV or DL becuase the program has finished its execution.

The elaboration of the output stream TERM OUT follows that of TERM IN. The two streams still correspond exactly. The correspondences with LOG FILE are as in Version One. The list of operations includes the diagnostic output operations. The allocation of operations is straightforward, as it always must be.

There are two recognition difficulties that must be confronted in the final step of the method, on the iteration component C-P-BADVENDSET and on the selection C-P-ITEM. The difficulty in the two cases is

very similar and is solved in the same way, as you can see in the complete solution.

A recognition difficulty is a condition that cannot be evaluated on the basis of a single record read ahead. A multiple read-ahead scheme can be used if the condition can be written, given knowledge of a fixed number of records. Otherwise, and alternatively, there is the backtracking technique.

A Brief Description of Backtracking. The central idea is not to let a recognition difficulty distort the static structure of the data that is appropriate to the problem. A classification of recognition difficulties is given in Chapter 2.4. Recognition difficulties are ignored until the fourth step, when the choice between multiple-read-ahead and backtracking is made. In backtracking, one of the paths past the condition is chosen as the posit path: during execution it will be chosen unconditionally. QUITs are inserted on this path at the points at which the hypothesis (that this path is the right one) may be disproved. The QUITs transfer control back to the branch point. A QUIT is a GOTO with an implied label. Finally, the side-effects of partial execution of the wrong path are identified and dealt with in a variety of ways.

This is the JSP answer to the question of the use of GOTOs. GOTOs (QUITs) may be used in a design when there is recognition difficulty that is being solved by backtracking. (GOTOs may be used in an implementation at will, though, obviously, elegant coding standards should be adopted wherever possible.)

Don't be put off by the number of steps needed to solve a problem with backtracking. The number of steps is a sign of success in separating concerns. The separation will give the method power when the problems are large and difficult. Even handling side-effects, which is sometimes messy (though less often than might be supposed) is easier when considered at the end of the other steps than when mixed up with all the other issues.

In this problem, the backtracking comes out very easily. In both cases there is a single QUIT, executed if the vendor/product is not found on the database. In both cases, the side-effects are beneficent. The database had to be looked up anyway.

When the arguments and discussions over principles are forgotten, a method justifies itself if, once learned, it makes the job easier. Focusing, for the moment, narrowly on backtracking and multiple read-ahead, we may say that they help the programmer by allowing him to choose simpler and more natural data structures.

In this example, this argument is even more powerful because the basic structure in Figure 2.3d was derived by applying the standard rules of error elaboration.

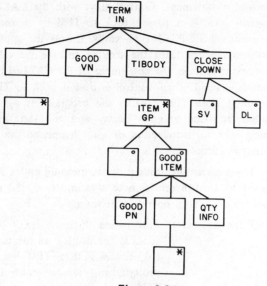

Figure 2.3d

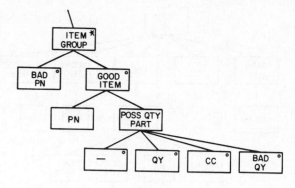

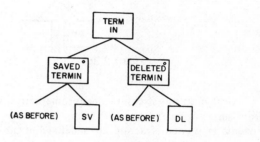

Figure 2.3f

Consider what changes would need to be made at each step of the development to accommodate the following specification changes.

(1) The null option for a quantity is not available if a wrong quantity for that product has already been entered.

(2) Any mistake in entering a quantity is to be interpreted in the same way as a CC, thus forcing the reentry of the PN line.

(3) For orders finishing with a DL, no records should be written to LOG FILE.

Each of the changes requires some change to the data structure of TERM IN and corresponding changes to TERM OUT. Appropriate data structures are Figures 2.3e, 2.3f, and 2.3g, respectively.

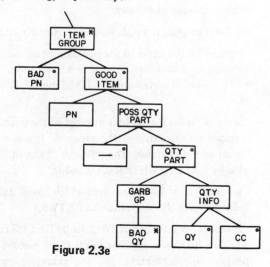

Figure 2.3e

Figure 2.3g

For the first two changes, there are also some obvious changes to the allocation of operations. In the third variation, the log record on the output LOG FILE now corresponds with POSS QTY on the SAVED branch of the structure. There is an obvious and massive recognition difficulty, which is deferred, as usual, to the fourth step of the method. The distinction between a SAVED file and a DELETED file cannot be made until the very last record. All the side-effects are beneficent except the writes on LOG FILE. These writes must be replaced by writes to an internal temporary file, which is reread and written to LOG FILE when the SV is input.

There is no real disadvantage in having to go back to the data structures and change them. The advantage is that the components that have to be changed are obvious, and a programmer is not inhibited from making a change to a middle level of the structure. Traditionally, maintenance programmers try to change as few lines of code as possible, and try to make all changes to the lowest levels of the program structure. When the changes do not belong in the lowest levels, the program soon becomes messy and full of structurally distorting switches.

Finally, you might at some stage have considered Figure 2.3h as the data structure for TERM IN. The incomplete item group is needed because otherwise the structure would imply that an SV or DL record could not immediately follow a bad product record.

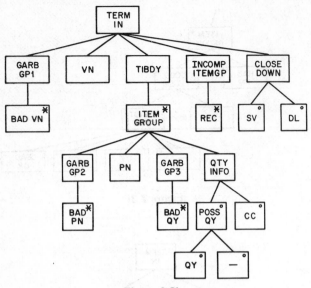

Figure 2.3h

An item in this structure means something different from an item in the given solution. Inevitably, components in a good structure are redefined as the structure is elaborated, and you must be careful to make sure you understand the new definition.

The structure in Figure 2.3h is good enough to solve the problem, but it is clumsier than the given solution. It also needs some backtracking because an ITEM GROUP cannot be distinguished from an INCOMPLETE ITEM GROUP on the basis of one or any other fixed number or records read ahead. Very briefly, the solution involves positting that the item group will be complete and quitting if there is a premature SV or DL. The side-effects are beneficent because the partial execution of a complete item group is exactly the required processing for an incomplete group, and so the whole incomplete item group component can be deleted from the program text.

2.3.3 Purchase Order Problem (Version 3)

Specification. After eighteen months' faithful service, POP is moved to a new home. The old computer is replaced by a new machine that uses sophisticated teleprocessing facilities. These, it has been argued, will dramatically improve response time for all on-line users. Consequently, you have been called in to convert POP to run under the new TP software. The name of the TP system is called TPM (TeleProcessing Monitor).

A program running under control of TPM does not acquire its input and dispose of its output by "reading" and "writing" data as in the case of the ACCEPT and DISPLAY verbs used in POP versions 1 and 2. Instead, data keyed-in is transmitted from the terminal device to TPM. TPM will know which program is to process this data and CALLs the appropriate program much in the same way as subroutines are called by applications

programs. The program CALLed by TPM is loaded from the program library and starts processing at the first executable statement. Control stays with the CALLed program until it is passed back to TPM by means of the standard RETURN-type verbs. Unless the application programmer takes the trouble to save the values of working storage, the core-image of the CALLed program is deleted when control is passed back to TPM. The next time TPM CALLs the program, it will be loaded from the program library and will start processing with no recollection of what happened the last time it was invoked.

When an applications program running under TPM wishes to send information to a terminal, special routines are used. They operate as follows:

PUTP(message-text): This passes "message-text" back to TPM for display on the terminal, requests that TPM issue a prompt, and returns control to TPM.

PUT(message-text): This passes "message-text" back to TPM for display on the terminal, does *not* request that TPM issue a prompt, and does *not* pass control back to TPM.

PUTE(message-text): This passes "message-text" back to TPM for display on the terminal, does *not* request that TPM issue a prompt, and returns final control to the operating system, terminating the program.

It is possible under TPM to save working storage needed by the applications program between invocations by TPM so that the program can continue processing the next time it is invoked by remembering where it had gotten to. The routines supplied under TPM to achieve this are as follows:

GETWS(prog-id, term-id, ws-area, if-ws-exi) where

"prog-id" is the name of the program being run. This can be expressed as either a literal or a data-name. The value of "prog-id" is obtainable by CALLing GETPRID(prog-id),

"term-id" is the logical unit number of the terminal being serviced by this copy of the program. It can be either a literal or a data-name. The value of "term-id" is obtainable by CALLing GETRMID(term-id),

"ws-area" is a data-name into which saved data will be loaded during the invocation of GETWS,

"if-ws-exi" is a two-valued flag set by GETWS to indicate whether there was any saved data to be retrieved for this prog/term combination. So, for example, on the first invocation of a program by TPM, no saved working storage would exist. The values of if-ws-exi are "Y" and "N" respectively.

PUTWS(prog-id, term-id, ws-area) where

"prog-id" and "term-id" are as explained above, and "ws-area" is a data-name you wish to save so that it will be available next time.

CREATEWS(prog-id, term-id, size) where

"prog-id" and "term-id" are as explained above.

"size" is the number of characters you wish to save.

The effect of this routine is to create a storage area (either on disk or in memory, depending on the loading of the system) in which one can save working storage addressable by "prog-id"/"term-id".

DELETEWS(prog-id, term-id)where

"prog-id" and "term-id" are as explained above. The routine deletes the storage area. Do this when it is no longer needed.

Handling multiple terminals is accomplished by the generation of reentrant versions of the program text. This feature of the system is fully automatic under TPM and means that when programs run under TPM are needed, one central copy of the program code is accessed with one copy of the program's data area available per terminal. These data areas are, however, as explained previously, only in existence whilst a terminal is actively being serviced by POP. On return to TPM, each terminal's data area is deleted. Multiprogramming of concurrently-running terminals is handled by TPM.

Redesign (or convert) POP2 to run under TPM with no specification changes.

Specification Comments/Solution Hints. If you are unfamiliar with mainframe on-line environments, you may find some of the features of TPM a little bizarre. In fact, TPM is very similar to the IBM CICS system and is not very different from the equivalent systems supplied by other manufacturers.

The central question in this exercise is whether a redesign is necessary, whether we must start again with the data structures. The answer is an emphatic no. No change need or should be made to any of the four steps that build the specification. The necessary changes are at the implementation stage, in which the program must be coded as an inverted program that is called by TPM when a record of TERM IN is available. Additional coding must also be added to ensure that values of the local variables of POP are retained between invocations from TPM and to ensure that POP starts at the beginning of its text on the very first invocation.

You may now want to read "Program Inversion and its Consequences", an extract from an MJSL technical brochure that introduces the inversion technique.

(One common misunderstanding about JSP is that inversion is a technique used only with boundary clashes. This is not so, as the present example shows.)

POP(3) Solution

To convert the POP program to run under TPM, it is necessary to perform two transformations on the code:

1) Invert the code so that POP becomes a record-processing subroutine that may be invoked by TPM.

2) Introduce code into the inverted POP program to save the local variables when control passes back to TPM and to restore them when POP is reentered.

The key point is that *no changes are required to the design of the program*; we are merely altering the way in which the same design is to be implemented in order to fit in with the new hardware/software environment.

The two steps are described in more detail below. This is followed by copies of the final POP code in both COBOL and PL/1.

1) Inverting POP to Run under TPM

The requirement here is to understand that POP is no longer running as a main program in the sense that the term is usually used. In version 3 of the specification, TPM is the main program which, in turn, calls POP each time someone has entered data into one of the terminals serviced by TPM. POP, as a subroutine, runs until it passes control back to TPM. What we have to do, therefore, is to change POP from a main program to a subroutine.

The relationship between TPM and POP is shown in the following diagrams.

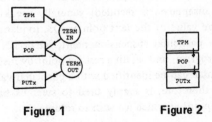

Figure 1   **Figure 2**

In Figure 1 we see the software modules as if they were main programs. We may ignore TPM and the PUTx software and concentrate on POP. This is the POP we have at the moment. Data is read from TPM by means of the ACCEPT verb and is passed to the PUTx routines by means of the DISPLAY verb. In Figure 2 we have redrawn the relationships between the software components to reflect the situation as it will have to be under TPM as implemented. POP is depicted as a subroutine called by TPM, and the PUTx set is shown as subroutines called by POP (actually, we knew this already from the version 3 specification).

Dealing first with the changes necessary to incorporate the PUTx set, we observe that the changes are quite simple: we substitute "CALL PUTx" for the DISPLAYs. However, a moment's thought makes us realise that PUTx is more than just a "write" in disguise. As well as PUTting the data on the screen, they may RETURN control to TPM. This return can be thought of as a return to get the next input message because, next time POP is called by TPM, the next input message will be available to POP. Therefore, a call to one of the PUTx routines, PUTP, is really a write and half-a-read.

We say that PUTP is a write followed by half-a-read because the read element only returns to TPM for the next message. It does nothing about actually returning the next message to POP when the next message is available. This is the other "half" of the read and is put into effect by TPM calling POP when the message is available. The "call" is the concern of TPM; however, it is up to us to ensure that, on being called, POP resumes control at the correct point in the program text. So we need to remember where we had reached in the program text at the point we passed control back to TPM, and we need to be able to get back to this point on being called the next time by TPM.

This is the classic problem that the technique of program inversion addresses: the requirement to interrupt a long-running program and resume it under the control of a piece of software "above" it in the calling hierarchy. We say that we are inverting POP with respect to its TERM-IN file.

In inversion, each I/O operation acting on the data stream that disappears is recoded: generally speaking, we update the value of the text pointer, QS, to identify uniquely the particular suspension point, RETURN to the calling program, and set up a resume point by inserting a label which can be identified with a particular value of QS. QS, therefore, is simply used to steer us back safely to the point at which we wish to resume.

In the case of inverting POP, we can see that the RETURN is a part of PUTP, so it will not appear explicitly in our text. We shall want to resume POP immediately after the call to PUTP, so this will be where the resumption point is located. We are told from the TPM

specification that PUT does not return to TPM; therefore, no inversion coding is required here. An ACCEPT which dynamically follows PUTP is deleted since the input record will already be available, but an ACCEPT not so preceeded will need an interrupt.

The names TERM-IN and TERM-OUT are no longer associated with physical files as they were in POP2. TERM-IN-REC is now passed down from TPM on each invocation and would be declared in the LINKAGE SECTION in COBOL, would be termed a "dummy" argument in FORTRAN, and would be a parameter passed to POP by TPM in PL/I. TERM-OUT-REC would be an argument passed down to PUT, PUTP, or PUTE.

2) Saving and Restoring the Local Variables

We know from the version 3 specification that when POP is invoked by TPM, reference to one central copy of the "code" part of the program is made, as far as controlling the logic is concerned, but that a copy of the "data" part of the program is made available for each active terminal. This means that under TPM, on entry to POP, the data area will be as defined in the DATA DIVISION, and this will be true for all invocations of POP. From this, it is clear that we need to use the working-storage routines explained in the version 3 specification to maintain intact values of working-storage data between invocations by TPM. The changes we need to make to the inverted POP program are

a. Prior to each return to TPM (whether this be by "GOBACK", "PUTP", or whatever), we need to save those working–storage variables that we shall need the next time POP is invoked. A convenient way of organising this data is to declare them so that they are contiguously located in a logical record held in working–storage. If we do this, we simply CALL PUTWS immediately before we return control to TPM,

b. At each entry to POP we need to retrieve the values of working-storage so that processing may resume from where it left off. Saved working–storage is automatically accessed by "prog-id"/"term-id", and "term-id" can be determined by CALLing GETRMID. "prog-id" can be either a constant declared at compilation time or a data name whose value is determined by a CALL to GETPRID. We therefore CALL GETWS at each entry and branch according to the value of QS. If, however, the "if-ws-exi" flag is returned with value "N", it means that POP is being invoked for the first time. In this case, we initialise QS to 1 and create a working-storage area by CALLing CREATEWS;

c. Immediately prior to the dynamically-last operation executed in one complete "pass" through POP (i.e. one pass through the data structures), we delete the working-storage area. Apart from reasons of good housekeeping and efficiency, we need to do this so that POP will be able to recognise its first invocation the next time a complete POP cycle is initiated.

```
POP (3): COBOL CODE

ID DIVISION
        :
ENVIRONMENT DIVISION
        :
DATA DIVISION
        :
WORKING-STORAGE SECTION
77 TERM-ID PIC X(4).
77 PROG-ID PIC X(4) VALUE 'POP3'.
77 IF-WS-EXI PIC X.
77 SIZE PIC 99 VALUE 24.
01 TERM-OUT-REC PIC X(80).
01 WS-AREA.
   03 QS PIC 99.
   03 IFVENDEXI PIC X.
   03 IFPRODEXI PIC X.
   03 WS-PROD-ID PIC X(6).
   03 WS-VEND-ID PIC X(6).
   03 WS-ORDER-ID PIC X(6).
   03 WS-QTY PIC 99.
LINKAGE SECTION.
01 TERM-IN-REC PIC X(80).
        :
        :
PROCEDURE DIVISION.
    ENTRY 'POP3' USING TERM-IN-REC.
    CALL 'GETRMID' USING TERM-ID.
    CALL 'GETWS' USING PROG-ID, TERM-ID, WS-AREA, IF-WS-EXI.
    IF IF-WS-EXI = 'Y' GO TO POP3-START.
*
*   INITIALISE WORKING STORAGE.
*
    MOVE 1 TO QS.
    CALL 'CREATEWS' USING PROG-ID, TERM-ID, SIZE.
*
*   MAIN PART OF POP STARTS HERE.
*
POP3-START.
    GO TO Q1 Q2 Q3 Q4 Q5 Q6 Q7 Q8 Q9 Q10 Q11
                DEPENDING ON QS.


Q1.
    OPEN EXTEND LOGFILE, INPUT DATABASE.
C-P-BADVENDSET-ITR.
    IF VN GO TO C-P-BADVENDBDY-ALT.
    MOVE BAD-VN-MSG TO TERM-OUT-REC.
    MOVE 2 TO QS.
    CALL 'PUTP' USING TERM-OUT-REC.
Q2.
    GO TO C-P-BADVENDBDY-END.
C-P-BADVENDBDY-ALT.
    CALL 'GETVEND' USING VEND-ID, VEND-REC, IFVENDEXI.
    IF IFVENDEXI = 'Y' GO TO C-P-BADVENDSET-END.
    MOVE VEND-ID TO VENDOR-ID IN NON-EXI-VEND-MSG.
    MOVE NON-EXI-VEND-MSG TO TERM-OUT-REC.
    MOVE 3 TO QS.
    CALL 'PUTP' USING TERM-OUT-REC.
Q3.
C-P-BADVENDBDY-END.
    GO TO C-P-BADVENDSET-ITR.
C-P-BADVENDSET-END.
    MOVE VEND-ID TO WS-VEND-ID.
    CALL 'NEXTORDID' USING WS-ORDER-ID.
    MOVE WS-ORDER-ID TO ORD-ID IN ORDER-MSG.
    MOVE ORDER-MSG TO TERM-OUT-REC.
    MOVE 4 TO QS.
    CALL 'PUTP' USING TERM-OUT-REC.
Q4.
C-TI-P-TO-P-LFBDY-ITR.
    IF SV OR DL GO TO C-TI-P-TO-P-LFBDY-END.
    IF PN GO TO C-P-BADITEMBDY-ALT.
    MOVE BAD-PN-MSG TO TERM-OUT-REC.
    MOVE 5 TO QS.
    CALL 'PUTP' USING TERM-OUT-REC.
Q5.
    GO TO C-P-BADITEMBDY-END.
C-P-BADITEMBDY-ALT.
    CALL 'GETPROD' USING PROD-ID, PROD-REC, IFPRODEXI.
    IF IFPRODEXI = 'Y' GO TO C-P-ITEM-ADMIT.
    MOVE PROD-ID TO PRODUCT IN NON-EXI-PROD-MSG.
    MOVE NON-EXI-PROD-MSG TO TERM-OUT-REC.
    MOVE 6 TO QS.
    CALL 'PUTP' USING TERM-OUT-REC.
Q6.
C-P-BADITEMBDY-END.
    GO TO C-P-ITEM-END.
C-P-ITEM-ADMIT.
    MOVE PROD-ID TO WS-PROD-ID.
    MOVE PROD-DESC TO TERM-OUT-REC.
    MOVE 7 TO QS.
    CALL 'PUTP' USING TERM-OUT-REC.
Q7.
C-P-BADQTYSET-ITR.
    IF CC OR SV OR DL OR PN OR
       (QY AND QTY >= MIN AND QTY <= MAX) GO TO C-P-BADQTYSET-END.
    IF QY GO TO C-P-BADQTYBDY-ALT.
    MOVE BAD-QTY-MSG TO TERM-OUT-REC.
    MOVE 8 TO QS.
    CALL 'PUTP' USING TERM-OUT-REC.
Q8.
    GO TO C-P-BADQTYBDY-END.
C-P-BADQTYBDY-ALT.
    MOVE RANGE-ERR-MSG TO TERM-OUT-REC.
    MOVE 9 TO QS.
    CALL 'PUTP' USING TERM-OUT-REC.
Q9.
C-P-BADQTYBDY-END.
    GO TO C-P-BADQTYSET-ITR.
C-P-BADQTYSET-END.
    IF CC GO TO C-P-POSSCANC-ALT.
    IF NOT QY GO TO C-P-POSSQTY-P-ITEMLOGBDY-ALT.
    MOVE QTY TO WS-QTY.
    MOVE 10 TO QS
    GOBACK.
Q10.
    GO TO C-P-POSSQTY-P-ITEMLOGBDY-END.
C-P-POSSQTY-P-ITEMLOGBDY-ALT.
    MOVE 1 TO WS-QTY  MOVE WS-PROD-ID TO PRODUCT IN DEFAULT-MSG.
    MOVE DEFAULT-MSG TO TERM-OUT-REC.
    CALL 'PUT' USING TERM-OUT-MSG.
C-P-POSSQTY-P-ITEMLOGBDY-END.
    MOVE WS-ORDER-ID TO ORD-ID IN LOG-REC.
    MOVE WS-PROD-ID TO PRODUCT-ID IN LOG-REC.
    MOVE WS-QTY TO QUANTITY IN LOG-REC.
    WRITE LOG-REC.
    GO TO C-P-POSSCANC-END.
C-P-POSSCANC-ALT.
    MOVE 11 TO QS.
    GOBACK.
Q11.
C-P-POSSCANC-END.
C-P-ITEM-END.
    GO TO C-TI-P-TO-P-LFBDY-ITR.
C-TI-P-TO-P-LFBDY-END.
    IF NOT SV GO TO C-CD-P-FM-P-PT-ALT.
    MOVE ORD-SV-MSG TO TERM-OUT-REC.
    MOVE WS-ORDER-ID TO ORD-ID IN TRL-REC.
    MOVE '*****' TO STARS.
    MOVE SPACES TO FILLER IN TRL-REC.
    WRITE TRL-REC.
    GO TO C-CD-P-FM-P-PT-END.
C-CD-P-FM-P-PT-ALT.
    MOVE ORD-DL-MSG TO TERM-OUT-REC.
C-CD-P-FM-P-PT-END.
    CLOSE LOGFILE, DATABASE.
    CALL 'PUTE' USING TERM-OUT-REC.
```

As with the above COBOL, the following PL/1 code is included to show the job is finished rather than as an elegant example of coding.

```
POP (3): PL/I CODE

POP3:
    PROC (TERM_IN_REC);
        .
        .
        .
    DCL  TERM_ID     CHAR (4);
    DCL  PROG_ID     CHAR (4)    INIT ('POP3');
    DCL  IF_WS_EXI   CHAR (1);
    DCL  SIZE        PIC '99'    INIT (24);
        .
        .
    DCL 1 WS_AREA,
          3 QS         PIC '99',
          3 IFVENDEXI  CHAR (1),
          3 IFPRODEXI  CHAR (1),
          3 WS_PROD_ID CHAR (6),
          3 WS_VEND_ID CHAR (6),
          3 WS_ORDER_ID CHAR (6),
          3 WS_QTY     PIC '99';
        .
        .
    CALL GETRMID (TERM_ID);
    CALL GETWS (PROG_ID, TERM_ID, WS_AREA, IF_WS_EXI);
    IF IF_WS_EXI = 'Y' THEN GO TO POP3_START;
/*                                                */
/*   INITIALISE WORKING STORAGE.                  */
/*                                                */
```

```
      QS = 1;
      CALL CREATEWS (PROG_ID, TERM_ID, SIZE);
/*                                              */
/*    MAIN PART OF POP STARTS HERE.             */
/*                                              */
POP3_START:
      GO TO Q (QS);   Q (1):
      OPEN FILE (LOGFILE), FILE (DATABASE);
C_P_BADVENDSET_ITR:
      IF VEND_MSG.MSG_CODE = 'VN' THEN GO TO C_P_BADVENDBDY_ALT;
      TERM_OUT_REC = BAD_VN_MSG_D;
      QS = 2;   CALL PUTWS (PROG_ID, TERM_ID, WS_AREA);
                CALL PUTP (TERM_OUT_REC);  Q2:
      GO TO C_P_BADVENDBDY_END;
C_P_BADVENDBDY_ALT:
      CALL GETVEND (VEND_ID, VEND_REC, IFVENDEXI);
      IF IFVENDEXI = 'Y' THEN GO TO C_P_BADVENDSET_END;
      NON_EXI_VEND_MSG.VENDOR_ID = VEND_ID;
      TERM_OUT_REC = NON_EXI_VEND_MSG_D;
      QS = 3;   CALL PUTWS (PROG_ID, TERM_ID, WS_AREA);
                CALL PUTP (TERM_OUT_REC);  Q(3):
C_P_BADVENDBDY_END:
      GO TO C_P_BADVENDSET_ITR;
C_P_BADVENDSET_END:
      WS_VEND_ID = VEND_ID;
      CALL NXTORDID (WS_ORDER_ID);
      ORDER_MSG.ORD_ID = WS_ORDER_ID;
      TERM_OUT_REC = ORDER_MSG_D;
      QS = 4;   CALL PUTWS (PROG_ID, TERM_ID, WS_AREA);
                CALL PUTP (TERM_OUT_REC);  Q(4):
C_TI_P_TO_P_LFBDY_ITR:
      IF (VEND_MSG.MSG_CODE = 'SV') | (VEND_MSG.MSG_CODE = 'DL')
          THEN GO TO C_TI_P_TO_P_LFBDY_END;
      IF VEND_MSG.MSG_CODE = 'PN' THEN GO TO C_P_BADITEMBDY_ALT;
      TERM_OUT_REC = BAD_PN_MSG_D;
      QS = 5;   CALL PUTWS (PROG_ID, TERM_ID, WS_AREA);
                CALL PUTP (TERM_OUT_REC);  Q(5):
      GO TO C_P_BADITEMBDY_END;
C_P_BADITEMBDY_ALT:
      CALL GETPROD (PROD_ID, PROD_REC, IFPRODEXI);
      IF IFPRODEXI = 'Y' THEN GO TO C_P_ITEM_ADMIT;
      NON_EXI_PROD_MSG.PRODUCT = PROD_ID;
      TERM_OUT_REC = NON_EXI_PROD_MSG_D;
      QS = 6;   CALL PUTWS (PROG_ID, TERM_ID, WS_AREA);
                CALL PUTP (TERM_OUT_REC);  Q(6):
C_P_BADITEMBDY_END:
      GO TO C_P_ITEM_END;
C_P_ITEM_ADMIT:
      WS_PROD_ID = PROD_ID;
      TERM_OUT_REC = PRODUCT_DESC;
      QS = 7;   CALL PUTWS (PROG_ID, TERM_ID, WS_AREA);
                CALL PUTP (TERM_OUT_REC);  Q(7):
C_P_BADQTYSET_ITR:
      IF (VEND_MSG.MSG_CODE = 'CC') | (VEND_MSG.MSG_CODE = 'SV') |
         (VEND_MSG.MSG_CODE = 'DL') | (VEND_MSG.MSG_CODE = 'PN') |
         ((VEND_MSG.MSG_CODE = 'QY') & (QTY >= MIN) & (QTY <= MAX))
          THEN GO TO C_P_BADQTYSET_END;
      IF (VEND_MSG.MSG_CODE = 'QY') THEN GO TO C_P_BADQTYBDY_ALT;
      TERM_OUT_REC = BAD_QTY_MSG_D;
      QS = 8;   CALL PUTWS (PROG_ID, TERM_ID, WS_AREA)
                CALL PUTP (TERM_OUT_REC);  Q(8):
      GO TO C_P_BADQTYBDY_END;
C_P_BADQTYBDY_ALT:
      TERM_OUT_REC = RANGE_ERR_MSG_D;
      QS = 9;   CALL PUTWS (PROG_ID, TERM_ID, WS_AREA);
                CALL PUTP (TERM_OUT_REC);  Q(9):
C_P_BADQTYBDY_END:
      GO TO C_P_BADQTYSET_ITR.
C_P_BADQTYSET_END:
      IF (VEND_MSG.MSG_CODE = 'CC') THEN GO TO C_P_POSSCANC_ALT;
      IF VEND_MSG.MSG_CODE = 'QY'
          THEN GO TO C_P_POSSQTY_P_ITEMLOGBDY_ALT;
      WS_QTY = QTY;
      QS = 10;  CALL PUTWS (PROG_ID, TERM_ID, WS_AREA);
                RETURN;  Q (10):
      GO TO C_P_POSSQTY_P_ITEMLOGBDY_END;
C_P_POSSQTY_P_ITEMLOGBDY_ALT:
      WS_QTY = 1;
      DEFAULT_MSG.MSG.PRODUCT = WS_PROD_ID;
      TERM_OUT_REC = DEFAULT_MSG_D;
      CALL PUT (TERM_OUT_REC);
C_P_POSSQTY_P_ITEMLOGBDY_END:
      LOG_REC.ORD_ID = WS_ORDER_ID;
      LOG_REC.PRODUCT_ID = WS_PROD_ID;
      LOG_REC.QUANTITY = WS_QUANTITY;
      WRITE FILE (LOGFILE) FROM (LOG_REC);
      GO TO C_P_POSSCANC_END;
C_P_POSSCANC_ALT:
      QS = 11;  CALL PUTWS (PROG_ID, TERM_ID, WS_AREA);
                RETURN;  Q (11):
C_P_POSSCANC:
C_P_ITEM_END:
      GO TO C_TI_P_TO_P_LFBDY_ITR;
C_TI_P_TO_P_LFBDY_END:
      IF VEND_MSG.MSG_CODE¬= 'SV' THEN GO TO C_CD_P_FM_P_PT_ALT;
      TERM_OUT_REC = ORD_SV_MSG_D;
      TRL_REC.ORD_ID = WS_ORDER_ID;
      STARS = '*****';
      TRL_REC.FILLER_1 = ' ';
      WRITE FILE (LOGFILE) FROM (TRL_REC);
      GO TO C_CD_P_FM_P_PT_END;
C_CD_P_FM_P_PT_ALT:
      TERM_OUT_REC = ORD_DL_MSG_D;
C_CD_P_FM_P_PT_END:
      CLOSE FILE (LOGFILE), FILE (DATABASE);
      CALL DELETEWS (PROGID, TERM_ID);
      CALL PUTE (TERM_OUT_REC);
      END POP3;
```

Note the position of the final "PUTE" operation. We know from the TPM specification that PUTE directs a data string to the terminal and returns to TPM for the last time. If we had called PUTE where the final DIS-PLAYs were in POP2, the program would never be called again to perform all subsequent operations. Therefore, having moved the appropriate data to the TERM-OUT-REC area, we delay the invocation of PUTE until the remaining operations of the program have been performed. Hence the position of PUTE as the dynamically last operation in the program.

Comments on the Solution.

The solution is presented in all the gory details of COBOL and PL/I.

Nest-free coding is needed because, to resume at a read in the middle of a program, the inversion mechanism needs a jump (yes, a GOTO, but remember this is implementation) from the beginning of the subroutine to the appropriate resume point. Entering most structured coding constructs from other than their beginning is prohibited.

You might like to look at these nest-free implementations of POP2 and satisfy yourself that, although the coding is ugly, they are nevertheless exact implementations of the structured program we have designed. An iteration does not cease to be an iteration just because it is implemented by a conditional GOTO at its head and an unconditional GOTO at its foot.

We cannot achieve elegant code in any commonly used language without abandoning or distorting the structure of the whole conversation. We see a choice here between good structure with ugly code and bad structure with good code. We unhesitantly choose the good structure despite the ugly code.

The JSP approach to the problem of on-line design is to draw structures of logically-connected conversations, the elementary components of which are individual transactions. The conventional approach is arboricidal. The individual transactions are specified independently; nowhere is the structure of the tree explicitly considered.

Some of the important ideas in JSD are anticipated in this third version of the problem. The program structure describes the whole lifetime of a conversation; in JSD a model structure describes the whole of an entity's life. The traditional approach is more piecemeal; chronological relationships are not captured. The long-running program is later transformed into a module that is fitted into the implementation environment by the technique of program inversion.

In chapter 2.4 there is a description of a further implementation technique applied to POP.

Having thought about the three versions of this problem separately, you might like to think of all the steps involved in the solution of the problem if it had been specified as a single problem. They would be:

Draw the system network diagram of the equivalent main program. (For a subroutine specification, the equivalent main program is the program that, when inverted, will give the subroutine.)

Draw the data structure of the good TERM IN.

Elaborate this data structure to include errors.

Draw the other data structures.

Define correspondences, and compose the data structures into the program structure.

List and allocate the operations.

Write the structure text of the program.

Add the conditions and do the backtracking.

Code in a nest-free inverted form.

Add coding to store local variables between invocations.

(There is bound to be some iteration within the early steps.)

This is what is meant by decomposition of the development process, as opposed to simply decomposition of the problem.

Chapter 2.4   Summary of JSP

The whole of JSP is described in The JSP Handbook, a pocket-sized booklet used by programmers as a concise reference. The JSP Handbook is reproduced in Section 2.4.1.

In Section 2.4.2, further explanation is given of some points that are not covered by examples elsewhere in this text. These points are dealt with in the same order as the topics in the Handbook.

2.4.1 The JSP Handbook

JSP HANDBOOK — CONTENTS

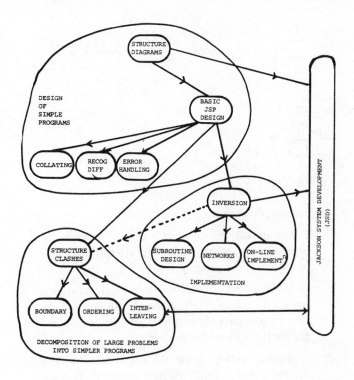

Relationship between JSP Topics

The diagram shows the main relationships between the various topics in JSP. An arrow from A to B means that A is a prerequisite for B.

There is a dotted line from inversion to structure clashes because inversion in needed only for some implementations of structure clash problems.

The topics in JSP which are most necessary for an understanding of JSD are also shown: interleaving clashes are closely related to JSD, but neither is exactly a prerequisite for the other.

Notations Used In JSP

System Network Diagram (SND)

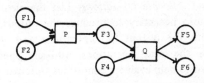

Circle: a serial data stream. Rectangle: a program.

Examples of serial data streams:

- a stream of messages input (or output) via a terminal

- a physical serial file

- a stream of segments or records serially accessed on a database

- a sequence of invocations of a subroutine

Structure Diagram   Structure Text

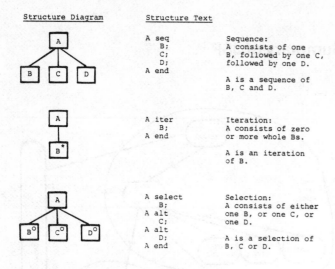

```
A seq              Sequence:
  B;               A consists of one
  C;               B, followed by one C,
  D;               followed by one D.
A end
                   A is a sequence of
                   B, C and D.


A iter             Iteration:
  B;               A consists of zero
A end              or more whole Bs.

                   A is an iteration
                   of B.


A select           Selection:
  B;               A consists of either
A alt              one B, or one C, or
  C;               one D.
A alt
  D;               A is a selection of
A end              B, C or D.
```

Basic Design Procedure

0. If not already drawn, draw a system network diagram showing all the serial data streams input and output from the program.

1. *Data Structures.* Draw a structure diagram for each serial data stream. The diagram should describe the view of that data stream which needs to be imposed for the purposes of this program.

2. *Program Structure.* Merge the several data structure diagrams into a single program structure diagram. To do this, correspondences are defined, corresponding components must form a single component in the program structure, and the program structure can be verified by recovering each data structure in turn.

3. *List and Allocate Operations.* List the elementary operations necessary to produce the output, starting with the output I/O operations and working back to the input operations. Add any operations required to help evaluate conditions. Allocate operations into the program structure.

4. *Text Step.* Transcribe the program structure diagram with allocated operations into structure text. Add conditions to selections and iterations.

5. *Implementation.* Include possible inversion, separate compilation of modules, possible optimisations, and program coding.

The whole of the basic design procedure may be preceded by a bout of *bottom-up design* which enhances the programming language and hence the power of the operations listed in step 3. The operations listed in step 3 are operations in the (possibly enhanced) program language.

Only use bottom-up design if the more powerful operations are of general use in the application area.

Checkpoints in the Basic Design Procedure

The two major checkpoints follow:

1. If there are not enough correspondences at step 2 to form a program structure, then either there is a structure clash or the data structures are not correct for this problem.

2. If some operation does not allocate in an easy and trivial manner, then the program structure is wrong, and probably the data structures are wrong also.

Direct Access Files

Files which are accessed directly by keys supplied by another serial input data stream may be omitted from the SND. Their data structures, if drawn, will not contribute to the program structure.

Files which are accessed directly by keys internally generated (e.g., in a linked list) must be in the SND and will therefore have data structures.

Correspondences

Two components (from different data structures) correspond if they must be processed quasi-simultaneously. Put another way, there must be

- some functional relationship between the components,

- the same number of each component in any one program instance, and

- the pairs of functionally related instances must occur in the same order.

Program Structure Verification

For each data structure,

1. remove from the boxes all text that does not refer to the data structure of interest,

2. delete any subtrees that contain no text at all,

3. apply transformations such as

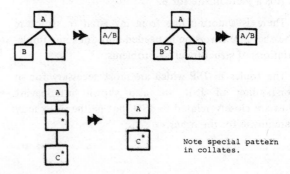

Note special pattern in collates.

and

4. verify that the result is the same as that in the original data structure.

Allocating Operations

Each operation is allocated to program components by asking the following questions:

- How often is this operation executed? Once per . . . .
- Where is it executed, relative to what is already there?

Note that we go down the list of operations, putting them into the structure. We don't scan the structure, inserting suitable operations.

Special Allocation of Read Operation

The above allocation rule places the read operation at the beginning of each C-RECORD component. This is the zero read ahead position.

The problem with zero read ahead is that there is an excessive amount of backtracking, which can be avoided by shifting reads forward in the structure. The following special cases cover most practical problems:

- *Single Read Ahead*

  For input streams, which have an "eof" or recognisable last record and which have no constraints on their I/O relative to other streams, allocate one read immediately after the open; allocate a read at the end of every C-RECORD components. If there are recognition difficulties, this rule can be replaced by the similar *multiple read ahead* rule.

- *Conversational Constraint*

  For input streams on which the reads must alternate with the writes on another output stream, the constraint prevents a shift of a read past a write on the other stream.

  In the body of the program allocate a read immediately after a write on the other stream. At the beginning and end of the program, allocate according to whether this program begins and/or ends the conversation.

  A trivial variation is when the conversation has several writes alternating with several reads.

- *Different Read Operations*

  In database environments (and also, e.g., FORTRAN), a variety of read operations are used to access a single serial data stream. Shifting reads sometimes must be contained within parts of the structure that use only one read. Sometimes a database can usefully be thought of as a set of serial streams.

Group-id Rule

If a structure contains a component that is a group of records all having the same value of a (usually sorted) identifier, then there must be an operation that stores the value of the identifier. This operation should be allocated once per group, at the beginning of group.

Nest-Free COBOL

Sequence

```
A seq                 ASEQ.
  B;                       B
A end                 AEND.

        For ordinary nested COBOL nothing needs to
        be coded for the A construct.
```

Iteration

```
A itr while (cond-B)  AITR.  IF NOT COND-B GO TO AEND.
  B;                           B
A end                        GO TO AITR.
                      AEND.

        For ordinary nested COBOL use PERFORM B
        UNTIL NOT COND-B. If the COND-B involves
        a variable which is incremented, perhaps use
        the VARYING option.
```

Selection

```
A sel (cond-B)        ASLCT. IF NOT COND-B GO TO AALT1.
  B;                           B
A alt (cond-C)               GO TO AEND.
  C;                  AALT1. IF NOT COND-C GO TO AALT2.
A alt (cond-D)               C
  D;                         GO TO AEND.
A end                 AALT2.
                             D
                      AEND.

        For ordinary nested COBOL use IF COND-B THEN B
        ELSE IF COND-C THEN C ELSE D.
```

Backtracking   (selection)

```
A posit               APOSIT.
  B                          B
A quit (cond-X)       AQUIT1. IF COND-X GO TO AADMIT.
  C                          C
A admit                      GO TO AEND.
  D                   AADMIT.
A end                        D
                      AEND.
```

Backtracking   (iteration) (posit another iterated part, only)

```
A itr                 AITR.
  B                          B
A quit (cond-X)       AQUIT1. IF COND-X GO TO AEND.
  C                          C
A end                        GO TO AITR.
                      AEND.
```

Nest-Free PL/I

Sequence

```
A seq                 ASEQ:
  B;                         B;
A end                 AEND:

        For ordinary nested PL/I nothing needs to
        be coded for the A construct.
```

Iteration

```
A itr while (cond-B)  AITR: IF ⌐ COND_B THEN GOTO AEND;
  B                         B;
A end                       GOTO AITR;
                      AEND:

        For ordinary nested PL/I use DO WHILE (COND_B);
        .... END;
```

Selection

```
A sel (cond-B)        ASLCT: IF ⌐ COND_B THEN GOTO AALT1;
  B;                         B;
```

47

```
A alt (cond-C)                      GOTO AEND;
    C;              AALT1:  IF 7 COND_C THEN GOTO AALT2;
A alt (cond-D)                      C;
    D;                              GOTO AEND;
A end               AALT2:
                                    D;
                    AEND:
```
For ordinary nested PL/I use a SELECT-group or optionally an IF statement for selections of only 2 parts.

<u>Backtracking</u> (selection)

```
A posit             APOSIT:
    B;                              B;
A quit (cond-X)     AQUIT:  IF COND_X THEN GOTO AEND;
    C;                              C;
A admit                             GOTO AEND;
    D;              AADMIT:
A end                               D;
                    AEND:
```

<u>Backtracking</u> (iteration) (posit another iterated part, only)

```
A itr               AITR:
    B                               B;
A quit (cond-X)     AQUIT1: IF COND_X THEN GOTO AEND;
    C                               C;
A end                               GOTO AITR;
                    AEND:
```

Hints in Drawing Data Structures

Most of the difficult thinking in JSP takes place at the data structure stage. If you are having problems here, the following suggestions may help.

1. Keywords. Look for the keywords in the specification and make sure they fit your structure.

   Some keywords for sequence: before, after, first, last, start, end, follows, precedes, and, next, and middle.

   Some keywords for selection: either, or, alternative, sometimes, possible.

   Some keywords for iteration: several, a number, many, and first or last of a group.

2. Make some instances of the data stream and see what groupings or associations suggest themselves. This is particularly useful for the terminal input and output streams in on-line problems.

3. Make sure your data structure is the one you want to impose on the data stream and that you are not unduly influences by some background, more physical structure.

4. Have you a selection in your structure where there should be an iteration?

5. Are you avoiding a recognition difficulty by trying to draw a complex dynamically motivated structure?

6. Draw the other data structures and see if they give you a hint.

7. Make a list of operations and ask yourself what sort of components will be necessary for a successful allocation.

8. Try to isolate the difficulty: solve a simpler problem, one which perhaps doesn't have the difficulty,

or attack the difficulty in isolation from the rest of the problem.

9. Talk to other people: show them the problem, not your diagnosis of the difficulty or your attempted solution. Don't pick holes in their solution—an imperfect solution may still hold the key to the difficulty.

10. Get a good night's sleep, and try again.

11. Think about what you might have done without JSP and then work back. Don't be like the centipede:

> The centipede was happy quite,
> Until the Toad in fun
> Said "Pray which leg goes after which?"
> And worked her mind to such a pitch,
> She lay distracted in the ditch
> Considering how to run.

Collating

A collating problem has two or more input data streams, which are consumed simultaneously, according to the value of a key.

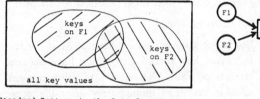

Standard Pattern in the Data Structures

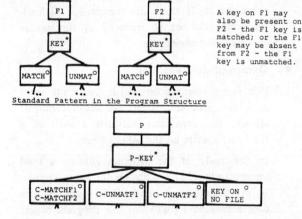

A key on F1 may also be present on F2 - the F1 key is matched; or the F1 key may be absent from F2 - the F1 key is unmatched.

Standard Pattern in the Program Structure

Notes

1. Usually the program is not concerned with keys which are on neither file. Sometimes it is only concerned with 2 or the 4 possible parts of the selection.

2. Often there are many records for one value of the key; there will be an iteration or other structure below the MATCH and UNMAT part of the data structure.

3. Store the "nextkey" at the beginning of P and the end of P-KEY. Use bottom-up components to handle key values.

Recognition Difficulties

Classification of Recognition Difficulties

1. Soluble by examining a fixed number of records ahead on an input stream.

2. Soluble only if a variable number of records can be examined.

3. Soluble only if certain operations (e.g. direct access on a database) are executed.

Multiple Read Ahead

Only usable on the 1st class of recognition difficulties.

— determine n—the no. of records to be read ahead

— declare n record areas, each with "eof" bit

— define Nread operation

— allocate n Nreads immediately after the open operation and 1 Nread at the end of C-RECORD component

Use of the Read Ahead Area

The $(n-1)$ records in the read ahead area, beyond the immediately next record, are only used for the evaluation of conditions. A record is only processed (used in assignments) when it has moved up to become the next record.

Example of Nread Operation ($n=3$)

```
NREAD seq
   move area1 to area0;
   move area2 to area1;
   NNEW select (not eof)
       read file into data2;
   NNEW alt (eof)
   NNEW end
   NEOF select (not eof)          i.e. still not eof
       set not-eof2;
   NEOF alt (eof)
       set eof2;                  A more sophisticated
   NEOF end                       nread might set pointers
NREAD end                         rather than move whole
                                  areas.
```

eof0	data0	area0	(=next/current)
eof1	data1	area1	(=next+1)
eof2	data2	area2	(=next+2)

Backtracking Procedure

1. Complete the design, ignoring the recognition difficulty. (Assume that there will be a helpful demon available when required.)

2. Posit one path, and insert quits at the points in the program text where the hypothesis might be disproved. (For a selection, replace select ... alt by posit ... admit, having first converted to 2-part selections, and possibly reordering the parts. For an iteration, make the while condition ="true" if we wish to posit the iterated part and ="false" if we wish to posit that there is no further iterated part.)

3. Identify and deal with side effects.

Note that the structure text at the end of step 1 of this procedure is the same as if we were using multiple read ahead.

Classification of Side Effects

An operation causes side effects if it changes the value of a data item or if it reads or writes a file where also

- the data item or file is not local to the posit path and

- the operation can be executed in a posit path before the execution of a quit.

Side Effects can be

- beneficent — usually can remove part of the admit path,

- neutral — usually can be ignored, or

- intolerable — when two basic techniques, pretend/really (pretend to do the operation in the posit path, really do it only after passing the last quit) and do/undo (undo the operation at the beginning of the admit path) are used.

A note/restore on a file is a way of undoing reads and writes. Otherwise, we usually must pretend to write by holding the records in a termporary store, and, similarly, to undo reads by allowing rereads from a temporary store.

Other Points

1. The introduction of a posit switch by generalising a backtracking structure is often a convenient and attractive optimisation.

2. Posit ordering rules for selection: specific before general, not exists before exists and, choose the easier order.

3. Posit rule for iteration: where possible, posit another part to the iteration.

4. When there are many quits and difficult, intolerable side effects, we may have to regularise the quit state

by moving some quits, by undoing some side effects within the quit construct, or by having a mixture of multiple read ahead and backtracking.

Error Handling

Good/Error Data: Good data is data input to the system as intended. Error data is input data that differs from what was intended.

Valid/Invalid Data: Valid data is data for which the operation of the program is specified. For invalid data, the operation is unspecified.

Some Principles

1. Programs check for error data, not invalid data. The range of validity of a JSP program is defined by the input data structure(s).

2. Programs can't diagnose errors with certainty. Diagnostics describe the way a program interprets given data. The wording of a diagnostic is essentially the same as the name of the data component to which it refers (and to which it is allocated).

3. The program structure must be based on data structures that describe all valid data, both good and erroneous. The full input data structure can be built up by successively elaborating the structure of good data.

4. Good data structures can be elaborated in different ways to favour different types of errors. Favouring one type of error usually implies misinterpretation of others.

Some Characteristic Data Structure Patterns

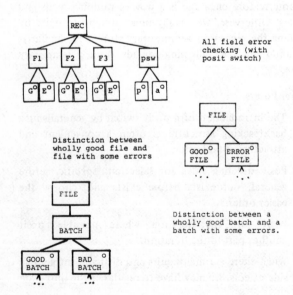

All field error checking (with posit switch)

Distinction between wholly good file and file with some errors

Distinction between a wholly good batch and a batch with some errors.

Elaboration of the good structure GF to accommodate errors of omission (FO), errors of insertion (FI), and errors of mispunching (FM). Note that most on-line errors are dealt with as if they were errors of insertion.

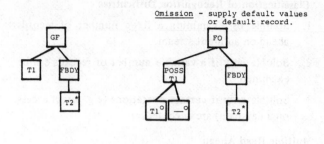

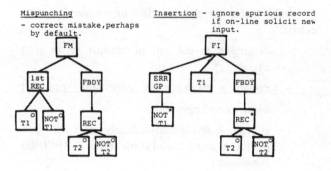

Program Inversion

Basic Idea

A simple program designed using JSP reads and writes serial data streams. During design, we probably think of the program as a module which runs without interruption from beginning to end; however, this is not necessarily so. The same program, built by the same design steps, can be inverted so that it partially executes, suspends itself, and then resumes where it left off on the next invocation. An inverted program is a program which has been coded in this resumable form.

Principle of Inversion Coding

A program can be inverted with respect to one or more of its data streams. The suspension points in the inverted program are (roughly) the reads and writes of these data streams. The records of these data streams are supplied and taken away by the invoking program.

Most inversion coding conventions introduce a single local variable (QS) and set it to a different value before each relevant I/O operation, place a label immediately after the I/O operation, and replace the I/O operation itself by a return to the invoking level. A branch point at the beginning of the program tests QS and directs control to the relevant label.

Some Uses of Program Inversion

1. Designing variable state subroutines
   - first specify the equivalent main program
   - design using standard JSP
   - invert to give the subroutine that meets the specification of the interface

2. Implementing on-line conversational programs in many (though not all) TP environments
   - JSP program design covers the whole of an on-line conversation, including what is often called on-line system design. The JSP program is inverted with respect to the terminal input stream to give the required module.
   - A conversational program can be inverted to give a pseudo-conversational program.

3. Implementing a network of programs as a single module

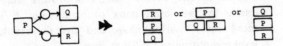

4. Producing interrupt-driven routines in low level software

5. Producing input and output modules for manufacturer's sort programs

Standard Inversion Coding (COBOL)

Standard Inversion coding is used for inversions

- which are made with respect to a single data stream,

- where the inversion does not have to satisfy an arbitrary interface, or

- where the coding in the invoking program also satisfies this standard.

The rules below refer to separately compiled inverted programs, invoked with a CALL. With only slight modifications, they also apply to sections or paragraphs invoked by a PERFORM.

Inversion with respect to an input data stream   **Inversion with respect to an output data stream**

In the calling program:

1. Declare 77 EOF PIC *X* VALUE SPACE.

2. For the open *F*, code nothing.

3. For each write FREC, CALL *"B"* USING EOF FREC.

4. For the close *F*, code: MOVE *"E"* TO EOF. CALL *"B"* USING EOF FREC.

3. For each read *F*, code: CALL *"A"* USING EOF FREC.

4. For the close *F*, code: CALL *"A"* USING EOF FREC.

In the inverted (called) program:

1. Declare 77 QS PIC S99 COMP VALUE 1.

2. At the beginning of the procedure division, code:
   GO TO Q1 Q2 .. Qn DEPENDING ON QS.
   Q1.

3. For the open *F*, code nothing.

4. For the 1st read *F*, code nothing. For the other read *F*, code: MOVE *n* TO QS. GOBACK. Qn.

5. For the close *F*, code nothing.

4. For each write *F*, code:
   MOVE *n* TO QS. GOBACK. Qn.

5. For the close *F*, code: MOVE *"E"* TO EOF. MOVE *n* TO QS. GOBACK. Qn.

6. At the end of the procedure division, code: GOBACK.

Standard Inversion Coding (PL/I)

Standard Inversion coding is used for inversions

- made with respect to a single data stream,

- where the inversion does not have to satisfy a nonstandard interface, or

- where the coding in the invoking program also satisfies this standard.

The rules below apply whether the inverted program is to be an external or an internal procedure.

Inversion with respect to an input data stream   **Inversion with respect to an output data stream**

In the calling program:

1. DECLARE EOF BIT(1) INIT ("O"B);
2. For the open F, code nothing.

3. For each write FREC, code: CALL B(EOF, FREC);

4. For the close F, code: EOF: ="1"B; CALL B(EOF,FREC);

3. For each read F, code: CALL A(EOF,FREC);
4. For the close F, code: CALL A(EOF,FREC);

In the inverted (called) program:

1. DECLARE QS BINARY FIXED STATIC INIT (1); DECLARE Q(m) LABEL;
2. At the beginning of the executable statements, code: GOTO Q(QS); Q(1):
3. For the open F, code nothing.

4. For the 1st read, code nothing. For the other read F, code: QS =n; RETURN; Q(n):
5. For the close F, code nothing.

4. For each write F, code: QS: =n; RETURN; Q(n) :
5. For the close F, code: EOF ='1'B; QS =n; RETURN; Q(n):
6. At the end of the executable statements, code: RETURN;

Complex Inversions

Multiple Inversions

A program can be inverted with respect to more than one of its serial data streams. Records of more than one data stream are then passed across the interface between invoking and invoked modules.

Introduce extra information into the interface to specify reason for returning to invoking level.

(In many subroutine problems the interface is already specified, and the inversion must be made to fit the given rules.)

Conversational Constraint

If F is an input and G is an output stream of P, then F and G satisfy the conversational constraint in P, if on every execution of P the reads on F strictly alternate with the writes on G.

Because the order of I/O operations on F and G is predictable on the other side of an interface, no extra information need be introduced if P is inverted with respect to both F and G.

Often, F will be written and G will be read by the same program Q, and they will satisfy the conversational constraint in Q as well. A standard inversion can make P a subroutine of Q, or vice versa, one record passing in each direction on each invocation. First, move the reads so that they pair with the writes; then apply standard inversion rules, replacing each write-read with the remember, return, and resume mechanism.

State Vector Separation

Used in many on-line environments and also as a common implementation of a problem with an interleaving clash.

1. Remove the working storage variables from the inverted program P (including QS); call the aggregate of storage so obtained the state vector of P.
2. Between invocations the state vector must be stored. In the on-line case, P will store the SV itself. In the interleaving problem case, P will move the SV into linkage and give the invoking level responsibility for SV storage.
3. Set up a mechanism to ensure that QS = 1 on the first invocation.

The effect is to allow a single piece of executable code to implement a number of similar processes that are running quasi-simultaneously.

On-Line Programming Environments

Ask these questions about an on-line programming environment.

1. Are you required to write an inverted program for acceptable efficiency? (Remember this program will deal with the whole of the conversation.)
2. If the answer to 1 is yes, where can the state vector be stored (in temporary storage, in a file, protected and invisible on the screen, etc.)?
3. If the answer to 1 is yes, do you ever have inverted programs which are too large for acceptable efficiency? If yes, what mechanism is available for specifying, on return from one module to the TP monitor, which module is to be called next (set TRANSID, . . .?)

On-line Dismemberment

To be used only when the answers to both questions 1 and 3 are yes, and then only as required.

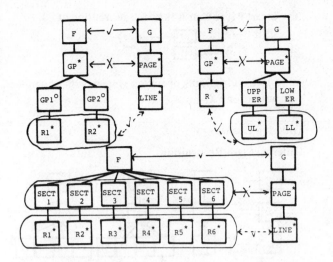

1. Make as many copies of the inverted program (or the structure text, for convenience) as there are values of QS. Name the *j*th copy *Pj*, where *P* was the old id.

2. On the *j*th copy, delete all code not reachable in one invocation, on entering at *Qj*.

3. On every copy add the mechanism "next module: = Pi;" beside each remaining assignment "QS: =-i;".

Now there are many small modules. Optionally we may reduce the number by the following methods:

4. If 2 modules are identical, except for the name, remove one, say Pk, leaving say Pl; then in all copies, simply replace "next module:=Pk;" by "next module:=Pl;".

5. If module Pk is a subset of Pl, then we may do the same as in 4.

6. If module Pk and Pl have a large common subset, then we may make a module Pkl the union of Pk and Pl and use "next module:= Pkl;" in all copies instead of both "next module:= Pk;" and "next module:= Pl;".

Boundary Clashes

Basic Recognition Pattern

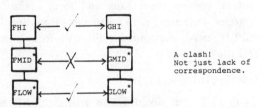

A clash!
Not just lack of
correspondence.

FMID and GMID must both be necessary components—each must have an operation which is allocated to it.

FMID and GMID cannot be related by sequence, selection, or iteration. There is no relationship between the boundaries of a FMID and a GMID.

Variations in the Recognition Pattern

There is rarely a direct correspondence at the lower level.

Boundary Clash Resolution

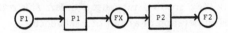

Two programs are connected by an intermediate data stream.

P1 will contain the structural component FMID.
P2 will contain the structural component GMID.

Define the contents of FX before starting seriously on the design of either P1 or P2. Use modelling arguments about what should be done in P1 and P2 to help with the definition of FX. Don't push extra work into P1 just because it is the first of the programs.

Information about FMID may appear in the records of FX and even may be partially processed in P2, but FMID may not appear structurally in P2. These tenets apply similarly for GMID in P1.

Sometimes there is more than one boundary clash, and three programs are needed for a successful resolution.

Boundary Clash Implementation

Common implementations

1. Run P1 and P2 as separate programs; FX is stored on a physical medium.

2. Invert P2, so that it runs as a subroutine of P1.

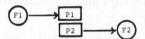

3. Invert P1, so that it runs as a subroutine of P2.

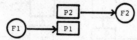

4. Use a multitasking operating system, with a bounded buffer for FX.

Ordering Clashes

Ordering Clash Recognition

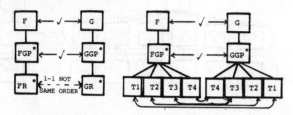

Essentially, the same components are in each structure, but they are in a rearranged order. This ordering can be as an iteration or as part of a sequence.

The GP level is not necessary for the clash. The lowest component which corresponds to and that which contains the misordering is called the *lowest containing component*.

Sometimes an ordering clash is not even exactly 1-1. For example, an on-line browse shows the following:

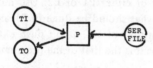

Ordering Clash Resolution

Make a sequence of components which communicate by some intermediate storage.

Either 1. The components are programs P1 and P2; the output of P1 is sorted to give the input to P2.

Sometimes we don't need both P1 and P2. P1(2) can be inverted with respect to FX1(2) to make a sort input (output) routine.

Or 2. The components are within the program, in sequence immediately below the lowest containing component. The left part of the sequence consumes the input and produces the intermediate storage; the right part consumes the storage and produces the output. Usually not all the lowest containing component needs to be stored.

Interleaving Clashes

Interleaving Clash Recognition

No structure can be imposed on the input data stream except:

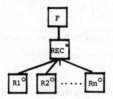

The problem is that useful structure can only be imposed on a subset of the data stream, and this subset is interleaved with other similar subsets. One subset contains the data associated with one entity.

The selection below REC can be either on entity-id or on record type within entity.

Interleaving Clash Resolution

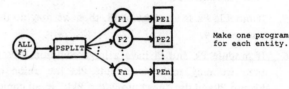

Make one program for each entity.

Interleaving Clash Implementations

1. If the complete ALLFj data stream is available, sort it; the program which reads the sorted file is an iteration of PEj.

2. Invert PEj with respect to Fj and separate out state vectors, passing them back and forth across the interface between PSPLIT and the subroutine PE. PSPLIT must put and get the SVs from a suitable file or database.

Interleaving Clashes and JSD

Using JSD, one would follow a slightly different path to the same solution. JSD would concentrate on the entity programs PEj, rather than on an analysis of input and output data streams.

Interleaving clashes lie on the boundary of JSP and JSD.

2.4.2 Miscellaneous Points

Notations. Structure diagrams are a limited language. For example, the number of instances of an iterated part cannot be defined, nor can the fact that two iteration components in the same structure have the same number of iterated parts, nor can all the instances of a given iterated part have the same value of an identifying field.

In a procedural language, we could add local variables to the data structure and annotate the diagram with the extra restrictions expressed in terms of the local variables. These local variables are normally needed for the evaluation of conditions rather than for the calculation of output. Sometimes we call the operations that assign their values "structure-derived" operations, to distinguish them from the operations that calculate the output. In a strict version of JSP, local variables of the two types are kept separate and therefore

> no local variable used in a condition is ever used directly or indirectly to calculate output,

> no local variable used to calculate output ever appears in a condition, and

> variables in an input record may not be used in any condition after they have been used on the right-hand side of any assignment statement.

These rules are slightly stricter than are used in practice, but they are usually satisfied by normal application of JSP. They are the result of the separation of recognition issues and functional issues.

Basic JSP Design. In the Purchase Order Problem, the database is directly accessed using keys taken from the TERM IN data stream. No structure diagram is drawn of the database stream. Such a diagram would not contribute to the program structure, as everything relevant about the database is already expressed in the structure of TERM IN. (The note on direct-access files in The JSP Handbook describes a class of data streams for which diagrams need not be drawn.)

If the read was allocated like any other operation, it would appear at the beginning of each C-RECORD component in the structure. We have used single read-ahead, to avoid excessive recognition difficulties. Single read-ahead is a dynamic shift of the reads forward in the execution of the program, so that input records are available earlier for the evaluation of conditions. Multiple read-ahead represents a further dynamic shift of the reads and is used as an alternative to backtracking.

Sometimes there are constraints inherent in a problem on the relative orderings of I/O operations on different data streams. The simplest and most common example is the conversational constraint, by which reads on one data stream must alternate with writes on another. Reads must never be shifted forward so that they violate this constraint. Multiple read-ahead can never be used with the conversational constraint. For some problems, even single read-ahead is enough to violate the constraint. The furthest a read can be shifted under the conversational constraint is up to the write that is constraining it. (The problems for which single read-ahead violates the conversational constraint are those in which the constrained input and output structures do not exactly correspond.)

In FORTRAN or in accessing databases, several different read operations may be used. This also implies some variant on the way reads are allocated. A global shift to the single read-ahead position will not be possible.

These comments refer to the notes on read allocation in The JSP Handbook.

Nest-Free Coding in COBOL and PL/I. A knowledge of nest-free coding is necessary for program inversion. Nest-free code is ugly and certainly need not be used outside these special circumstances.

Hints in Drawing Data Structures. The hints reflect the central importance of finding a suitable data structure in JSP and the fact that this is the most difficult and potentially discouraging of the steps.

Collating. Optimisation of the standard collating structure is possible when the matched case is processed the same way as the sum of the unmatched cases. For example, three input files each containing a monotonic sequence of integers (including duplicates) are to be processed to output a file with one copy only of each integer that is on any file. The optimised structure uses only the matched structure, excluding the other possible parts to the selection.

Usually, for multiple file collates, only some of the possible two-to-the-nth-power components remain in the program structure selection. Here is an example. Four files are to be collated. One is the day's input of invoices, and one is the day's input of payments on the invoices. The other two are, respectively, the unmatched invoices and the unmatched payments leftover from the previous day's run. Assume that payments are for a unique invoice and completely clear the invoice. The problem is to match payments to invoices and to output the leftovers for the next day. If there can be no match between the two leftover files, and if there can be no match between the leftover payments and the new payments or between the leftover invoices and the new invoices, and if we are not interested in keys that are on no file at all, how many of the sixteen possible parts to the selection in the four-file collate are present? The answer is seven.

Recognition Difficulties. As discussed in Section 2.3.2, the QUIT is a GOTO with an implied target label.

Backtracking can be avoided, but only at the cost of drawing structures that are artificial and do not reflect the problem. For example, suppose good groups are to be written to a file and bad groups dropped. A good group contains exactly five records, each of which satisfies certain conditions (different for each record). The JSP structure of the input stream is Figure 2.4a. The alternative structure, avoiding any recognition problem, is Figure 2.4b. This daisy chain structure, so called

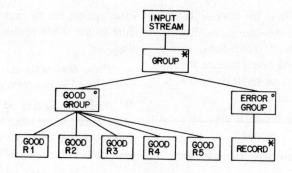

Figure 2.4a

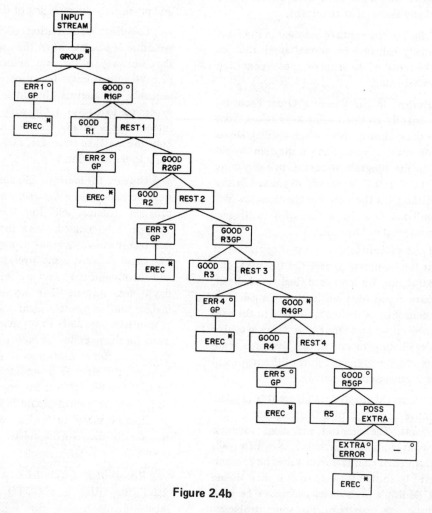

Figure 2.4b

because of the shape of the chain of selections, is not the reflection of any user's view of the problem. The structure is coloured by the dynamic view of the execution of the program.

The structure in Figure 2.4b would not be chosen if we were going to use multiple read-ahead.

The choice in method is between a structure that does not reflect the problem and recognition difficulties

that may require backtracking and GOTOs. JSP chooses the latter. As remarked earlier, the choice must justify itself, not only in principle but also by practical use. The example shows that the freedom to draw data structures that ignore recognition difficulties allows a considerable simplification.

In general, if the handling of side-effects is very difficult, an even more explicit separation of recognition issues and functional issues may be made. In Figure 2.4c, suppose that PCPT is a program component that has a recognition difficulty with horrific side-effects. PCPT may be decomposed into PRECOG, which outputs a copy of F on H and the answer to the recognition question on J, and into PFN, which performs the functional part of PCPT. This arrangement is shown in Figure 2.4d. PRECOG and PFN both have the same structure as PCPT. PRECOG has the same recognition problem, but now the side-effects are all beneficent. PFN has no recognition problem, because it reads J before H. The solution is essentially a two-pass solution because H must be buffered (since PRECOG writes J after H). Many error-vetting problems, for which the traditional solution is to put a group of records in a table and then make a second pass of the table, are recognition problems of this type.

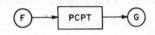

Figure 2.4c

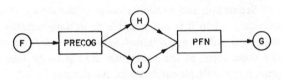

Figure 2.4d

Error Handling. The difference between good/error and valid/invalid is important, even if different terms are used. (The almost universal use of "to validate", meaning to check for errors, suggests that the JSP choice of words is not the most fortunate.) Error data are possible but unfortunate. Invalid data are impossible, or, at any rate, are data for which there is no specified response.

If a program is considered as a mathematical function (though this is not encouraged in JSP), the domain of the function is the valid data. Elaborating an input data structure for errors simply extends the domain.

Various patterns of error elaboration are shown in The JSP Handbook.

All-field error checking is an irresistibly attractive example of optimisation by generalising the structure and introducing a switch. Suppose a choice has to be made between a totally error-free record and a record with errors; all the fields on an error record must be checked and diagnosed. The correct structure is shown in Figure 2.4e. The GFs are shown in the structure only for clarity. The field structure of an error record is necessary because individual fields are diagnosed. This is an example in which the structure of the stream does extend

below the level of the record. As is commonly true in diagnostic programs, the error structure does not explicitly show that there must be at least one error.

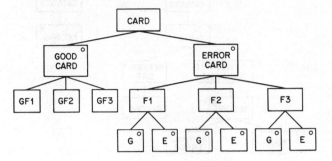

Figure 2.4e

The optimised structure is the first structure in the Error Handling section of The JSP Handbook. The posit switch, psw, is set to "p" initially and to "a" at any point at which there would have been a QUIT to the admit part. The two values of psw allow one structure to do duty for two. At the end, psw is tested so that operations allocated to either GOODCARD only or ERRORCARD only can be executed correctly. This optimisation depends on all the side-effects of the underlying backtracking problem being beneficend.

Figures 2.4f and 2.4g show two common (unoptimised) error-handling structures. In Figure 2.4f, any error is enough to mess up the file, but we are still interested in distinguishing good and error groups in an error file, and good and error records in an error group. In Figure 2.4g, there are three levels of error. For a catastrophic error, processing is abandoned on the whole file; for a serious error, processing is abandoned on the group; and for a normal error, processing is abandoned only for that record.

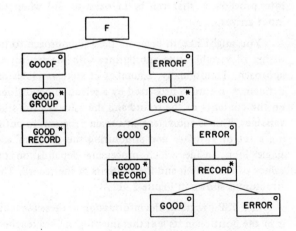

Figure 2.4f

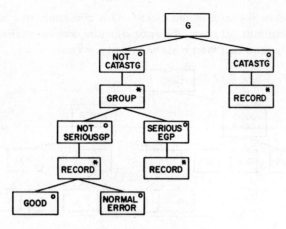

Figure 2.4g

Program Inversion. Program inversion converts a program into a variable-state subroutine. To design a variable-state subroutine in JSP, first recognise the main program to which it is equivalent, design it using the usual JSP steps, and then invert to give the desired subroutine.

Program inversion is used in this way in many on-line environments (as for POP3), for interrupt driven routines in low-level software (as in the reprint at the end of Part Three), for input–output procedures (IBM access methods), for input or output procedures to sorts, and, no doubt, in other circumstances as well.

Program inversion can also be used to implement in a single hierarchy any network of programs that form a tree. For many applications, a network decomposition is more natural than hierarchical decomposition (e.g. edit-update-print). Program inversion allows the use of network decomposition, in traditional programming languages, without any necessary accompanying I/O overhead.

We shall see that, in JSD, inversion is used to turn processes, whose input takes many years to accumulate, into procedures that can be invoked as and when the input arrives.

You might like to compare the JSP approach to the design of variable-state subroutines with the traditional approach. Traditionally, a number of state variables are defined. A record is processed by a selection conditional on the contents of the record and the values of the state variables. This is equivalent, in a main program, to defining a set of switches and structuring the program as a single loop, inside which processing depends on the values of the switch and the contents of the record. This structure is shown in Figure 2.4h.

In a JSP program, the information in these switches is in the position in its text that the program has reached. The organisation and layout of the text of the program

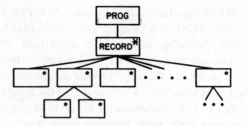

Figure 2.4h

(dare one say the "structure" of the program?) is so arranged that processing can continue correctly without needing to test a set of switches. The position in the text, the text pointer, contains the necessary information. For the subroutine, the text pointer is stored explicitly and is conventionally named "QS". Traditionally subroutine development starts with the specification of these state variables. In JSP, QS emerges at the end, as a result of the program inversion.

Complex Inversions. The state vector (also known as the activation record) is the collective term for the local variables of a program, including the text pointer QS.

Separation and explicit storage of the state vector is necessary when it is not possible to declare variables so that their values are retained between invocations or if the same copy of the procedure text is to be used to implement multiple instances of the process.

On-line Programming Environments. On-line dismemberment is a technique used in environments that require inversion for large conversational programs. The inverted program may be uncomfortably large, in which case it can be dismembered, that is, implemented in several pieces. In the standard form of dismemberment described in The JSP Handbook and illustrated in the reprint for the Purchase Order Problem, each piece always processes a complete input record (a screen) and is able to specify unambiguously as it returns control to the teleprocessing monitor which piece (perhaps itself) is to process the next record.

The idea is not so much to cut one piece of text into parts as it is to have many copies of the text, removing from each the portions that are not needed. In the simplest cases, groups of the remaining texts are identical or at least very similar; similar remainders may be combined into a single module. In the Purchase Order Problem the presence of the null component leads to a complication; some remaining texts are proper subsets of others. If there were no null option there would be three almost disjoint groups of the eleven residues.

People who use the large TP environments for which dismemberment is relevant have different opinions about how much, if any, dismemberment is necessary in practice. Certainly there is no need to do any without good cause.

Traditionally, an analyst cuts up the conversation into chunks and specifies the data interfaces; then a programmer programs the individual chunks. In JSP terms, the local variables of the whole conversational program are specified before anything else, and the lower-level parts of the structure are dealt with in isolation, without any reasonable understanding of the overall structure. This is bad. If you need to dismember, wait until there is a clear definition of what has to be dismembered. If you want to make a jigsaw, you paint the whole picture on the board before cutting it up into pieces, not vice versa.

This arboricide of important tree structures and the premature decomposition to meet implementation constraints is a recurrent characteristic of conventional system design. The JSD approach to systems emphasises the preservation of complete tree structures throughout the specification phase and the dismemberment and restructuring during the later implementation phase. Some ideas central to the JSD approach to systems are illustrated in microcosm in the JSP approach to those on-line developments that have to run under the constraints imposed by typical mainframe teleprocessing environments.

Boundary Clashes. Boundary clashes are well illustrated by the Microfiche case study in Part Three.

Many examples of boundary clashes are caused by some unit of data storage (a page, a block) clashing with some more application-oriented unit. However, boundary clashes are not an artifact of computer systems. The calendar contains the boundary clash between weeks and months or years. Accountants solve this sometimes by decreeing that some years have 52 weeks and some have 53.

The natural units of your work do not necessarily fit well with the sessions you have to do it in. You break off doing something to go to lunch and finish it in the middle of the afternoon.

Inversion is only one way of implementing the two or more programs that result from boundary clashes. You can use a physical data set, a bounded buffer, a pipe if you are running under the UNIX† operating system, or coroutines if you have them; or you can use Ada tasks.

_____
†UNIX is a Trademark of Bell Laboratories.

The central point about a boundary clash is that there is something in the problem that leads you to uncouple the program into two or more programs in the development of the design/specification. There are many ways of implementing the two programs.

Ordering Clashes. There is no specific example of an ordering clash in this book, but this is the most intuitively obvious of the three types of structure clashes, and examples are easy to imagine. The basic solution is to have two components in sequence, one that sets up some *intermediate* storage, the other that reads it. The components may be somewhere within a program structure, or they may be programs with a sort program to rearrange the intermediate storage.

The browsing ordering clash mentioned in The JSP Handbook occurs when a file is only serially accessible and the problem demands arbitrary scanning backwards and forwards on a terminal over the file contents.

Interleaving Clashes. Suppose that you take the input streams for two completely separate programs or two completely separate instances of the same program and arbitrarily *interleave* them on the same data stream. This is an interleaving clash, and the solution is obvious. Separate the single stream into the individual streams again, and input the separate streams to the separate programs or to separate instances of the same program.

The world is full of interleaving clashes, and so are computer systems. The many customers of a bank perform interleaved transactions on their respective accounts. The input from many users of an on-line system is interleaved when it arrives to be processed. The references to a variable in a program are interleaved one with another. Any single view of a set of parallel activities will result in interleaving clashes. The idea that separate activities should be represented by separate processes is central to JSD. Interleaving clashes lie on the boundary of JSP and JSD.

If an interleaved input stream is sorted so that the whole input stream is an iteration of the separate input streams, the overall solution will be an iteration of the separate individual programs. This is a particular scheduling of the individual programs. This approach is only possible if no output is required before all the input is collected, a condition that is sometimes but not often true.

The Car Rally/Golden Handshake pair of examples that are discussed in Chapter 4.1 are examples of interleaving clashes.

Chapter 2.5   More on the Ideas Underlying JSP

2.5.1 The Static/Dynamic Distinction

In the context of programming, there is no real distinction between designing a program, developing an algorithm, and formalising a specification. According to taste and circumstance, JSP is a method for doing any or all of these three tasks. In this section a number of examples are discussed to illustrate this equivalence and to make some further points about the distinction between the static and dynamic properties of programs and specifications. (See also Section 2.2.2.)

A Bad Specification

See Figure 2.5a. The input file K is sorted on the key PNO.

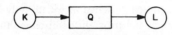

Figure 2.5a

(1) Open the files. Write a header on L. Set PCOUNT to zero. Read the first record of K. Store PNO.

(2) If there are no records on K, see paragraph (8) below.

(3) Process the first record by adding PQTY to PCOUNT if PTYPE = "R", otherwise subtract PQTY from PCOUNT.

(4) Process subsequent records according to whether they are normal records or control-break records. Normal records have a PNO equal to the stored PNO. Control-break records have a PNO not equal to the stored PNO.

(5) Process normal records by adding PQTY to PCOUNT if PTYPE = "R", otherwise subtract PQTY from PCOUNT.

(6) Process control-break records as follows:

Output stored PNO and PCOUNT to L.

If PTYPE = "R" set PCOUNT to PQTY, else set PCOUNT to –PQTY.

Store new PNO.

(7) On reading end-of-file on K, output the stored PNO and PCOUNT.

(8) Output the trailer on L.

(9) Close the files.

Discussion. The problem is stated very dynamically. Everything is in terms of processing the next record. There is an implicit "and then do" between most of the paragraphs. In fact, the whole specification is a program, albeit one written in an imprecise and highly ambiguous language. Faced with such a text, a programmer has two possible courses of action. He can code the program as it stands, translating from one language into another for which he has a compiler, or he can try to figure out what the problem is for which this is a solution. If he chooses the latter, he will eventually realise that the problem is no more than a very distorted statement of the Stores Movement Problem (Chapter 2.1). If he chooses the former, he will head in the direction of a program whose structure is something like that depicted in Figure 2.5b. Figure 2.5b is the structure of the English text in the above specification. Without doubt, the correct structure for this problem is the one developed in Chapter 2.1; the structure is shown in Figure 2.5c.

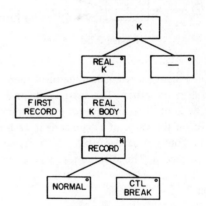

Figure 2.5b

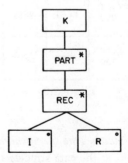

Figure 2.5c

Portions of this Chapter are excerpted from previously unpublished Michael Jackson Systems Limited (MJSL) internal documents with permission from MJSL.

Interim Conclusions

(1) We are aiming to base the structure of the program on the structure of the problem. This is not necessarily the same as the apparent structure of some so-called specifications.

(2) Specifications are poor if they describe the problem in terms of the dynamics of a solution.

This example is a particularly bad specification of a particularly simple problem. Unfortunately, this style of specification is very common, even in installations that have adopted some form of structured programming. Connoisseurs of this style will enjoy paragraph (2), which contains a GOTO branching to paragraph (8).

Choosing a Record from Multiple Keygroups

Specification. (See Figure 2.5d.) The file, F, is sorted on a key. The program P has to remove multiple instances of the key. The algorithm for choosing which record of a multiple record group should be kept, that is, written to the file G, is as follows: Initially designate the first record of a multiple record group as the kept record. Successively compare the next record of the group with the kept record, rejecting one of the pair and making the

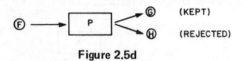

Figure 2.5d

other the new kept record. Continue until there are no more records in the group. The surviving kept record is the one to be kept. The rejection of one or other of the pair depends on the value of a type code in each record. The table in Figure 2.5e describes which of the pair is the new kept record. The rejected records are written to the file H. They must be written out in the order they appeared on F.

NEXT RECORD / KEPT RECORD	TYPE = 999	TYPE ≠ 999
TYPE = 999	KEPT	NEXT
TYPE ≠ 999	KEPT	KEPT

Figure 2.5e

Solution that matches the specification. Figure 2.5f is an initial attempt at the data structures of the files F, G, and H.

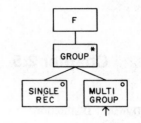

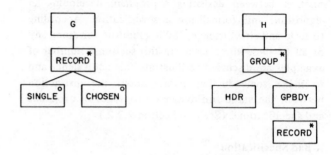

Figure 2.5f

For our present discussion we are only interested in the structure of the program component that processes a multiple record group. However, the reader may note, in passing, the following points:

(1) The structure does match the problem. The problem is about groups: multiple-record groups must be distinguished from single-record groups.

(2) There is a recognition difficulty in the GROUP selection.

(3) The recognition difficulty can be solved by backtracking or by multiple read-ahead. In this case, the latter is by far the simpler method; two records ahead are sufficient.

(4) In the data structure step, the recognition difficulty is ignored; so is the eventual choice between the two methods of resolving the difficulty.

Now consider the data structure of the MULTI-GROUP component of F. The statement of the specification leads in the direction of Figure 2.5g. The condition

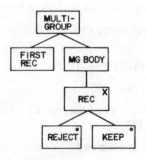

Figure 2.5g

62

on the RECORD selection is written using the information in the table in Figure 2.5e.

Records are rejected in a different order than they appear on F, and therefore are rejected in a different order than they must appear on H. If a record is kept for a while, and is then rejected, it will appear later than it should on H. There is therefore an ordering clash between Figure 2.5g and the structure of the output file, H. This ordering clash can be solved by storing the whole or part of the MULTI-GROUP before writing the rejected records of the group H. However, one is left with the feeling that this solution is not very elegant and that the original problem is not really an ordering clash problem.

The choice of which record of a MULTI-GROUP is to be kept is expressed dynamically by an algorithm. The question that needs to be asked is "Which record is kept?" After some thought you will come to the answer, "If all the records are type 999, keep the first, and otherwise keep the first that has type not equal to 999". This suggests the structure in Figure 2.5h for the input file, F. There is a big recognition difficulty between the two kinds of MULTI-GROUP, but this is not relevant at the data structure step.

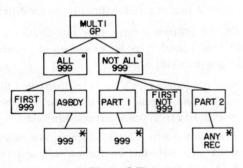

Figure 2.5h

Possibly the user really does see his problem in the terms of the original specification. If so, then it would be appropriate to structure the program as in 2.5d. If possible, we should ask him. A strong indication that he does not view the problem in this way is the requirement that records on H should be in the same order they were on F. If a user saw his problem in terms of the algorithm, he would surely want the records on H in the order they are rejected. The structure in Figure 2.5h is almost certainly correct in the JSP sense that it exactly matches the problem.

At the risk of labouring the point, here is another formulation of the specification for choosing the kept record of the MULTI-GROUP. The function KEPT applied to the MULTI-GROUP delivers the required record. The (t_j), (h_j), and (f_j) are all families of functions also with the MULTI-GROUP as their argument.

Let R_k be the kth record of the GROUP
Let max be the number of records in the GROUP

$$t_j: \{GROUP\} \rightarrow \{0,1\}$$
$$h_j: \{GROUP\} \rightarrow \{0,1\}$$
$$f_j: \{GROUP\} \rightarrow \{R_k\}$$

$$t_j(GROUP) = \begin{cases} 1 \text{ if } R_j \text{ is of TYPE '999'} \\ 0 \text{ otherwise} \end{cases}$$

$$h_{max}(GROUP) = t_{max}(GROUP)$$
$$h_j(GROUP) = h_{j+1}(GROUP) * t_j(GROUP)$$
$$\text{for } j < max$$

$$f_{max}(GROUP) = R_{max}$$
$$f_j(GROUP) = \begin{cases} R_j \text{ if } t_j(GROUP) = 0 \\ \qquad\qquad\qquad \text{for } j < max \\ f_{j+1}(GROUP) \text{ otherwise} \end{cases}$$

$$KEPT(GROUP) = \begin{cases} R_1 \text{ if } h_1(GROUP) = 1 \\ f_1(GROUP) \qquad\quad \text{otherwise} \end{cases}$$

The obvious order of evaluation is first the t_j, next the h_j, then the f_j if necessary, and finally KEPT. The structure of this algorithm is shown in Figure 2.5i. Operations could be listed and allocated to this structure; we could document the algorithm using JSP notations. But this is only partly JSP. JSP is a method of developing algorithms; you don't need it if you already have an algorithm. If you do use JSP to solve the problem for which this algorithm is a solution, then you'll have a structure like that in Figure 2.5h.

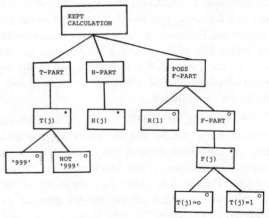

Figure 2.5i

The Limits of the Static View. Of course the strictly static view of data has its limitations. Suppose, for example, that an input stream, F, consists of records each with a field F-QTY. A program, P, has to output

63

the single record from F that has the highest value of F-QTY. It is guaranteed that no two records in F have the same value of F-QTY.

The only reasonable structure to adopt for this problem is one like that shown in Figure 2.5g. A structure like the NOTALL999 part of Figure 2.5h would not be suitable because it poses a near-insoluble recognition difficulty.

The shift from dynamic thinking to static thinking is not absolute. The choice of data structures for some problems relies on a degree of intuition about the dynamics of the intended algorithm. Such problems are close to the boundary of applicability of *pure* JSP.

2.5.2 Comparison of JSP and the Functional Approach

The hand-in-hand method of program and proof construction (Dijkstra [1] is a pure example of the functional approach to programming, in which programs are viewed as implementations of mathematical functions. The following example (slightly simplified) is taken from Gries [1].

A program has to right-justify a line of text. The input line consists of two or more words separated by single spaces, starting with a word at the left but having extra spaces to the far right. The output line has to contain the same words spread out as evenly as possible on the line, with the last word ending on the last character of the line. A word is a string of consecutive nonspace characters. This specification is informal and incomplete. "As evenly as possible" certainly needs a clearer definition.

The approach taken in Gries [1] is, quite reasonably, to formalise the specification. However, because the approach is functional, the specification is formalised as a function. The function maps the vector $A(j)$ of the starting positions of the words on the input line to the vector $B(j)$ of their starting positions on the output line. In the formalised specification and in the subsequent development all reference to lines, words and characters are excluded.

By contrast, using JSP, the sequential relationships between lines, words, and characters are not ignored; they are formalised in input and output data structures. Direct consideration of the function of the program is deferred. (Figure 2.5j shows the output data structure for the case in which all the shorter gaps are at the beginning of the line.)

One difference between the hand-in-hand method of program and proof construction (Gries [1]) and Dijkstra [1]) and JSP is this. In the former method, programs are viewed as abstract algorithms about abstract objects. The first step is to throw away all

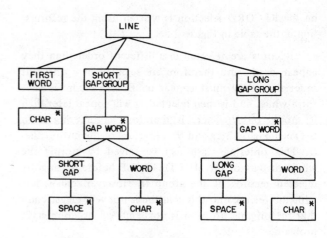

Figure 2.5j

reference to the objects that give meaning to the desired functional transformation. In JSP, the objects that give meaning to the functional transformation are given central importance. The structure of the program is based on the relationships between them.

With the former view, there doesn't seem to be any concept of maintenance. A small change to the list of assertions that comprise the specification may allow a completely different proof. Every program is different.

Of the following three new specifications, which would you consider to be examples of maintenance on the line-justifying problem?

(1) Now the longer gaps have to be distributed throughout the line. (Again this is imprecise, but the exact new specification is not our concern here.)

(2) The input line is now free-format, that is, the first word may not start on the far left, and the gaps between words may be more than one space.

(3) A number of packages of weight $C(j)$ are to be loaded on to an aircraft. They are to be arranged along the central axis of the aircraft, so that the weight distribution along the aircraft's hull is as even as possible. The program is to take the vector $C(j)$ as input and output the vector $D(j)$ of distances from the nose end of the cargo area.

We would argue that the first two changes are examples of program maintenance and that the third is not, even if, by a fluke, the changes necessary to meet the third specification are smaller than the changes necessary to meet the first two. The third modification is not one that you would reasonably expect to be able to make. Nobody will complain that your program is unmaintainable if you are unable to adapt it to do arbitrary nonlinear vector transformations. However, they might complain if you could not do the first two.

What allows you to think of maintenance at all is the persistence of the underlying objects (the lines, the words, the characters) through a number of related statements of functional requirement. The statements are related precisely because they refer to the same objects, the objects that comprise the JSP model. Maintenance will not be so easy if reference to these objects is not an integral part of the program development.

2.5.3 Limits on the Applicability of JSP

JSP uses sequential relationships in the subject matter as the basis of program structure. Not all programming problems have such readily identifiable sequential relationships. Consider the following example.

Inverting a Matrix. The problem is to write a program to invert a matrix. We can understand this specification only if we already understand matrix multiplication. The inverted output matrix must have the property that it yields the identity matrix when multiplied by the input matrix.

The specification "invert a matrix" conjures up an implicit mathematical world. To solve the problem, properties, relations and facts about objects in this world have to be made explicit, so they can be exploited in proving the equivalence of a different statement of the problem. For example, the far from obvious fact that the square matrices that do not have inverses are those for which the determinant is zero will presumably have to be made explicit. Is this programming or is it mathematics? Certainly it is not part of JSP.

The part of "programming" that JSP does not address is the invention, construction, or discovery of suitable models appropriate for given functional transformations. Abstract mathematical algorithmic programming is excluded because most of that job is the invention of objects with suitable sequential relationships. Line justifying algorithms are included because the objects that will make up the model—lines, words, characters—are obvious and don't need to be invented.

Sometimes JSP can be used on the part of the problem that remains when suitable objects have been discovered. The reprinted example, Integration Using Simpson's Rule, shows the use of JSP in a mathematical problem. The relationships in the model are the groups of abcissa values on the conceptual (i.e. constructed or invented) ABS-FILE. Having recognised or invented this data stream and the groups within it, JSP works perfectly for the rest of the problem.

2.5.4 JSP and Applicative Or Non-Procedural Languages

The emphasis placed in JSP on the static features of problems and programs suggests that applicative or non-procedural languages should fit well with JSP. To some extent, using JSP with a procedural language is programming in a procedural language with an applicative style.

The following are some comments on how JSP might be used with a non-procedural language. At step three, instead of listing and allocating operations from the programming language, define the functional part of the program as an applicative language function. To do this, assume that the data structures of the input and output streams are syntactically recognisable. At step four, define a recogniser function that converts an input data stream into a form in which the desired data structure is syntactically recognisable. The final program is the composition of the recogniser function and the function defined in the third step.

The recogniser function can be derived directly from the desired data structure, except for some functions that are exactly equivalent to the conditions that are normally added in step four of the method for a sequential language. The following is one way of deriving the recogniser function. (There may be better ways.)

We want to define a function

recogX: CARDFILE --> X

where

CARDFILE = CARD* and X is the data structure we wish to impose on the CARDFILE.

For every component, Z, in the data structure of X, define two functions, recogZ and unusedZ, as follows:

recogZ: CARD*--> Z
unusedZ: CARD*--> Z

If Z is elementary,

recogZ [cs] = first [cs]
unusedZ [cs] = rest [cs]

where "first" takes the first of the stream and "rest" all but the first.

If Z is a sequence,

recogZ [cs] = (recogA1[cs1], recogA2[cs2], ...)
unusedZ [cs] = unusedAn[csn]

where $cs1=cs$ and $csj+1 = unusedAj[csj]$.

If Z is a selection of A1, A2, ... An,

define ZSEL[cs] as an *n*-valued function (that evaluates the selection) and

recogZ [cs] = recogAj[cs]
unusedZ [cs] = unusedAj[cs]

if ZSEL[cs] has the value j.

If Z is an iteration of B,

define ZITR[cs] as a two-valued function (to evaluate if there is another B) and

recogZ[cs] = (recogB[cs] , recogZ[unusedB[cs]])
    or null

unusedZ[cs] = unusedZ[unusedB[cs]]
    or (cs)

both according to the value of ZITR.

Note the following points.

(1) In general (for example in collating problems), the recogniser function for one data stream needs information from the others. ZSEL and ZITR have arguments from more than one data stream.

(2) For a recognition difficulty, the recogniser function must run ahead of the program function. This causes a problem if some of the side effects are beneficent, especially if, as in on-line problems, the beneficent side-effects cannot be delayed.

(3) For a boundary clash, the problem is broken into two or more parts, each with its own recogniser function and program function. The output from one part is the input to the next.

(4) Applicative languages highlight the separation in JSP between recognition issues and functional issues.

Good languages are not enough. To solve programming problems like the case studies in Part Three consistently well, we need a method. You may like to try any of the case studies using the applicative language of your choice.

CONSTRUCTIVE METHODS OF PROGRAM DESIGN

M. A. Jackson

Abstract Correct programs cannot be obtained by attempts to test or to prove incorrect programs: the correctness of a program should be assured by the design procedure used to build it.

A suggestion for such a design procedure is presented and discussed. The procedure has been developed for use in data processing, and can be effectively taught to most practicing programmers. It is based on correspondence between data and program structures, leading to a decomposition of the program into distinct processes. The model of a process is very simple, permitting use of simple techniques of communication, activation and suspension. Some wider implications and future possibilities are also mentioned.

1. Introduction

In this paper I would like to present and discuss what I believe to be *a more constructive method of program design*. The phrase itself is important; I am sure that no-one here will object if I use a LIFO discipline in briefly elucidating its intended meaning.

'Design' is primarily concerned with structure; the designer must say what parts there are to be and how they are to be arranged. The crucial importance of modular programming and structured programming (even in their narrowest and crudest manifestations) is that they provide some definition of what parts are permissible: a module is a separately compiled, parameterized subroutine; a structure component is a sequence, an iteration or a selection. With such definition, inadequate through they may be, we can at least begin to think about design: what modules would make up that program, and how should they be arranged? Should this program be an iteration of selections or a sequence of iterations? Without such definitions, design is meaningless. At the top level of a problem there are P^N possible designs, where P is the number of distinct types of permissible part and N is the number of parts needed to make up the whole. So, to preserve our sanity, both P and N must be small: modular programming, using tree or hierarchical structures, offers small values of N; structured programming offers, additionally, small values of P.

'Program' or, rather 'programming' I would use in a narrow sense. Modeling the problem is 'analysis'; 'programming' is putting the model on a computer. Thus, for example, if we are asked to find a prime number in the range 10^{50} to 10^{60}, we need a number theorist for the analysis; if we are asked to program discounted cash flow, the analysis calls for a financial expert. One of the major ills in data processing stems from uncertainty about this distinction. In mathematical circles the distinction is often ignored altogether, to the detriment, I believe, of our understanding of programming. Programming is about computer programs, not about number theory, or financial planning, or production control.

'Method' is defined in the Shorted OED as a 'procedure for attaining an object'. The crucial word here is 'procedure'. The ultimate method, and the ultimate is doubtless unattainable, is a procedure embodying a precise and correct algorithm. To follow the method we need only execute the algorithm faithfully, and we will be led infallibly to the desired result. To the extent that a putative method falls short of this ideal it is less of a method.

To be 'constructive', a method must itself be decomposed into distinct steps, and correct execution of each step must assure correct execution of the whole method and thus the correctness of its product. The key requirement here is that the correctness of the execution of a step should be largely verifiable without reference to steps not yet executed by the designer. This is the central difficulty in stepwise refinement: we can judge the correctness of a refinement step only be reference to what is yet to come, and hence only by exercising a degree of foresight to which few people can lay claim.

Finally, we must recognize that design methods today are intended for use by human beings: in spite of what was said above about constructive methods, we need, now and for some time to come, a substantial ingredient of intuition and subjectivity. So what is presented below does not claim to be fully constructive - merely to be 'more constructive'. The reader must supply the other half of the comparison for himself, measuring the claim against the yardstick of his own favored methods.

2. Basis of the Method

The basis of the method is described, in some detail, in (1). It is appropriate here only to illustrate it by a family of simple example problems.

Example 1

A cardfile of punched cards is sorted into ascending sequence of values of a key which appears in each card. Within this sequence, the first card for each group of cards with a common key value is a header card, while the others are detail cards. Each detail card carries an integer amount. It is required to produce a report showing the totals of amount for all keys.

Solution 1

The first step in applying the method is to describe the structure of the data. We use a graphic notation to represent the structures as trees:

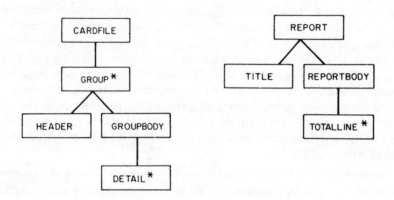

The above representations are equivalent to the following (in BNF with iteration instead of recursion):

$$<cardfile> ::= \{<group>\}_0^\infty$$
$$<group> ::= <header> <groupbody>$$
$$<groupbody> ::= \{<detail>\}_0^\infty$$
$$<report> ::= <title> <reportbody>$$
$$<reportbody> ::= \{<totalline>\}_0^\infty$$

The second step is to compose these data structures into a program structure:

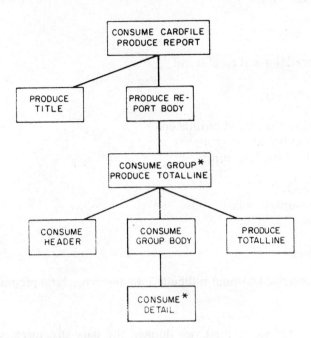

This structure has the following properties:

• It is related quite formally to each of the data structures. We may recover any one data structure from the program structure by first marking all nodes lying in a path from a marked node to the root.

• The correspondences (cardfile : report) and (group : totalline) are determined by the problem statement. One report is derivable from one cardfile; one totalline is derivable from one group, and the totallines are in the same order as the groups.

• The structure is vacuous, in the sense that it contains no executable statements: it is a program which does nothing; it is a tree without real leaves.

The third step in applying the method is to list the executable operations required and to allocate each to its right place in the program structure. The operations are elementary executable statements of the programming language, possibly after enhancement of the language by a bout of bottom-up design; they are enumerated, essentially, by working back from output to input along the obvious data-flow paths. Assuming a reasonably conventional machine and a line printer (rather than a character printer), we may obtain the list:

1. write title

2. write totalline (groupkey, total)

3. total := total + detail.amount

4. total := 0

5. groupkey := header.key

6. open cardfile

7. read cardfile

8. close cardfile

Note that every operation, or almost every operation, must have operands which are data objects. Allocation to a program structure is therefore a trivial task if the program structure is correctly based on the data structures. This triviality is a vital criterion of the success of the first two steps. The resulting program, in an obvious notation, is:

```
CARD-REPORT sequence
    open cardfile;
    read cardfile;
    write title;
    REPORT-BODY iteration until cardfile.eof
        total := 0;
        groupkey := header.key;
        read cardfile;
        GROUP-BODY iteration until cardfile.eof
                        or detail.key ≠ groupkey
            total := total + detail.amount;
            read cardfile;
        GROUP-BODY end
        write totalline (groupkey, total);
    REPORT-BODY end
    close cardfile;
CARDFILE-REPORT end
```

Clearly, this program may be transcribed without difficulty into any procedural programming language.

Comment

The solution has proceeded in three steps: First, we defined the data structures; second, we formed them into a program structure; third, we listed and allocated the executable operations. At each step we have criteria for the correctness of the step itself and an implicit check on the correctness of the steps already taken. For example, if at the first step we had wrongly described the structure of cardfile as

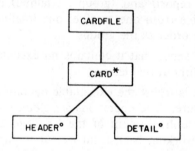

(that is: $<cardfile> ::= \{<card>\}_0^\infty$

   $<card> ::= <header> | <detail>$),

we should have been able to see at the first step that we had failed to represent everything we knew about the cardfile. If nonetheless we had persisted in error, we would have discovered it at the second step, when we would have been unable to form a program structure in the absence of a cardfile component corresponding to a totalline in report.

The design has throughout concentrated on what we may think of as a static rather than a dynamic view of the problem: on maps, not on itineraries, on structures, not on logic flow. The logic flow of the finished program is a by-product of the data structures and the correct allocation of the 'read' operation. There is an obvious connection between what we have done and the design of a very simple syntax analysis phase in a compiler: the grammar of the input file determines the structure of the program which parses it. We may observe that the 'true' grammar of the cardfile is not context-free: within one group, the header and detail cards must all carry the same key value. It is because the explicit grammar cannot show this that we are forced to introduce the variable groupkey to deal with this stipulation.

Note that there is no error-checking. If we wish to check for errors in the input we must elaborate the structure of the input file to accommodate those errors explicitly. By defining a structure for an input file we define the domain of the program: if we wish to extend the domain, we must extend the input file structure accordingly. In a practical data processing system, we would always define the structure of primary input (such as decks of cards, keyboard messages, etc) to encompass all physically possible files: it would be absurd to construct a program whose operation is unspecified (and therefore, in principle, unpredictable) in the event of a card deck being dropped or a wrong key depressed.

Example 2

The cardfile of example 1 is modified so that each card contains a card-type indicator with possible values 'header', 'detail' and other. The program should take account of possible errors in the composition of a group: there may be no header card and/or there may be cards other than detail cards in the group body. Groups containing errors should be listed on an errorlist, but not totaled.

Solution 2

The structure of the report remains unchanged. The structure of the errorlist and of the new version of the cardfile are:

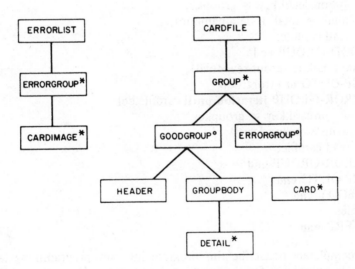

The structure of cardfile demands attention. Firstly, it is ambiguous: anything which is a goodgroup is also an errorgroup. We are forced into this ambiguity because it would be intolerably difficult - and quite unnecessary - to spell out all of the ways in which a group may be in error. The ambiguity is simply resolved by the conventions we use: the parts of a selection are considered to be ordered, and the first applicable part encountered in a left-to-right scan is chosen. So a group can be parsed as an errorgroup only if it has already been rejected as a goodgroup. Secondly, a goodgroup cannot be recognized by a left-to-right parse of the input file with any predetermined degree of lookahead. If we choose to read ahead R records, we may yet encounter a group containing an error only in the R+1'th card.

Recognition problems of this kind occur in many guises. Their essence is that we are forced to a choice during program execution at a time when we lack the evidence on which the choice must be based. Note that the difficulty is not structural but is confined to achieving a workable flow of control. We will call such problems 'backtracking' problems, and tackle them in three stages:

● Ignore the recognition difficulty, imagining that a friendly demon will tell us infallibly which choice to make. In the present problem, he will tell us whether a group is a goodgroup or an errorgroup. Complete the design procedure in this blissful state of confidence, producing the full program text.

- Replace our belief in the demon's infallibility by a sceptical determination to verify each 'land-mark' in the data which might prove him wrong. Whenever he is proved wrong we will execute a 'quit' statement which branches to the second part of the selection. Those 'quit' statements are introduced into the program text created in stage a.

- Modify the program text resulting from stage b to ensure that side-effects are repealed where necessary.

The result of stage a, in accordance with the design procedure used for example 1, is:

```
CFILE-REPT-ERR sequence
    open cardfile;
    read cardfile;
    write title;
    REPORT-BODY iteration until cardfile.eof
        groupkey := card.key;
        GROUP-OUTG select goodgroup
        total := 0;
        read cardfile;
        GOOD-GROUP iteration until cardfile.eof
                or detail.key ≠ groupkey
            total := total + detail.amount;
            read cardfile;
        GOOD-GROUP end
        write totalline (groupkey, total);
        GROUP-OUTG or errorgroup
            ERROR-GROUP iteration until cardfile.eof
                    or card.key ≠ groupkey
                write errorline (card);
                read cardfile;
            ERROR-GROUP end
        GROUP-OUTG end
    REPORT-BODY end
    close cardfile;
CFILE-REPT-ERR end
```

Note that we cannot completely transcribe this program into any programming language, because we cannot code an evaluable expression for the predicate goodgroup. However, we can readily verify the correctness of the program (assuming the infallibility of the demon). Indeed, if we are prepared to exert ourselves to punch an identifying character into the header card of each goodgroup - thus acting as our own demon - we can code and run the program as an informal demonstration of its acceptability.

We are now ready to proceed to stage b, in which we insert 'quit' statements into the first part of the selection GROUP-OUTG. Also, since quit statements are not present in a normal selection, we will replace the words 'select' and 'or' by 'posit' and 'admit' respectively, thus indicating the tentative nature of the initial choice. Clearly, the landmarks to be checked are the card-type indicators in the header and detail cards. We thus obtain the following program:

```
CFILE-REPT-ERR sequence
    open cardfile;
    read cardfile;
    write title;
    REPORT-BODY iteration until cardfile.eof
        groupkey := card.key;
        GROUP-OUTG posit goodgroup
            total := 0;
            quit GROUP-OUTG if card.type ≠ header;
            read cardfile;
            GOOD-GROUP iteration until cardfile.eof
                    or card.key ≠ groupkey
                quit GROUP-OUTG if card.type ≠ detail;
                total := total + detail.amount;
                read cardfile;
            GOOD-GROUP end
            write totalline (groupkey, total);
        GROUP-OUTG admit errorgroup
            ERROR-GROUP iteration until cardfile.eof
                    or card.key ≠ groupkey;
                write errorline (card);
                read cardfile;
            ERROR-GROUP end
        GROUP-OUTG end
    REPORT-BODY end
    close cardfile;
CFILE-REPT-ERR end
```

The third stage, stage c, deals with the side-effects of partial execution of the first part of the selection. In this trivial example, the only significant side-effect is the reading of cardfile. In general, it will be found that the only troublesome side-effects are the reading and writing of serial files; the best and easiest way to handle them is to equip ourselves with input and output procedures capable of 'noting' and 'restoring' the state of the file and its associated buffers. Given the availability of such procedures, stage c can be completed by inserting a 'note' statement immediately following the 'posit' statement and a 'restore' statement immediately following the 'admit'. Sometimes side-effects will demand a more ad hoc treatment: when 'note' and 'restore' are unavailable there is no alternative to such cumbersome expedients as explicitly storing each record on disk or in main storage.

Comment

By breaking our treatment of the backtracking difficulty into three distinct stages, we are able to isolate distinct aspects of the problem. In stage a we ignore the backtracking difficulty entirely, and concentrate our efforts on obtaining a correct solution to the reduced problem. This solution is carried through the three main design steps, producing a completely specific program text: we are able to satisfy ourselves of the correctness of that text before going on to modify it in the second and third stages. In the second stage we deal only with the recognition difficulty: the difficulty is one of logic flow, and we handle it, appropriately, by modifying the logic flow, and we handle it, appropriately, by modifying the logic flow of the program with quit statements. Each quit statement says, in effect, 'It is supposed (posited) that this is a goodgroup; but if, in fact, this card is not what is ought to be then this is not, after all, a goodgroup'. The required quit statements can be easily seen from the data structure definition, and their place is readily found in the program text because the program structure perfectly matches the data structure. The side-effects arise to be dealt with in stage c because of the quit statements, producing discontinuities in the context of the computation and hence side-effects. The side-effects are readily identified from the program text resulting from stage b.

Note that it would be quite wrong to distort the data structures and the program structure in an attempt to avoid the dreaded four-letter word 'goto'. The data structures shown, and hence the program structure, are self-evidently the correct structures for the problem as stated: they must not be abandoned because of difficulties with the logic flow.

3. Simple Programs and Complex Programs

The design method, as described above, is severely constrained: it applies to a narrow class of serial file-processing programs. We may go further, and say that if defines such a class - the class of 'simple programs'. A 'simple program' has the following attributes:

- The program has a fixed initial state; nothing is remembered from one execution to the next.

- Program inputs and outputs are serial files, which we may conveniently suppose to be held on magnetic tapes. There may be more than one input and more than one output file.

- Associated with the program is an explicit definition of the structure of each input and output file. These structures are tree structures, defined in the grammar used above. This grammar permits recursion in addition to the features shown above; it is not very different from a grammar of regular expressions.

- The input data structures define the domain of the program, the output data structures its range. Nothing is introduced into the program text which is not associated with the defined data structures.

- The data structures are compatible, in the sense that they can be combined into a program structure in the manner shown above.

- The program structure thus derived from the data structures is sufficient for a workable program. Elementary operations of the program language (possibly supplemented by more powerful or suitable operations resulting from bottom-up designing) are allocated to components of the program structure without introducing any further 'program logic'.

A simple program may be designed and constructed with the minimum of difficulty, provided that we adhere rigorously to the design principles adumbrated here and eschew any temptation to pursue efficiency at the cost of distorting the structure. In fact, we should usually discount the benefits of efficiency, reminding ourselves of the mass of error-ridden programs which attest to its dangers.

Evidently, not all programs are simple programs. Sometimes we are presented with the task of constructing a program which operates on direct-access rather than on serial files, or which processes a single record at each execution, starting from a varying internal state. As we shall see later, a simple program may be clothed in various disguises which give it a misleading appearance without affecting its underlying nature. More significantly, we may find that the design procedure suggested cannot be applied to the problem given because the data structures are not compatible: that is, we are unable at the second step of the design procedure to form the program structure from the data structures.

Example 3

The input cardfile of example 1 is presented to the program in the form of a blocked file. Each block of this file contains a card count and a number of card images.

Solution 3

The structure of blockedfile is:

74

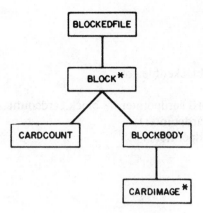

This structure does not, of course, show the arrangement of the cards in groups. It is impossible to show, in a single structure, both the arrangement in groups and the arrangement in blocks. But the structure of the report is still:

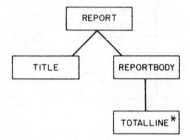

We cannot fit together the structures of report and blockedfile to form a program structure; nor would we be in better case if we were to ignore the arrangement in blocks. The essence of our difficulty is this: the program must contain operations to be executed once per block, and these must be allocated to a 'process block' component; it must also contain operations to be executed once per group, and these must be allocated to a 'process group' component; but it is impossible to form a single program structure containing both a 'process block' and a 'process group' component. We will call this difficulty a 'structure clash'.

The solution to the structure clash in the present example is obvious: more so because of the order in which the examples have been taken and because everyone knows about blocking and deblocking. But the solution can be derived more formally from the data structures. The clash is of a type we will call 'boundary clash': the boundaries of the blocks are not synchronized with the boundaries of the groups. The standard solution for a structure clash is to abandon the attempt to form a single program structure and instead decompose the problem into two or more simple programs. For a boundary clash the required decomposition is always of the form:

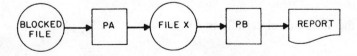

The intermediate file, file X, must be composed of records each of which is a cardimage, because cardimage is the highest common factor of the structures blockedfile and cardfile. The program PB is the program produced as a solution to example 1; the program PA is:

75

```
PA sequence
    open blockedfile;
    open fileX;
    read blockedfile;
    PABODY iteration until blockedfile.eof
        cardpointer := 1;
        PBLOCK iteration until cardpointer > block.cardcount
            write cardimage (cardpointer);
            cardpointer := cardpointer + 1;
        PBLOCK end
        read blockedfile;
    PABODY end
    close fileX;
    close blockedfile;
PA end
```

The program PB sees file X as having the structure of cardfile in example 1, while program PA sees its structure as:

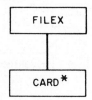

Comment

The decomposition into two simple programs achieves a perfect solution. Only the program PA is cognizant of the arrangement of cardimages in blocks; only the program PB of their arrangement in groups. The tape containing file X acts as a cordon sanitaire between the two, ensuring that no undesired interactions can occur: we need not concern ourselves at all with such questions as 'what if the header record of a group is the first cardimage in a block with only one cardimage?', or 'what if a group has no detail records and its header is the last cardimage in a block'; in this respect our design is known to be correct.

There is an obvious inefficiency in our solution. By introducing the intermediate magnetic tape file we have, to a first approximation, doubled the elapsed time for program execution and increased the program's demand for backing store devices.

Example 4

The input cardfile of example 1 is incompletely sorted. The cards are partially ordered so that the header card of each group precedes any detail cards of that group, but no other ordering is imposed. The report has no title, and the totals may be produced in any order.

Solution 4

The best we can do for the structure of cardfile is:

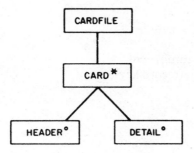

which is clearly incompatible with the structure of the report, since there is no component of cardfile corresponding to totalline in the report. Once again we have a structure clash, but this time of a different type. The cardfile consists of a number of groupfiles, each one of which has the form:

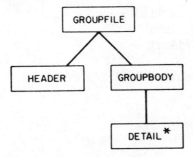

The cardfile is an arbitrary interleaving of these groupfiles. To resolve the clash (an 'interleaving clash') we must resolve cardfile into its constituent groupfiles:

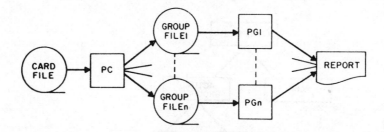

Allowing, for purposes of exposition, that a single report may be produced by the n programs PG1, ... PGn (each contributing one totalline), we have decomposed the problem into n+1 simple programs; of these, n are identical programs processing the n distinct groupfiles groupfile1, ... groupfilen; while the other, PC, resolves cardfile into its constituents.

Two possible versions of PC are:

77

```
PC1 sequence
    open cardfile;
    read cardfile;
    open all possible groupfiles;
    PC1BODY iteration until cardfile.eof
        write record to groupfile(record.key);
        read cardfile;
    PC1BODY end
    close all possible groupfiles;
    close cardfile;
PC1 end
```

and

```
PC2 sequence
    open cardfile;
    read cardfile;
    PC2BODY iteration until cardfile.eof
        REC-INIT select new groupfile
            open groupfile(record.key);
        REC-INIT end
        write record to groupfile(record.key);
        read cardfile;
    PC2BODY end
    close all opened groupfiles;
    close cardfile;
PC2 end
```

Both PC1 and PC2 present difficulties. In PC1 we must provide a groupfile for every possible key value, whether or not cardfile contains records for that key. Also, the programs PG1, ... PGn must be elaborated to handle the null groupfile:

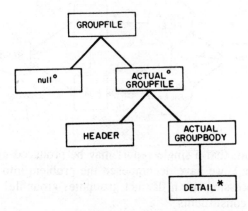

In PC2 we must provide a means of determining whether a groupfile already exists for a given key value. Note that it would be quite wrong to base the determination on the fact that a header must be the first record for a group: such a solution takes impermissible advantage of the structure of groupfile which, in principle, is unknown in the program PC; we would then have to make a drastic change to PC if, for example, the header card were made optional:

78

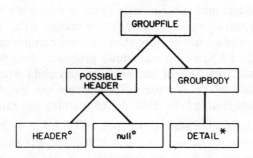

Further, in PC2 we must be able to run through all the actual key values in order to close all the groupfiles actually opened. This would still be necessary even if each group had a recognizable trailer record, for reasons similar to those given above concerning the header records.

Comment

The inefficiency of our solution to example 4 far outstrips the inefficiency of our solution to example 3. Indeed, our solution to example 4 is entirely impractical. Practical implementation of the designs will be considered below in the next section. For the moment, we may observe that the use of magnetic tapes for communication between simple programs enforces a very healthy discipline. We are led to use a very simple protocol: every serial file must be opened and closed. The physical medium encourages a complete decoupling of the programs: it is easy to imagine one program being run today, the tapes held overnight in a library, and a subsequent program being run tomorrow; the whole of the communication is visible in the defined structure of the files. Finally, we are strengthened in our resolve to think in terms of static structures, avoiding the notoriously error-prone activity of thinking about dynamic flow and execution-time events.

Taking a more global view of the design procedure, we may say that the simple program is a satisfactory high level component. It is a larger object than a sequence, iteration or selection; it has a more precise definition than a module; it is subject to restrictions which reveal to us clearly when we are trying to make a single program out of what should be two or more.

4. Programs, Procedures and Processes

Although from the design point of view we regard magnetic tapes as the canonical medium of communication between simple programs, they will not usually provide a practical implementation.

An obvious possiblity for implementation in some environments is to replace each magnetic tape by a limited number of buffers in main storage, with a suitable regime for ensuring that the consumer program does not run ahead of the producer. Each simple program can then be treated as a distinct task or process, using whatever facilities are provided for the management of multiple concurrent tasks.

However, something more like coroutines seems more attractive (2). The standard procedure call mechanism offers a simple implementation of great flexibility and power. Consider the program PA, in our solution to example 3, which writes the intermediate file X. We can readily convert this program into a procedure PAX which has the characteristics of an input procedure for file X. that is, invocations of the procedure PAX will satisfactorily implement the operations 'open file X for reading', 'read file X' and 'close file X after reading'.

We will call this conversion of PA into PAX 'inversion of PA with respect to file X'. (Note that the situation in solution 3 is symmetrical: we could equally well decide to invert PB with respect to file X, obtaining an output procedure for file X.) The mechanics of inversion are a mere matter of generating the appropriate object coding from the text of the simple program: there is no need for any modification to that text. PA and PAX are the same program, not two different programs. Most practicing programmers seem to be unaware of this identity of PA and PAX, and even those who are familiar with coroutines often program as if they supposed that PA and PAX were distinct things. This is partly due to the baleful influence of the stack as a storage allocation device: we cannot jump out of an inner block of

PAX, return to the invoking procedure, and subsequently resume where we left off when we are next invoked. So we must either modify our compiler or modify our coding style, adopting the use of labels and go to statements as a standard in place of the now conventional compound statement of structured programming. It is common to find PAX, or an analogous program, designed as a selection or case statement: the mistake is on all fours with that of the kindergarten child who has been led to believe that the question 'what is 5 multiplied by 3?' is quite different from the question 'what is 3 multiplied by 5?'. At a stroke the poor child has doubled the difficulty of learning the multiplication tables.

The procedure PAX is, of course, a variable state procedure. The value of its state is held in a 'state vector' (or activation record), of which a vital part is the text pointer; the values of special significance are those associated with the suspension of PAX for operations on file X—open, write and close. The state vector is an 'own variable' par excellence, and should be clearly seen as such.

The minimum interface needed between PB and PAX is two parameters: a record of file X, and an additional bit to indicate whether the record is or is not the eof marker. This minimum interface suffices for example 3: there is no need for PB to pass an operation code to PAX (open read or close). It is important to understand that this minimum interface will not suffice for the general case. It is sufficient for example 3 only because the operation code is implicit in the ordering of operations. From the point of view of PAX, the first invocation must be 'open', and subsequent invocations must be 'read' until PAX has returned the eof marker to PB, after which the final invocation must be 'close'. This felicitous harmony is destroyed if, for example, PB is permitted to stop reading and close file X before reaching the eof marker. In such a case the interface must be elaborated with an operation code. Worse, the sequence of values of this operation code now constitutes a file in its own right: the solution becomes:

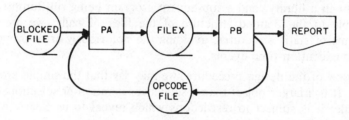

The design of PA is, potentially, considerably more complicated. The benefit we will obtain from treating this complication conscientiously is well worth the price: by making explicit the structure of the opcode file we define the problem exactly and simplify its solution. Failure to recognize the existence of the opcode file, or, just as culpable, failure to make its structure explicit, lies at the root of the errors and obscurities for which manufacturer's input-output software is deservedly infamous.

In solution 4 we created an intolerable multiplicity of files—groupfile1,... groupfilen. We can rid ourselves of these by inverting the programs PG1,...PGn with respect to their respective groupfiles: that is, we convert each of the programs PGi to an output procedure PGFi, which can be invoked by PC to execute operations on groupfilei. But we still have an intolerable multiplicity of output procedures, so a further step is required. The procedures are identical except for their names and the current values of their state vectors. So we separate out the pure procedure part—PGF—of which we need keep only one copy, and the named state vectors SVPGF1, ... SVPGFn. We must now provide a mechanism for storing and retrieving these state vectors and for associating the appropriate state vector with each invocation of PGF; many mechanisms are possible, from a fully-fledged direct-access file with serial read facilities to a simple arrangement of the state vectors in an array in main storage.

5. Design and Implementation

The model of a simple program and the decomposition of a problem into simple programs provides some unity of viewpoint. In particular, we may be able to see what is common to programs with widely different implementations. Some illustrations follow.

a.   A conversational program is a simple program of the form:

The user provides a serial input file of messages, ordered in time; the conversation program produces a serial file of responses. Inversion of the program with respect to the user input file gives an output procedure 'dispose of one message in a conversation'. The state vector of the inverted program must be preserved for the duration of the conversation: IBM's IMS provides the SPA (Scratchpad Area) for precisely this purpose. The conversation program must, of course, be designed and written as a single program: implementation restrictions may dictate segmentation of the object code.

b.   A 'sort-exit' allows the user of a generalized sorting program to introduce his own procedure at the point where each record is about to be written to the final output file. An interface is provided which permits 'insertion' and 'deletion' of records as well as 'updating'.

We should view the sort-exit procedure as a simple program:

To fit it in with the sorting program we must invert it with respect to both the sortedfile and the final output. The interface must provide an implementation of the basic operations: open sortedfile for reading; read sortedfile (distinguishing the eof marker); close sortedfile after reading; open finaloutput for writing; write finaloutput record; close finaloutput file after writing (including writing the eof marker).

Such concepts as 'insertion' and 'deletion' of records are pointless: at best, they serve the cause of efficiency, traducing clarity; at worst, they create difficulty and confusion where none need exist.

c.   Our solution to example 1 can be seen as an optimisation of the solution to the more general example 4. By sorting the cardfile we ensure that the groups do not overlap in time: the state vectors of the inverted programs PGF1, ... PGFn can therefore share a single area in main storage. The state vector consists only of the variable total; the variable groupkey is the name of the currently active group and hence of the current state vector. Because the records of a group are contiguous, the end of a group is recognizable at cardfile.eof or at the start of another group. The individual groupfile may therefore be closed, and the totalline written, at the earliest possible moment.

We may, perhaps, generalize so far as to say that an identifier is stored by a program only in order to give a unique name to the state vector of some process.

d.   A data processing system may be viewed as consisting of many simple programs, one for each independent entity in the real world model. By arranging the entities in sets we arrange the corresponding simple programs in equivalence classes. The 'master record' corresponding to an entity is the state vector of the simple program modelling that entity.

The serial files of the system are files of transactions ordered in time: some are primary transactions, communicating with the real world, some are secondary, passing between simple programs of the system. In general, the real world must be modelled as a network of entities or of entity sets; the data processing system is therefore a network of simple programs and transaction files.

Implementation of the system demands decisions in two major areas. First a scheduling algorithm must be decided; second, the representation and handling of state vectors. The extreme cases of the first are 'real-time' and 'serial batch'. In a pure 'real-time' system every primary transaction is dealt with as soon as it arrives, followed immediately by all of the secondary and consequent transactions, until the system as a whole becomes quiet. In a pure 'serial batch' system, each class (identifier set) of primary transactions is accumulated for a period (usually a day, week or month). Each simple program of that class is then activated (if there is a transaction present for it), giving rise to secondary transactions of various classes. These are then treated similarly, and so on until no more transactions remain to be processed.

Choosing a good implementation for a data processing system is difficult, because the network is usually large and many possible choices present themselves. This difficulty is compounded by the long-term nature of the simple programs: a typical entity, and hence a typical program, has a lifetime measured in years or even decades. During such a lifetime the system will inevitably undergo change: in effect, the programs are being rewritten while they are in course of execution.

e. An interrupt handler is a program which processes a serial file of interrupts, ordered in time:

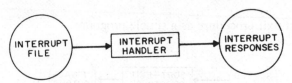

Inversion of the interrupt handler with respect to the interrupt file gives the required procedure 'dispose of one interrupt'. In general, the interrupt file will be composed of interleaved files for individual processes, devices, etc. Implementation is further complicated by the special nature of the invocation mechanism, by the fact that the records of the interrupt file are distributed in main storage, special registers and other places, and by the essentially recursive structure of the main interrupt file (unless the interrupt handler is permitted to mask off secondary interrupts).

f. An input-output procedure (what IBM literature calls an 'access method') is a simple program which processes an input file of access requests and produces an output file of access responses. An access request consists of an operation code and, sometimes, a data record; an access response consists of a result code and, sometimes, a data record. For example, a direct-access method has the form:

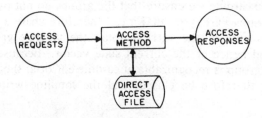

By inverting this simple program with respect to both the file of access requests and the file of access responses we obtain the desired procedure. This double inversion is always possible without difficulty, because each request must produce a response and that response must be calculable before the next request is presented.

The chief crime of access method designers is to conceal from their customers (and, doubtless, from themselves) the structure of the file of access requests. The user of the method is thus unable to determine what sequences of operations are permitted by the access method, and what their effect will be.

g.   Some aspects of a context-sensitive grammar may be regarded as interleaved context-free grammars. For example, in a grossly simplified version of the COBOL language we may wish to stipulate that any variable may appear as an operand of a MOVE statement, while only a variable declared as numeric may appear as an operand of an arithmetic (ADD, SUBTRACT, MULTIPLY or DIVIDE) statement. We may represent this stipulation as follows:

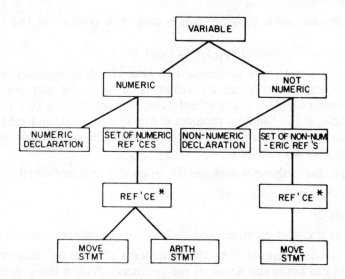

The syntax-checking part of the compiler consists, partly, of a simple program for each declared variable. The symbol table is the set of state vectors for these simple programs. The algorithm for activating and suspending these and other programs will determine the way in which one error interacts with another both for diagnosis and correction.

6. A Modest Proposal

It is one thing to propose a model to illuminate what has already been done, to clarify the sources of existing success or failure. It is quite another to show that the model is of practical value, and that it leads to the construction of acceptable programs. An excessive zeal in decomposition produces cumbersome interfaces and pointlessly redundant code. The "Shanley Principle" in civil engineering (3) requires that several functions be implemented in a single part; this is necessary for economy both in manufacturing and in operating the products of engineering design. It appears that a design approach which depends on decomposition runs counter to this principle: its main impetus is the separation of functions for implementation in distinct parts of the program.

But programs do not have the intractable nature of the physical objects which civil, mechanical or electrical engineers produce. They can be manipulated and transformed (for example, by compilers) in ways which preserve their vital qualities of correctness and modifiability while improving their efficiency both generally and in the specialized environment of a particular machine. The extent to which a program can be manipulated and transformed is critically affected by two factors: the variety of forms it can take, and the semantic clarity of the text. Programs written using today's conventional techniques score poorly on both factors. There is a distressingly large variety of forms, and intelligibility is compromised or even destroyed by the introduction of implementation-orientated features. The justification for these techniques is, of course, efficiency. But in pursuing efficiency in this way we become caught in a vicious circle: because our languages are rich the compilers cannot understand, and hence cannot optimize, our programs; so we need rich languages to allow us to obtain the efficiency which the compilers do not offer.

Decomposition into simple programs, as discussed above, seems to offer some hope of separating the considerations of correctness and modifiability from the considerations of efficiency. Ultimately, the objective is that the first should become largely trivial and the second largely automatic.

The first phase of design would produce the following documents:

- a definition of each serial file structure for each simple program (including files of operation codes!);

- the text of each simple program;

- a statement of the communication between simple programs, perhaps in the form of identities such as

$$\text{output } (p_i, f_r) \equiv \text{input } (p_j, f_s).$$

It may then be possible to carry out some automatic checking of self-consistency in the design—for instance, to check that the inputs to a program are within its domain. We may observe, incidentally, that the 'inner' feature of Simula 67 (4) is a way of enforcing consistency of a very limited case. More ambitiously, it may be possible, if file-handling protocol is exactly observed, and read and write operations are allocated with a scrupulous regard to principle, to check the correctness of the simple programs in relation to the defined data structures.

In the second phase of design, the designer would specify, in greater or lesser detail:

- the synchronization of the simple programs;

- the handling of state vectors;

- the dissection and recombining of programs and state vectors to reduce interface overheads.

Synchronization is already loosely constrained by the statements of program communication made in the first phase: the consumer can never run ahead of the producer. Within this constraint the designer may choose to impose additional constraints at compile time and/or at execution time. The weakest local constraint is to provide unlimited dynamic buffering at execution time, the consumer being allowed to lag behind the producer by anything from a single record to the whole file, depending on resource allocation elsewhere in the system. The strongest local constraints are use of coroutines or program inversion (enforcing a single record lag) and use of a physical magnetic tape (enforcing a whole file lag).

Dissection and recombining of programs becomes possible with coroutines or program inversion; its purpose is to reduce interface overheads by moving code between the invoking and invoked programs, thus avoiding some of the time and space costs of procedure calls and also, under certain circumstances, avoiding replication of program structure and hence of coding for sequencing control. It depends on being able to associate code in one program with code in another through the medium of the communication data structure.

A trivial illustration is provided by solution 3, in which we chose to invert PA with respect to file X, giving an input procedure PAX for the file of cardimages. We may decide that the procedure call overhead is intolerable, and that we wish to dissect PAX and combine it with PB. This is achieved by taking the invocations of PAX in PB (that is, the statements 'open fileX', 'read fileX' and 'close fileX') and replacing those invocations by the code which PAX would execute in response to them. For example, in response to 'open fileX' statement in PB can be replaced by the statement 'open blockedfile'.

A more substantial illustration is provided by the common practice of designers of 'real-time' data processing systems. Suppose that a primary transaction for a product gives rise to a secondary transaction for each open order item for that product, and that each of those in turn gives rise to a transaction for the open order of which it is a part, which then gives rise to a transaction for the open order of which it is a part, which then gives rise to a transaction for the customer who placed the order. Instead of having separate simple programs for the product, order item, order and customer, the designer will usually specify a 'transaction processing module': this consists of coding from each of those simple programs, the coding being that required to handle the relevant primary or secondary transaction.

Some interesting program transformations of a possibly relevant kind are discussed in a paper by Burstall and Darlington (5). I cannot end this paper better than by quoting from them:

"The overall aim of our investigation has been to help people to write correct programs which are easy to alter. To produce such programs it seems advisable to adopt a lucid, mathematical and abstract programming style. If one takes this really seriously, attempting to free one's mind from considerations of computational efficiency, there may be a heavy penalty in program running time; in practice it is often necessary to adopt a more intricate version of the program, sacrificing comprehensibility for speed. The question then arises as to how a lucid program can be transformed into a more intricate but efficient one in a systematic way, or indeed in a way which could be mechanized."

"...We are interested in starting with programs having an extremely simple structure and only later introducing the complications which we usually take for granted even in high level language programs. These complications arise by introducing useful interactions between what were originally separate parts of the program, benefiting by what might be called 'economies of interaction'." ■

References

1. Principles of Program Design; M A Jackson; Academic Press 1975.

2. Hierarchical Program Structures; O-J Dahl; in Structured Programming; Academic Press 1972.

3. Structured Programming with *go to* Statements; Donald E Knuth; in ACM Computing Surveys Vol 6 No 4 December 1974.

4. A Structural Approach to Protection; C A R Hoare; 1975.

5. Some Transformations for Developing Recursive Programs; R M Burstall & John Darlington; in Proceedings of 1975 Conference on Reliable Software; Sigplan Notices Vol 10 No 6 June 1975.

2. The Importance of Program Structure

2.1 A Simple Program Specification

A program has to process a single input file and produce one report. The input file has been sorted by customer identifier (CUST-ID). For each customer on the input file there is a header record which comes first and then some number of transaction records. Each transaction record contains a product identifier (PROD-ID) and a QTY field which indicates the number of the product that the customer has ordered. A database can be directly accessed on the key PROD-ID to find the value of one unit of the product. There are two types of customer, discount customers and normal customers, which are distinguished by a code (value 'D' or 'N') in the header record. The header records also contain a field, DEBT, which is the customer's outstanding debt. 'D' type header records also have a discount field which is the percentage discount the customer gets on all items.

The summary consists of one line for each normal customer, two lines for each discount customer and two overall summary lines. The normal customer summary line has the total value of the transactions, the old debt and the new debt. The first line of a discount summary has the total value of the transactions, the discount level, and the discounted value. The second line has the old debt and the new debt. The overall summary totals the debts and values.

It isn't relevant here, but the input file actually consists of segments from a data base.

2.2 The Correct Program Structure

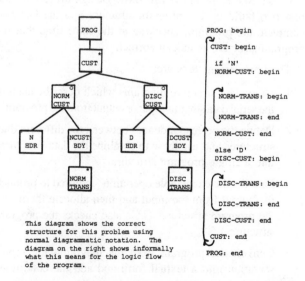

This diagram shows the correct structure for this problem using normal diagrammatic notation. The diagram on the right shows informally what this means for the logic flow of the program.

Structure diagrams are used both to describe serial streams of data and to describe the pattern of logic flow within a program. The above diagram describes the

program structure (i.e. the pattern of logic flow) of a solution to the small problem we have set ourselves. The informal picture on the left helps explain what the logic flow looks like.

Note that this logic flow could be implemented either by in-line code or by nested subroutine calls. A program structure diagram specifies the pattern of logic flow but defers this implementation choice.

In a short overview like this, we cannot fully justify our claim that this structure is the correct one for this problem. However the following observations support the claim even if they do not fully prove it:

— The problem is about customers; there are two types of customer; for each customer there can be a number of transactions. The program structure reflects this problem structure. The parts of the program which deal with different parts of the external reality (e.g. a discount customer, one transaction of a normal customer) are easily recognised and are separable from the rest of the program.

— The clarity of this program structure makes it obvious how often each program operation will be executed (once per discount customer, once per transaction of a normal customer). Most program bugs are caused by some operation which is executed either once more or once less than it should be.

— Compare our correct structure with the alternative shown below. No one is saying that a solution to our problem cannot be based on this structure. However, consider how much more difficult the structure is to understand, how it doesn't at all reflect the problem structure, how much more likely it is to fail a test (e.g., a customer with no transactions). Remember, we are in the business of mastering complexity.

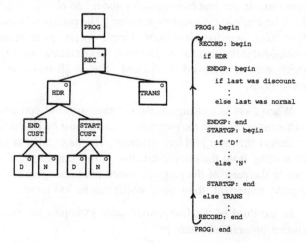

2.3 Program Maintenance

A correctly structured program is much easier and cheaper to maintain than a wrongly structured program. Reduced maintenance costs are the main cost justification for introducing JSP. Consider the following amendments to the specification of our small problem:

— The report must now include copies of the input transaction records for discount customers only. The output for a discount customer is now the transaction records followed by the two summary lines as before.

— Separate reports are needed, one for discount customers and one for normal customers. The output per customer is the same as in the original specification. The two overall summary lines now appear at the end of each report and total only the debts and values of customers which appear on that report. (There are separate discount and normal customer summaries.)

— The original specification stated that the input was sorted on unique customer identifier. In fact, the input is now sorted on unique customer identifier within area code. A further summary line is to be produced for each area detailing the total value and total discounted value of the transactions for that area.

— Now there is a third type of customer, a special discount customer, whose discount is calculated in a more complicated way.

Specification changes divide themselves crudely into two categories: those in which there is a change in that part of the external world which concerns the program; and those in which there is only a change in the way information about the same external world is analysed and presented. Of the four above examples, the first two are of this latter type. In the third, there is a change in the external world. Customers are grouped into areas where before they were not. In the fourth there is also a change. There are three types of customer where before there were only two.

Specification changes of the second type are very easy to handle if the program structure exactly matches the problem structure. In the first two examples above, no change at all need be made to the program structure. The pattern of logic flow stays the same. Some extra simple operations must be embedded in the structure and some of the operations already there must be removed or replaced. That is all that needs to be done.

When there is a change in the external world of concern to the program, then the program structure must be changed to reflect this new problem structure. The huge advantage of starting from the correct structure is that one can easily isolate the parts of the program which need changing and, equally important, those parts which can be left alone.

In the third of the four maintenance examples the new correct program structure is:

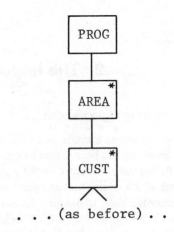

. . .(as before). .

And in the fourth of the examples the new program structure is:

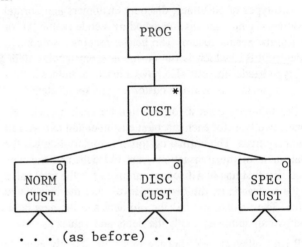

. . . (as before) . .

2.4 The JSP Basic Design Procedure

Of the four steps in the JSP Basic Design Procedure, the first two build up the program structure and the last two complete the program, checking at the same time that the program structure is indeed correct.

The four design steps are:

1. Draw data structure diagrams which describe each of the serial data streams input or output from the program.

2. Define the correspondences between the different data structures and use these to combine the data structures into a single program structure.

3. First list the executable operations required to produce the output from the input and then allocate them into the program structure. (This also checks the program structure.)

4. Convert the program from the diagrammatic representation into a textual form and add the conditions to iteration and selection components.

The JSP solution to the small Customer Accounts Summary problem is as follows.

1. Data structures step.

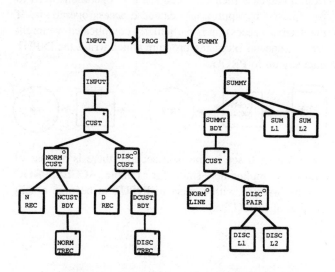

RECORD	VARIABLES
INREC	INOLDDEBT, DISCLEVEL, PROD-ID, QTY
NORMSUMLINE	N-TOTVAL, N-OLDDEBT, N-NEWDEBT
DISCSUML1	D-TOTVAL, D-DISCLEVEL, DISCVAL
DISCSUML2	D-OLDDEBT, D-NEWDEBT
OVERSUML1	TOTOLDDEBT, TOTNEWDEBT
OVERSUML2	TOTGROSSVAL, TOTDISCVAL

```
 1.   open SUMMY
 2.   close SUMMY
 3.   write OVERSUML1
 4.   write OVERLUML2
 5.   write DISCSUML1
 6.   write DISCSUML2
 7.   write NORMSUMLINE
 8.   N-OLDDEBT := INOLDDEBT
 9.   N-NEWDEBT := N-OLDDEBT + N-TOTVAL
10.   N-TOTVAL := 0
11.   N-TOTVAL := N-TOTVAL + TRANSVAL
12.   TRANSVAL := QTY X PRICE
13.   GET PRICEREC (PROD-ID)
14.   D-TOTVAL := 0
15.   D-TOTVAL := D-TOTVAL + TRANSVAL
16.   D-DISCLEVEL := DISCLEVEL
17.   DISCVAL := D-TOTVAL - (D-TOTVAL X DISCLEVEL)
18.   TOTOLDDEBT := 0
19.   TOTOLDDEBT := TOTOLDDEBT + D-OLDDEBT
20.   TOTOLDDEBT := TOTOLDDEBT + N-OLDDEBT
21.   TOTNEWDEBT := 0
22.   TOTNEWDEBT := TOTNEWDEBT + D-NEWDEBT
23.   TOTNEWDEBT := TOTNEWDEBT + N-NEWDEBT
24.   TOTGROSSVAL := 0
25.   TOTGROSSVAL := TOTGROSSVAL + N-TOTVAL
26.   TOTGROSSVAL := TOTGROSSVAL + D-TOTVAL
27.   TOTDISCVAL := 0
28.   TOTDISCVAL := TOTDISCVAL + N-TOTVAL
29.   TOTDISCVAL := TOTDISCVAL + DISCVAL
30.   CURRENT-CUST-ID := CUST-ID
31.   open INPUT
32.   close INPUT
33.   read INREC
```

2. Forming the program structure. The correspondences in this problem are between INPUT and SUMMY; CUST and CUST; NORM CUST and NORM LINE; and DISC CUST and DISC PAIR. A correspondence is a functional association between components of different structures. For two components to correspond, they must occur the same number of times in any single execution of the program. The program structure contains each of the data structures within it; a pair of corresponding data components forms a single program component.

In making this list, no attempt has been made to optimise for efficiency in any way which would sacrifice some simplicity.

— The prefixes C- and P- mean Consume- and Produce-respectively and distinguish the components which originate from the input and output data structures.

3. In making the following list of operations it is assumed that the following variables have been declared within the appropriate records.

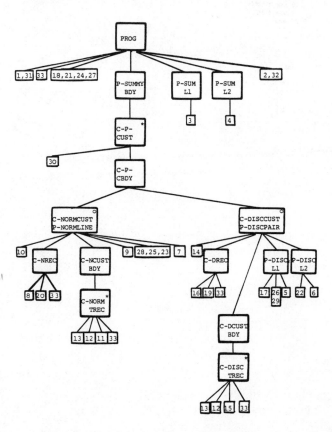

Program Structure with Operations Allocated

4. *Completing the program by converting the diagram into a textual form.* The following structure text notation is very useful because it does not prejudice the choice of coding style.

```
PROG seq
    open SUMMY; openINPUT; read INREC;
    TOTOLDDEBT := O; TOTNEWDEBT := O; TOTGROSSVAL := O; TOTDISCVAL := O;
    P-SUMMYBDY iter while not eof-INPUT
        C-P-CUST seq
            CURRENT-CUST-ID := CUST-ID;
            C-P-CBDY select(CODE = 'N')
                C-NORMCUST-P-NORMLINE seq
                    N-TOTVAL := O;
                    N-OLDDEBT := INOLDDEBT; TOTALOLDDEBT := TOTALOLDDEBT
                    TOTALOLDDEBT := TOTALOLDDEBT + N-OLDDEBT;
                    read INREC;
                    C-NCUSTBDY iter while (CURRENT-CUST-ID = CUST-ID)
                        GET PRICEREC (PROD-ID);
                        TRANSVAL := QTY X PRICE;
                        N-TOTVAL := N-TOTAL + TRANSVAL;
                        read INREC;
                    C-NCUSTBDY end
                    N-NEWDEBT := N-OLDDEBT + N-TOTVAL;
                    TOTDISCVAL := TOTDISCVAL + N-TOTVAL;
                    TOTGROSSVAL := TOTGROSSVAL + N-TOTVAL;
                    TOTNEWDEBT := TOTNEWDEBT + N-NEWDEBT;
                    write NORMSUMLINE;
                C-NORMCUST-P-NORMLINE end
            C-P-CBDY alt (CODE = 'D')
                C-DISCCUST-P-DISCPAIR seq
                    D-TOTVAL := O;
                    D-DISCLEVEL := DISCLEVEL;
                    TOTOLDDEBT := TOTOLDDEBT + D-OLDDEBT;
                    read INREC;
                    C-DCUSTBDY iter while (CURRENT-CUST-ID = CUST-ID)
                        GET PRICEREC (PROD-ID);
                        TRANSVAL := QTY X PRICE;
                        D-TOTVAL := D-TOTVAL + TRANSVAL;
                        read INREC;
                    C-CUSTBDY end;
                    DISCVAL := D-TOTVAL - (D-TOTVAL X DISCLEVEL);
                    TOTGROSSVAL := TOTGROSSVAL + D-TOTVAL;
                    TOTDISCVAL := TOTDISCVAL + DISCVAL;
                    write DISCSUML1;
                    TOTNEWDEBT := TOTNEWDEBT + D-NEWDEBT;
                    write DISCSUML2;
                C-DISCCUST-P-DISCPAIR end
            C-P-CBDY end
        C-P-CUST end
    P-SUMMYBDY end
    write OVERSUML1;
    write OVERSUML2;
    close SUMMY;
    close INPUT;
PROG end
```

If, as was suggested, the input file consists of segments from a database then the 'read INPUT' operations need to be replaced by appropriate database access operations. If the database accessing is particularly complicated we might create a special accessing program which writes the INPUT data stream to PROG.

As we shall see in the next section, there is no loss of efficiency implied here since, for example, ACCESSPROG can be inverted with respect to INPUT to become a subroutine of PROG.

3. Program Inversion and Its Consequences

3.1 Meaning of Program Inversion

Up to now it may appear that we have a technique of limited application: fine for batch programs but little else.

Inversion is a programming tool which extends the range of applicability of basic JSP design into the areas of subroutine design and on-line programming and which allows the use of the long running program as the basic tool in the JSD approach to systems.

An inverted program is a resumable program—that is to say it does not execute continuously from beginning to end but instead is suspended and resumed at a number of points within its text. An immediate consequence is that the data streams which are input and output (and on which the JSP design is based) need not be stored in their entirety on a serial medium. If, for example, a program is suspended each time it tries to read a record of its input file, then whoever or whatever produces that record has time to produce it and pass it to the program (which now resumes) without placing it meanwhile on any storage medium.

For example, an on-line program may be viewed as a resumable program which suspends itself each time it is ready to read another input from the operator. Or a variable state subroutine may be seen as a resumable program which suspends itself each time it returns control to the invoking program.

Program inversion is the technique of converting an ordinary program into this resumable form.

The huge benefit of program inversion is that the underlying seriality of almost all programming problems need not be distorted by the piecemeal execution of the program. The normal JSP tools can be used to analyse this seriality and design a program which must then be inverted to give the module required by the implementation environment.

3.2 The Inversion Mechanism

Suppose that P is a program which outputs a serial data stream F which is read by the program Q. We want to invert P so that it is a subroutine of Q and the records of F pass, one for each invocation, across the subroutine linkage.

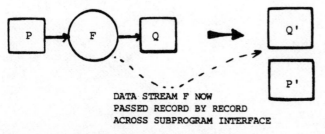

DATA STREAM F NOW
PASSED RECORD BY RECORD
ACROSS SUBPROGRAM INTERFACE

In essence the inversion mechanism is this. At each write statement in P's text the position in the text must be remembered explicitly. On the next invocation the program must be made to resume at that point. Since a subprogram starts each invocation at the beginning of its text, there must be a conditional jump from the beginning of the program text to the relevant resume point. There is a little more to it than that, but not much.

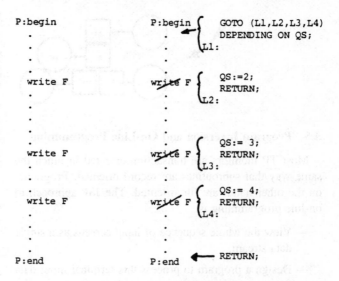

The variable QS is the text pointer. QS identifies at which resume point the program was suspended.

3.3 Program Inversion and the Design of Variable State Subroutines

Using JSP a variable state subroutine is designed by first specifying the main program equivalent to it, designing it, and then inverting it to give the required subroutine. For example, if the variable state subroutine is:

'Q requires a subroutine P which returns the first prime on the first invocation and the next prime on each of 999 further invocations.'

then the equivalent main program is:

'F is a file of the first 1000 prime numbers, in ascending order, one per record. P creates F. Q reads F.'

Again, if the subroutine specification is:

'Q requires a subroutine, P', which will scan the database and return, one for each invocation, all database customer segments which belong to an area making a profit and which satisfy . . .'

then the equivalent program is:

'P writes a file F (read by Q) of all database customer segments which belong to an area making a profit and which satisfy . . .'

3.4 Program Inversion and the Implementation of Networks in a Hierarchy

Often a problem can very conveniently be split into a network of small simple programs. Program inversion allows a straightforward implementation of this network as a hierarchy of subroutines.

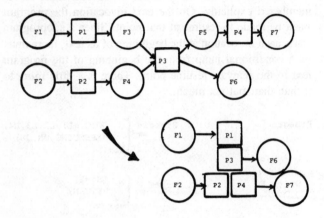

3.5 Program Inversion and On-Line Programming

Most TP monitors are transaction oriented in much the same way that subroutines are record oriented. Programs, on the other hand, are file oriented. The JSP approach to on-line programming is:

— View the whole sequence of input screens as a single data stream.

— Design a program to process this terminal input data stream.

— Invert the program so that the TP monitor sees a transaction oriented module as required.

3.6 Program Inversion and System Design

Program inversion allows the designer to take a bird's eye view of data streams which may only be created piecemeal over a substantial period. An on-line designer draws data structures of the terminal input file which might, if the operator is lazy, take all afternoon to input.

In system design this freedom is exploited to the full. One of the key building blocks in Jackson System Development (JSD) is the long running program. A long running program processes all the input relevant to an entity. If the entity is, for example, a customer at a bank, or a mortgagor at a building society, or an employee, or a car in a company fleet, or indeed almost anything, then the input will take many years to create. No matter. A program can still be designed, based on a data structure of the entire input data stream. This program takes many years of elapsed time to complete its execution. However, there is no inefficiency. When inverted the program is suspended for most of this time, and only need be resumed when there is input for it.

An example, taken from chapter 11 of 'Principles of Program Design', is of a customer of a bank who conducts a series of negotiations with the bank, invariably reaches agreement, and then is allowed to take out a series of loans, one at a time. Each loan has an initial payment, a number of repayments and a final repayment. The whole process takes many years.

The long running program processes a file of all the customer's transactions.

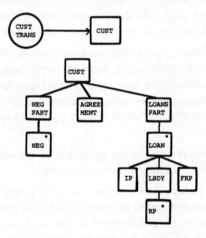

That part of the loans system which deals with one customer is viewed as a single program which is resumed, partially executed and suspended during a number of different load modules throughout the lifetime of the system.

Getting It Wrong—A Cautionary Tale
Michael Jackson

There is a very simple kind of programming problem which appears everywhere in data processing: you have a serial file of transactions, sorted into ascending order by some group identifier, and you have to print a summary showing the total for each group. It's the kind of problem everyone knows about—at least everyone who has been around in programming for more than a month or two—and those who don't know about it can read how it should be solved in that admirable book, *Principles of Program Design* (by M.A. Jackson, Academic Press, 1975).

Well, this story is about a programmer who was such a novice that he hadn't seen the problem before. So when it came his way he just did a nice simple piece of top-down design, and arrived at the following structured coding:

```
PA: open INFILE; display 'SUMMARY'; read INFILE;
    do while not eof-INFILE
        if new group
            end old group
            start new group
        else process record
        endif
        read INFILE
    enddo
    display 'END SUMMARY';
    close INFILE
end PA;
```

Now you, my learned readers, can probably see at once that something here is not quite right; but our hero was only a novice. So he went right ahead and coded his solution in COBOL, and compiled it, linked it and ran it. What came out was a little surprising (to our hero, though not to any of us more experienced programmers):

```
SUMMARY
$$..V/*     V..K$/K
A172632        +15
A195923        -60
...
Z749321      +8755
END SUMMARY
```

What, he wondered, could that curious second line be? In quite a short time he understood: it was, of course, the effect of ending the old group before the first group, only there was no old group before the first group. But how to make it disappear? Luckily, he knew his COBOL quite well: the first part of the curious line was, of course, the group-id, and could be removed by setting a VALUE clause in the WORKING-STORAGE item

```
02  PREVIOUS-RECORD-ID PIC X(7) VALUE SPACES.
```

while the right-hand part of the line was the total, and required slightly more subtle treatment:

```
02  GROUP-TOTAL PIC S9(6)
        VALUE ZERO
        BLANK WHEN ZERO.
```

After a recompilation he reran the test, and was delighted to see:

```
SUMMARY
A172632        +15
A195923        -60
A198564
A200135       -157
...
Z749321      +8755
END SUMMARY
```

He was poring happily over this printout, when his manager happened to come by. 'What's this?' asked the manager, pointing to the total for group A198564, 'why is the total blank?'. 'That's zero' said the programmer. 'No it isn't' said the manager, 'it's blank, and I want it to print as zero, not as blank'. Our hero, although a novice, was very quick to learn the tricks of the programmer's trade, and, as quick as a flash, he replied 'well, there are technical reasons why it has to print as blank'. This was a testing moment for the manager; he might have made the catastrophic mistake of asking 'what technical reasons?'. But he was cleverer than that; so he just said 'technical reasons or no technical reasons, it must print as zero'.

So it was back to the drawing board for our hero. Luckily, he happened to overhear one of his colleagues at lunch talking about something called a 'first-time switch'; he had never heard of such a thing before, but, being very intelligent, he saw at once what the name implied and how such a device could help him. That afternoon he added one to his program:

```
PA: open INFILE; display 'SUMMARY'; read INFILE;
    move 0 to switch1;
    do while not eof-INFILE
        if new group
            if switch1 = 1
                end old group
            else move 1 to switch1
            endif
            start new group
        else process record
        endif
        read INFILE
    enddo
    display 'END SUMMARY';
    close INFILE
end PA;
```

When he ran it again, the output looked really fine, and the program went into production running. It ran happily for six months, and then one day a clerk from the user department came to see our hero. 'Look' said the clerk, pointing to the end of that week's report, 'there's no total for the last group'. Well, I expect that all of you readers knew all along that this was going to happen: after all, the end-group and start-group operations had originally been paired, and the introduction of switch1 removed one of the end-groups; so there must have been a group which was being started but not ended. And indeed there was, and it was the last group in the file.

Of course, the error had been there on every one of the twenty five reports produced since the program had been put into production, but no-one had noticed it before; there's a lot of computer printout which nobody reads in most installations. The programmer, of course, didn't like to say anything about this to the clerk, so he just said 'OK, I'll fix it'. Why had the programmer not noticed the error in testing? Really, because he was too conscientious. He had decided to test the program thoroughly, by using the whole of last year's actual data as test data. This is a special kind of testing, called 'volume testing' or 'soak testing'. It's a special kind of testing because you run the program on the input, but you don't look at the output. After all, who could look all through a pile of paper five inches high? What you do when you get five inches of output is this: you throw away the front two sheets, because they're JCL, which no ordinary mortal understands (experts sometimes look to see that the system completion code is zero, but not everyone's an expert); you check to see that there is no core dump; you look at the first and last lines; you spot-check a few of the totals; then you riffle through the whole five inches by raising the edge of the pile and letting the sheets peel off against your thumb, to make sure that if there is anything really nasty, like forty consecutive pages on which every line is printed with zeros all across the page, it will force itself on your attention. And that's all. So the error had remained undetected.

But it was very easily fixed. At the end of the program the programmer inserted the statements to end the last group:

```
        ...
        read INFILE
     enddo
     end last group
     display 'END SUMMARY';
     close INFILE
 end PA;
```

and the job was done.

All went well for the next seventeen months. And then the program showed that it was sensitive to something you wouldn't have expected a program to be sensitive to: the Bicentennial celebrations. What happened was that the company gave everyone a week's vacation; the next Monday morning they came back to work and ran the program, just like they ran it every Monday morning. What came out was:

```
SUMMARY
$$..V/*   ..D$K./
END SUMMARY
```

It was immediately obvious that something was wrong. There had been no transactions the previous week, so there were no groups, and the mystery line was, of course, the result of ending the last group—only there wasn't a last group. But again the problem was easily solved.

Our hero, more experienced by now, was tempted to do something clever with switch1, but he resisted the temptation. He had heard about 'defensive programming'. Defensive programming is a theory based on the idea that when you are programming you don't have the faintest idea whether what you are doing is right or not, so you ought to do something that won't cause too much harm. In accordance with this admirable principle, which he felt was clearly applicable in his own case, he resisted the temptation to do something with switch1, and instead introduced switch2:

```
PA:  open INFILE; display 'SUMMARY'; read INFILE;
     move 0 to switch1; move 0 to switch2;
     do while not eof-INFILE
        if new group
           if switch1 = 1
              end old group
           else move 1 to switch1
           endif
           start new group
        else process record
              move 1 to switch2
        endif
        read INFILE
     enddo
     if switch2 = 1
        end last group
     endif
     display 'END SUMMARY';
     close INFILE
 end PA;
```

After recompiling, he ran the program again in the empty file and produced the hoped-for result:

```
SUMMARY
END SUMMARY
```

Clearly, his tribulations were not at an end. The program ran happily and successfully for the next nineteen months, and no complaints were heard.

Then, one day, he was sitting quietly in his programming cubicle—Gerry Weinberg would have had something to say about that, I think—reading the job advertisements, when along came the clerk from the user department. 'Look', he said, 'the last group has been left off the printout again'. And indeed it had.

The diagnosis was easy. Somehow the program library had been messed up, and it was an old, incorrect version of the program that had been run that week. But not so.

After a couple of days of detective work our hero established beyond doubt that it was the current version which had been run. However, he also established that the program had been recompiled with the new version 6 compiler, for which the installation was a field test site. It must have been the compiler which was at fault! With the help of the systems programmer our hero went through the object code, hexadecimal character by hexadecimal character, and related it to the source code. The job took only nine hours, which they did in one marathon stretch, thus earning a bonus from their appreciative management. But the result was to prove that the object code was a perfectly reasonable compilation of the source COBOL text! Only one possibility was left: it had to be a transient error in the hardware or the operating system. Now, people don't like to come to that conclusion if they can avoid it; but I have to say that I have never found a programmer who, in private conversation with only one other programmer, refused to admit that he could remember at least one occasion in the past when something funny happened in one of his programs which had to be put down to that cause. And this seemed to be one of those occasions.

Certainly the error hadn't occurred before—at least, since the 'end last group' statements were added to the program. And it didn't happen again.

However, something funny did happen recently. The clerk from the user department came to see the programmer. 'I've been wondering', he said 'about that week we lost the last group from the printout. I got hold of the card input—which we always keep for a few months—and I discovered that there were exactly 843 cards'. 'So?' said the programmer. 'Well', the clerk went on, 'there were 842 group totals on the printout that week, and there should have been 843'. 'I don't see that that's relevant' said the programmer, 'but it's kind of you to mention it. Thank you for your trouble'. That night he took the program listing home secretly, and looked it over carefully. Suddenly the answer dawned on him. Of course! If there were 843 cards and 843 groups, then each group contained exactly one card; so the condition 'new group' would be true on every card, and it would always be the 'if' which was executed, and never the 'else'. But the instruction to set switch2 to 1 was only in the 'else' clause! So switch2 was never set on, and the last group was never ended.

The problem, once identified, was easily solved. In accordance with the principles of defensive programming, another statement 'move 1 to switch 2' was added to the

first clause of the 'if–else', leaving the original statement untouched in the 'else' clause. So the program was now:

```
PA:  open INFILE; display 'SUMMARY'; read INFILE;
     move 0 to switch1; move 0 to switch2;
     do while not eof-INFILE
         if new group
             if switch1 = 1
                 end old group
             else move 1 to switch1
             endif
             start new group
             move 1 to switch2
         else process record
             move 1 to switch2
         endif
         read INFILE
     enddo
     if switch2 = 1
         end last group
     endif
     display 'END SUMMARY';
     close INFILE
end PA;
```

Obviously, the program is now perfect and correct. But, of course, it has been running only for three months in its new form, and I will keep you posted if there are any new developments.

* * * *

And the moral? Well, it's this. The structure of the program is one we often see:

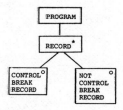

and this structure is wrong. Not inferior; not inelegant; just plain wrong. The difficulties were all caused by the 'end group' instructions. Now, how often should we end a group? Why, once per group! Where, in this program structure, is there a component which processes each group? There is no such component, and the 'end group' instructions cannot therefore be correctly allocated to the program structure. That's what all the difficulty was about.

Now, all of you good readers are experienced folk, and you wouldn't have made these mistakes—not, at least, on this small and well-known problem. But I know some very experienced programmers who make just this kind of mistake on bigger and more obscure programs; in fact, a lot of the mistakes they make are of exactly this kind—having the wrong program structure. But I don't suppose that any of those programmers are reading this cautionary tale, are they?

On-Line Program Dismemberment

If it turns out that the program code products for the Purchase Order Problem under TPM (see POP(3) in Section 2.3.3) is too large for operational efficiency then it may be dismembered into a number of parts. Only one of the parts need be loaded for each input transaction.

This technique of on-line dismemberment is a technique for modularising inverted programs. It should only be used when the efficiency gains are both important and demonstrable. The factors affecting efficiency are often complex. For example, a large module may be less likely to be swapped out of main storage and therefore is more likely still to be there when the next transaction comes in.

The diagram below shows the program structure of POP. The numbers 1–11 denote the eleven resume points in the inverted program. We analyse which parts of the program are reachable from each resume point on a single invocation. In general, though not in this example, we have to be careful of the effect of quit statements.

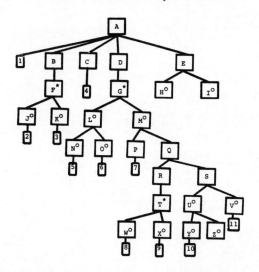

Elementary components reachable from each resume point (1 to 11) are:

1. J, K, and C
2. J, K, and C
3. J, K, and C
4. N, O, P, H, and I
5. N, O, P, H, and I
6. N, O, P, H, and I
7. W, X, Y, Z, N, O, P, H, and I
8. W, X, Y, Z, N, O, P, H, and I
9. W, X, Y, Z, N, O, P. H, and I
10. N, O, P, H, and I
11. N, O, P, H, and I.

The analysis of elementary components reachable from each resume point suggests two modules:

Module I containing J, K, and C

Module II containing W, X, Y, Z, N, O, P, H, and I.

Note the effect of the null component, the Z component. In the design there is no read allocated to the null component, therefore there is no resume point in the inverted program, and therefore we may resume at points 7, 8 or 9 and reach for example component P (on entry of a good PROD ID) or component H (on entry of a SV).

If our teleprocessing environment has some mechanism for moving from module to module without the input of a new transaction (e.g. XCTL in CICS) we may dismember POP into three parts as follows. The component Z in the third module has such a dynamic link to the second module.

M1 contains J, K and C.
M2 contains N, O, P, H and I.
M3 contains W, X, Y and Z.

Integration by Simpson's Rule

When designing what are commonly called "data processing" programs using Jackson Structured Programming (JSP), the data streams upon whose structures the program is to be based are fairly obvious. However, when one is designing "mathematical" programs, the situation can be somewhat different; finding the data streams can be the hardest part of the design process. As an illustration, consider how one would construct a program to evaluate an integral between finite limits by Simpson's Rule. This rule is discussed in any elementary calculus or numerical analysis book and states that such an integral can be approximated as follows:

Let $I = \int_a^b f(x)\, dx$ and I^* be the approximation by Simpson's Rule, then

$$I_1^* = \frac{h}{3}[f(a) + 4f(a+h) + f(b)] \qquad (1)$$

where $h = \frac{b-a}{2}$

Graphically, this is shown as:

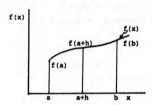

The approximation (1) is constructed by approximating $f(x)$ between a and b by a parabola and evaluating the integral of the approximating parabola. Greater accuracy can be achieved by applying Simpson's Rule to the two intervals $[a, a+h]$, and $[a+h, b]$ separately and adding the results. The resulting approximation is

$$I_2^* = \frac{h_1}{2}[f(a) + 4f(a+h_1) + 2f(a+2h_1) + 4f(a+3h_1) + f(b)] \quad 2$$

where $h_1 = \frac{h}{2}$

If we continue to halve the intervals to generate successively more accurate approximations, the following pattern coefficients as shown in Table 1 results.

Table 1

Approxi-mation		Coefficients of f(x) at x =								
	a	a+h/4	a+h/2	a+3h/4	a+h	a+5h/4	a+3h/2	a+7h/4	b
I_1^*	1				4				1
I_2^*	1		4		2		4		1
I_3^*	1	4	2	4	2	4	2	4	1
I_4^*	1	4	2	4	2	4	2	4	2	4	2	4	2	4	1

This table could of course be extended indefinitely. The program we wish to write will read one card containing a, b, and ϵ. The program will compute successive approximations, I^*, until the relative difference between two successive approximations is less than ϵ. The program will write one line containing a, b, ϵ, and the last I^* computed. The trivial System Network Diagram is:

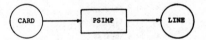

These files, being essentially unstructured, tell nothing about the required structure of PSIMP. We look for another file upon which to model the program. Looking again at Table 1, we can see that each value of $f(x)$ is multiplied by 1, 2, or 4. The values multiplied by 1 are the same in each approximation; the values multiplied by 2 are the same as those multiplied by 2 or 4 in the previous approximation; the values multiplied by 4 are new in each approximation. Because of the constancy of the points multiplied by 1 and the relationship between points multiplied by 2 and 4, we believe that we can concentrate on the conceptual file of abcissa values corresponding to those values of $f(x)$ that are multiplied by 4. Call this file ABS-FILE. The revised System Network Diagram becomes:

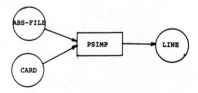

The data structure for ABS-FILE is:

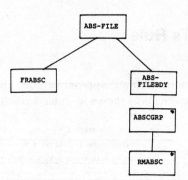

The program structure will be the same as that of ABS-FILE. Letting T1, T2, T4 represent the total of function values multiplied by 1, 2, and 4 respectively; n be the approximation number; h be the step size; and x be a dummy variable, we generate the following operations list:

Operations

1. $x: = a+h$
2. $x: = x+2h$
3. $n: = 1$
4. $n: = n+1$
5. $T1 = f(a) + f(b)$
6. $h: = (b-a)/2$
7. $h: = h/2$
8. $T4 = 0$
9. $T4: = T4 + f(x)$
10. $I^*: = \frac{h}{3} (T1 + 2T2 + 4T4)$
11. $T2 = 0$
12. $T2: = T2 + T4$
13. read CARD
14. Write a, b, ε, I^*
15. $CURRI^*: = I^*$
16. open CARD
17. close CARD
18. open LINE
19. close LINE
20. $CURRI^*: = 0$

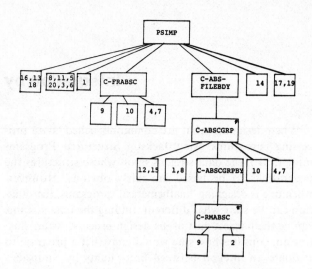

Structured text for some hypothetical computer is

```
PSIMP seq
        open CARD; open LINE; read CARD;
        T4: = 0; T2: = 0; T1: = f(a) + f(b); CURRI*: = 0;
        n: = 1; h = (b-a)/2; x: = a + b;
    C-FRABSC seq
            T4: = T4 + f(x);
            I*: = h/3 (T1 + 2T2 + 4T4);
            n: = n+1;
            h: = h/2;
    C-FRABSC end
    C-ABS-FILEBDY itr while ((n<2) | (n>2 & abs(I-CURRI*/I*)>ε))
        C-ABSCGRP seq
            T2: = T2 + T4;
            CURRI*: = I*;
            x: = a + h; T4: = 0;
            C-ABSCGRPBDY itr while (x < b)
                C-RMABSC seq
                    T4: = T4 + f(x);
                    x: = x + 2h;
                C-RMABSC end
            C-ABSCGRPBDY end
                I*: = h/3 (T1 + 2T2 + 4T4); n: = n+1; h: = h/2;
        C-ABSCGRP end
    C-ABS-FILEBDY end
            write a, b, ε, I*; close CARD; close LINE;
PSIMP end
```

100

PART THREE

JSP CASE STUDIES

Chapter 3.0   Introduction to Part Three

This part of the book illustrates the use of JSP in practice. The JSP solutions to three moderately complicated programming problems are developed and discussed in considerable detail. A fourth problem is fully dealt with in one of the reprints.

Two of the examples are real application programs that have been modified only slightly for inclusion here. The microfiche problem is a batch program that prepares input for the production of microfiches. The On-line Case Study is a slightly simplified and rewritten version of a real problem that was implemented under CICS, one of IBM's main teleprocessing environments.

The third example, Infix to Postfix, illustrates the application of JSP to a problem from compiler writing and also the use of recursion in a JSP program.

Of the four reprints at the end of Part Three, three are the MJSL (Michael Jackson Systems Limited) course solutions to these three problems. The fourth, "Structured Programming Techniques in Interrupt-Driven Routines", describes the application of JSP to the design of a microcode module and illustrates again the range of application of the method.

If you think you know JSP already, then these problems will be a good test of your understanding. If this book is your introduction to JSP, you will probably find these problems quite hard if you try them without looking at the solutions. However, if you can do them you will certainly be able to practice JSP successfully.

Chapter 3.1 The Microfiche Problem

First read the one-and-a-half-page specification of the microfiche problem.* The specification is not a particularly good example of technical writing, not, unfortunately, is it the worst specification ever written. A method must not assume that some previous piece of work that falls outside its scope has been done superbly, otherwise the utility of the method will be severely limited. We have to be able to work with bad technical descriptions as well as good ones.

When they are given this specification to program, as opposed simply to reading it in a book, most people feel a certain insecurity or mild panic. Their very sane reaction is to break off work and go and make a cup of coffee. (Certainly this is what happens on courses.) They feel like this because they have no ideas what a solution might look like to a problem that is understood only enough to see that it might be nasty. Only the experienced and the self-confident avoid all feelings of insecurity when they know they have to solve a problem and they cannot see an answer. As has been emphasised many times, a method of software development is not a way of writing down solutions that come in a flash of inspiration or memory. JSP is supposed to be a way of working toward solutions, a way of analysing specifications so that you can begin to understand them and expose their ambiguities, and a way of moving toward a solution without having to see the whole thing immediately. For this reason the technical description of the microfiche problem is the right sort of testing ground for JSP or any other method.

You can still panic of course, but you may do it slightly less so because you know you are not supposed to see the whole solution yet.

Begin by drawing the System Network Diagram showing the input and output data streams for the problem. Then start analysing the specification by drawing fragments of data structures. This will either crystallise your understanding of parts of the specification or expose ambiguities about which you will have to ask or make some explicit decision yourself.

Read the first part of the solution to clarify some points in the specifications. You will realise that many of the details and complications of microfiche production are not in fact part of this problem. The gathering together of all the T3 records to make the index frame

*This reprint appears on pages 117-118.

at the end is not part of this program, nor is the large task of rearranging the contents of a microfiche so that it can be produced column by column part of this program. Our program has to add some summary records for the customer and item groups and various header and trailer records to divide the output into the groups that will form the frames and fiches. The problem is larger than most course examples, but it isn't really large or complicated.

An initial attempt at the data structures will look something like the diagram on the second page of the solution. Perhaps your structure for OF1 was more like Figure 3.1a, which has extra T1 selection lower in the structure.

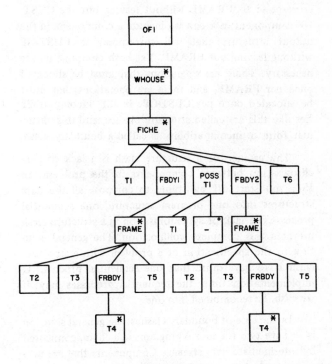

Figure 3.1a

The component T4SET in FRAMEBDY is the set of T4 records that may not be split between frames. You may or may not have this extra iteration at this stage. You may also have eliminated the DATE-GP component from the INPUT structure. Although the input is sorted on this key, it turns out that this grouping is not significant for the problem.

Portions of this Chapter are excerpted from previously unpublished Michael Jackson Systems Limited (MJSL) internal documents with permission from MJSL.

When you have data structures like these, or the variants just described, and there is nothing obviously wrong or inadequate about them, you should look for correspondences. If the correspondences are there, the data structures can be combined, and the development can proceed. If they cannot be found, then the lack of correspondences may give some clue about the necessary changes to one or more of the data structures. Alternatively, the lack of correspondences may lead to the recognition of a structure clash.

There are very few correspondences between our input and output data structures, nor can the structures be easily changed so that they can be fitted together. We would like, for example, to include a FRAME component in the input structure. If we did, we would either have to leave out the CUST-GP component or find a way of fitting CUST-GP and FRAME into the same structure. Here is the crunch. Because of the way their boundaries overlap in arbitrary ways, these components cannot be fitted into the same structure diagram. We cannot include a component in the input structure that will correspond to FRAME without leaving out the CUST-GP component, nor can we include a component in the output structure that will correspond to CUST-GP without leaving out FRAME. Yet both components are necessary. There are operations that must be allocated once per FRAME, and there are operations that must be allocated once per CUST-GP. In JSP, incompatibilities like this are called structure clashes, and this particular form of incompatibility is called a boundary clash.

The essence of a structure clash is a lack of synchronisation between components in the problem. In JSP, you start off by trying to compose all the data structures into one program structure, one sequential process. The lack of synchronisation in a structure clash prevents this complete composition. The general solution to the specification of a problem with a structure clash is to have more than one sequential process. At implementation time, the sequential processes may, if we wish, be recombined into one.

In the case of boundary clashes, the general solution is to have two (or more) programs in a chain, connected by intermediate data streams. Components that are necessary and that will not fit together in one program structure must be put in different program structures. There is a concise overview of boundary clashes in the JSP Handbook, reprinted in Section 2.4.1.

To make progress with the microfiche problem, the boundary clashes must be resolved and the intermediate data streams, specified. This is the key to the whole problem.

To analyse boundary clashes, it is helpful to draw skeleton structures such as are shown on the third page of the solution.

These show a correspondence between RECORD on input and T4SET on output. We might also have made a selection between different types of T4 record on output, and corresponded RECORD with the T4 records that came directly from RECORDs. The correspondence below the clash in a boundary clash is not always so easy to state exactly.

A clash is not the same as a lack of correspondence. ITEM-GP on input does not correspond with WAREHOUSE on output, but they don't clash. Some integral number of ITEM-GPs make up a WAREHOUSE.

In the same way, ITEM-GP on input does not clash with FRAME on output. An ITEM-GP consists of an integral number of FRAMES.

There is a clash between ITEM-GP and FICHE, between CUST-GP and FICHE, and between CUST-GP and FRAME.

Had there also been a clash between ITEM and FRAME, two programs would have been sufficient for the solution. One program would have dealt with CUSTOMERs and ITEMS and written a data stream to another program that would have dealt with FICHES and FRAMES. The data stream would have consisted (roughly) of T4 records. However, there is the ITEM/FRAME relationship to consider. Because information about ITEM boundaries is necessary for the definition of the FRAME boundaries, the program that creates FRAMES must have ITEMs as components, and this cannot be the same program that has CUST-GPs in its structure (because of the CUST/FRAME clash) nor can it be the same program that has FICHEs in its structure (because of the ITEM/FICHE clash). So we have three programs, one concerned with CUSTOMERs and ITEMs, one with ITEMs and FRAMEs, and one with FRAMEs and FICHEs.

You may have considered solving the problem with only two programs. Perhaps, you may suppose, the first program could add a special marker record, an S record, at the end of each ITEM and have the second program use the S record to help it create the FRAME boundaries. The structure of the second program would be something like that shown in Figure 3.1b.

This is fine in that the intermediate data stream can be specified and both the programs can be completed using JSP. But something has been lost. The ITEM/FRAME relationship has been replaced by an S RECORD/FRAME relationship. A relationship of interest

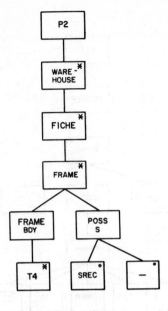

Figure 3.1b

in the application area has been partially lost. Just as in the "Getting It Wrong" story, we can identify the end of the component in the program, but not the start. The S record identifies the end of the ITEM component, but there is nothing in the program containing FRAME that identifies the start of ITEM. (The S records don't. If you start to try to make them, you will exactly repeat the mistakes of the "Getting It Wrong" story. Something must be introduced at the beginning of the whole program to deal with the beginning of the first item, and something special must be introduced at the end of the whole program because the last S record is not the beginning of a new item.)

Arguably, in the microfiche problem, this is less serious because the component ITEM at least appears explicitly with a start and an end in another program. However, consider such a simple change as adding the FRAME count within ITEM to each T2 record. (There is already a similar FICHE count within WAREHOUSE on each T1 record.) Now there is something to be allocated at the beginning of each ITEM (initialisation of the FRAME counter) in the program that creates T2s. This forces us to recognise the ITEM/FRAME relationship, which we ought to have done anyway, and therefore to have three programs.

In practice, and certainly on courses, a programmer may not analyse the pattern of boundary clashes as precisely as this. But faced with the choice of a two-program solution and a three-program solution, he can (and ought to) choose the three-program solution on general grounds of simplicity. A boundary clash forces the decomposition of a problem into a network, but sometimes this same network decomposition is attractive when there is no clash or when the exact nature of the clash is not clear.

Indeed one of the important uses of inversion in conventional COBOL and PL/I environments is to allow this form of decomposition without being committed to the I/O overhead of reading and writing the intermediate data streams. A programmer may make an initial decomposition into only two programs. Then later one of the programs is further decomposed giving the three-program solution.

The intermediate data stream between P1 and P2 must be specified before either P1 or P2 can be designed. The intermediate data stream between P2 and P3 must be specified before either P2 or P3 can be designed. We know the main components of the three programs, and we know the approximate job each program has to do. Specifying the intermediate data streams makes this approximation precise. The standard solution to a boundary clash is to have records on the intermediate data stream for the highest nonclashing component below the level of the clash. On questions of detailed specification, we try to ensure that issues are being dealt with in the appropriate program. For example, in this problem, do not specify the groups of T4 records that cannot be split between FRAMEs in P1. Leave it to P2, the program that is concerned with the definition of FRAME boundaries.

Two errors are common at this stage of the development. One is starting the detailed JSP design of the separate programs before the intermediate data streams are properly specified. Even if the best choice is not clear, a provisional choice must be made for the later work to make sense. The other error is defining the data streams so that more of the processing than is appropriate is done in the first program of the chain. There is no virtue in doing the hard part first, in P1, if the hard part does not belong in P1. If you have not already done so, you should read the middle part of the solution (the ninth and tenth pages), which discusses the specification of the intermediate data streams.

In this solution, all the eventual T4 records are produced in P1. If the extra T4 records associated with customer and item summaries are only blank lines, then arguably, they should be produced in P2, as they are concerned with FRAME layout. They would then be associated with certain types of T4 record (customer and item summary types) in P2 instead of with groupings of T4 records (customer and item groups) in P1. Certainly this would be the correct view if there were additional rules, for instance, to suppress the production of blank lines at the bottom of a FRAME, if this allows an extra CUSTOMER or ITEM group to fit.

With the given definitions of the intermediate data streams you may want to develop each of the three programs yourself before looking at the rest of the solution.

There is nothing especially interesting or difficult about the program P1. In program P2, we have to deal with the requirement that certain groups of T4 records must not be split between FRAMEs. In the reprinted solution, FRAMEBDY is a simple iteration of T4 records. The recognition problem is simply whether a given T4 is part of this FRAME or not. The problem is solved by reading ahead seven records. The QUIT statements in the solution are used simply to break up the large condition on the iteration. There is no real backtracking. Optimisation of this condition is possible, and it may be desirable.

Another approach is to introduce into the structures of IM1 and IM2 the groups of records (T4SETs in some previous structures) that cannot be split between FRAMEs. This works well for this problem and leads to the same recognition problem as that specified in the reprinted solution. A reason for not choosing this solution is that the groups of T4 records do not really have any meaning in the application area. A user understands FRAMES and ITEMs but probably does not understand NON SPLITABLE T4GROUP. The groups are our construction from the individual user-imposed constraints such as do not split a normal T4 record from the A-type T4 record, do not start a page with an item summary, and so on.

The final program, P3 inserts the T1 and the T6 records to define the FICHE boundaries and writes the output files OF1 and OF2. The main point of interest is the production of the second T1 record. In the reprinted solution, the selection is made at the FICHE level between a FICHE with and a FICHE without the appropriate item change. This is the cleanest and clearest solution. The requirement for a second T1 is a property of the FICHE as a whole, or at least the whole first part of the FICHE. Figure 3.1a is an alternative structure for OF1. The selection of the second T1 is at a lower level.

Figure 3.1c is another possible structure for OF1. This is not a good description of OF1. The T1 record is described as a possible FRAME trailer and is therefore being associated with FRAMEs instead of FICHEs. The

structure implies there might be many T1 records, not just one or two.

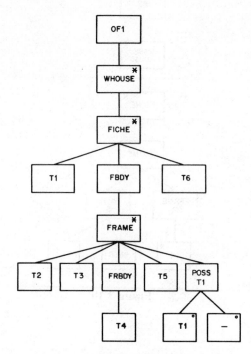

Figure 3.1c

Our solution consists of three programs. The second has a recognition difficulty solved by multiple read ahead. The third has a recognition difficulty solved by backtracking. In conventional environments, the implementation choice is between running the programs in sequence, using some physical medium to store the intermediate data streams and combining the programs together using program inversion so that the data streams pass record by record across subroutine interfaces. Any one of the three programs can be made the main program. If P1 is the main program, P2 is inverted with respect to IM1, and P3 is inverted with respect to IM2; P1 calls P2 to dispose of IM1 records, and P2 calls P3 to dispose of IM2 records. If P2 is the main program, P1 is inverted with respect to IM1, and P3 is inverted with respect to IM2; P2 calls P1 to access IM1 records, and P2 calls P3 to dispose of IM2 records. If P3 is the main program, P1 is inverted with respect to IM1, and P2 is inverted with respect to IM2; P3 calls P2 to access IM2 records, and P2 calls P1 to access IM1 records. In other environments, there are more possibilities for the implementation of three programs that communicate by data streams.

Finally, consider the following question on program maintenance. Suppose that there was also a boundary clash between ITEMs and FRAMEs and that a solution was implemented using two programs. Then the specification changes to the current statement. Is it not a disadvantage of the whole approach that such a relatively small change forces the radical change from two to three programs in the solution?

The change from two to three programs is mainly a repackaging of the same set of components. The executable operations are also little changed, although they are now divided between three programs. There is some clerical work redrawing the structure diagrams and making the new operation lists, but the difficulty of making the amendment is not significantly greater than the difficulty for a specification change that is confined to only one of the programs.

Chapter 3.2 An On-Line Case Study

Start by reading the six-page specification of the On-Line Case Study.* You may want to try the problem yourself, before reading on.

As always we start with a System Network Diagram to clarify and name the input and output data streams. In this problem, as for most on-line problems, the input and output streams from the terminal are the most important in that they contribute most to the program structure.

In the Purchase Order Problem discussed in Chapter 2.3, the units of terminal I/O are lines. In this problem, the units of I/O on the terminal data streams are whole screens. On input, the unit of I/O is a concatenation of the screen and the identity of the function key that is pressed to transmit it. The leaves of the structure diagram that describe the terminal input will therefore each be a screen and a function key.

(The implementation may actually be more complicated, but this doesn't affect the definition of the data structures. For some function keys no screen is transmitted, and the object on the data stream is the identity of the function key alone. In general, the whole screen may not be sent; only changes from the previous screen may be transmitted, allowing an up-to-date screen image to be maintained at the other end of the line.)

There may be some structure below the level of the screen to analyse errors within a screen, in the same way that in a batch program there may be some structure below the level of a record.

As explained above, this problem is taken from an IBM CICS environment, where it has to be implemented in pseudo-conversational form. That means (essentially) that the program must be in the form of a subroutine that is called to process single input screens. Our approach is the normal JSP approach to the design of variable-state subroutines. We develop a main program and then invert it to give the desired subroutine. We also have to separate the state vector and store it explicitly in some storage area because local variables of the subroutine are not retained between invocations. In CICS terms, we develop a fully-conversational program and then invert it so that it is pseudo-conversational.

The problem also contains error processing. In the usual way, we start with the input structure of good data only, and later elaborate it to include errors.

*This reprint appears on pages 125-130.

You might start with a structure like Figure 3.2a. The selection between AMEND and LOOK ONLY is at the SECTION level. The decision is made at the beginning of the section and applies to the whole of the SECTION part of the input stream. In many traditional solutions, this selection would be made lower in the structure, on the basis of a variable set at the beginning of a section, and tested repeatedly within. This two-valued variable is a switch. By making the selection at the correct level, we remove the need for a switch. During the execution of the program, the information that would have been in the switch is in the text pointer of the program, that is, in the position reached in one branch or the other of the program text.

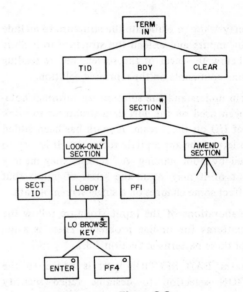

Figure 3.2a

Notice that the section and security code input is in sequence below the SECTION selection. This input record is like a batch header that takes two values, thus defining two types of batch. The batch header is part of the batch. Having this screen in sequence above the level of the SECTION selection is a sign of thinking too dynamically about the data stucture. You are thinking, "First the program reads this screen, and then decides which type of SECTION". The better, static view approach is something like "The main part of the stream consists of SECTIONs of two types distinguishable by the contents of their header".

Portions of this Chapter are excerpted from previously unpublished Michael Jackson Systems Limited (MJSL) internal documents with permission from MJSL.

In the AMEND SECTION of the data structure, you have to describe the following:

The operator is not obliged to make changes to any screen. He may browse just as if he were in a LOOK ONLY SECTION.

When changes are made, there is a basic sequence. First the changes are input on the screen (and checked for errors), and then the changes are confirmed. Two inputs are necessary to make changes on one screen.

A series of changes may be made on a single screen of data before the whole series is confirmed. There is still the basic sequence of CHANGEDATA and CONFIRM, but CHANGEDATA is an iteration of inputs. (Each one of these inputs may change some number of lines on the screen.)

Taking these points into account, we reach the structure shown in Figure 3.2b. This is still only the structure of good data. You should reread the example conversation in the specification if you are puzzled in any way by this structure.

You may want to elaborate the structure to include error screen inputs and extend the structure to include structure below the level of the screen, before reading the following comments on the reprinted solution.

To help understand the solution, an informal notation has been used on the TIN data structures to mark the units of I/O on the stream. A mark has been added to the top left of the appropriate rectangles. It is easy to be confused by poor naming. A "screen" may mean a single input or it may mean the series of inputs that together effect some changes on a single screen of data.

The elaborations of the input structure follow the standard patterns for on-line problems. There is a description of these patterns in Section 2.3.2.

An extra BAD SECTION part is added to the SECTION selection to describe failed security codes. In the given solution this component does not describe wrong function keys, implying that the security input will be accepted with any function key. It is easy to add a fourth part to the selection if this extra check is needed.

A WRONG (function) KEY and two RANGE ERROR components are added to the LO BROWSE KEY selection and to the AM BROWSE KEY selection.

An extra iteration component is added below CHANGE SET ATTEMPT. The new iterated component, BAD CHANGE, is a screen on which changes have been made, but not all are correct. There are now three levels of iteration in AMEND

SECTION: over the screenfuls of data retrieved from the CTLFILE; within these, over the series of good CHANGESET inputs that may precede the CONFIRM input; and within these, over the series of errors that an operator may make before getting a single CHANGESET right.

The structure is elaborated below the level of the screen in two places. When the changes are CONFIRMed, they must be made on the CTLFILE and recorded on the LOGFILE. The input component CONFIRM CHANGE SET must be extended to show the structure of lines within the screen. Detailed diagnostics are output to the operator in the form of highlighted fields, so the BAD CHANGE input component must be extended to show an appropriate structure of good and error fields.

The structure of BAD CHANGESET DATA is an example of the use of the posit switch (see Chapter 2.4) in typical circumstances. A distinction has to be made at a high level between a screen that has no errors and a screen which has at least one error. However, error checking must not stop when the first error is found. All the errors on the screen must be highlighted.

Suppose now that the data part of one line of the screen is instead defined as one field, so that the whole data part is highlighted as a single unit. In this case, there is no need to continue diagnosis of one line of the screen, once one error is found. The structure of the INS/AMD component is shown in Figure 3.2c.

In the given version of the problem, a CLEAR function key is accepted only after the initial screen is displayed, either at the end of a SECTION or at the beginning of the program. Similarly, a PF1 is accepted only after a good set of changes has been made. Suppose that a PF1 can be input at any time to abandon a SECTION and which a CLEAR can be entered at any time to abandon the whole program. This does not mean that CLEAR components have to be added all over the structure. Although, dynamically, a CLEAR can be input at any time during the execution of the program, statically, there is still only one CLEAR, and it is still the last input on the TIN data stream. The correct data structure for TIN for this new problem is shown in outline in Figure 3.2d. An INCOMPLETE SECTION is a section that does not finish normally with a PF1, but which is stopped in the middle by the input of a CLEAR.

There is a recognition difficulty over the condition on the TINBDY iteration. How can a COMPLETE SECTION be distinguished from an INCOMPLETE SECTION? This example needs backtracking in iteration. We posit that the SECTION will be COMPLETE, and quit when this hypothesis is disproved, by the input of a

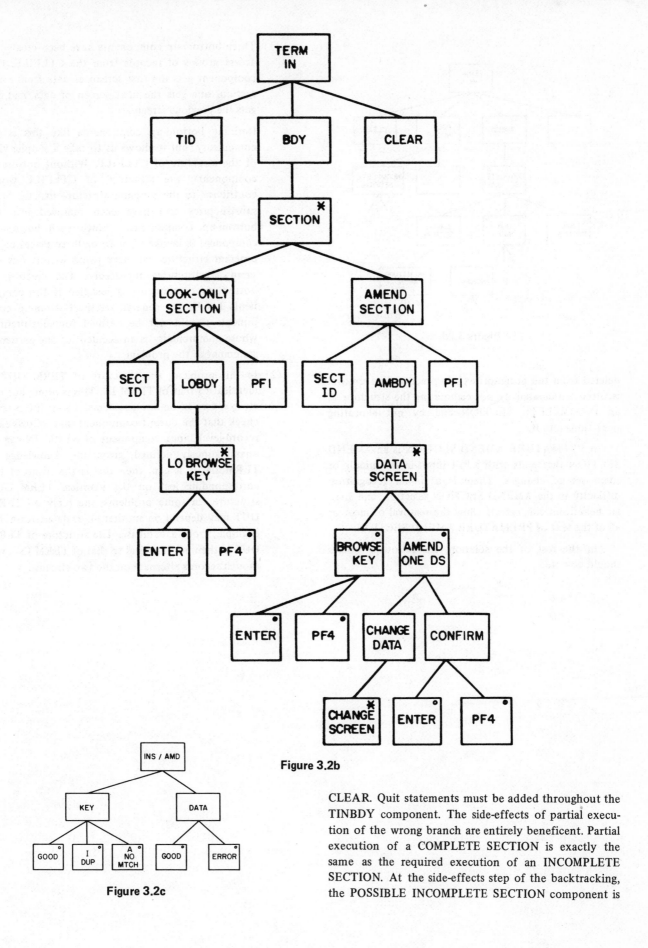

Figure 3.2b

Figure 3.2c

CLEAR. Quit statements must be added throughout the TINBDY component. The side-effects of partial execution of the wrong branch are entirely beneficent. Partial execution of a COMPLETE SECTION is exactly the same as the required execution of an INCOMPLETE SECTION. At the side-effects step of the backtracking, the POSSIBLE INCOMPLETE SECTION component is

113

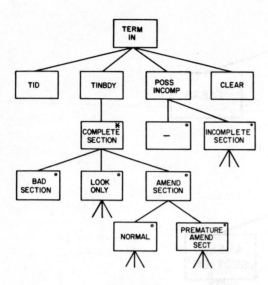

Figure 3.2d

deleted from the program text. In practice, this removal is often anticipated by not elaborating the structure of an INCOMPLETE SECTION and by not allocating operations into it.

A PREMATURE AMEND SECTION is an AMEND SECTION that ends with a PF1 input in the middle of some set of changes. There is a similar recognition difficulty in the AMEND SECTION selection, and similar beneficent side-effects allow the removal of most or all of the text of PREMATURE AMEND SECTION.

In the rest of the solution, the following points should be noted:

(1) Three bottom-up components have been created to access groups of records from the CTLFILE. One component gets the first screen of data from a new section, one gets the next screen of data, and one gets the previous screen.

Defining bottom-up components like this is not compulsory, but it allows us to take a simpler view of the structure of CTLFILE. Without bottom-up components, the structure of CTLFILE would contribute to the program structure exactly those substructures that have been removed into the bottom-up components. Since each bottom-up component is invoked in two or three places in the program structure, we have saved writing out the same substructures repeatedly. The creation of bottom-up components is justified if the components have some general utility. Bottom-up components should not be defined for substructures whose commonality is an accident of one particular statement of the problem.

(2) In this problem, the structure of TERM OUT is identical to that of TERM IN. This is often, but not always, true in on-line problems. To see if it is true, check that the output component that follows each record-level input component of TERM IN can be unambiguously defined, given only knowledge of TERM IN. If it can, then this is the name of the corresponding leaf on the identical TERM OUT structure. In some problems, the reply on TERM OUT may depend on another input data stream, for example, from a database. The structure of TERM OUT is then not identical to that of TERM IN, even though records alternate on the two streams.

Chapter 3.3   Infix to Postfix

The problem* is to take an arithmetic expression in which the operators are between the operands (Infix) and convert it to one in which the operators are after the operands (Postix). The detailed statement of the problem in the reprint contains several examples of Infix expressions and their Postfix equivalents. You should read this problem statement, perhaps try the problem yourself, and then read the solution in the reprint. The following miscellaneous comments elaborate on some aspects of the solution.

The BNF definition of A given in the problem statement is, of course, a data structure. The use of a textual rather than a diagrammatic notation is not important. The trouble is that it is completely the wrong data structure because although it describes the syntax of an A, it doesn't describe the groupings that are important for this problem.

We use recursion or iteration in a data structure according to the relationships between data components that are appropriate for the problem. Generalising grossly, most problems do not have important recursive

---

*This reprint appears on pages 131-132.

relationships. This one does, but only in the use of parentheses. Recursion is not appropriate in the description of an expression without parentheses.

The dots in the full program structure indicate that the entire substructure ZPRL is to be repeated, as is the entire substructure SUBEXP.

The final IF statement in the sample of recursion coding is a little misleading. If $S > 1$, S is to be decremented, the value of the SV is to be taken from the STACK, and the branching GOTO is to be executed. Otherwise the program ends.

The issue of GOTOs in the code is exactly the same as the issue of GOTOs in inversion coding. This is one of the reasons the example is included in the book. (See Section 2.3.3 and Chapter 2.4 for a discussion of inversion.)

In moving from POP2 to POP3 in Chapter 2.3, nothing in the problem changed. Only the implementation environment changed. The move was equivalent to moving in this problem from a language that supports recursion to one which doesn't.

A Microfiche Problem

A company which owns a number of large warehouses has to create each month a set of microfiches containing information about the stock movements of the various items which they store. These items are stored (for a fee of course) on behalf of the company's customers. The total stock of one item in any given warehouse may belong to several different customers. Similarly, though it is not relevant here, one customer may own some of several different items in one or more different warehouses.

Each record on the input file has eight fields:

W – the warehouse identifier

I – the item identifier

C – the customer identifier

D – the date of the stock movement

Q – the quantity of the item moved

T – the type of movement (= R for receipt, = I for issue)

E – a code identifying the company employee who supervised the movement

A – a field for an additional description. This field is often left blank.

The file is sorted by the warehouse identifier, W; for one value of W, the records are sorted by the item number I; for one value of W and I they are sorted by the customer identifier C; for one value of W, I and C they are sorted by the date D.

There are two output files OF1, which will be input to the program which actually creates the fiches, and OF2 which will be input to a program which creates a special master fiche.

There are six different types of record in the output file OF1:

T1 – a fiche header record

T2 – a frame header record

T3 – an index frame record

T4 – a frame detail record

T5 – indicates the end of the current frame

T6 – indicates the end of the current fiche

Before describing the structure of the output files it will be helpful to first look at the microfiches which are eventually produced. Each fiche is composed of a header line, 269 ordinary frames and one index frame. Each ordinary frame has a frame header line and room for up to 62 detail lines. The program which produces the fiche does so column by column, starting from the left.

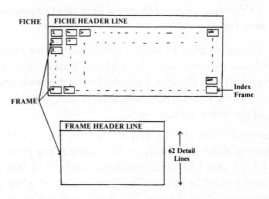

An input record whose field A is blank gives rise to one ordinary frame record in OF1 (and eventually to one detail line on a frame). This T4 output record contains information from the fields C, E, D, Q and T. An input record whose field A is not blank gives rise to two T4 records, the first contains information from the fields C, E, D, Q and T as above on the second contains the field A. In addition two T4 records are written to OF1 at the end of each group of input records which have the same customer identifier. The first of these contains the word TOTAL followed by the total net movement of the relevant item for the customer. The second T4 record only contains blanks. Finally three T4 records are written to OF1 at the end of each group of input records which have the same item identifier. The first two such records contain only blanks (except of course for the type information) and the third contains the item identifier, the words TOTAL NET MOVEMENT and the total net movement of in the particular warehouse.

A group of T4 records in F1 which are to make up the detail lines of a frame must be preceded by a T2 record and are followed by a T5 record. The T2 record (which will be printed as the frame header) will contain I, the item identifier and the number of the frame within the fiche (i.e. a number between 1 and 269). The group of T4 records in OF1 between a T2 and a T5 record will number 62 or as many as possible subject to the following constraints.

- if an input record has information in the A field and therefore directly gives rise to 2 output T4 records, then this pair of records must not be split between frames.

- the pair of customer summary records must not be split and they must appear on the same frame as the last ordinary detail record of that customer group. Similarly the triple of item summary records must not be split and must appear on the same frame as the last ordinary detail record for that item (and the summary pair for the last customer within that item).

- T4 records referring to a new item must appear on a new frame.

A T3 record must be output immediately after each T2 record and must contain the same two data items as that T2 record (1 and the frame number). The program which reads OF1 will hold this record back and output it as part of the index frame.

There remains the T1 and T6 records to consider. A T6 record must be output to OF1 after every group of T2, T3, T4 and T5 records which will make up a fiche. A new fiche must be taken after 269 frames or when the warehouse number changes. The header which will appear on the microfiche contains the following information—the company's name, an item number, the word WARE-HOUSE, the warehouse identifier relevant to this fiche,

the symbol # and the number of the fiche relative to the first fiche for this warehouse. The item number referred to is the second item number to appear in the fiche if the second item number appears in the first 30 frames, otherwise the first item number to appear.

Either one or two T1 records will be output to OF1 for every fiche. One T1 record is output at the beginning of the group of records which will make up one fiche and this will contain the first item number to appear in the fiche together with all the other header information. If necessary a second T1 record must be written with the new item number and this must be output at the latest before the 31st frame group of records. The reason for this bizarre criterion is that the fiche is printed column by column, the company's name appears at the beginning of the header line (hence the first T1 record) and the item number appears above the 31st frame (hence the criterion on the item number change). In the program which reads OF1 the second T1 record will overwrite the part of store in which the first T1 was held.

Finally one record per fiche is to be written to the file OF2. This record is to contain much the same information as will be on the fiche header—the item number as above, the word WAREHOUSE, the warehouse identifier, the symbol # and the number of the fiche relative to the first fiche for this warehouse.

The Microfiche Problem Solution

See Figure 1

- The program we are asked to design is only part of a system.

- We have to design PMF. The output files of this program are input to programs P1F and P2F which are assumed already to exist.

- The INPUT file is easy to understand. All the records are the same type. Each has eight fields. The file is sorted on the first four of these fields.

- The OUTPUT files are more difficult to understand. The contents of the output files only make sense when we know something about the FICHES which are eventually to be produced.

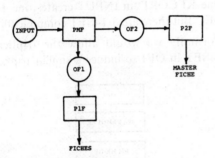

Figure 1

The Output File OF1

First we examine T4 records

- A T4 record will give rise to exactly one detail line in one frame of the finished fiche.

- Either one or two T4 records are produced from each input record, depending on whether the field A is blank.

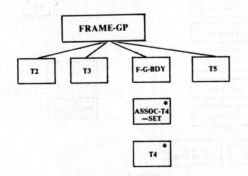

Figure 2

- Additionally two T4 records are produced at the end of each customer group of input records and three T4 records are produced at the end of each item group of input records.

- There are no other T4 records. The program PMF is not required to reorder these records in any way.

There is one T2, one T3 and one T5 record for every FRAME.

- In OF1 the T4 records are arranged into groups. Each group will eventually produce one frame.

- No FRAME-GP in OF1 can contain records referring to different ITEMS.

- A FRAME-GP can contain up to 62 T4 records.

- A FRAME-GP will only contain less than 62 T4 records if the ITEM number changes or if there are not enough spaces left on the frame for a set of associated T4 records which must not be split between frames.

- If the last record referring to a particular item number has a non blank A field there will be a total of 7 records which must not be split between FRAME-GPs. These 7 records comprise one ordinary T4 record, one for the A field, two for the customer summary (the end of an item is also the end of a customer) and three for the item summary.

- The maximum number in such an associated group of records is 7.

- The T5 is a simple trailer.

- The T2 record is a header containing two simple items of information.

- The T3 record is like the T2 record but will be used by another program for a different purpose—to create the INDEX FRAME. There is an ORDERING clash to be resolved when the INDEX FRAME is created. The T3 records are mixed up among all the other trecords in OF1. This is a matter for the other programs in the system, not for PMF.

- Records in OF1 are also arranged in groups which correspond to the FICHES which will eventually be produced.

- Each FICHE-GP has a T1 record as a header and a T6 record as a trailer. Sometimes there is an extra T1 record in the middle of the group.

- We start a new FICHE-GP after 269 FRAMES or when we start a new WAREHOUSE number.

- The FICHE is produced column by column. There is an ORDERING CLASH here but it is not for PMF to resolve it. It is the concern of the other programs in the system.

- Information on the FICHE header is visible to the naked eye. The item number is to help an operator find the correct fiche quickly.

- The criterion for choosing the item number is strange for 2 reasons

  - I can't see why it would be more difficult for the operator if simply the first item number was given.

  - It looks as though the analyst thought that the criterion given was identical to 'the first new item number in each fiche'. It isn't in the case where a new item number begins on the first frame.

- We shall use the rule as stated but consider alternatives as well.

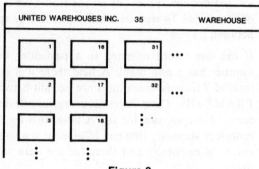

Figure 3

A First Look at the Data Structures (see Figure 4)

- Both components of the structure OF2 correspond to components in the structure OF1.

- OF2 is therefore easily composed either directly with OF1 or with any composite structure which contains OF1. We can concentrate on INPUT and OF1.

- There are correspondences at the top level between INPUT and OF1 and between the respective WAREHOUSE groups.

- There is no correspondence between ITEM-GP and FICHE-GP.

  - Records referring to one item may be spread over more than one fiche.

- One fiche may contain information from several item groups.

- There is no special relationship between the beginning of an item and the beginning of a group.

- There is a boundary clash between ITEM-GP and FICHE-GP.

- There is a similar boundary clash between CUST-GP and FRAME.

- The situation is complicated by the possible extra T1 record which makes FICHE-GP a selection of two parts and which creates 3 components in OF1 of which describes a FRAME.

- This triplication does not affect the boundary clash. The boundaries of CUST-GP clash with the boundaries of FRAME irrespective of the fact that there are 3 types of FRAME.

- However the triplication stops us finding a perfect 1-1 correspondence between a record in INPUT and any component in OF1.

  - One RECORD in INPUT creates one T4SET in OF1. But there are 3 T4SET components in OF1.

  - Normally we would allow the triplication of T4SET in OF1 to induce a similar triplication of

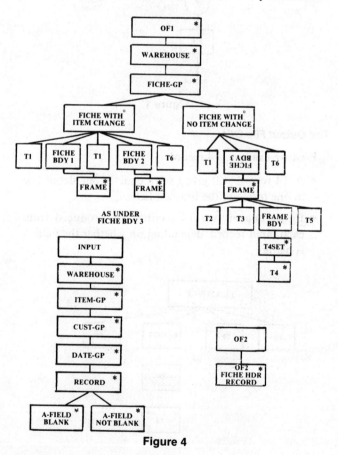

Figure 4

120

RECORD in INPUT. But we cannot mirror, in INPUT, a splitting into 3 types of FRAME unless the level FRAME already exists in INPUT and the level FRAME cannot exist in any structure describing INPUT because it clashes with CUST-GP.

- Conclusions from all this are—
  - The first attempt at the data structures was rather inadequate.
  - Progress is to be made by first resolving the boundary clashes.

Resolving the Structure Clashes

- The skeleton data structures are shown in Figure 5.
- The level DATE has been retained, although there do not seem to be any operations which must be allocated to it.
- There are operations which must be allocated to CUST-GP and ITEM-GP. (e.g. the extra T4 records). These levels are clearly necessary in the structure.
- So are all the levels shown in the structure of OF1.

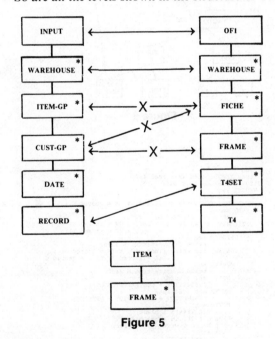

Figure 5

- We have a DOUBLE BOUNDARY CLASH.
- Can it be resolved in one step like an ordinary single boundary clash?
  - The answer is no, it cannot.

- The reason is that there is already a relationship between two of the components. There is no relationship between CUST-GP and FICHE.

  This is another boundary clash.

- There is a relationship between ITEM-GP and FRAME. ITEM-GP is an iteration of FRAME.
- Knowledge of the ITEM-GP boundaries is needed to create the FRAME boundaries. Some program in the system must know about FRAMEs and about ITEM-GPs.
- A single step solution would have two programs: the first would know about ITEM-GP and CUST-GPs only and the second would know about FRAMEs and FICHEs only.

- We need at least three programs in the PMF system. In fact we need exactly three.
  - One program to know about ITEM-GPs and FRAMEs.
  - One program to know about CUST-GPs—different from the first because of the CUST-GP/FRAME clash.
  - One program to know about FICHEs—different from the first two because of the ITEM-GP/FICHE and the CUST-GP/FICHE clashes.
  - These three programs completely solve the boundary clashes.

The System Network Diagram and the Intermediate Files

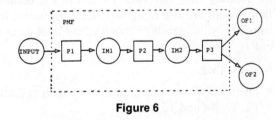

Figure 6

- P1 knows about ITEMS and CUSTOMERS but not about FRAMES or FICHES.
- P2 knows about ITEMS and FRAMES but not about CUSTOMERS or FICHES.
- P3 knows about FRAMES and FICHES but not about ITEMS or CUSTOMERS.
- Roughly, P1 will create the T4 records, P2 will create the frame boundaries by adding in the T2, T3 and T5 records, and P3 will create the fiche boundaries

by adding in the T1 and T6 records. P3 will also create OF2.

- The intermediate files IM1 and IM2 must be specified.

- First we consider IM1.

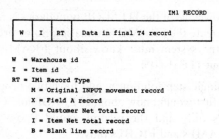

IM1 RECORD

| W | I | RT | Data in final T4 record |

```
W  = Warehouse id
I  = Item id
RT = IM1 Record Type
     M = Original INPUT movement record
     X = Field A record
     C = Customer Net Total record
     I = Item Net Total record
     B = Blank line record
```

Figure 7

- Figure 7 shows the IM1 record format.

- There is one record in IM1 for each eventual T4 record.

- The warehouse and item identifiers are retained in the records of IM1 because warehouse and item groups must be recognized in P2.

- The five record types will allow P2 to ensure that associated lines (eg MCB) are not split between frames.

- A Customer Net Total record (type C) must be created once per customer. The associated operations can only be correctly allocated to the Customer component in P1. There are less compelling reasons for creating Item Net Total records in P1, because Item groups are also recognized in P2. However, for consistency, we decide to create all net total records in P1.

- Now for IM2.

  - There will be one record in IM2 for each eventual T2, T3, T4 and T5 record.

  - The warehouse identifier is retained because warehouse groups must be recognized in P3.

  - The format of a IM2 record is shown in Figure 8.

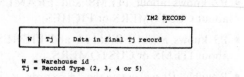

IM2 RECORD

| W | Tj | Data in final Tj record |

```
W  = Warehouse id
Tj = Record Type (2, 3, 4 or 5)
```

Figure 8

- Other specifications of IM1 and IM2 would alter the detail in P1, P2, and P3, but would not change the way these three programs solve the structure clashes.

- The largest group of consecutive lines that must not be split between frames is, in terms of the IM1 record types, MXCBBBI. P2 will therefore read 7 records ahead.

- Note how the structure clashes were resolved before the recognition difficulties were even considered.

The Program P1:

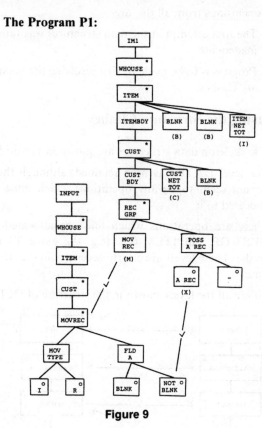

Figure 9

```
P1 seq
    open INPUT; open IM1; read INPUT;
    P1BDY itr while (not eof)
      WHOUSE seq
            store W;
        WHOUSEBDY itr while ((not eof) & (W = stored W))
        ITEM seq
            store I; ITEMNETTOT = zero;
          ITEMBDY itr while ((not eof) & (W = stored W)
                                        & (I = stored I))
          CUSTOMER seq
                store C; CUSTNETTOT = zero;
            CUSTBDY itr while ((not eof) & (W = stored W) &
                                (I = stored I) & (C = stored C))
              MOVREC seq
                    build & write type M rec;
                MVTYP sel (issue)
                    CUSTNETTOT = CUSTNETTOT - QTY;
                MVTYP alt (receipt)
                    CUSTNETTOT = CUSTNETTOT + QTY;
                MVTYP end
                FLDA sel (field A blank)
                FLDA alt (field A not blank)
                    build & write type X rec;
                FLDA end
                    read INPUT;
              MOVREC end
            CUSTBDY end
                build & write type C rec;
                ITEMNETTOT = ITEMNETTOT + CUSTNETTOT;
                build & write type B rec;
          CUSTOMER end
          ITEMBDY end
                build & write type B rec;
                build & write type B rec;
                build & write type I rec;
        ITEM end
        WHOUSEBDY end
      WHOUSE end
    P1BDY end
        close INPUT; close IM1;
P1 end
```

Figure 10

122

The Program P2:

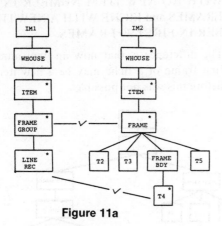

Figure 11a

In P2, each LINE REC in IM1 is considered to be a possible candidate for inclusion in the current frame. A type M record is included in the current frame only if the cluster of which it is the first record will completely fit in the current frame. The five FRAMEBDY quit statements in P2 refer to the following clusters respectively:

```
MCB
MCBBBI
MX
MXCB
MXCBBBI
```

Anything else requires only a single line.

The program P3:

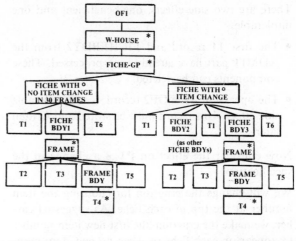

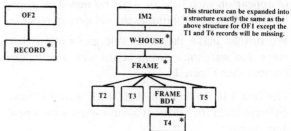

This structure can be expanded into a structure exactly the same as the above structure for OF1 except the T1 and T6 records will be missing.

Figure 12

The composite program structure is identical to the structure of OF1

```
P2 seq
      open IM1; open IM2; read IM1;
      read IM1; read IM1; read IM1; read IM1; read IM1; read IM1;
    P2BDY itr while (not eof)
      WHOUSE seq
            store W;
        WHOUSEBDY itr while ((not eof) & (W = stored W))
          ITEM seq
              store I;
            ITEMBDY itr while ((not eof) & (W = stored W)
                                         & (I = stored I))
              FRAME seq
                    build & write T2 rec;
                    build & write T3 rec;
                    REM = 62;
                FRAMEBDY itr while ((not eof) & (W = stored W) &
                                    (I = stored I) & (REM > zero))
                  FRAMEBDY quit ((type (0) = M) & (not eof (1)) &
                                  (type (1) = C) & (REM < 3))
                  FRAMEBDY quit ((type (0) = M) & (not eof (1)) &
                                  (type (1) = C) & (not eof (5)) &
                                  (type (5) = I) & (REM < 6))
                  FRAMEBDY quit ((type (0) = M) & (not eof (1)) &
                                  (type (1) = X) & (REM < 2))
                  FRAMEBDY quit ((type (0) = M) & (not eof (1)) &
                                  (type (1) = X) & (not eof (2)) &
                                  (type (2) = C) & (REM < 4))
                  FRAMEBDY quit ((type (0) = M) & (not eof (1)) &
                                  (type (1) = X) & (not eof (2)) &
                                  (type (2) = C) & (not eof (6)) &
                                  (type (6) = I) & (REM < 7))
                      build and write T4 rec;
                      REM = REM - 1;
                      read IM1;
                FRAMEBDY end
                    build and write T5 rec;
              FRAME end
            ITEMBDY end
          ITEM end
        WHOUSEBDY end
      WHOUSE end
    P2BDY end
      close IM1;
      close IM2;
    P2 end
```

Figure 11b

```
P3 seq
      open IM2; open OF1; open OF2; read IM2;
    P3BDY iter  until eof
      WHOUSE seq
          store W; FCH:=0;
        WHOUSEBDY iter  while (W=stored W) & (not eof)
          FICHE seq
              FRM:=0; FCH:=FCH+1;
            FICHEBDY posit
                NOCHANGEFICHE seq
                    write T1; store item no; store OF2 record;
                  NCFBDY iter  while (not eof) & (W=stored W) & (FRM<269,
                    NCFRAME seq
          FICHEBDY      quit if item no ≠ stored item no & FRM < 30
                          FRM:=FRM+1;
                          write T2; read IM2; write T3; read IM2;
                        NCFBDY iter  while T4
                            write T4; read IM2;
                        NCFBDY end
                        write T5; read IM2;
                    NCFRAME end
                  NCFBDY end
                  write T6; write stored OF2 record;
                NOCHANGEFICHE end
            FICHEBDY admit
                CHANGEFICHE seq
                  do P-Q1; do P-FICHEBDY2;
                  write T1; write OF2 record;
                  CFICHEBDY iter  while (not eof) & (W=stored W) & (FRM<269)
                    CFRAME seq
                        FRM:=FRM+1;
                        write T2; read IM2; write T3; read IM2;
                      CFBDY iter  while T4
                          write T4; read IM2;
                      CFBDY end
                      write T5; read IM2;
                    CFRAME end
                  CFICHEBDY end
                  write T6;
                CHANGEFICHE end
            FICHEBDY end
          FICHE end
        WHOUSEBDY end
      WHOUSE end
    P3BDY end
      close IM2; close OF1; close OF2;
    P3 end
```

Figure 13

On the Program P3

- There are two side effects, one beneficial and one intolerable.

    - The first T1 record and FICHEBDY2 from the ADMIT part have already been processed. These components can be deleted.

    - The operation write OF2 record; is an intolerable side effect. This record must be stored and written later.

- Now consider the effect on P3 of a change in the specification.

- We will change the criterion for choosing the item number at the top of each fiche. As suggested earlier, we make the criterion 'the first new item number to appear on each fiche or when no new item number appears within 30 frames the old item number'

- We further make the reasonable assumption that every new warehouse group begins with a new item number. See Figure 14.

- The first FICHE in each WHOUSE group is now different from the others. It always starts with a new item number.

- The component FICHE is now a selection of FICHE WITH NO NEW ITEM NUMBER IN FIRST 30 FRAMES and FICHE WITH A NEW ITEM NUMBER IN FIRST 30 FRAMES.

- The difference is that now an item number in the first frame of a fiche may be a new item number; before this was not possible.

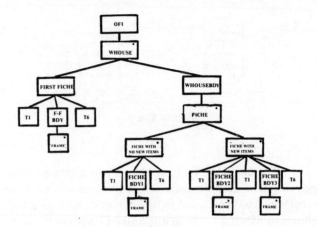

Figure 14

124

On-Line Case Study

A program is needed which will allow an operator (according to the value of his security code) either to examine a file, CTLFILE, or both to examine and update CTLFILE.

There are two display formats: one for entering the operator's security code and the id of the section of the CTLFILE which he wants; the other for displaying up to 15 records of the specified section and for amending and deleting existing CTLFILE records and inserting new ones. The format of these screen layouts is shown below.

Here is a typical conversation which illustrates the required operation of the program.

- Key in transaction ID. Press ENTER.
  - Empty initial screen appears.
- Key in security code and section id. Press ENTER.
  - Display screen with first 15 records of that CTLFILE section appears. (Suppose that the security code was good for examination only.)
- Press ENTER.
  - Display 2nd 15 records (i.e. records 16-30) of this CTLFILE section.
- Press ENTER.
  - Display next 15 records of CTLFILE (i.e. 31-45).
- Press function key PF4.
  - Display previous 15 records of CTLFILE (i.e. 16-30 again). In this context PF4 means move 1 page backwards.
- Press ENTER.
  - Display next 15 records of CTLFILE (i.e. 31-45).
- Press function key PF1.
  - Initial screen. In this context PF1 means that the operator has finished with this section of CTLFILE and wants the initial screen to enter a new security code and section id.
- Key in security code and section id. Press ENTER.
  - Display screen with 1st 15 records of the specified CTLFILE section. (Suppose that for this section the operator may both examine and update.)
- Press ENTER.
  - Display next 15 records of CTLFILE (i.e. 16-30). Even though updating is now allowed, the operator is not obliged to make changes. He may page backwards and forwards by pressing PF4 and ENTER as if he were in look-only mode.

- Press ENTER.
  - Display next 15 records (i.e. 31-45)
- Press ENTER.
  - Display next 15 records (i.e. 46-60)
- Key in amendments to 3 of the records, and delete another 2. Press ENTER.
  - Display same 15 records. When changes are first entered, they are checked for errors, but CTLFILE is not updated. Here we assume the changes were error free.
- Press ENTER.
  - Display next 15 records (i.e. 61-75). The program has now updated CTLFILE and paged forward. Had the operator pressed PF4 instead of ENTER, the program would have updated CTLFILE and paged backward (records 31-45).
- Press ENTER.
  - Display next 15 records (i.e. 76-90)
- Press ENTER
  - Display next, and final 8 records of the section.
- Key in amendments to 2 of the records, delete 1, and insert 3 records on the empty spaces in the screen. ENTER.
  - Display same screen (assume changes were all error free). Note that insertions can only be made at the end of a section because only here is there space to make the insertions.
- Key in 2 more amendments. Press ENTER.
  - Display same screen (assume changes were error free). The operator may make a whole succession of changes, each group of which is vetted for errors when ENTER is pressed, but which are only processed when PF4 or ENTER is pressed with no accompanying changes.
- Key in 3 deletions. Press ENTER.
  - Display same screen.
- Press PF4.
  - Display previous 15 records. All the changes (4 amendments, 4 deletions and 3 insertions) are now processed and CTLFILE updated.
- Press PF1.
  - Display Initial screen.
- Press CLEAR.
  - End of program message.

In the above conversation, the operator made no errors. Four types of errors are possible:-

– Security violation. The security code entered is not sufficient even to allow the operator to access that section in look-only mode. The initial screen should be redisplayed with a message 'SECURITY VIOLATION' at the bottom. A subroutine SECHECK can be called with section id and security code as parameters; the subroutine will return a flag value 0,1,2 meaning violation, look only and look and update respectively.

– The operator tries to ENTER on the last page of the section or PF4 on the first page. The same page is redisplayed with a message either 'FORWARD RANGE ERROR' or 'BACKWARD RANGE ERROR'.

– A function key other than ENTER, PF4, PF1 or CLEAR is pressed. Redisplay the same page with a message 'WRONG FUNCTION KEY'.

– Some of the updates the operator makes are wrong:—

  – The key for an inserted record may already be in CTLFILE.

  – The amend or delete function code may be used for a record not on the screen i.e. by mistake when the operator is trying to insert.

  – The data within an amended or inserted record must be in the right format, and have values in the allowed ranges.

  The display format allows the program to hilite the function code, the key or the record data of any of the 15 lines. Error checking must be for the whole screen, the offending fields should be hilited, a message 'UPDATING ERRORS' should appear at the bottom of the screen, and the page redisplayed.

Insertions can only be made after paging forward until the end of that section of CTLFILE. If a page is full, either because there are 15 x n records in the section originally, or because what space there was has been filled with inserts, then pressing ENTER will give a blank new page. There is only a forward range error if the page is partly or fully empty.

When paging backwards after changes have been made what records should appear on the screen? Records may have been deleted; inserted records of any key may have been added at the end. On any page there is a lowest and highest key, as originally accessed from CTLFILE—i.e. ignoring insertions. Paging back (PF4) should access the 15 keys immediately lower than the lowest key; paging forward the 15 keys higher than the highest.

The access commands available for CTL-FILE are:

Find first CTL-FILE (SECTION):	Locates the first record in a section.
Find CTL-FILE (KEY):	Locates a record with a specified key.
Find next CTL-FILE:	Locates the sequentially next record.
Find previous CTL-FILE:	Locates the sequentially previous record.

These operations do not result in the located record being read into buffer. This is done by issuing a command 'Retrieve CTL-FILE into RECORD-AREA' once the desired record has been located.

The following commands are used to update CTL-FILE:

Replace CTL-FILE (KEY) by RECORD-NAME.

Insert RECORD-NAME into CTL-FILE (KEY).

Delete CTL-FILE (KEY).

There is another output file to be written by this program, the LOGFILE. This is a sequential file which records all the changes—amendments, insertions, and deletions—made to CTL-FILE. Each record contains the function code (A, I, or D) and the old, new or both records as appropriate.

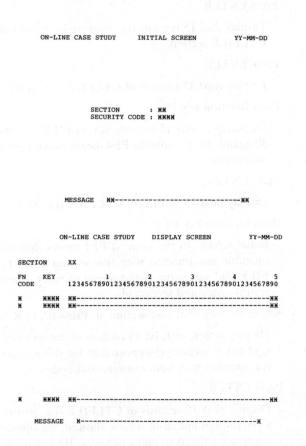

On-Line Case Study—Solution

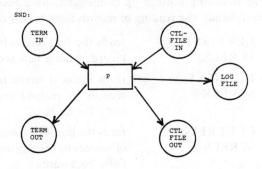

SND:

1. Data Structures

TERM-IN
The data structure for TERM-IN is shown below.

TERM-OUT
The data structure for TERM-OUT is identical to that for TERM-IN. This is established by annotating each record level component of the TERM-IN structure with the name of the corresponding TERM-OUT record. This has been done on the TERM-IN structure overleaf.

CTL-FILE IN
The data structure for CTL-FILE IN defines the accesses required to CTL-FILE to build the output screens shown on the TERM-OUT structure. By defining new bottom up components which, in one call, perform all the accesses required to build a complete output data screen, the structure for CTL-FILE IN becomes a simple subset of TERM-OUT. The CTL-FILE OUT structure can be derived from TERM-OUT by deleting all record level components from TERM-OUT except those called:

 - FIRST DATA SCREEN

 - NEXT DATA SCREEN

 - PREVIOUS DATA SCREEN

We have not, therefore, drawn a separate structure.

CTL-FILE OUT
The data structure for CTL-FILE OUT defines the accesses required to update the CTL-FILE. There accesses will be made directly based on the key obtained from the screen. This structure will not, therefore, contribute to the program design and may be omitted.

LOGFILE
A record is written to the LOGFILE for every update made to the CTL-FILE. The LOGFILE structure will be:

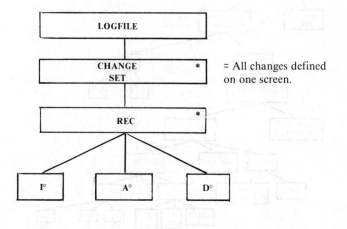

= All changes defined on one screen.

Terminal Input and Output Data Structures

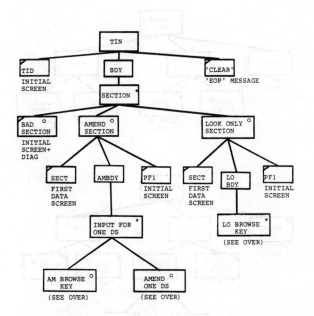

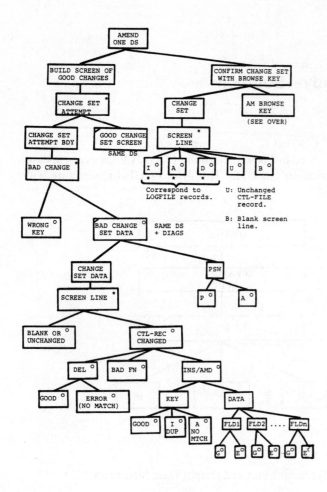

2. Program Structure

The program structure is identical to the composite TERM-IN/ TERM-OUT structure described.

3. Operations

The following bottom up components have been defined to handle the reading of records from CTL-FILE:

GET-FIRST-SCREEN:	reads the first screen full of records from a new section.
GET-NEXT-SCREEN:	reads the next screen full of records by reading sequentially forwards.
GET-PREV-SCREEN:	reads the previous screen full of records by reading sequentially backwards.

The parameters used by these components are:

SECTION:	the current CTL-FILE section.
DS-AREA:	the working storage to hold the current set of up to 15 CTL-FILE records for display or amendment.
HIKEY LOWKEY	define the range of keys last accessed from CTL-FILE
OORFLAG:	a flag used by GET-NEXT-SCREEN and GET-PREV-SCREEN to indicate that no more records are held for the current section.

In addition, the component GET-BLANK-SCREEN has been defined. This component returns a blank screen and is for use in the event that the operator pages beyond the end of the records available when amending a section and his current screen is already full.

As an example, structure text for GET-PREV-SCREEN is given below. The other components have similar structure to this. Note that this component fills the working storage from the bottom upwards and, when no more CTL-FILE records are available, space fills the unused storage.

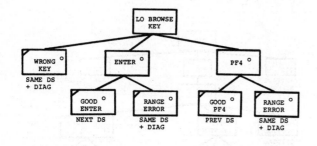

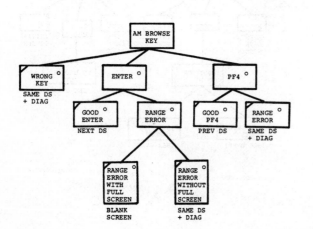

```
GPS seq
    find CTL-FILE(LOWKEY);
    find previous CTL-FILE;
    BDY sel ((not found) or (change of section))
        OORFLAG:='Y';
    BDY else
        OORFLAG:='N';
        retrieve CTL-FILE into DS-REC(15);
        HIKEY:= DS-REC-KEY(15);
        find previous CTL-FILE;
        I:= 14;
        RECFILL itr while (I > 0 and found and same section)
```

```
        retrieve CTL-FILE into DS-REC(I);
        find previous CTL-FILE;
        I:= I-1;
     RECFILL end
     LOWKEY:= DS-REC-KEY(I+1);
     SPACEFILL itr while (I > 0)
        DS-REC(I):= spaces;
        I:= I-1;
     SPACEFILL end
  BDY end
  return;
GPS end
```

Operations List

1. open TERM-OUT
2. close TERM-OUT
3. write INITIAL-SCREEN to TERM-OUT
4. move 'SECURITY VIOLATION' to IS-MESSAGE
5. call GET-FIRST-SCREEN
6. call GET-NEXT-SCREEN
7. call GET-PREV-SCREEN
8. call GET-BLANK-SCREEN
9. write DATA-SCREEN to TERM-OUT
10. move 'USE ENTER OR PF4' to DS-MESSAGE
11. move 'FORWARD RANGE ERROR' to DS-MESSAGE
12. move 'BACKWARD RANGE ERROR' to DS-MESSAGE
13. move 'UPDATE ERRORS' to DS-MESSAGE
14. open LOGFILE
15. close LOGFILE
16. write LOGREC to LOGFILE
17. I:= 1
18. I:= I+1
19. move DS-FUNCODE(I) to LOGREC-FUNCODE
20. move DS-REC(I) to LOGREC-NEWREC
21. retrieve CTL-FILE(DS-REC-KEY(I)) into LOGREC-OLDREC
22. LOGREC:= spaces
23. replace CTL-FILE(DS-REC-KEY(I)) by DS-REC(I)
24. delete CTL-FILE(DS-REC-KEY(I))
25. insert DS-REC(I) into CTL-FILE(DS-REC-KEY(I))
26. hilite DS-FUNCODE(I)
27. hilite DS-REC-KEY(I)
28. hilite DS-REC-FLD1(I)
29. hilite DS-REC-FLD2(I)
30. hilite DS-REC-FLDn(I)
31. read TERM-IN into TID-REC
32. read TERM-IN into IS-REC
33. read TERM-IN into DS-REC
34. open TERM-IN
35. close TERM-IN
36. write 'END OF PROGRAM' to TERM-OUT

Program Structure with Operations Allocated

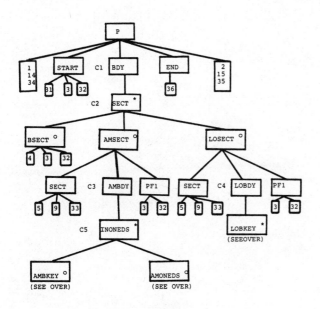

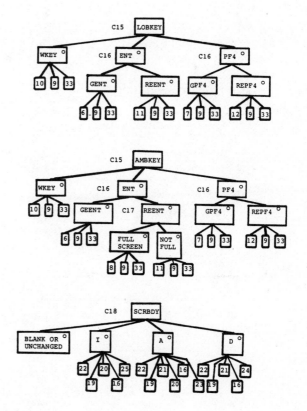

129

Evaluation of Conditions

C1. Itr while (not CLEAR).

C2. Evaluated directly by calling SECHECK.

C3. Itr while (not PF1).

C4. Itr while (not PF1).

C5. Evaluated directly by testing for modified data on the terminal read.

C6. Itr while not ((ENTER or PF4) and (no modified data since last read)).

C7. Evaluated by backtracking, using the posit switch. The posit switch is set to 'P' at the beginning of WDATA and is changed to 'A' if any error is found on the screen (i.e. immediately after execution of each of operations 26 thru 30). The posit switch is tested in the component PSW and, if it is still set to 'P', a quit (i.e an unconditional branch) is executed to the end of CSATT-BDY. There are no side effects associated with the backtracking.

C8. Evaluated directly by testing the terminal read for ENTER or PF4.

C9. Itr while (I $\leq$ 15).

C10. Evaluated directly based on DS-FUNCODE (I).

C11. Evaluated directly based on DS-FUNCODE (I).

C12. Evaluated directly by accessing CTL-FILE using the key of the record to be updated to ensure that the key exists for a record to be deleted or amended, or that the key does not exist for a record to be inserted.

C13. Evaluated according to the validation rules specified for each field.

C14. Itr while (I $\leq$ 15).

C15. Evaluated directly by testing the terminal read for ENTER or PF4.

C16. Evaluated directly by calling the appropriate 'GET-SCREEN' component and testing the OOR-FLAG.

C17. Evaluated directly by examination of the current screen.

C18. Evaluated directly based on DS-FUNCODE (I).

130

Infix to Postfix

The problem is to take an arithmetic expression in which the operators are between the operands and convert it to an expression in which the operators come after the operands.

Examples

Infix	Postfix
7	7
7+6	76+
((7+6))	76+
(3+4)*(7+2)	34+72+*
(3+(4+(5+(6+7))))	34567++++
3+4*7+2	347*+2+
(3–6+8)*2*(5+7+9)	36–8+2*57+9+*

As a definition of an infix expression, A, you are given:

$<A>$ :: = $<z>$ | $<TERM>$ $<op>$ $<A>$ | $<TERM>$
$<TERM>$ :: = $<z>$ | $<"(">$ $<A>$ $<")">$
$<op>$ :: = $<"+">$ | $<"–">$ | $<"*">$ | $<"/">$
$<z>$ :: = integer

You are expected to follow the normal rules of precedence of operators.

Infix to Postfix Solution

In the following discussion the word "bracket" is used synonymously with "parenthesis."

We assume that one input stream consists of the characters of one infix expression. The program has to produce an output stream consisting of the characters of the corresponding postfix expression. We must draw data structures of these input and output streams.

The definition of an infix expression, shown previously, is a data structure, but not the correct data structure for this problem. It is true, but not true enough.

The problem is inherently recursive, in that any integer can be replaced by a bracketed expression to make another legal expression.

The following is one way of working towards the final correct data structures. First draw a structure of expressions that have no brackets. The parts of the expression connected by "*" or "/" must appear separately in the structure because precedence is given to these over "+" or "–".

Some thought needs to be given also to "/", which is not an associative operator. What precedence rules are deemed to be in force? Or are some expressions considered illegal? Ignoring "+" and "–" for a moment, the structure

in the figure below seems appropriate for the definition of subexpression with only "*" and "/". It describes only those expressions in which the non-associativity of "/" does not leave room for ambiguity.

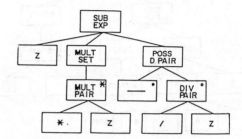

If left to right evaluation is assumed, except for the precedence of "*" and "/" over "+" and "–" than expressions like

$$8/4/2$$

and

$$8/4*2$$

are permissible. The appropriate structure is show below:

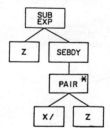

We shall assume this latter case.

The structure of an expression with no brackets is shown in the following diagram:

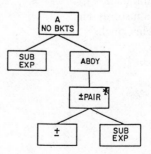

where SUBEXP is defined above.

The intermediate components of this structure, for example SUBEXP, are the components past which the operator is moved. They are the components that have meaning for this problem.

The full structure of the input stream was shown in the preceding diagram with each z replaced by a selection of a z or a bracketed A. The full structure is shown in the following diagram:

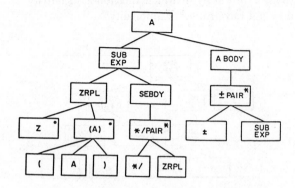

where ZPRL and SUBEXP are only written out in detail once.

The structure of the output is identical except that the order of all sequence components PAIR is reversed, and there are no brackets components. Correspondences are obvious. The program structure is identical to the input structure except that each PAIR component in the program structure is a sequence of three.

The full program structure with operations allocated is shown in the following diagram.

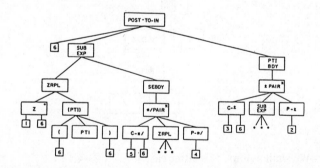

The operations list is:

1. write from inchr
2. write from store+−chr
3. store+−chr :=inchr

4. write from store*/chr
5. store*/chr :=inchr
6. read into inchr

Writing the conditions completes the JSP design. There are no recognition difficulties.

Here, in outline, is a way, of implementing this specification in a language that has no recursive constructs.

Declare an extra local variable QS. Collect the local variables together, including QS, and designate them SV (for state vector). Declare an explicit stack, in the form of a table STACK(j) in which the state vectors of the various instances of the program can be stored. Declare a variable S to keep track of how deep we are in the STACK.

```
X seq
.                   S:=1;
.                   XLABEL:
.
.
doX
.                   QS:=1;
.                   STACK(S):=SV;S:=S+1;
.                   GOTO XLABEL;
.                   Q1:
.
.                   .
.
doX
.                   QS:=2;
.                   STACK(S):=SV;S:=S+1;
.                   GOTO XLABEL;
.                   Q2:
.
.                   IF(S>1)S:=S-1;SV:=STACK(S);
.                   GOTO(Q1,Q2,...) DEPENDING ON QS;
X end
```

For each recursive invocation of X in the text, a variable QS, is set to remember exactly which of several possible textual calls the invoking level is at; the local variables of the invoking level are stored in the STACK; S is incremented. At the end of an X for which S>1, S is decremented, the local variables of the higher level X are recovered from the stack, and the higher level X is resumed where it left off. If S>1 is not true the programs ends.

Of course, you don't have to do this if your language supports recursion; and even for a language like COBOL there might be a better way than this.

The important point is that the problem is inherently recursive. Some of the relationships between the objects that form the subject matter of the problem are recursive. The correct model for the problem, the correct data structures, and the correct JSP specification must all reflect this recursion whether or not the language support it.

Structured programming techniques in interrupt-driven routines

P.F.Palmer

Product Development Group (Southern Development Division), Bracknell

Abstract

The application of structured programming techniques to the production of interrupt-driven code is illustrated by the design of a microcode module, recently implemented on the 2903/4. The Jackson method used provides a powerful means of developing an accurate design and well structured microcode

1 Introduction

Structured programming techniques are popular in some areas of software development, less so in others. These techniques are often analysed in the context of high-level languages and 'commercial' software. However, much system software has characteristics quite unlike the software used as examples of structured programming. Although there is always a trend towards more structured designs, many of the ideas of structured programming have still to find a place here. One area where formal structured programming techniques are little used is the area often called 'firmware' — the low-level system software, including the microcode of machines like the 2903/4. One aspect of this code is that it is frequently interrup-driven; and as will be shown in Section 3, interrupt-driven code is inherently difficult to structure cleanly.

In May 1978 the 2903 microcode team started on the development of a new microcode module to drive a communications coupler, called an SMLCC, a new addition to the set of 2903/4 peripherals. In an effort to improve still further our design techniques we chose to experiment with a design using Jackson structured programming techniques.[1] This paper is the story of how the design went and what was achieved. The result of the experiment was a success, rather more so than had been expected at the outset. As well as producing a self-documenting design and well organised code it elucidated several features of the interrupt-driven code.

The Jackson techniques turned out to be almost purpose-designed for our application. The paper presents the design of the new microcode module from the initial stages of writing down the data structures representing the way the microcode views the transmission blocks on the line, to the point of writing the microcode. The design technique throws light on several aspects of the code, and some of the features which come out of the design are clearly relevant to any interrupt-driven package. Comparison with other 2903/4 microcode shows that the code produced is at least as good as other implementations. With the benefit of such a clear design methodology the approach must be strongly recommended.

2 The problem

In this Section we outline the way in which the microcode module fits into the 2903/4 system. Of necessity some understanding of programming terms is required; a glossary is given in Appendix 1.

The microcode we are going to discuss drives an SMLCC coupler which is connected to a communications line on which there may be several terminals, say 7181 videos or 7502 remote job entry terminals. The line protocol can be ICLC01, ICLC02, or ICLC03, with the 2903/4 acting as the primary; for a definition of these protocols see, for example, Reference 2. The coupler is operated in a character-by-character manner, interrupting the microcode when it requires the next character. An interrupt mechanism is a fundamental part of all modern computers and it is not the purpose of this paper to describe it. However, to set the context for which our design is intended we shall describe the operation in a little more detail.

When the 2903/4 executive wishes to communicate with a terminal it passes the addresses of two buffers to the microcode with a special START instruction. The first buffer contains data to be transmitted to the line, for example a status poll. The second is a buffer for the response of the terminal, say a status response. The microcode's function is to move data from the output buffer to the SMLCC until it recognises a character which terminates the output. This character is transmitted, followed by a block-check character (BCC) if required. The microcode then stops transmitting, puts the line into receiving mode and waits for a response. Incoming data are transferred from the coupler to the store until again a terminating character is detected, when the microcode desynchronises the line.

The SMLCC handles one ISO line character at a time. On output, when it has serialised a character onto the line, it interrupts the microcode, requesting another character. The microcode fetches the next character from the store, passes it to the coupler and exits from the interrupt. This sequence continues until the end of the transmission block. Reading data works in a similar way.

When the SMLCC requests an interrupt the hardware of the 2903/4 stops the execution of the system in its basic level and automatically switches the microcode into its interrupt level which then starts executing from the interrupt entry point. The microcode runs on in interrupt level until the character from the SMLCC has been processed and then obeys a special INTERRUPT EXIT instruction which causes the hardware to restart the basic level at the point at which it was when the interrupt occurred. A timing diagram for this process is given in Fig. 1.

As can be seen the interrupt servicing microcode is executed in a series of paths, each one separated from the next by an interval spent executing a quite different piece of microcode. The design problem that is specific to such interrupt-driven code is to decide how to remember what happened between one interrupt and the next.

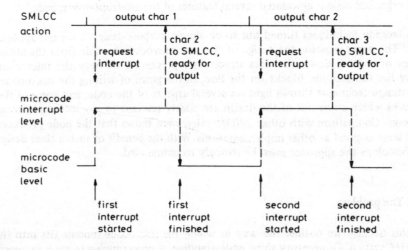

Fig. 1   Timing diagram

3 The microcode design

3.1 Method

The design method adopted was based on some of the ideas expounded by M.A.Jackson.[1] The basic technique is to write down the design first as a simple structured diagram and then as pseudocode. The latter, however, is written not as if it were interrupt-driven but as if the data were always available and could just be written or read as a serial file, using READ or TRANSMIT routines. At this level the fact that the code is interrupt-driven is completely disguised and as a result the structure is clear and easy to follow. The program is then 'inverted' to produce pseudocode which is interrupt-driven but has a less obvious structure. This 'inversion' is a purely mechanical process and may be viewed as just an implementation of the design; it is explained in more detail in Section 3.3. The term is due to Jackson; it does not have the same meaning as, for example, inversion of an indexed file. After the inversion, additional features for handling interrupts, such as timers, are added.

3.2 Initial design

First we have to describe the transmission blocks in more detail. The notation used by Jackson[1] is suitable for this; to summarise, it uses a tree diagram for the data, as in Fig. 2.

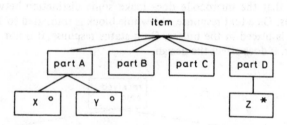

Fig. 2 Tree diagram

Fig. 2 shows 'item' made up of a *sequence* part A, part B, part C, part D. A small circle indicates a *selection*, so part A is shown as made up of X *or* Y. A box with an asterisk means that the item may be repeated an unspecified number of times; thus part D is Z or ZZ or ZZZ etc. 'Item' could therefore be, for example, X part B part C ZZ or Y part B part C ZZZ. In this notation the microcode's-eye view of the transmission is given in Figs. 3-5. Terms such as SYN, ETB are defined in the Glossary, Appendix 1.

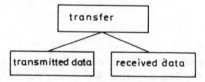

Fig. 3 Data tree

To the microcode, there is no significance in the different types of transmission block, say between a poll or a select, although they will be significant to higher levels of software. A full definition of the data may be found in several places, for example, Reference 2.

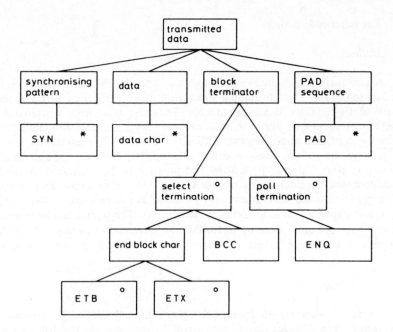

Fig. 4

Note however that the microcode does make some distinction between text and status responses. On a text response, the whole block is translated to 2903/4 3-shift code before it is placed in the buffer. On a status response, it is not. Although the reason is minor, it does affect the design.

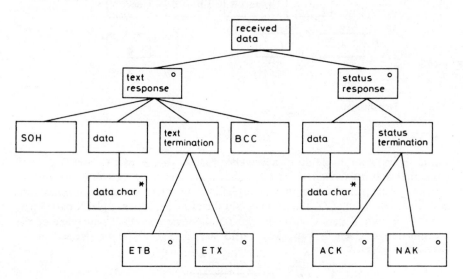

Fig. 5

Once we have the data structure, again following Jackson, we draw a tree diagram for the code based on the data structure. We did not use the code tree very much in our original design, since it is relatively easy to write down the pseudocode directly from the data diagram. For a problem where the actions to be performed are more intricate, a code tree is a useful tool. For completeness a simplified code diagram is given in Figs. 6-8. Notice how the structures match those of Figs. 3-5.

The next step is to represent the design in more detail as pseudocode. For our problem, this step is straightforward, and the code is given in Fig. 9. Notice again how the structures of Figs. 6-8 and Fig. 9 match. Boxes with ° map onto conditional

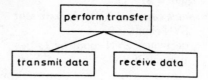

Fig. 6 Simplified code tree

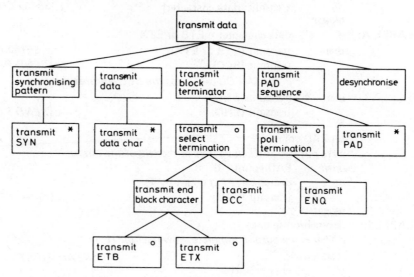

Fig. 7 Simplified code tree

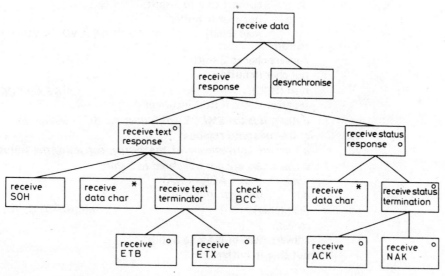

Fig. 8 Simplified code tree

statements (*if . . fi*), boxes with an asterisk map onto loops (*until do repeat*). For the first time, we can see how the choice on selections is made, and how loops terminate.

The 'transmit' and 'read' calls in Fig. 9 are the way data are output to, and taken from the line. Representing the input and output in this way is a major feature of the design method. We know the final microcode cannot look like this, since it is interrupt-driven. However, pretending it can makes the pseudocode clear and easy to follow.

```
              set SYN count = 2;
              c In the simple case, two SYN chars are sent
              until     SYN count = 0
              do        decrement SYN count by 1;
                        transmit (SYN)                              c{SEND SYN}
              repeat;
              c Two SYN chars have been output. Now the data can be sent.
              until     fetch next data character from store;
                        data character = ETB or ETX or ENQ
              do        transmit (data character)                  c{SEND CHAR}
              repeat;
LABEL A:      if        data character = ETB or ETX
              then      transmit (ETB or ETX);                     c{SEND BCC}
                        transmit (BCC)                             c{SEND PAD1}
                        c The SMLCC calculates the BCC automatically
              else      c Assume ENQ
                        transmit (ENQ)                             c{SEND PAD2}
              fi;
              set PAD count = 2;
              c We put two PAD characters at the end of the output
              until     PAD count = 0
              do        decrement PAD count by 1;
                        transmit (PAD)                             c{SEND PAD3}
              repeat;
LABEL B:      desynchronise line;
              c That is the output complete, now read the reply.
              read (char);                                  c{READ FIRST CHAR}
              if        char = SOH
              then      until     char = ETB or ETX
                        do        convert char to 3-shift;
                                  put char in buffer;
                                  read (char)      c{READ CHAR AND CONVERT}
                        repeat;
                        convert char to 3-shift;
                        put char in buffer;
                        read (BCC);                          c{READ BCC}
                        set error status if BCC incorrect
                        c Again it is the SMLCC which does the BCC calculation.
              else      c Assume status response
                        c For the convenience of the system software, the status
                        c characters are not translated to 3-shift.
                        until     char = ACK or NAK
                        do        put char in buffer;
                        read (char)                          c{READ CHAR}
                        repeat;
                        convert ACK or NAK to 3-shift;
                        put char in buffer
              fi;
              desynchronise the line;
              c The transfer is complete.
```

Fig. 9   Structural pseudocode

3.3   Inversion about the read/transmit routines

Fig. 9 shows the design so far. In some ways, it can be regarded as the complete
design, since all the essential flow is there. For example, if it became necessary to
modify the design to terminate a status response on an additional character, then
the place to change Fig. 9 is clear. However, it assumes data are available by means
of subroutines when it is required; an assumption that is incorrect because it is the
SMLCC that decides when a character is wanted, and interrupts.

To obtain the interrupt-driven code we 'invert' Fig. 5 about the read/transmit routines. This inversion is performed below. Its great importance is that it is a mechanical process which can be performed in a systematic way on the pseudocode.

We achieve the inversion by a systematic substitution of code. First, we pick out and label uniquely each read or transmit call. In Fig. 9 the label is enclosed in { } as a comment. Now we pick one word of store which we call a *state variable*. We use this state variable as a row of flags. To each of the labelled calls we picked out earlier, we associate a flag. Now, we take, for example,

$$\text{transmit (ENQ) } c \; \{ \text{SENDPAD2} \} . \, c$$

For this call, we substitute the code in Fig. 10.

```
            give character to SMLCC;
            set 'sendpad2' flag in state variable;
            interrupt exit;

SENDPAD2:   clear 'sendpad2' flag.
```

Fig. 10

In addition, at the interrupt entry point we add the code

$$\textit{if 'sendpad2' flag set } \textit{then goto } \text{SENDPAD2} \, \textit{fi}$$

Notice that we have used the convention writing the labels introducing the inversion in italics to make them stand out.

We make this substitution at all the marked calls in Fig. 9. The code is expanded somewhat, so in Fig.11 we show only the expansion of the code between LABEL A and LABEL B.

In Fig. 11, we can see for the first time how the individual interrupts are routed. Notice how the interrupts cut right across the block structure; an interrupt will start by jumping into the middle of one block and finishing in the middle of another. The diagram illustrates vividly why interrupt-driven code is difficult to structure.

The purpose of our state variable is to remember from one interrupt to the next where one finished and where the next should start. A state variable is a standard feature of any interrupt-driven code, although in many examples of such code, it is not always clear quite what constitutes the state variable.

The flag word we used is only one way of implementing a state variable. The state variable could have been a value to be used as an index to a jump table, or could have been the microprogram address of the return point. This is an implementation decision. We chose this implementation on 2903/4 because there are some excellent conditional-jump-on-bit instructions, but implementing a jump table is costly.

```
     if data character = ETB or ETX
        then                          give char to SMLCC;
                                      set 'send BCC' flag in state variable;
                                      interrupt exit;
        SEND BCC:                     clear 'send BCC' flag;
                                      c This completes the first transmit.
                                      c Now start the next transmit.
                                      tell SMLCC to send BCC;
                                      set 'send pad1' flag in state variable;
                                      interrupt exit;
        SEND PAD1:                    clear 'send pad1' flag;
                                      c This completes the second transmit.

        else c Assume ENQ.

                                      give char to SMLCC;
                                      set 'send pad2' flag in state variable;
                                      interrupt exit;
        SEND PAD2:                    clear 'send pad2' flag;
        fi;
        set pad count = 2;
        until pad count = 0
        do                            decrement PAD count by 1;
                                      tell SMLCC to send PAD;
                                      set 'send pad3' flag in state variable;
                                      interrupt exit;
        SEND PAD3:                    clear 'send pad3' flag
        repeat;
        c That is the end of that code.
        c At the interrupt entry point we will have the code.
        INTERRUPT ENTRY:    if 'send BCC' flag set then goto SEND BCC   fi;
                            if 'send pad1' flag set then goto SEND PAD1 fi;
                            if 'send pad2' flag set then goto SEND PAD2 fi;
                            if 'send pad3' flag set then goto SEND PAD3 fi;
```

Fig. 11   Inverted pseudocode

3.4   Completion of pseudocode

The pseudocode is only two stages away from completion. First we implement all
the *do repeats* and *if then fi* with simple *if then goto fi* statements. Once this is
finished, looking at Fig. 12 we can see some obvious optimisations to make. For
example, having returned to label SENDPAD1 on interrupt entry, the code jumps
smartly to SENDPAD. The optimisation is to jump directly to SENDPAD on interrupt entry.

To finish the design we add one more feature. The microcode must be resilient to
an expected interrupt not appearing, perhaps because the modem has failed or the
terminal does not respond. Therefore, before each exit, on transmission paths, a
timer is started, and is cleared when the next interrupt occurs. On read the whole
message is timed out. The timer fail code is not shown. In the microcode module
we are designing, if a timer fail occurs, the whole transmission is aborted, and in our
design we did not use Jackson techniques for this relatively easy part of the code.
However it is easy to see ways to introduce the timer fail case, if it were necessary.

Addition of the timer code completes the pseudocode and our design. Fig. 13
shows the final version of the code in Fig. 11. Appendix 2 contains all the final
pseudocode.

```
                           if data character = ETB or ETX
                           then goto TRANSMIT ENQ fi;
                           give char to SMLCC;
                           set 'send BCC' flag in state variable;
                           interrupt exit;
            SEND BCC:      clear 'send BICC' flag;
                           tell SMLCC to send BCC;
                           set 'send PAD1' flag in state variable;
                           interrupt exit;
           SEND PAD1:      clear 'send PAD1' flag
                           goto TRANSMIT PAD;
       TRANSMIT ENQ:       c Assume ENQ.
                           give char to SMLCC;
                           set 'send PAD2' flag in state variable;
                           interrupt exit;
          SEND PAD2:       clear 'send PAD2' flag;
       TRANSMIT PAD:       set PAD count = 2;
            SEND PAD:      if PAD count = 0 then goto END OF OUTPUT fi;
                           decrement PAD count by 1;
                           tell SMLCC to send PAD;
                           set 'send PAD3' flag in state variable;
                           interrupt exit;
          SEND PAD3:       clear 'send PAD3' flag;
                           goto SEND PAD;
  END OF OUTPUT:
  c That is the end of that code.
  c At the interrupt entry point we will have the code.
     INTERRUPT ENTRY:    if 'send BCC'  flag set then goto SEND BCC   fi;
                         if 'send PAD1' flag set then goto SEND PAD1 fi;
                         if 'send PAD2' flag set then goto SEND PAD2 fi;
                         if 'send PAD3' flag set then goto SEND PAD3 fi;
```

Fig. 12   Pseudocode before optimisation

```
                           set PAD count = 2;
                           if data character = ETB or ETX
                           then goto TRANSMIT ENQ fi;
                           give char to SMLCC;
                           set 'send BCC' flag in state variable;
                           start timer; interrupt exit;
            SEND BCC:      clear timer; clear 'send BCC' flag;
                           tell SMLCC to send BCC;
                           set 'send PAD' in state variable;
                           start timer; interrupt exit;
       TRANSMIT ENQ:       give char to SMLCC;
                           set 'send PAD' in state variable;
                           start timer; interrupt exit;
           SEND PAD:       clear timer; clear 'send PAD' flag;
                           if PAD count = 0 then goto END OF OUTPUT fi;
                           decrement PAD count by 1;
                           tell SMLCC to send PAD;
                           set 'send PAD' in state variable;
                           start timer; interrupt exit;
  END OF OUTPUT:
  c That is the end of that code.
  c At the interrupt entry point we will have the code.
     INTERRUPT ENTRY:   if 'send BCC' flag set then goto SEND BCC fi;
                        if 'send PAD' flag set then goto SEND PAD fi;
```

Fig. 13   Final pseudocode after optimisation and addition of timers

4   Characteristics of the design

The steps to the final design were:

Step 1   produce data structure diagrams
        2   produce code structure diagrams
        3   write pseudocode based on structure diagram, treating data as if it were from an immediately accessible serial file
        4   invert the pseudocode
        5   add interrupt specific code.

We took the opportunity to optimise at several of these stages, and examination of the final pseudocode shows no obvious design-induced inefficiencies. In Section 5 we compare the microcode produced from this design with other microcode, and show that it is at least as good when measured in terms of size and pathlengths.

The final pseudocode superficially shows none of the structure visible earlier. The nesting, clear in Fig.9, has all but disappeared. However, should we ever have to modify the code, we will be able to use the diagrams from step 3.

If the final pseudocode is examined, there is still visible a consistent organisation which is inherited from the earlier stages. We suggest these are characteristics which improve the structure of any interrupt driven code.

Characteristic 1

A path through the code is clearly partitioned into the sequence

(*a*) interrupt handling code
(*b*) switch code, from interrupt to inline code
(*c*) inline code
(*d*) interrupt exit.

The code itself is structured into units of independent inline code, with each unit performing only one action. Diagrammatically this can be represented as in Fig.14.

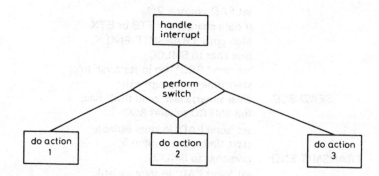

Fig. 14   Structure of code

Characteristic 2

The state variable is handled consistently. There are some implied rules:

Rule 1   state variables are clearly identified and not intermingled with other flags
Rule 2   state variables are accessed once only during each interrupt
Rule 3   state variable for next interrupt is set after in-line code.

In our pseudocode, Rule 2 above was enforced by actually clearing the flag after use. This keeps the flag word tidy. The rule is:

(a) interrupt pending   - one and only one flag set
(b) interrupt being actioned - no flags set.

Rule 3 above is important structurally. Consider the difference between the two pieces of pseudocode in Figs. 15 and 16.

        set state variable
        Action 1
        Action 2
        exit

        Fig. 15

                                    Action 1
                                    Action 2
                                    set state variable
                                    exit

                                    Fig. 16

In execution, there can be no difference. However the code of Fig. 15 is structurally weaker. Once it is implemented, changing action 2 so that it has a choice of exits will have a drastic effect.

There is one further point to be made. In Fig. 9 we used the technique suggested in Reference 1 of 'reading ahead' for the first character of the incoming block. The read ahead is the first read after turning round the line.

Following the read ahead through the inversion shows that the effect is to introduce a special once-entered read-first-character piece of code. In the final version, this code has the special actions of clearing the timer used to detect no response from the terminal and starting the timer on the whole input message. It is instructive to see how this read-ahead rule generates this code in a natural way, and that first-character actions do not have to be inserted in an *ad hoc* fashion.

5   Resulting microcode: assessment and comparisons

The microcode which has its design described in Section 3 represents just under half the final microcode written for the SMLCC. The other half is the code which supports the 2903/4 Executive, makes the line connection, updates timers etc. This has a simple structure and the pseudocode was produced by writing it down directly. We are able to compare the two halves and Table 1 gives the number of errors discovered during testing and validation.

Here, design error means an error where the microcode faithfully represented the intention of the design but the intention was later found to be incorrect. Coding error means an error where the microcode did not faithfully represent this intention.

Table 1

	code designed using techniques of this paper	code designed conventionally
number of design errors	1	6
number of coding errors	15	31

The improvement in design accuracy vindicates the method. The improvement in coding accuracy is also a direct benefit of having a design which has been carefully worked through and which is available in detail. The one design error noted was actually an undocumented hardware restriction which was discovered the hard way on the machine — it had nothing to do with the design method.

We are also in a position to compare our new code with another module written earlier to drive the integrated communications coupler. Direct comparison is difficult: the couplers are different, the line-connection and error-reporting facilities are improved in the newer module. In addition, the way the data are held differs: the earlier module has four dedicated 'working store' locations while the new one has none and consequently requires more instructions to access a given piece of data. The comparison is therefore subjective but is still worth making.

The earlier code has obviously been carefully optimised to reduce the length of the most common path, and the other paths have increased lengths. The new code is more even over all path lengths and there is still room for reducing the lengths of the frequently used paths by jumping on the less frequent cases. When we measure the number of changes of control (jumps) between different parts of the code in one interrupt, we find the two are the same on the standard paths but the new code has fewer jumps on the unusual paths, for example when an ACK or ETB is received. As we showed in Section 4 (Fig. 14), we should expect our design method to give this improvement.

The new code is larger, but this is mainly accounted for by the differences in couplers and facilities mentioned above. Overall, the new code is clear and has an obvious organisation.

Given the fact that some reduction in path lengths is still possible, the comparison shows that the new code is at least as good as the earlier module; and we expect, of course, to have the benefits of easier maintenance from our design.

6 Conclusions

We have used a structured programming technique,[1] to provide a design for an interrupt-driven microcode module for 2903/4.

The strategy is to produce a block-structured design which disguises the interrupts by assuming the communications coupler can be driven as a serial file. This design is then 'inverted' to produce the interrupt-driven code.

The idea of inversion is crucial to the technique. It provides a simple mechanism to identify conceptually the two different types of code organisation, and a procedure for converting from one to the other. The code can be designed in a block-structured way, which gives substantial benefits in having a 'self-documenting' design and well organised code.

The application of this technique to the 2903/4 microcode was very successful, and produced high-quality code which contained almost no design errors.

Structured programming techniques are not widely used in low-level firmware. Our example shows that they can be used with good effect, and that the Jackson technique in particular should always be considered when interrupt-driven code is being designed.

Acknowledgments

A.W.Radgick, Senior Programmer, implemented the SMLCC microcode.

References

1   JACKSON, M.A. *Principles of program design* (Academic Press)
2   TAS 11 ICL. XBM

Appendix 1

Glossary

This paper assumes some understanding of programming terms. This glossary offers additional explanations, especially of the communications terminology.

pseudocode	Code written to represent the microcode. It is not compiled, but used as a template for the final microcode. We choose to write it to look like S3.
flag	A piece of store to remember a true or false condition. The flag can be set (true) or clear (false).
SMLCC	A communications coupler, i.e. a piece of hardware connected to the communications line, which operates the line under the control of the microcode.
ISO codes	One particular way of encoding data onto a communications line. The ISO characters mentioned in this paper are:

	SYN	a character transmitted at the start of all blocks to get the two ends of the line in step (synchronisation).
	ETB, ETX	two characters used to mark the end of test blocks. As far as the microcode is concerned, the two are interchangeable.
	BCC	Block check character, used to detect errors in a block. Small blocks, like status response, do not have a BCC.
	ACK, NAK, ENQ	ENQ marks the end of a poll, ACK or NAK marks the end of a status response.
	SOH	a character put at the beginning of a text block.
	PAD	the character used to round off all blocks.

Appendix 2 Final pseudocode

```
c The code starts initially in the basic level, processing
c the 'START' command from the 2903/4 executive.
                              set SYN count = 1;
                              give SYN to SMLCC;
                              set 'send SYN' flag in state variable;
                              start timer;
c This first SYN wakes up the SMLCC.
c It will output this SYN and then interrupt for all subsequent
c characters.
                              continue processing 2903/4 program;
c The transfer has been started. The basic level goes on to
c do other work.
c All the following code is obeyed in interrupt level.
                 SEND SYN:    clear timer; clear 'send SYN' flag;
                              if SYN count = 0 then goto SEND CHAR fi;
                              decrement SYN count by 1;
                              give SYN to SMLCC;
                              set 'send SYN' flag in state variable;
                              start timer; interrupt exit;
                 SEND CHAR:   clear timer; clear 'send char' flag;
                              fetch next data character from buffer;
                              if char = ETB or ETX
                              then goto TRANSMIT ETBX fi;
                              if char = ENQ then goto TRANSMIT ENQ fi;
```

```
                               c some changes here from fig. 13 for optim—
                               isation
                               give char to SMLCC;
                               start timer; interrupt exit;
TRANSMIT ETBX:                 give char to SMLCC;
                               set 'send BCC' flag in state variable;
                               start timer; interrupt exit;
    SEND BCC:                  clear timer; clear 'send BCC' flag;
                               tell SMLCC to send BCC;
                               set 'send PAD' flag in state variable;
                               start timer; interrupt exit;
TRANSMIT ENQ:                  give char to SMLCC;
                               set PAD count = 2;
                               set 'send PAD' flag in state variable;
                               start timer; interrupt exit;
    SEND PAD:                  clear timer; clear 'send PAD' flag;
                               if PAD count = 0 then goto END OF
                               OUTPUT fi;
                               decrement PAD count by 1;
                               tell SMLCC to send PAD;
                               set 'send PAD' flag in state variable;
                               start timer; interrupt exit;
END OF OUTPUT:                 desynchronise SMLCC;
c That is the whole output block transmitted.
c The SMLCC will automatically synchronise on the incoming message.
c All we have to do is wait for the interrupt.
                               set 'receive first char' flag in state variable;
                               start timer; C Allowing time for the terminal
                               to respond. interrupt exit;
RECEIVE FIRST CHAR:            clear timer; clear 'receive first char' flag;
                               start timer on whole of input message;
                               c There is time for a 2000 character message.
                               take char from SMLCC;
                               if char = SOH
                               then goto RECEIVE STATUS fi;
                               goto RECEIVE TEXT;
READ CHAR AND CONVERT:         clear 'read char and convert' flag;
                               take char from SMLCC;
RECEIVE TEXT:                  if char = ETB or ETX
                               then goto RECEIVE ETBX fi;
                               convert char to 2903/4 3-shift;
                               put char in buffer;
                               set 'read char and convert' flag in state variable;
                               interrupt exit;
RECEIVE E\XTB                  convert char to 2903/4 3-shift;
                               put char in buffer;
                               set 'check BCC' flag in state variable;
                               interrupt exit;
    CHECK BCC:                 clear 'check BCC' flag;
                               if BCC incorrect then set error status fi;
                               c. The SMLCC does this calculation for us.
                               goto DESYNCHRONISE;
    READ CHAR:                 clear 'read char' flag;
                               take char from SMLCC;
RECEIVE STATUS:                c This path is taken if the first char of the
                               c incoming block is not SOH, implying a status
                               c response.
                               c The status characters are not translated but
                               c the terminating ACK or NAK is.
```

```
                                if char = ACK or NAK
                                then goto RECEIVE ACK NAK fi;
                                put char in buffer;
                                set 'read char' flag in state variable;
                                interrupt exit;
    RECEIVE ACK NAK:            convert char to 2903/4 3-shift;
                                put char in buffer;
    DESYNCHRONISE:             desynchronise SMLCC;
                                clear timer;
c That is the end of the transmission. After tidying, a peripheral interrupt is set to
c the 2903/4 executive. There is then the final interrupt exit.
                                interrupt exit;
c At the interrupt entry point there is the code.
INTERRUPT ENTRY:              if 'send SYN' flag set then goto SEND SYN fi;
                                if 'send char' flag set then goto SEND CHAR fi;
                                if 'send BCC' flag set then goto SEND BCC fi;
                                if 'send PAD' flag set then goto SEND PAD fi;
                                if 'receive first char' flag set
                                then goto RECEIVE FIRST CHAR fi;
                                if 'read char and convert' flag set
                                then goto REACH CHAR AND CONVERT fi;
                                if 'check BCC' flag set then goto CHECK BCC fi;
                                if 'read char' flag set then goto READ CHAR fi;
```

PART FOUR

JSD PRINCIPLES
AND SMALL EXAMPLES

Chapter 4.0   Introduction to Part Four

Part Four describes the JSD method and illustrates it by small examples. Most of the examples refer to a data-processing system, the Widget Warehouse Company system. Reference is also made to the Car Rally/Golden Handshake systems and a microprocessor-controlled Lift (Elevator) system, both of which are described in the single reprinted paper, "Two Pairs of Examples in the Jackson Approach to System Development".

Chapter 4.1 introduces JSD notations and some basic concepts and techniques, independently from a detailed description of the JSD steps. The JSD notations introduced are for interprocess communication as used in System Specification Diagrams (SSDs) (Section 4.1.2) and for describing transformations by System Implementation Diagrams (SIDs) (Section 4.1.3). Chapter 4.2 describes the steps of the method. Chapter 4.3 illustrates the method using the Widget Warehouse Company system, concentrating on steps one, four, and six. Chapter 4.4 discusses and illustrates the major aspects of the method not covered in Chapter 4.3. Chapter 4.5 consists of arguments that justify the JSD approach.

You do not have to read all the preceding Chapters to understand the arguments in Chapter 4.5. One approach to this Part is to read Chapter 4.1; read Chapter 4.2 quickly; read Chapter 4.3, referring back to Chapter 4.2; and then skip to Chapter 4.5. Having absorbed the method in outline and understood its rationale, Chapters 4.2, 4.3, and 4.4 (and the case studies in Part Five) can be studied in more detail.

Chapter 4.1   Basic Concepts and Notations of JSD

4.1.1 Long-Running Programs

We are used to the idea that a program may be swapped in and out of main storage during execution and may have a much longer elapsed time than execution time. We are used to the idea that an on-line program may have a long elapsed time because the operator is slow to supply input and the program is waiting for this input most of the time. We are less used to the idea of specifying programs whose input is gradually accumulated over a long period, perhaps over several decades. The idea is less familiar but is different only in degree from that of the first two.

JSD specifications are expressed in terms of processes that have a long elapsed time because their input is only gradually accumulated. For most of the time, these processes will have partially executed and will be waiting for new input.

The Car Rally/Golden Handshake systems are a pair of examples that illustrate the use of long-running programs in specification. They are described in the third section of the reprinted paper, "Two Pairs of Examples . . .". You should now read Sections 3.1–3.3 of that paper. The point of the comparison in the paper is that, except for the time dimension, the statements of the two problems are identical.

In the JSD specification of the Car Rally/Golden Handshake, there is one process per car/employee. The input for this process comes, albeit indirectly, from the real car/employee. The process therefore has an elapsed time of the order of an afternoon/thirty years.

For the Car Rally problem, an implementation environment is easily imagined in which the n car processes (one for each real car) may run concurrently throughout the afternoon, each being invoked when there is appropriate input. In such an environment the specification can be executed directly; the specification is the system.

For the Golden Handshake system, the implementation problem is more difficult. The usual implementation environments do not allow the concurrent execution of a large number of very long-running processes,

and if they did, the inefficiency would probably be unacceptable. The JSD implementation phase is largely concerned with building a special-purpose implementation environment under which the specification processes can be executed efficiently. An example of a special-purpose environment for this system is described in Section 4.1.4.

In JSD, all systems are real-time systems. Data processing systems are just rather slow real-time systems. In both the Car Rally/Golden Handshake systems, outputs are required before all the inputs are collected. There are response time constraints on the outputs. By any reasonable definition both are real-time systems.

4.1.2 Notations Used in JSD Specifications

JSD specifications consist of sequential processes. The notations used to define individual sequential processes are the same as those used in JSP, namely structure diagrams and structure text. For a description of these notations, see Chapter 2.1. This section describes JSD notations for the two basic means of process communication: by reading and writing data streams, and by state vector inspection.

Figure 4.1a shows a data stream F that is written by the process P and is read by the process Q. A data stream is an infinitely buffered First-In-First-Out queue. Data stream communication has the following characteristics. Everything written by P must eventually be read by Q. Records read by Q are read in the same order in which they are written. Because infinite buffering is assumed, the writer P can never be blocked on a write operation. If Q tries to execute a read operation and no record is available, then Q will be blocked until the record is available. There is no way of testing the contents of the buffer before reading. The initiative for the communication lies with the writer P. Q cannot use the data stream F to influence when or what P writes. (Data stream communication is also used in JSP. See Section 2.4.1 and the microfiche problem in Chapter 3.1.)

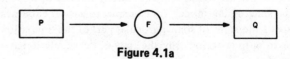

Figure 4.1a

Portions of this Chapter are excerpted from previously unpublished Michael Jackson Systems Limited (MJSL) internal documents with permission from MJSL.

Figure 4.1b shows the process S inspecting the state vector of the process R. The state vector of a process is the collective name for the local variables of the process, including the text-pointer. The text-pointer of a partially executed process is the position that it has reached in its text. When S inspects the state vector of R by an operation of the form "get SV of R", the values of the state vector are made available to S.

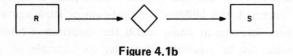

Figure 4.1b

State vector communication has the following characteristics: The accessing of the state vector does not affect the process R. There is no operation in R that is executed when a state vector inspection is made. The examination by S is invisible to R. The initiative for the communication lies with the inspecting process S. If, for some reason, S fails to execute any "get SV of R" operations, then no backlog of information builds up. S simply misses what has been happening in R.

State vector inspection is the special case of communication by shared variables in which only one of the communicating processes may write the variables. All the variables of R are shared between R and S, but only R may change their values. A further restriction on the access of the shared variables can ensure that only states judged to be coherent as a whole can be returned as a result of a "get SV" operation. It is enough that the only states returned to S are those just before an I/O operation in R.

A common implementation of SV inspection is to make a second copy of the state vector and to use the second copy to give the results of "get SV" operations. The inspected process can continue to execute, and only periodically is the second copy of the state vector updated to the value of the "real" state vector.

State vector connection is a loose means of communication in the sense that the inspecting process does not know exactly how up-to-date the values are that it accesses. State vector inspection can only be used where this indeterminacy is acceptable in the specification.

JSD specifications are like specifications of simulations in which part of the specification, the model part, defines what is being simulated. Another part of the specification defines an information system on the model. In this context it is perfectly natural to inspect the state of the model, for example, to answer enquiries about the state of some particular part of the simulation or to output periodically the state of the simulation as a whole.

In JSD notation, double lines on one side of the circle or diamond denote a relative multiplicity between the connected processes. In Figure 4.1c, the process P, over its whole lifetime, writes data streams to many processes of type Q. The process S, over its whole lifetime, examines the state vectors of many processes of type R. Nothing is implied in the notation about the absolute number of processes of the various types. There may or may not be many instances of P or R. Figure 4.1c does imply that each Q is connected to only one P and that each R is connected to only one S. Figure 4.1d has double bars on both sides of the circle and diamond. This implies that many processes of type P each write data streams to many processes of type Q and that many processes of type S each inspect many state vectors of type R.

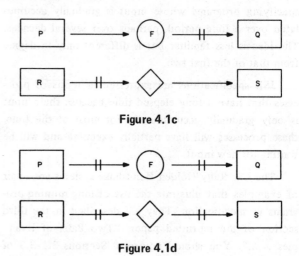

Figure 4.1c

Figure 4.1d

The final piece of JSD specification notation concerns the way two or more input streams appear to the reading process. In Figure 4.1e, the arrows from F and G to the process R have been joined, and there is only one arrowhead. This means that R reads F and G as if they were one data stream. The algorithm by which F and G are merged is not specified. F and G are said to be "rough-merged".

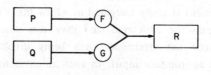

Figure 4.1e

A process that reads a rough-merged stream must be specified so that it can handle any rough-merging algorithm. In this way JSD addresses the problem of "race conditions", in which one input may unexpectedly arrive before another.

(We shall see that a common implementation of rough-merging is to invert R with respect to the joint input stream, thus making R a common subroutine of P and Q. The way F and G are merged will then depend on the relative scheduling of P and Q.)

In Figure 4.1f, there are separate arrows from F and G into the process R. This means that R reads F and G using separate "read" operations. The relative speed of consumption of the F and G data streams is determined in R by the ordering of the "read F" and "read G" operations in the execution of R.

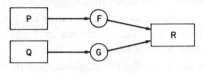

Figure 4.1f

Figure 4.1g shows the processes R each writing a data stream H to the process S. Perhaps the notation should be extended to distinguish whether the H streams are rough-merged and S reads them as if they were one stream or whether S reads each stream individually. Usually in these circumstances, S reads a single rough-merged stream.

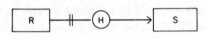

Figure 4.1g

4.1.3 Transformations

JSD specifications are executable. They consist of well-defined sequential processes that communicate in well-defined ways. (This is not completely true. The timing constraints introduced in the System Timing step are not executable.)

The implementation phase is concerned with finding a way, and choosing a good way, of running the specification processes on a given target hardware/software configuration. An important element in the implementation phase is the transformation of the specified processes so that they can fit into an appropriate implementation framework. The most important of these transformations are program inversion and state vector separation, which are also used under certain circumstances in JSP. In this section these and some other transformations are reviewed, and suitable notations are introduced. The example in Section 4.1.4 shows that even the extra scheduler processes introduced in the implementation phase sometimes undergo transformations.

Program Inversion. (See also Sections 2.3.3, 2.4.1, and 2.4.2.) Program inversion is the transformation of a process into a variable-state procedure by adding a suspend-and-resume mechanism. When an inverted program is invoked for the first time, it starts execution at its beginning and continues until it reaches the (dynamically) first suspension point, where it returns to the invoking level. On subsequent invocations, the inverted program resumes where it left off and continues to the next suspension point, where it again returns to the invoking level. The overall effect is that the process executes piecemeal.

Suspension points are always identified with I/O operations of one or more data streams. If suspension points are associated with the data streams F and G, we say that the program is "inverted with respect to F and G". If P is inverted with respect to F and G, records of F and G pass in the appropriate direction between the invoking and the invoked levels. Commonly in JSD, a program is inverted with respect to its single input data stream. For most of its lifetime the process is suspended, waiting for its next input. When the invoking level has an input record and chooses to invoke the inverted program, it does so with the input record as parameter. The inverted program then executes until it reaches its next read operation, when it returns to the invoking level.

The mechanism for inverting with respect to a single data stream is fully illustrated by the example in Section 2.3.3. The single data stream case is simpler because the invoked program always returns to the invoking level for the same reason, to read or write a record of the single data stream.

The mechanism for multiple inversion is more complicated because the interface must include information about the reason for the suspension, for example, to distinguish between a return to write a record of F and a return to read a record of G. None of the examples in this book use multiple inversion in their final implementation, and no detailed example of the transformation is included. The interested reader is referred to Jackson [2].

The JSD notation used for program inversion is shown in Figure 4.1h. The number of lines between the upper, invoking box and the lower, invoked box is one more than the number of data streams involved in the inversion. Thus P is inverted with respect to a single data stream, and Q is inverted with respect to three data streams. B and C are both invoked by A: B is inverted with respect to one data stream, C is inverted with respect to two.

Figure 4.1h

State Vector Separation. JSD specifications usually contain many instances of processes of the same type. These processes have the same text but, during execution, have different values of their local variables and text-pointer. Multiple processes of the same type can be implemented by a single copy of the process text and multiple copies of the process state vectors. The transformation that does this is called "state vector separation".

Starting with an inverted program, the local variables and text-pointer are moved into the interface between invoking and invoked levels. Instead of invoking the inverted program with, say, the input record it has been waiting for, the invoking level invokes the generalised, inverted program with both the input record and the state vector of the appropriate instance of the process. When the generalised program returns, it passes back the updated state vector to the invoking level. With this arrangement, the invoking level is responsible for the storage and retrieval of the state vectors. The operations that must be executed in the invoking level are of the form

> load SV of P-id into PSV
> call P (REC, PSV)
> store PSV as SV of P-id

where P-id identifies the process instance that is to read the record REC.

A variation in this arrangement makes the inverted generalised program responsible for the storage and retrieval of its own state vectors. In the example referred to in Section 2.3.3, there is a full illustration of state vector separation with such an arrangement.

Figure 4.1i shows a notation for the separation of the state vectors for *P* where the invoking level *S* has responsibility for storing and retrieving the state vectors. (The symbol for PSV denotes any storage medium and is not to be construed as referring to only a disk.)

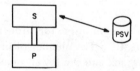

Figure 4.1i

Program Dismemberment. Program dismemberment is a transformation that results in the implementation of a single process by two (or more) separate pieces of program text. A particular form of program dismemberment is introduced and illustrated in Chapter 2.4 in the context of on-line programming. In that example the idea of cutting up a single copy of the text is misleading. Instead, many identical copies of the text are created, each to be used under different circumstances. The unnecessary

parts of each copy are then deleted. One copy is created, at least initially, for each entry point into the inverted program. With this form of dismemberment, the dismembered part that will process the next record can be specified by the dismembered part that processed the preceding record.

A simple variation on this basic scheme is to create one copy of the text for each type of input record and then to delete from each copy unnecessary text. Each input record has to be tested to find out which of the dismembered components should process it.

A different style of dismemberment is used to create batch-processing components. Consider the long-running process whose structure is shown in Figure 4.1j and whose inputs accumulate at a rate that allows one complete execution of the iterated component WEEK per week. A likely implementation is to dismember PROG into two parts, the upper iteration and the WEEK component. The upper iteration can be implemented by operator instructions, for example. "Run the program WEEK every week on the accumulated input". The WEEK component becomes the weekly program. In particularly simple cases, there are no local variables that retain their values from week to week, and this is all that has to be done. In general, the weekly program has to retrieve and store at least part of the state vector of PROG. The text-pointer does not have to be stored because each weekly run leaves PROG at the same point of its text, at the beginning of the WEEK component.

Figure 4.1j

Figure 4.1k shows two more notations that are used in the JSD implementation phase. The small letter suffices, "a" and "b", indicate that PROGa and PROGb are both dismembered parts of the process PROG. The diagram also implies that PROGa invokes PROGb and that, when it does, PROGb executes completely. This contrasts with the normal invocation of an inverted program, which only partially executes on a single invocation. In this example PROGa is the operator instructions and PROGb is the weekly batch program. The separate notation is useful because toward the end of implementation, we must arrive at processes that can be run on a computer and that do execute completely when they are invoked. We must end up with a system cast in familiar form, with operator instructions and JCL controlling the invocations of a collection of programs, each of which runs to completion when invoked once.

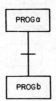

Figure 4.1k

There are examples of this form of dismemberment in the next section and in Chapter 4.3.

Other Transformations. Just as a single process can be implemented by several separate pieces of program text, so also can a state vector be split up and the parts stored in separate places. This transformation is called "state vector dismemberment". The four transformations —inversion, state vector separation, program dismemberment, and state vector dismemberment—are more than enough to implement satisfactorily a very wide range of systems. State vector dismemberment is discussed further in Section 4.4.4.

The range of potential transformations, though, is very wide. Other transformations may prove to be useful, particularly in specialised implementation environments. The following is a single example.

A function process answers enquiries by adding the values of a variable from all the state vectors of a given process type. On request, it outputs the total of the balances of all the accounts held in a bank. In a distributed implementation, the state vectors of the accounts may be stored in a number of computers, one located in each branch of the bank. The centralised function may access the account state vectors over some communication link. A transformation, based on the fact that a grand total equals the sum of its subtotals, would add up a total for each branch and send only the subtotal over the link to the centralised function. The centralised function is transformed into $(n+1)$ parts.

4.1.4 Scheduling

One of the main issues running through the JSD Implementation phase is the definition of a special-purpose scheduling scheme for the many processes that make up the specification.

For most systems, a completely general purpose scheduler, even if one existed, would be too inefficient. A special-purpose scheduling scheme therefore has to be built, and scheduling decisions have to be fixed at system build-time. There is an obvious trade-off. The more special-purpose we make our scheduling, the more effi-

cient it will be; however, it becomes more likely that it will have to be changed if the specification changes. We shall see that the scheduling schemes we adopt are relatively general, even though the scheduling is completely fixed.

We have met scheduling issues in a restricted form in JSP examples. In the microfiche problem (Chapter 3.1) the solution is defined by three processes. An implementation with inversion fixes the scheduling in one way, an implementation with coroutines fixes the scheduling in a similar way, an implementation with physical datasets fixes the scheduling in a quite different way, an implementation with Ada tasks leaves the scheduling decisions to run-time.

Languages today (1982) either force a developer to leave scheduling decisions to run-time or to mix up scheduling statements with specification statements. Really, there should be two languages, a specification language and a metalanguage, to describe how the specification is to be implemented.

Consider again the Car Rally/Golden Handshake problems from the third section of the paper, "Two Pairs of Examples ...".

The specification consists of n processes, one for each car/employee. We start with two basic transformations. Each specified process is inverted with respect to its input data stream, and the state vectors are separated so that there is only one copy of the process text. The single, generalised subroutine is invoked by an operation of the form:

CALL CAR (FREC, SV)

The specified system is partially executed by one of these CALLs. The system is completely executed by a whole succession of such CALLs. Figure 4.1l shows the result of these transformations.

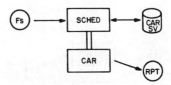

Figure 4.1l

We now describe three different scheduling schemes in which the succession of CALLs is ordered in different ways. In all three, we assume that the implementation is to use only one processor.

Scheduler (1). In this scheduling, everything is kept up to date. Records coming into the SCHEDuler program are passed immediately to the inverted CAR (or EMPEE) process. The structure for this scheduler is shown in Figure 4.1m. The data stream *F*s consists of all the *F* streams that are input to the CAR processes. The operations list (main operations only) is

1. load CARSV (C-id) into CSV
2. CALL CAR (FREC,CSV)
3. put CSV into CARSV (C-id)
4. read *Fs*

This is an on-line scheduler for a bare machine. In a real on-line environment, a teleprocessing (TP) monitor supplies the upper iteration, and the developer has only to supply FREC modules.

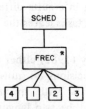

Figure 4.1m

Scheduler (2). The list of operations referred to in Figure 4.1o is

1. load CARSV (C-id) into CSV
2. CALL CAR (FREC,CSV)
3. put CSV into CARSV (C-id)
4. read *Fs&T*
5. write FREC to BUFFER
6. write end-marker to BUFFER
7. read BUFFER

This is a batch scheduling. The batch periods are defined by the arrival of a *T* record on the SCHEDuler input stream *Fs&T* that is shown on the SID in Figure 4.1n. The *T* records are for the scheduler only. They are not input to any specified process. (Eventually, they will probably be implemented by operator instructions.)

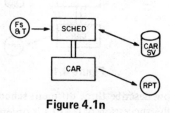

Figure 4.1n

In this batch scheme the records are used in the same order in which they arrived. The scheduling is like the on-line scheduling but is delayed until the end of the batch period.

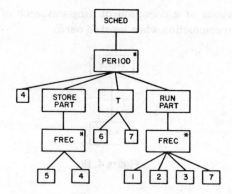

Figure 4.1o

Scheduler (3). The list of operations referred to in Figure 4.1p is

1. read next OLDCARSV into CSV
2. CALL CAR (FREC,CSV)
3. write CSV to NEWCARSV
4. read *Fs&T*
5. write FREC to A-BUFFER
6. write end-marker to A-BUFFER
7. exec SORT (A-BUFFER, B-BUFFER)
8. read B-BUFFER
9. create new CSV

This is a batch scheduling in which the batch periods are defined by the *T* records on the *Fs&T* data stream. Each batch of input is sorted. This allows the serial access of the CAR state vectors within each batch period. The sort must be a stable sort, in which the sequencing of records with the same key is preserved. The collate part is an absolutely standard JSP collate between the B-BUFFER and the serial OLD CARSV file. (See Chapter 2.4 for a brief

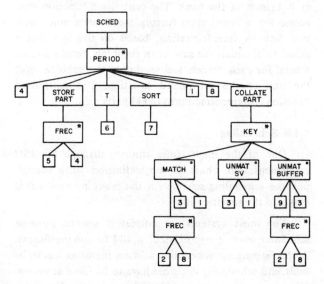

Figure 4.1p

description of JSP collating.) Unlike the first two schedulers, we have chosen in this one to include the creation of new state vectors. The specified system is still executed by invoking the inverted CAR program. The framework within which these invocations are embedded is more complicated. This scheduling scheme is more plausible for the Golden Handshake system than it is for the Car Rally system.

A likely implementation of this SCHEDuler process involves the dismemberment of its text into four parts. This dismemberment is briefly described at the end of the third section of the reprinted paper, "Two Pairs of Examples ...". The four parts are the upper iteration, which will be implemented by operator instructions; the store part, which could be operator instructions but is more likely to be an on-line data-collection program; the sort part, which is a manufacturer-supplied program; and the collate part, which will be the update program in the system.

The operator instructions for the upper iteration will be something like "Run the on-line data entry program every day until 6 pm, then run the accumulated input through the sort program. The sorted transactions file is one of the two inputs to the updating program; the other input is the serial master file that was the output from yesterday's updating program. Run the updating program with these inputs, keeping the updated master file for the next day's run".

The finished system consists of an updating program and a combination of software and operating instructions to prepare the input. The whole of the specification of the system is in the subroutine invoked by the updating program. The upper structure of the updating program, the collate, is not defined until the implementation phase. We shall see that the structure of the subroutine would have been defined in the modelling phase and that the detailed operations would have been added in the function phase.

Using a conventional approach, a designer would specify an updating program and a programmer would program it, filling in the details of the specification as he went along. The designer would be creating or working within an implementation framework. There would not be the same separation of specification and implementation, let alone the separation of model and function, in the programmer's work on the updating program.

The three schedulers discussed here are all fairly general purpose. Each could be used (at least) for any system that consists of multiple instances of a single process type.

4.1.5 Storage and Access of State Vectors

The storage and access of state vectors is the third of the three main issues in the JSD implementation phase (the other two being transformations and scheduling).

Separated state vectors have to be accessed by whichever processes call the inverted generalised subprogram. They must also be accessed by processes that inspect the state vectors via a state vector connection.

Suppose that a function process, F, has a state vector connection to a set of model processes of type P. One execution of F contains an ordered set of "get SV" operations, each of which returns a state vector of a P process. An execution of F defines what we call an "access path" through the state vectors of the P processes. The set of possible executions of F defines a set of possible access paths. In the implementation phase, file or database designs must be chosen so that the process F can access the state vectors in a way that is acceptably efficient.

For example, consider the following three functions that could be added to the Golden Handshake system. (The system specification diagram for each of the three functions is shown in Figure 4.1q. To complete the specification, we must add the structure and text of the three F processes.)

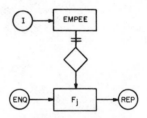

Figure 4.1q

$F1$ is a function process that answers a stream of enquiries about specified employees. For each enquiry, $F1$ must access one state vector, the state vector of the employee whose identifier is on the input enquiry record.

An input to $F2$ specifies an employee grade (clerk, manager, etc.). $F2$ must then print out an alphabetical list of all employees of that grade. For each input record, $F2$ must access all the state vectors of employees in the specified grade, and it must access them in alphabetic order. (The employee grade is part of the text-pointer of the process, although we may introduce another local variable that duplicates information in the text-pointer but whose information content is more accessible.)

An input to $F3$ specifies a date. $F3$ prints out a list of all employees who started their employment on or before that date, in increasing order of starting date. For each input record, $F3$ must access a particular subset of the state vectors in increasing order of starting date. (We will have to ensure that the starting date is kept as a local variable of the employee process.)

At implementation time, we may choose a file organisation that can directly support the access paths defined by these function processes. In this example, we may choose a file organisation that allows direct access by employee-id, allows serial alphabetic access within grade, and allows serial access by ascending starting date. Alternatively, a simpler file organisation may be chosen and the access paths realised by extra software such as sorts and programs that remove unwanted state vectors.

The central point is this: function processes that have state vector connections to other processes define access pathways through these state vectors, the definition of the required access pathways is therefore part of the JSD function phase and the choice of which access paths should be directly realised in a database or file organisation is made in the implementation phase.

The choice will inevitably involve trade-offs that depend on numbers of state vectors, expected frequencies of enquiries of various types, and the performance and characteristics of available file or database management systems. The file or database design decisions will be that much more complicated if the state vectors of some processes are dismembered and the dismembered parts are stored separately. Examples of the transition from JSD specification to file design and the subsequent implementation decisions are given in Section 4.3.4.

Chapter 4.2   The JSD Method

This chapter is intended to be used as a reference to JSD. For an initial description of the method, read only the "Concise Statement" and the "General Description" of each step. Then refer to the other subsections such as the Widget Warehouse example developed in Chapters 4.3 and 4.4.

There are six main steps in the JSD method:*

1. Entity/Action and Entity Structure Step
2. Initial Model Step
3. Interactive Function Step
4. Information Function Step
5. System Timing Step
6. Implementation Step

Steps 2, 3, and 4 can be performed largely in parallel. The decisions in any one of these steps are independent of the decisions in the other two. Each step is now discussed in turn.

4.2.1 Entity/Action and Entity Structure Step

Concise Statement. The purpose of the first major step in the JSD method is to define a model that is rich enough to support the functional requirements of the system. The model consists of a set of action definitions and a number of disconnected sequential processes that describe the time constraints between the actions.

The model is, indirectly, a specification of a coherent range of functions, from which the actual functional requirement must be chosen. By defining the possible, and therefore the acceptable, sequences of actions, the model is also a specification of part of the error handling of the system.

General Description. Attention is focused first on the subject matter of the system and not on the system itself. For example, the subject matter of payroll system probably consists of the employees, their contracts, and their pension agreements. The subject matter is dynamic; things happen. Employees clock on, clock off, go sick, go and come back from holiday, are promoted, go and

work for a subsidiary, return from such assignments, and make choices about the options on their pension scheme

In the Entity/Action and Entity Structure step, we make an abstraction of the subject matter, concentrating on its time dimension. The abstraction is formal in that it is well defined and is expressed in a precise language. To make an abstraction, questions must be answered about the range of the abstraction (how much of the world to include?) and about its accuracy (is the description of what is included correct?). In JSD the abstraction of the subject matter is called the "model".

Only if the explicit aim is to automate existing procedures will the subject matter of a payroll system be the existing system for doing the payroll. We could call this a "payroll department administration system" rather than an "employee work compensation system". The point is not that JSD stops you from building one or the other of these systems; rather it is that in the first major step of JSD you decide what the subject matter of the system is to be. The subject matter is not the same as the system itself, and therefore the correct choice of subject matter will never be the computer or administrative system that is to be replaced.

Detailed Procedure. In what follows, we shall use the term "problem area input" to refer to facts, decisions, and information that have been gleaned from interviews with users, from knowledge of the application area, from reading existing documents on the purpose and subject matter of the system, and from any other available sources. The idea is not that the developer should make specification decisions himself, but that he should guide the user(s) towards making the decisions in an appropriate order.

In JSD, an "action" is an event in the world that forms the subject matter of the system and about which the system must produce or use information. Actions in JSD are regarded as atomic. An "entity" is a person, organisation, or object that performs or suffers an interesting time sequence of actions.

Use problem area input to make a list of candidate actions, that is, verbs that describe events that seem as though they may be part of a suitable model. Make a similar list of candidate entities. Refine the lists independently and by cross referencing the actions with the entities. Some reasons for rejecting actions and entities are set out below. Write out definitions of the actions. The

---

*The organisation into steps given here differs slightly from that in Jackson [2]. There the Entity/Action and Entity Structure steps are separated into distinct steps [steps 1 and 2]. What is simply the function step there [step 4], is here divided into the Interactive Function and Information Function steps [steps 3 and 4]. The first of these changes is purely cosmetic. The second reflects a small change in view, the association of interactive functions with model realisation as well as with information functions.

Portions of this Chapter are excerpted from previously unpublished Michael Jackson Systems Limited (MJSL) internal documents with permission from MJSL.

action definitions form the basis of a glossary used by everyone involved in the development of the specification. Include in the action descriptions any data associated with the action. For example, DEPOSIT may be an action in a banking system. The date and amount of the DEPOSIT are associated data. We call such data "attributes" of the action. Attributes that occur naturally to the developer at this stage will help in the informal definition of the actions. Extra attributes can be added later, especially during the function steps.

Describe the time constraints between the actions by one or more structure diagrams for each entity. The entity is the root component of a structure diagram, and the actions are the leaves. Extra entities may be added to the list if there are time constraints between actions that cannot be expressed in terms of the existing entities. The action and entity lists may be further refined as a result of drawing these structures.

Documentation Output.

Candidate lists of actions and entities with reasons for rejection.

Final lists of actions and entities.

Action descriptions with associated attributes.

Entity/action cross reference.

At least one structure diagram for each entity.

Hints/Comments. The following are some reasons a verb may be removed from the action list. A candidate action may be one of the following:

(1) Outside the model boundary. We use the term "outside the model boundary" for actions and entities that are deliberately excluded from the abstraction of the subject matter. They could be actions or entities in another system but not in the one under consideration.

(2) A system output, that is, something the system does, not something in the subject matter of the system.

(3) The state of an entity, rather than the action of an entity.

(4) The verb form of a noun that is or should be in the entity list.

(5) The synonym of another action.

There are many variations on the basic reason for rejecting an entity, which is, that it does not perform or suffer an interesting sequence of actions. The following are some more detailed reasons a noun may be removed from the entity list. A candidate entity may be one of the following:

(1) A system output.

(2) Outside the model boundary.

(3) An implementation feature of the current system.

(4) The noun form of a verb that is or should be in the action list.

(5) A collective term, perhaps of entities, that has no actions of its own.

(6) A synonym of another entity.

(7) A term that describes part of the life of another entity or that describes only some of the instances of an entity.

(8) An attribute of some action.

(9) A noun that may later become the local variable of an entity process as a result of imposing or embedding a function.

(10) A time period associated with the function or the implementation of the system or with part of the life of some entity.

Two candidate entities may be replaced by a single entity if they have the same structures of the same actions. For example, if the candidate entities "car" and "truck" have the same structures, they may be replaced by the single entity "vehicle". Two actions may be replaced by a single action, if there are no time constraints on one of the actions that do not also apply to the other.

Often more than one structure is necessary to describe the time constraints on the actions of an entity. Sometimes, to describe the time constraints fully, the same action must appear in more than one structure diagram.

4.2.2 Initial Model Step

Concise Statement. The purpose of this and the next step is to realise the abstraction defined in the previous step as a set of processes within the system. We call these processes "the realised model".

There must be an input to the realised model for each action in the model. In the initial model step, the actions are divided into two types, those that correspond to events (employee goes sick, employee clocks on) that are genuinely external to the system and those that are to be generated automatically by the system (perhaps adding the interest to an account). In the initial model step, a connection is defined between the external reality and the realised model so that inputs to the realised model are created when external actions happen. In the next JSD step, the interactive function step, processes are defined to generate inputs for the second type of action.

The realised model is the basis of the specification and will be a central part of the final implementation.

General Description. Input is collected for external actions to synchronise and coordinate the realised model with the external reality. When the real employee goes sick, the employee process in the realised model gets an input that enables it to remain an accurate and up-to-date model of the real employee.

If all actions are externally generated, the realised model is purely a reflection of the external reality. If all the actions are internally generated, the system will be a simulation of the model defined in the first step.

The connection between the external reality and the realised model will probably be error-prone. At best, extra error-handling software must be specified to filter out input errors and to make the connection between the external reality and the realised model more reliable. At worst, we may have to recognise that the desired model cannot be realised, and we have to amend it to something that can.

A model may be unrealisable for many reasons: perhaps an action in the external world cannot be detected, or cannot be detected economically; perhaps the data-collection system does not preserve the ordering of inputs for two actions; or perhaps an action cannot be detected without also picking up spurious inputs that do not refer to genuine actions. Extra software can detect most, but not all, of the spurious inputs. For example, in a banking system, error-handling software cannot detect the mis-typing of an account number that unluckily results in the perfectly acceptable account number of another customer. There must be extra (managerial) actions that can compensate for these errors. If the model does not already include these actions, it must be amended so that it does.

Detailed Procedure. We use the term "level-0" model for the abstraction of the external world and the term "level-1" model for the processes in the realised model. Thus we use the suffixes "-0" and "-1" to distinguish a particular external process, for example, the abstraction of the real employee, from the realised process in the system that models the employee.

For each external action in the model, work out in principle how that action can be detected in the external world. (This may be easy. Each action may be associated with writing out a document of some kind or with the use of some piece of equipment whose operation can be directly detected by the computer.)

Where an action is common to two or more structure diagrams in the model, define a way of replicating the input for that action so that each process in the realised model that contains the action gets an input.

If the model cannot be realised, elaborate or amend it to one that can.

Define error-handling processes to filter out the spurious inputs that can be detected. Use JSP to define these processes fully.

Use JSP to design programs such as data-entry programs that fit in the input subsystem between the level-0 and the level-1 processes.

(There is room for further refinement in the detailed JSD procedure for defining the input subsystem, which contains the main interface with the user.)

Documentation Output.

Possible revision of the earlier documentation if the model needs amendment.

An SSD (system specification diagram) showing the connections between the external reality and the realised model, including the extra processes that have been introduced to filter errors and replicate input.

Structure diagrams and text for the extra processes. (The detailed construction of the extra processes may be delayed or done in parallel with the later function steps, which depend on the fact that the model can be realised, not on exactly how it will be realised.)

Hints/Comments. There are two possible patterns for the replication of inputs of actions that appear in more than one structure. One is to have separate input subsystem processes that distribute and replicate the records. The other is to allow one level-1 process to write records to another (see Figure 4.2a).

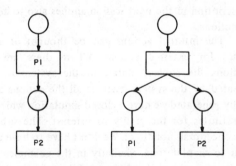

Figure 4.2a

Sometimes the input record for an action does not need to contain information identifying the action, or information identifying it fully. Figure 4.2b is a model of traffic lights. Because the next action is always determined, the records of F need only be timing signals. They don't need to identify the action that has occurred.

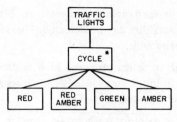

Figure 4.2b

Sometimes the connection between level-0 and level-1 is by state vector inspection. (See the Lift system in the reprinted paper, "Two Pairs of Examples ...", for an example.) An existing system can form part of the external world for a new system, and this can also lead to state vector connections between level-0 and level-1.

4.2.3 Interactive Function Step

Concise Statement. Extra processes are added to the specification to generate inputs for the internally generated actions. Together the initial model step and the interactive function step realise the abstraction defined in step one as a set of processes within the system.

General Description. Sometimes actions can be internally generated without interaction with the model. For example, in a pure simulation, inputs for some actions may be created by an independent random number generator.

In most cases the timing, the identity, and the attributes of the generated actions depend on information in the realised model. Interactive functions are just like information functions except that, instead of producing outputs, they generate inputs that help to realise the model. Everything in the information function step description in the next session applies also to interactive functions.

The internal actions can be thought of as substitutes for external actions. Where there are internal actions the subject matter of the system is, in part, created by the system itself. If all the actions are internally generated we have a closed simulation which totally substitutes for the reality of interest. The substitution is conceptual, not direct. We don't have to have a nuclear war to simulate one. Similarly in the examples of interactive functions in Section 4.4.3 we may define the internal actions ALLOCATE (Widget Warehouse system) and RESET (Lift system) without there ever existing a reality in which they are external.

A JSD developer does not have to analyse the question, "Why did this external action happen?". The initial model step establishes a connection that allows the system to know an action has happened and, therefore, also to synchronise and coordinate a realised model of the external reality.

Of course an external action may happen partly because of the outputs of the system. A lift may move upwards because the Lift system sent a stimulus to the motor. You may pay a bill because an accounting system sent you a reminder. But the distinction must be made very carefully between an output which is intended to cause an event and the event itself. Safety systems, in particular, depend on the distinction. Perhaps a safety mechanism has to be activated because an output was sent to the motor and the lift has not moved.

In contrast, the developer is concerned with the reasons internally generated actions happen. The reasons are precisely defined by the interactive function processes. There can also be no argument over whether an internal action has happened. If the system says it has happened, then it is deemed to have happened. That is the consequence of having the system create part of its own subject matter.

The relationships between level-0 objects, the model, interactive functions, and information functions are illustrated in Figure 4.2c. The dotted lines show the influences on the behaviour of level-0 objects; these influences are not the concern of the developer. The diagram is schematic. In a real system there are many

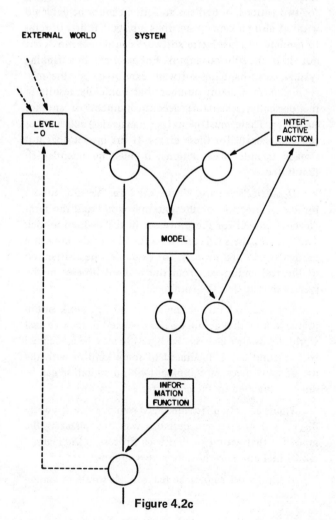

Figure 4.2c

processes of each type, and the connections are not all by simple data streams.

Detailed Procedure. For each action to be internally generated, ask "When should this action be generated?" The answer may be in terms of other model actions or in terms of external input. Often several different actions have the same answer to this question; they are generated by the same interactive function process. Ask also what information must be extracted from the model to decide which actions should be generated and what should be the values of their attributes. This will help to establish the nature of the connection between the interactive function process and the realised model processes. Just as for information functions (see Section 4.2.4), the specification of the function process can be completed using JSP.

Documentation Output. Exactly the same as that for information functions.

Hints/Comments. An information function may examine the state of a model process to supply output. Almost certainly, state vector connection is appropriate. Often an interactive function must generate an action for a model process that depends on the state of the model. If state vector connection is not appropriate because it is too loose, communication between the processes must be by conversational exchange of messages on two data streams.

Sometimes part of the model is used by interactive functions and not at all by information functions. There is a danger some of this part of the model may be missed on the first attempt.

4.2.4 Information Function Step

Concise Statement. Extra processes are added to the specification to extract information from the model processes by data stream and state vector connection and to calculate the required outputs.

General Description. The outputs of the system are finally included in the specification. The requirement for a system output can always be expressed in the general form

"When x,y,z happens, output a,b,c".

The "a,b,c" must be expressible at least indirectly in terms of the model. The model defines the subject matter of the system as agreed to with the user, so it is important that the outputs can be defined in terms of this model. The quantity on a paycheck output from the system must be definable in terms of the actions of the model and their attributes. The definitions of the actions and their attributes are the foundations on which the whole specification is built.

The "x,y,z" may be expressible in terms of the model, in which case the stimulus for the output will come from a data stream output by the model. Alternatively, the "x,y,z" may be the input of an enquiry record, in which case the stimulus does not come from the model, and the likely connection with the model is by state vector inspection. Considering the "x,y,z" helps establish the way new function processes are connected to model processes.

Just as the listed operations in JSP are chosen from whatever language is going to be used, so also in the function steps of JSD the developer is free to define function processes in any appropriate language. In particular, special-purpose languages like report generators and screen formatters may be used for some of the functions.

Detailed Procedure. For each required stream of output, analyse which processes in the model contain the necessary information and what type of connection (state vector or data stream) is appropriate for extracting it. Tentatively assume that a single function process is all that is needed, and define data stream and state vector connections from the model processes to the function process. Use JSP to complete the specification of the function process. A JSP data structure can be drawn of the stream of state vectors resulting from a state vector connection. In many cases, the function process must be decomposed into several processes as a result of JSP structure clashes.

Documentation Output. In JSD, functions are highly independent one from another. For each function the documentation consists of

> an SSD showing the extra function processes, their connections with the model processes, and their connections with each other;

> elaboration of the model process documentation (structure diagram with operations allocated and list of operations) to show extra local variables and calculations used for embedded output or to hold information for state vector inspection;

> the structure and text of the extra function processes; and

> a concise statement of access paths on state vectors defined by the function processes.

Hints/Comments. A classification of simple functions follows:

(1) Imposed enquiry function, with only one SV examined per enquiry.

(2) Imposed enquiry function that examines a whole set of state vectors per enquiry. Often the input stimuli

to these function processes are regular, for example, each day or each week.

(3) Embedded output directly from the model, with no new process needed.

(4) Embedded output gathered together from many instances of a single entity type and read by a process that produces the function output. Almost always the function process consumes a rough-merged stream of marker records to divide the output into reports.

(5) An extra process is needed for each entity instance, to describe some more complicated structure for at least some of the entity actions. The process may or may not have an extra rough-merged input stream of marker records.

(6) The extra processes as in (5) may have their embedded output gathered together and further processed as in (4).

(7) The extra processes as in (5) may have their state vector examined as in (1) or (2).

(8) The function may be connected to more than one entity type, thus permitting all variety of combinations of the above.

There are examples of most of these types of functions in Chapter 4.3.

4.2.5 System Timing Step

Concise Statement. In the system timing step, timing constraints are expressed that must be satisfied in the implementation step.

General Description. The output of the previous development steps is a network of processes communicating by buffered data streams and by state vector inspection. This specification is incomplete in that it contains nothing about the desired speed of execution of the various components of the system.

The following examples of requirements statements all imply constraints on the speed of execution of the specification processes.

(1) The response to a given input must occur within x seconds. This implies a complicated constraint on the partial execution of (potentially) a whole chain of processes.

(2) The information in the response to a given input must be no more than y hours out of date. A state vector connection implies an inherent arbitrariness in how up to date the information is that is accessed. However, we may wish to impose some overall constraints. The constraints are effectively on the speed of execution of the processes in the input subsystem

between the level-0 reality and the level-1 process and on the implementation of the state vector connection.

(3) Level-1 processes that are connected to their level-0 real-world entities by state vector connection must execute "get SV" operations with a certain minimum frequency.

(4) The rough-merges in the specification may need to be specified more accurately, or at least the unfairness of the merging may need to be limited, to ensure that today's report contains all of today's embedded output.

In the present state of JSD, most of the constraints are specified informally. Where a constraint is specified more formally, extra time marker streams are introduced as input to processes. The time marker streams are written by special clock processes. There are extra constraints on the buffering of these time marker streams; probably there needs to be zero buffering.

The problem is not so much finding a way to specify these timing constraints more formally; rather it is finding a pathway to an implementation in which the formally expressed timing constraints are preserved. Everything else in a JSD specification is preserved in the final implementation by the transformations in the implementation phase.

Detailed Procedure. For each output stream, define constraints on the speed of the output and how up to date the information in the output has to be. For each input stream, define the constraints on the input subsystem that must be satisfied to ensure that all the input is collected and all necessary orderings are preserved.

Documentation Output. A set of informal timing constraints on the implementation step.

4.2.6 The Implementation Step

Concise Statement. The purpose of the implementation step is to fit the specification developed in the previous steps to the target hardware/software environment so that it runs efficiently enough and meets the performance constraints defined in the system timing step. The main issues in a JSD implementation are the scheduling of the processes in the specification, the transformation of specification processes, and the organisation of the storage of the state vectors of processes.

General Description. The three main issues in implementation have been described in Sections 4.1.3, 4.1.4 and 4.1.5.

In practice a further issue is the use that can be made of available general-purpose software. A database

166

query language may be used to implement directly a set of access paths defined by function processes. An operating system or a teleprocessing monitor may ease the implementation by making available many virtual processors.

Detailed Procedure. The detailed procedure in implementation is more difficult to specify than it is for other steps because of the very wide range of target environments and the wide range of different criteria that might be the most critical.

Here is a commonly used, but not universal, ordering of implementation decisions.

(1) Allocate processes in the specification to the available (possibly virtual) processors. If there is more than one processor, deduce from the specification the interfaces between the processors.

(2) For each processor that has more than one process assigned, there must be a scheduler to run the processes. For each scheduler, define transformations on the specified processes to be scheduled, so that they can be invoked easily by the scheduler.

(3) Specify each scheduler by drawing its structure and then listing and allocating operations as in JSP.

(4) Analyse the access paths on the state vectors defined by the function processes and use them as the basis for a file or database design.

(5) Elaborate the function processes or add extra processes for access paths not directly realised by the file or database design.

(6) Do the transformations on the specified programs that have been specified in (2), and express the result in the programming language.

(7) Do the same for the schedulers that have been introduced and designed in (3), expressing the result in programming language, Job Control Language (JCL) and operator instructions.

Documentation Output. Whatever the detailed ordering of decisions in implementation, this step is a progression of transformations on the specification, accompanied by the specification of extra implementation-framework software. The transformations are documented by SIDs (System Implementation Diagrams) and by the results of the transformations. (SID notations for inversion and dismemberment were introduced in Section 4.1.3.) The result of a chain of transformations is code of the finished system.

Extra implementation processes are documented as in JSP: by structure diagrams, lists of operations, and diagrams with operations allocated and structure text. If they too undergo transformations, there will be more SIDs. The result of these transformations will be the program code, JCL, and operator instructions of the final system.

Hints/Comments. We may distinguish between the ordering and organisation of decisions that are imposed by a method and the actual making of the decisions. During the specification steps, the distinction is between the user who is deciding what system he wants and the developer who is guiding the decisions and formally writing them down. Sometimes the same person plays both roles and therefore needs to be doubly clear about the distinction between them.

In the implementation step the same person or group usually acts as both decision organiser and decision taker (an exception is the specialised database designer). JSD may dictate that now a scheduling decision must be taken, but the calculation of the trade-off between storage and execution time necessary to make the decision is not part of JSD. Here, too, the distinction between the roles must be kept clear.

Many of the processes in the specification may be tested before they are transformed. This is particularly useful for model processes because it allows many years of the system's execution to be tested.

An organised approach to testing involves adding extra processes to generate input for what would otherwise be external actions and external functional input, thus turning the whole system into a simulation. Usually these extra processes are noninteractive and are scheduled separately to produce the familiar "test data files", but there is no reason why this must be so.

Chapter 4.3   The Widget Warehouse Company

4.3.1   Entity/Action and Entity Structure Step

The first of the following two items is an introductory description of the Widget Warehouse Company. A problem area is described. Although there is some indication of the area that is to be the focus of attention, this description could hardly be called a specification. It is, however, an appropriate starting point for JSD.

The second item gives more information about the Widget Warehouse Company and sets up a specific exercise: to build a model (any model) that is reasonably consistent with the given information.

The Widget Warehouse Company

The Widget Warehouse Company is less specialized than its name suggests. In addition to widgets, it deals also in gadgets, fidgets, flanges, grommets, and many other products which its customers find indispensable. Some of the products are even manufactured or assembled in the company's workshops.

The company's customers order these products from the company, often by telephone but sometimes by other means such as mail or a personal visit to the company's warehouse. There is a company rule that separate orders are required for separate products. The customers are happy with this rule, because few customers have a use for more than one of the products: a dedicated user of widgets is unlikely to find a purpose for gadgets or flanges.

Customers sometimes amend their orders, changing the quantity or the requested delivery date. Occasionally, a customer may cancel an order.

Within the company, operational responsibility is divided between the director looking after the manufacture, assembly, external supply, and storage of the products and the director of marketing who is responsible for everything to do with customers. These two directors are not on speaking terms. Their animosity is a byword within the company, and the ramifications of their feud occupy many hours of contented speculation in the canteen and in the public houses nearby. For a while it seemed that any new computer system would have to deal exclusively with one or the other's area of responsibility. But then people remembered that one of the suggested uses of the new system would be to help plan production schedules by supplying information not just about the warehouse inventory but also about outstanding orders. Distressingly often, stock levels have been too low to meet customers' orders, and there has been plenty of mutual recrimination as a result.

At the moment the company employs a clerk, whose job is to deal with the customers and to allocate the available stock to outstanding orders. This clerk has access to information about the available stock of each product. He can telephone the warehouse to ask how much of any product is currently in the associated warehouse location. This enquiry is usually answered with reasonable reliability.

At the warehouse there is another clerk who records the issue of a batch of products from the warehouse; the receipt of a delivery by the warehouse from the workshops or from an outside supplier; the introduction of a new product; and occasionally, the effects of fire, flood, bacteria, insects, and metal fatigue on the precious fidgets, grommets, and other products.

Both directors have grandiose plans for the new system. The marketing director dreams of a huge system keeping track of all his contacts and customers, generating mailshots, action lists for his salesmen, cost effectiveness graphs for his advertisements, invoices for his customers, and much more besides. The other director feels that life would be much easier if the system could supply him with information about the complete production process from the ordering of materials and sub-assemblies from external suppliers, through the assembly and manufacturing processes in the workshops, to the storage of the finished product in the warehouse.

Widget Warehouse Company—Modelling (1)

The managing director of the company, who is an accountant, has decreed that the first version of this system should not be overambitious. He has also said that the designers should concentrate on those activities of the company close to the boundary of the two warring directors' areas of responsibility. He has observed that the company is least efficient in matters requiring the cooperation of the two directors, and therefore most in need of data-processing assistance.

Certainly the marketing department will need information about stock levels so that it can allocate stock to orders, and the manufacturing department will need information about outstanding orders so that it can plan

Portions of this Chapter are excerpted from previously unpublished Michael Jackson Systems Limited (MJSL) internal documents with permission from MJSL.

its production schedules. The managing director was overheard to remark, "If they won't tell each other what is going on, at least they'll be able to get some information from this computer system".

Some further investigation reveals that at present the clerk responsible for allocating stock to orders makes a list each day of the orders due for delivery the next day or of those already overdue. After checking with the warehouses about the stock levels, he takes each order and either allocates stock to it or delays it. When an order is delayed, he normally contacts the customer to explain the situation. When an order is allocated, the product will normally be delivered the next day.

On the whole, overdue orders are given priority over other orders, but the clerk has assured us that the decisions he makes in allocating stock to orders are so complex and so subtle that we cannot hope to automate them.

Bearing in mind the managing director's comments, carry out the entity/action and entity structure steps of JSD for this system.

Solution

Initial lists.

Entities	Actions
product	place (an order)
customer	amend
workshop	cancel
company	allocate
warehouse	issue (stock)
order	receipt
stock	introduce
clerk	write off
	delay
	deliver
	contact (customer)

We have decided (tentatively) to use product instead of widget, flange, etc., and to use write off instead of be burnt, eaten by insects, etc.

Activities concerned with salesmen and marketing activity have been ruthlessly excluded. So has everything to do with widget assembly and grommet manufacture.

After more analysis we decide on the following definitions:

Entities

product	a synonym of stock
customer	outside the model boundary (omb) for this system. The actions of a customer are also actions of order.
workshop	omb. We are not concerned with what happens to a product before it arrives in the warehouse.
company	no actions of company. a collective.
warehouse	again no actions. a collective.
order	selected
stock	selected
clerk	omb. Many of his actions would also be actions of order

Actions

place	action of order. Customers place orders. attributes: product-id, quantity, customer, requested delivery date, ...
amend	change the requested date or quantity of an order; product-id cannot be changed. action of order. attributes: code, new quantity of date, ...
cancel	action of order. attributes: ...
allocate	allocate product stock to order. action of order; could also be action of stock, but we choose to exclude allocation from our view of stock. attributes: quantity, ...
issue	issue quantity of stock from warehouse. action of stock attributes: quantity, vehicle no, ...
receipt	action of stock attributes: quantity, who from, ...
write off	any spoilage of stock while in warehouse action of stock attributes: quantity, reason, ...
introduce	new product in warehouse action of stock attributes: ...
delay	delay an order because stock is not available for it to be allocated. action of order attributes: ...
deliver	deliver ordered product to customer. action of order; could also be action of stock, but we choose to exclude it.
contact	omb. especially as both customer and clerk are omb as entities.

Entity Structures

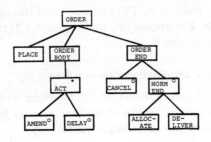

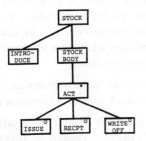

Comments on the Solution

The managing director's comment shows some insight into the nature of data-processing systems. He plans to circumvent the lack of direct communication between the directors by giving each access to a model of the other's area of responsibility.

The model in the solution certainly cannot be deduced from the information in the three pages of application description and problem statement. It is the technical documentation of the first step of a JSD development that has been written down by a developer as a result of problem area input supplied by the user organisation. This model is (approximately) the smallest imaginable consistent with the given description.

The implications of excluding an action are clear. No input will be collected for that action, and no function will be able to produce information that depends on knowledge of that action. Thus the decision to exclude actions referring to the manufacture of the stock items means that the system cannot be a production-control system.

All the actions of ORDER take place within the marketing director's area of responsibility. The actions of STOCK are the responsibility of the production director.

To ALLOCATE an order is not to take stock out of the warehouse; it is to decide that stock in the warehouse is to be used to meet that order. We might presume that as a result of an ALLOCATE there is an ISSUE of stock from the warehouse and subsequently a DELIVER

to the customer. Such presumption concerns the reasons actions happen and is strictly outside the model boundary. The model does not exclude the ALLOCATION of an order and the subsequent DELIVERY of the order from stock held somewhere other than our warehouse.

The action DELAY needs further explanation. Each day a clerk must either DELAY or ALLOCATE each order that is due or overdue. An order for which there is no stock for a period will therefore be repeatedly DELAYed.

The other actions have the obvious meaning.

An alternative model might redefine ISSUE so that it is an action of both STOCK and ORDER and not just an arbitrary output of stock from the warehouse. Why was this alternative model not chosen? Perhaps it was rejected because the company wanted the simplest, cheapest system; perhaps because the marketing director refused to accept that anything under the control of the other director should be an action of one of his ORDERs.

Choosing the simpler model means that only a smaller set of functions can be supported. We cannot have outputs to tell us whether allocated-but-not-yet-delivered ORDERs have had stock taken out of the warehouse for them. Also, because ISSUEs are not associated with ORDERs, we have no way of knowing how much of the remaining STOCK has been allocated to ORDERs.

The exclusion of customer and clerk from the entity list also has implications for the range of functions the model can support. By excluding customer as an entity, we are deciding that there is nothing interesting about a customer except that, as an attribute of PLACE, he is associated with the ORDERs he makes and that he is under no time constraints except those expressed in the ORDER structure. These decisions are made by the user with the guidance of the developer. They delimit the scope of the system.

"Widgets" is one instance of STOCK; "grommets" is another. An individual widget is not an instance of STOCK. The attribute of ISSUE, QTY is the number of widgets issued. The structure of ORDER implies that an AMEND or a CANCEL cannot happen after an ALLOCATE, nor can a DELAY happen after a CANCEL. When we consider the initial model step, we shall see that this implies that AMEND inputs that follow an ALLOCATE input must be filtered out by error-handling software; it cannot refer to a real AMEND.

There needs to be a local variable in the stucture to express the constraint that the sum of the quantities of the RECPTs must exceed the sum of the quantities of the ISSUEs and the WRITE OFFs. This is an example of a constraint that cannot easily be expressed by a structure diagram. We add a local variable to the structure and express the constraint informally by a note referring to the values of the local variable. Here the variable is STOCK-LEVEL, and the constraint is that it must always be nonnegative. (In real stock-control systems this constraint is not usually imposed.)

4.3.2 Initial Model and Interactive Function Steps

The Widget Warehouse Company has real customers who PLACE, AMEND, and CANCEL real ORDERs. There is a real warehouse where real STOCK is ISSUED, RECEIVED, and WRITTEN OFF. Unless we have chosen to build a simulation of the company, almost all the actions are external-world actions detected by collecting input from the external world. The only possible exceptions are DELAY and ALLOCATE. Because the clerks have assured us that the decisions made in allocating stock are too subtle to be computerised, we will assume for the moment that these actions are also external-world actions, performed on the ORDERs by the clerks.

Since all the actions are external-world actions, the interactive function step is null.

For this first run through the development of the system, we will assume, reasonably, that there is no difficulty creating an input record for each action in the model, and we will assume, unreasonably, that this can be done with perfect accuracy without introducing extra spurious input or reordering input for an individual STOCK item or ORDER. By assuming a perfect data-collection system, the initial model step is effectively null. We shall return to the problem of error handling in Section 4.4.2.

The diagram in Figure 4.3a is an SSD (System Specification Diagram) for the realised model. The level-0 processes are the abstractions of the real STOCK and the real ORDER. The level-1 processes are inside the system and have the same structure as the level-0 abstractions. They are synchronised and coordinated with their real-world counterparts by data stream connection.

There is one ORDER-0 and one ORDER-1 process per order and one STOCK-0 and one STOCK-1 process per stock item. The notation is not rich enough to show this. The double bars (see Section 4.1.2) refer to relative multiplicity.

4.3.3 Information Function Step

In the solution to the following function exercise, Functions (1), two of the functions are fully developed and two are described in outline only.

Widget Warehouse Company—Functions (1)

Show on an SSD how each of the following functions may be specified and where new processes are involved; draw their structure to whatever level of detail is known. Note also what extra local variables are needed within the model processes.

1. The clerk wants to be able to make simple enquiries about the stock level of a particular product.

2. He also wants to be able to specify a product and be given a list of the orders for that product that are due for delivery the next day or are already overdue, as well as a total quantity needed to satisfy these orders.

3. He wants a simple printed acknowledgement to be sent to a customer when he places an order.

4. He wants a daily list to be sent to the warehouse of all the allocations made for delivery the next day. The format of the daily list is to be specified by the warehouse foreman and will fit the sequence in which he picks the products from the various parts of the warehouse.

Widget Warehouse Company—Functions (1) Solution

1. Ad hoc enquiries on stock level.

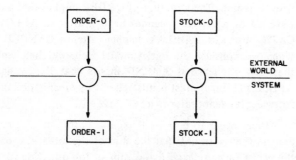

Figure 4.3a

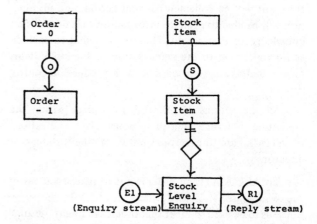

Data Structures:

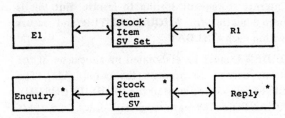

Program Structure:

```
        ┌──────────┐
        │  Stock   │
        │  Level   │
        │ Enquiry  │
        └────┬─────┘
             │
        ┌────┴─────┐
        │  C-Enq  *│
        │ P-Reply  │
        └──────────┘
```

Operations:

1. write 'Stock level for', STOCK-ID 'is', STOCK-LEVEL
2. get STOCKSV (STOCK-ID)
3. read E1

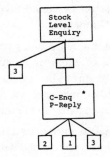

Text:

```
      SLE seq
         read E1;
         SLE-BODY itr (forever)
            get STOCKSV (STOCK-ID);
            write 'Stock level for', STOCK-ID, 'is',
                  STOCK-LEVEL;
            read E1;
         SLE-BODY end
      SLE end
```

Note: The state vector of Stock Item must have STOCK-LEVEL
      as a local variable. The model process is now:-

```
      SI-1 seq
         read S;
         STOCK-LEVEL: = INTRO-QTY;
         read S;
         STOCK-BODY itr (forever)
            ACTION set (ISSUE)
               STOCK-LEVEL: = STOCK-LEVEL-ISSUE-QTY;
               read S;
            ACTION alt (RECEIPT)
               STOCK-LEVEL: = STOCK-LEVEL+REC-QTY;
               read S;
            ACTION alt (WRITE-OFF)
               STOCK-LEVEL: = STOCK-LEVEL-WO-QTY;
               read S;
            ACTION end
         STOCK-BODY end
      SI-1 end
```

2. List of orders to be delivered on the next day or overdue for delivery, plus the total quantity of stock needed:

SSD:

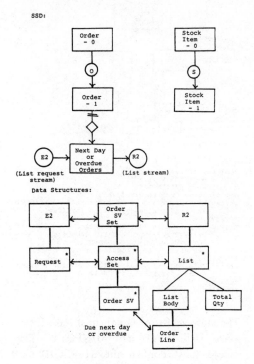

Data Structures:

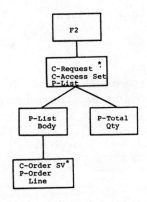

Due next day or overdue

Program Structure:

```
              ┌──────────┐
              │    F2    │
              └────┬─────┘
                   │
         ┌─────────┴──────────┐
         │  C-Request       * │
         │  C-Access Set      │
         │  P-List            │
         └─────────┬──────────┘
             ┌─────┴──────┐
        ┌────┴────┐  ┌────┴────┐
        │ P-List  │  │ P-Total │
        │  Body   │  │   Qty   │
        └────┬────┘  └─────────┘
             │
        ┌────┴──────┐
        │ C-Order SV*│
        │ P-Order    │
        │ Line       │
        └───────────┘
```

Operations:

1. write 'Total quantity needed for tomorrows & overdue orders for item', STOCK-ID, 'is', TOT-QTY
2. write 'List of orders to be delivered', TOMORROW, 'and orders overdue for item', STOCK-ID
3. write ORDER-ID, DUE-DATE, ORD-QTY
4. TOT-QTY: = 0
5. TOT-QTY: = TOT-QTY+ORD-QTY
6. get first SV from required set
7. get next SV from required set
8. TODAY: = SYSTEM-DATE
9. TOMORROW: = SYSTEM-DATE + 1
10. read E2

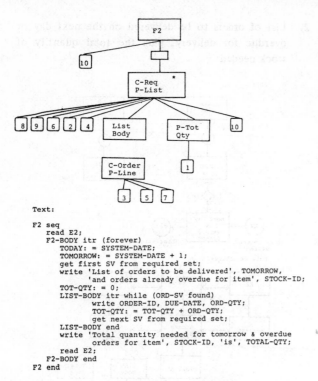

```
Text:

F2 seq
   read E2;
   F2-BODY itr (forever)
      TODAY: = SYSTEM-DATE;
      TOMORROW: = SYSTEM-DATE + 1;
      get first SV from required set;
      write 'List of orders to be delivered', TOMORROW,
            'and orders already overdue for item', STOCK-ID;
      TOT-QTY: = 0;
      LIST-BODY itr while (ORD-SV found)
            write ORDER-ID, DUE-DATE, ORD-QTY;
            TOT-QTY: = TOT-QTY + ORD-QTY;
            get next SV from required set;
      LIST-BODY end
      write 'Total quantity needed for tomorrow & overdue
            orders for item', STOCK-ID, 'is', TOTAL-QTY;
      read E2;
   F2-BODY end
F2 end
```

Notes: The state vector of Order must have local variables DUE-DATE and ORD-QTY. The E2 record must contain the STOCK-ID used to select the orders to appear on the list.

3.

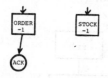

Unusually, no extra process is needed to specify this function. The detail of the acknowledgement may need some extra attributes of PLACE and hence extra local variables of ORDER-1.

4.

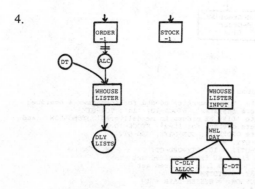

Only the upper part of the input data structure of WHOUSE LISTER is shown. There may well be an

ordering clash within each day which requires considerable internal storage or sorting to resolve. But this is an internal matter for WHOUSE LISTER and occurs only within each WHLDAY.

ORDER-1 must be elaborated by allocation of the operations needed to produce the output ALC. The DLYLISTS will certainly need the PROD-ID, CUST-ID, and QUANTITY for each allocated order, and these will have to be local variables of ORDER-1. According to the detail of the final output, there may need to be some others as well.

Comments on the Solution

The four functions illustrate, respectively, a function with state vector connection that makes one state vector access per enquiry, a function with state vector connection that makes many state vector accesses per enquiry, a function whose output can be directly produced by embedding write operations in the realised model, and a function that gathers together and further processes data streams that are output from the model.

Functions that have only data stream connection with the model are called "embedded" functions. Functions that have only state vector connection with the model are called "imposed" functions.

Each function process is a long-running process that answers the whole stream of enquiries or outputs the whole set of daily lists to be sent to the warehouse. Each process in a JSD specification only executes once. Each function can be added independently to the model.

Function processes may require extra attributes of model actions. They may also require the definition of local variables of the model processes. The first function needs the QTY attribute of ISSUE, RECPT, and WRITE OFF and the STOCK-LEVEL local variable. STOCK-LEVEL is defined in terms of the QTY attributes: STOCK-LEVEL is the cumulative sum of the RECPT QTYs and the negative ISSUE and WRITE OFF QTYs. Definitions like this are entered into the user/developer glossary. Only words defined in terms of the actions and their attributes may be used to describe functions. (In fact the QTY attribute had already been defined; so had STOCK-LEVEL, to express an extra constraint on the ordering of actions.)

PLACE is given the attributes PROD-ID, QTY, and DUE-DATE, and AMEND is given the attributes QTY and DUE-DATE. Probably PLACE also needs the attributes CUST-ID and perhaps also CUST-ADDRESS. Notice that although CUSTOMER was rejected as a JSD entity in this system, it may still appear as the attribute of some actions.

Information in the text pointer of a process may be duplicated by the introduction of local variables. These variables may be examined (when the state vector is inspected) instead of the text pointer, whose implementation may be obscure.

Each state vector connection with the model defines an access path through the state vectors. Over its lifetime the first function process accesses many STOCK state vectors in random order. Direct access of STOCK state vectors is assumed in the STOCK LEVEL ENQUIRY process. In the second function process, the access path is over all due or overdue orders for a random iteration of products. In the implementation step, these access paths must be realised either directly or indirectly.

If it is known that a particular database query language is to be used, then imposed functions may be expressed directly in terms of this query language and its full power may be exploited. In the absence of a given query language, JSD sets a default for the type of state vector accessing available for the definition of function processes. The default is that any set of state vectors specifiable in terms of constraints on the values of their constituent variables may be accessed in any order specifiable by using the constituent variables as sort keys. The text pointer is one of the constituent variables. The others are added during the function steps and may be added specifically to define access paths.

For example, we can access all orders with a given value of the PROD-ID local variable that have not yet been allocated or cancelled and whose local variable DUE-DATE is less than the current date, and we may do so in ascending order of QTY within CUST-ID. However, we may not access using set properties. Thus if we want all the orders of all the customers who have placed more than ten orders, we have to access more than just these.

The various ALC data streams are rough-merged with each other and with the marker stream DT as they are input to WHOUSE LISTER. The DT stream has the effect of dividing the merged ALC stream into groups, probably daily groups. WHOUSE LISTER needs these markers to delimit the input for each daily list. The rough-merging is perfectly acceptable in the specification; an allocation falling near the boundary of two days may appear on either daily list.

If the orders on a daily list have to appear in a particular order (for example, if the daily list is a picking list for the warehouse), then the reordering is internal to the WHOUSE LISTER process. There are never sort programs in SSDs because all specification processes are long-running, and sorts can only sensibly apply to parts of SSD data streams. In this case the sort component

(if a sort component is used) will appear inside the WHL DAY component of WHOUSE LISTER. (In the implementation it may appear as a separate program if a particular dismemberment is chosen.)

The function processes specified at this stage are formalisations of the outline descriptions given to the developer by the user.

Note the following different interpretation of the fourth function. Instead of periodic lists of all the ALLOCATions made since the last list, we might have specified the slightly different, imposed function, "On request list all the orders that were allocated today". The difference is that two requests on the same day will produce reports containing (most of) the same orders; that there must be a DATE attribute of the ALLOCATE action; that today's date must be on the request record or otherwise available to the function process; and that, if no request is made one day, then orders ALLOCATED that day will appear on no report. The formal definition of function processes is necessary to avoid this kind of ambiguity.

Here is a second function exercise.

Widget Warehouse Company—More Functions

For each of the following functions,

- draw an SSD showing how the outputs may be produced from the model, either directly or via other function processes;

- where new processes are involved, draw their structure to whatever level of detail is known; and

- list and allocate whatever operations are necessary in the ORDER process to support these functions.

At the end, summarise the contents of the ORDER state vector.

1. A printed apology note to be sent to a customer when his order is delayed.

2. Ad hoc enquiries about a particular order. When the order-id is entered, a screen is displayed with the following information: the order-id; the customer; the product; the quantity; the due date; the delivery address; the status (outstanding, allocated, cancelled, delivered, unknown); the date the order was placed; the original quantity; the original due date; the date of the last amendment (if any); and the values of the quantity, due date, and delivery address before the last amendment.

3. A list of those products and the total quantities that have been ordered by a specified customer and that were delivered during a specified period. The input

transaction contains the customer-id and the first and last dates of the required period.

4. For a specified product, a list of customers who have outstanding orders for that product, the total quantity each customer has outstanding, and the total outstanding quantity for all customers.

5. A weekly report on products whose stock level is less than the sum of the outstanding orders for that product. For each such product, the report should also show the date on which the stock will first be too low to satisfy the orders (assuming no stock receipts) and by how much, and the report should also show the current stock level, the total ordered quantity, and the excess of ordered quantity over stock.

6. The printed apology note in "1." above is only to be sent to a customer the first time his order is delayed after he has placed the order or amended the due date. On any subsequent delays, an apology should not be sent.

7. A periodic report that summarises the orders that have been cancelled or delivered since the last report. The following information is to be listed for each order:

   - customer, product
   - due date and quantity when the order was first placed
   - if cancelled, the date of the cancellation and the number of times the order was delayed
   - if delivered, either a line saying delivered as originally ordered or a line giving the date of delivery and the quantity delivered and another line giving the number of delays.

   The report is to be paginated. The information about an order may be split between pages. Each page header is to contain the number of the report within that year.

Widget Warehouse Company—More Functions Solution

1.

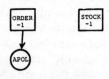

The address of the customer may have to be considered as an attribute of PLACING an order and held as a local variable of ORDER-1, if the address is part of the printed apology.

2.

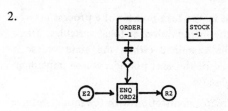

Many local variables have to be introduced into the ORDER-1 processes including one that duplicates information only in the text pointer. Suitable operations are allocated into ORDER-1 to keep the variables up to date, as is shown at the end of this solution.

3.

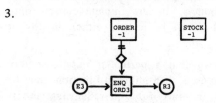

The wording implies that the date an order is delivered must be kept as a local variable of ORDER-1. The PRODs within DATERANGE are those whose delivery date is in the specified range.

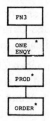

The ORDERs accessed by this function process are only those that contribute to the output lists: the orders for the specified customer which were delivered between the two specified dates. Moreover, they are accessed in product-id sequence.

4.

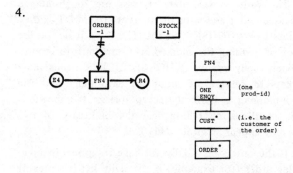

For ONEENQY, the FN4 process examines all the outstanding ORDER SVs for the specified product grouped by cust-id.

5.

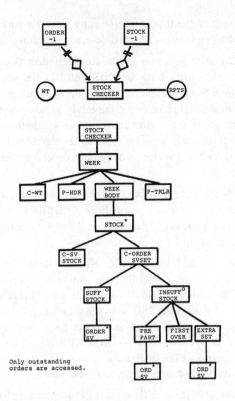

Only outstanding
orders are accessed.

Note the backtracking in the component C-ORDERSV-
SET.

6.

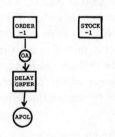

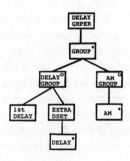

The model should not be complicated by extra structure
needed solely for functional reasons.

The data stream OA contains records of only two types:
DELAY records and AM records written for each
AMEND which changes the due date.

7.

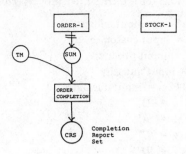

The TM (time marker) stream contains both period
markers, which define the reporting periods, and year-
end markers.

This is a boundary clash within **ORDER COMPLETION**
between **ORDER** and **PAGE** leading to the following
decomposition.

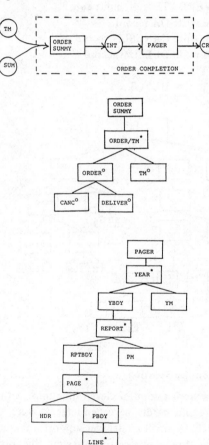

PAGER has a local variable initialised each YEAR and
incremented each report. The value of this variable is
printed on the HDR of every PAGE.

List of operations for the ORDER-1 process

1. read input
2. build & write APOL message

177

List of operations for the ORDER-1 process (*cont*)

3. ADDRESS : = input address
4. CUST : = input customer
5. PROD : = input product
6. QTY : = input quantity
7. DUEDATE : = input due date
8. STATUS : = 'O'
9. STATUS : = 'A'
10. STATUS : = 'C'
11. STATUS : = 'D'
12. PLACE DATE : = input date
13. ORIGQTY : = input quantity
14. ORIGDUEDATE : = input duedate
15. LADATE : = input date
16. LAQTY : = QTY
17. LADUEDATE : = DUEDATE
18. LAADDRESS : = ADDRESS
19. DELIVERDATE : = input date
20. build & write OA record
21. build & write CANCSUM record
22. build & write DELSUM record
23. DLYCT : = O
24. DLYCT : = DLYCT + 1

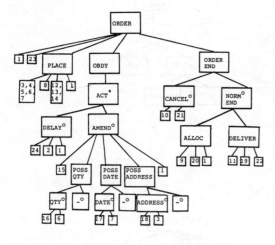

Comments on the Solution

We now have a total of eleven functions. Although the system could hardly be called large, it is no longer trivially small. A small model can support a reasonably sized system. In data-processing systems, the ratio of numbers of model process types (not instances) to function process types is often around one to ten.

Note again how each function process can be defined independently.

The first example is a simple embedded function. The second, third, and fourth examples are all imposed functions on the ORDER processes, each defining a different access path through the ORDER state vectors. The statement of the third function is particularly ambiguous and admits a number of possible interpretations.

The fifth example is the first function that needs information from both ORDER and STOCK processes. Had there been no such functions, the system could have been implemented in two completely separate parts. (In passing, note the following principle of methodology: if two completely separate systems are developed as one, nothing in the development should preclude their later separation.)

The function process for the fifth example, STOCK CHECKER, contains a recognition difficulty that is soluble by backtracking. (See Section 2.3.2 for a description of backtracking.)

We are only interested in STOCK items for which there are excess ORDERS; we are only interested in ORDERs with a PROD-ID for which there is insufficient stock. The default JSD accessing language, described above, does not support an access path through only these state vectors. STOCK CHECKER has to access all the outstanding ORDER state vectors and work out for itself which products have insufficient stock.

Several of the functions refer to "outstanding" orders. What is an outstanding order? From the point of view of a customer, an order is outstanding if it has been PLACED but not yet CANCELLED or DELIVERED. From the point of view of the clerk who is ALLOCATING and DELAYING orders, an order is outstanding if it has been PLACED but not yet CANCELLED or ALLOCATED. One of the strengths of JSD is that it forces the resolution of such ambiguities. In this development, the user said that he meant the second of the two definitions. "Outstanding" is entered into the user/developer glossary with this definition.

The sixth example introduces a new idea, an extra process per ORDER. The function demands an abstraction of ORDER that contains a grouping of DELAY records, a grouping that is necessary only for this function and that is not defined by time constraints on the external-world actions. An extra process type is introduced to define this grouping. The suffix "-2" is used to denote any process that has extra function-oriented structure and is one-to-one with level-0 and level-1 processes. There will therefore be two state vectors for ORDER. They may be stored separately or together.

The seventh function has boundary clash (between ORDER and PAGE) and also a local variable whose value is retained from report to report throughout the year.

As the specification is elaborated to include these functions, extra local variables are added to the ORDER-1 processes. The full ORDER-1 structure with operations allocated is shown at the end of the solution. Most of the extra variables are needed for the second function of this second set. The extra structure below AMEND reflects the assumption that any combination of QTY, DATE, and ADDRESS can be changed on one AMEND.

4.3.4 System Timing and Implementation Steps

In this example we leave out an explicit system timing step. We avoid perverse implementation decisions and assume the timing that results is acceptable.

The following questions cover a range of implementation issues.

Widget Warehouse Company—Implementations Question

The following SSD describes the model and functions developed in the first set of function exercises.

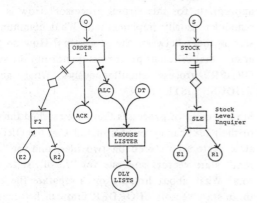

The following diagrams describe a uniprocessor implementation of this system in which the two enquiry processes, F2 and SLE, are run on-line and the ORDER, STOCK, and WHOUSE LISTER processes are run in daily batch. All the processes in the specification are inverted with respect to their single input data stream. The ORDER state vectors are separated and stored on a file that supports direct access by ORDER-ID and indexed sequential access with PROD-ID as the index. The STOCK state vectors are separated and stored on a file that supports direct access by PROD-ID.

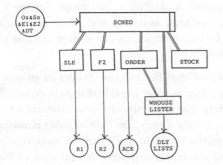

The ORDER processes invoke the WHOUSE LISTER process directly with the ALC records. WHOUSE LISTER is only invoked directly by the scheduler with the DT records.

The ORDER and STOCK state vector files are not shown on this SID. The ORDER state vectors are accessed by F2 to answer enquiries and by the scheduler for passing as a parameter to the inverted ORDER process. Similarly, the STOCK state vectors are accessed by SLE and by the scheduler.

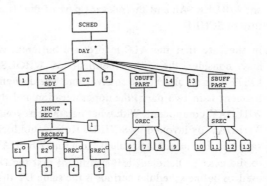

Main operations only

1. read input
2. call SLE (INREC)
3. call F2 (INREC)
4. write INREC to OBUFF
5. write INREC to SBUFF
6. get ORDER-SV (j)
7. call ORDER (OREC, ORDER-SV)
8. put ORDER-SV (j)
9. read OBUFF into OREC
10. get STOCK-SV (j)
11. call STOCK (SREC, STOCK-SV)
12. put STOCK-SV (j)
13. read SBUFF into SREC
14. call WHOUSE LISTER (DT)

Questions.

1. The access methods available on the ORDER SV file are less powerful than those assumed in the function process F2. In what way? What must be added to F2 to compensate?

2. Why is direct access by ORDER-ID required on the ORDER SV file?

3. Suppose that ORDER state vectors are updated by collating the sorted OBUFF with the serially accessed ORDER SV file. Amend the relevant part of the SCHED structure for this case.

4. Suppose the specification is to be implemented on two processors, one for the ORDER processes, F2

and WHOUSE LISTER, the other for the STOCK processes and SLE. What communication is required between the processors? How many schedulers must be designed? Draw the structure of this (these) scheduler(s).

5. Suppose that the ORDER processes write the ALC records directly into a buffer ALCBUFF instead of calling WHOUSE LISTER using them as parameters; SCHED then reads ALCBUFF and invokes WHOUSE LISTER. Draw an SID to describe the new relationships between SCHED, WHOUSE LISTER, and ORDER. Amend the relevant part of the structure of SCHED.

6. In the case that the ALC records are buffered, we may consider the dismemberment of WHOUSE LISTER as an alternative to inversion. The dismemberment is in two parts, the upper iteration and the WHLDAY component. With what parameters would WHLDAY by invoked by SCHED? How would local variables that retain their values from one WHLDAY to the next be handled? Is it significant that the DT used to define scheduler periods is the same DT that is input to WHOUSE LISTER?

7. Is dismemberment an alternative to inversion also for SLE and $F2$?

8. Is dismemberment an alternative to inversion for WHOUSE LISTER if the ALC records are not buffered?

9. Suppose WHOUSE LISTER has the following structure:

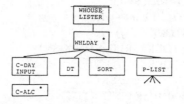

The day's input of ALC records is buffered until the DT arrives, the buffer is sorted, and the list is produced from the sorted buffer. Can WHOUSE LISTER be dismembered into more parts than just WHLDAY and the upper iteration?

10. Consider that SCHED resulting from question 3 above is further amended so that the STOCK state vectors are also updated by collating the serially accessed STOCK SV file. What dismemberment of SCHED leads to the most likely implementation? What happens to the upper iteration of SCHED in this implementation?

11. Suppose that the time markers input to WHOUSE LISTER are weekly, not daily, but that the ORDER processes are still to be executed in daily batch runs. Draw the structure of a suitable scheduler.

12. If $F2$ and SLE are to be executed on one processor and all other processes are on a second processor, what communication must there be between the two machines? Does it make any difference if the two processors are actually virtual processors? Draw suitable schedulers for this arrangement. The specification is changed so that there are n identical instances each of $F2$ and SLE to be run on n processors, making $(n+1)$ processors in all. Amend the scheduler structures as appropriate. What communication is required between the $(n+1)$ processors?

13. In an on-line implementation, each terminal has a virtual processor to run its own version of $F2$ and SLE and to share in the execution of the ORDER and STOCK processes. What scheduler structure is appropriate for this virtual processor? How is this scheduler usually implemented? What communication is there between the processors? How do you ensure that different processors do not run the same ORDER process simultaneously? What about WHOUSE LISTER?

14. State vectors of processes that have reached the end of their text can never be updated. Can the ORDER state vectors be stored on two files, one for "current" state vectors and one for "fossil" state vectors? What about holding on a separate file only those state vectors of ORDER that can be accessed by $F2$, thereby making this access much more efficient?

15. Suppose we want an old-fashioned batch system in which the only access possible on state vector files is serial. Describe the sorts and collates inside a scheduler that runs the ORDER processes and $F2$ on the accumulated input at the end of each day.

16. Five of the function processes defined so far ($F2$ in the first set; FN2, FN3, FN4, and STOCK CHECKER in the second set) inspect the state vectors of the ORDER processes. Summarise the access paths they define.

17. Describe in outline a file design for the ORDER state vectors, assuming that all these functions are to be implemented on-line with reasonable response times.

18. Suppose that the average lifetime of an order is ten days, that most of the ORDER state vectors describe orders that have already been delivered or are cancelled, that a response time of a day is adequate for enquiries input to FN3 and for enquiries input to FN2 on orders delivered or cancelled at least two

weeks previously, and that the other imposed functions must be implemented on-line. For these reasons it has been decided to store old ORDER state vectors separately on an archive file. Outline a possible file design for both the archive file and the current file. You may assume that all the on-line functions and data entry are scheduled on separate virtual processors. This leaves the model processes, the embedded function processes, FN3, and part of FN2 to be run in batch. Draw an SID to show the relationships between a single batch scheduler and these processes. Draw a suitable scheduler structure.

Widget Warehouse Company Implementation Questions —Solutions

1. *F*2 accesses only those state vectors for the relevant PROD-ID that are outstanding and are due or overdue. Indexed sequential access allows serial access of all the state vectors of the relevant PROD-ID. *F*2 can be elaborated so that the extra SVs are read and selected out.

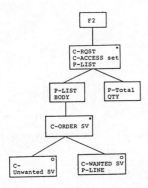

Alternatively, an extra program can be inserted between the file and *F*2 to select out these unwanted state vectors.

2. Direct access is needed on the order SV file because ORDER state vectors are updated in the same sequence as the records on the *O* stream arrive, i.e., in random sequence.

3.

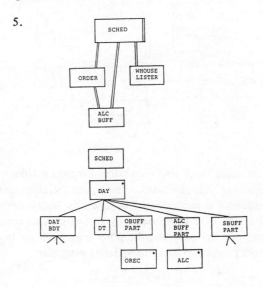

OBUFF PART is an absolutely standard collating structure.

Operations 6 and 8 will be replaced by

   6.   read (next) ORDER-SV FILE

   8.   write ORDER-SV

Extra operations will be needed, e.g.:

   15. EXEC SORT (OBUFF)

   16. store current KEY value

4. The two parts of the specification are unconnected, so no communication is necessary. Both processors are to run more than one process, so two schedulers are required.

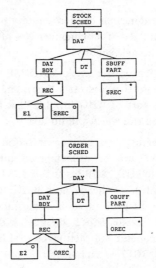

These schedulers assume the same type of scheduling as in the original implementation. Either of the BUFFPARTs could be replaced by a sort and collate.

Note that the DT input to STOCK SCHED is created solely for the scheduler and is not input to any specification process.

5.

6. WHLDAY is invoked by SCHED with the whole of ALCBUFF as a parameter. If there were local variables that retained their values from one WHLDAY to the next, then these would need to be stored as the state vector of WHOUSE LISTER. This state vector could also be a parameter when WHLDAY is invoked in the same way that a state vector is often a parameter when an inverted program is invoked.

This type of dismemberment only works when the periodicity of the scheduler is the same as that of the function process. If WHOUSE LISTER's DT was not also used by the SCHEDULER, then the contents of ALCBUFF would not be exactly one WHLDAY's input.

7. Yes, the upper iterations of these enquiry processes can be dismembered. The remainder is a procedure that processes a single enquiry.

8. No, the ORDER processes invoke WHOUSE LISTER to process one ALC record (at a time), and there is no convenient part of WHOUSE LISTER that can be dismembered and which will do this.

9. Further dismemberment and optimisation is possible. WHLDAY can be dismembered into three parts: C-DAYINPUT, SORT, and P-LIST. Since the ALC records have already been buffered by the scheduler, the first of these is superfluous. The scheduler can invoke SORT directly with ALC-BUFF as a parameter and then invoke P-LIST with the sorted ALCBUFF as a parameter.

If the scheduler used a sort and collate scheme for running the ORDER processes (as in question 3), then the SORT in ALCBUFF would be unnecessary in the unlikely case that the sort in the scheduler on OBUFF is on the same keys as the sort inside WHOUSE LISTER.

10.

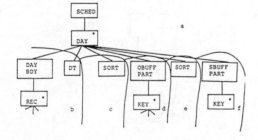

The most likely implementation involves a dismemberment into six parts. The upper iteration and sequence is implemented by operator instructions; the DAYBDY component, by an on-line date entry and enquiry program; the other four parts are two SORTs and two standard updating programs.

11.

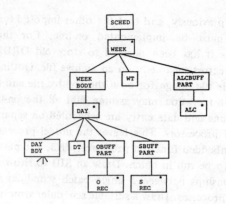

12. The machine running $F2$ and SLE must be able to access the ORDER SV file and the STOCK SV file. Since $F2$ and SLE do not amend these files, this is not too difficult.

Virtual processors are treated exactly as if they were separate physical processors.

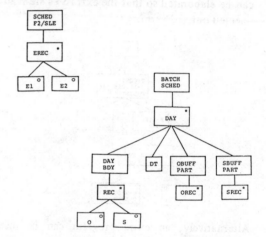

No change is necessary to the scheduler structures. There are simply n instances of SCHED $F2$/SLE, each of which has access to the ORDER SV file and the STOCK SV file.

This arrangement of on-line enquiries and batch updating is typical. Each terminal has its own virtual processor.

13.

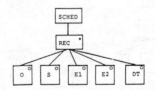

This scheduler is usually implemented as part of the teleprocessing monitor system (e.g. CICS, IMS DC, TIP, TDS, etc.).

The processors must all have access to the ORDER SV file and the STOCK SV file. In question 12 it was assumed, reasonably, that the specification had one *F2* and one SLE per terminal. Each scheduler ran its own version of *F2* and SLE. Each ORDER and STOCK process, however, can be run on any of the (virtual) processors, that is, updated from any terminal. Some mechanism must ensure that two processors do not run the same process at the same time and that one will pick up where the other left off. The mechanism is the familiar locking and unlocking of state vectors on the ORDER SV file and the STOCK SV file.

The most likely implementation for WHOUSE LISTER is to run it in background on another virtual processor. The inverted ORDER processes write ALC records into ALCBUFF. On receipt of a DT record, the relevant SCHED initiates the dismembered WHLDAY component with ALCBUFF as a parameter.

14. Yes, in fact, until more functions are added, the fossil state vectors are not used for anything and could be deleted.

A state vector file can be divided into any number of physical files if this is convenient or efficient. Alternatively, copies of parts of the file can be made periodically for use by enquiry processes.

A scheduler could make a copy of the state vectors used by *F2* each day at the end of OBUFFPART, and this may well lead to improved efficiency.

15.

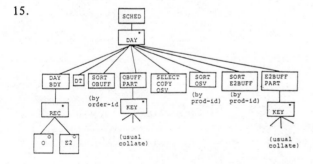

In outline: After the ORDER SV file is updated, a copy is made of outstanding state vectors that are due or overdue. This subset is sorted by prod-id; the input *E2* records are also sorted by prod-id. The two files are collated in E2BUFFPART which invokes the *F2* process.

16. Five of the functions have state vector connections with the ORDER processes. They define access paths as follows.

F2   By PROD-ID, all outstanding orders that are due or overdue.

FN2   Direct access by ORDER-ID.

FN3   By CUST-ID, all the delivered orders whose delivery date falls in the specified period, in PROD-ID sequence.

FN4   By PROD-ID, all outstanding orders, in CUST-ID sequence.

STOCK All outstanding orders, in ascending order
CHKER of due-date within PROD-ID.

17. Almost certainly, all the above access paths must be supported directly to guarantee reasonable response time. In other words, the file or DB system must support indexing of CUST within PROD, indexing of PROD within CUST, access by DUEDATE within PROD, and direct access by ORDER-ID. Ideally, there should be a means of only accessing state vectors that satisfy a condition like "outstanding" or "delivery date LE given date".

18. The essential point of the separation of the archive part of the file is that there is no need to maintain customer indexing on the remainder. The design of this nonarchive part is therefore considerably simplified. Given that FN2 enquiries still have to be answered on-line for recently delivered orders, the best arrangement is probably to add the state vectors to the archive file as soon as the order is cancelled or delivered, but only delete the state vector from the nonarchive file two or more weeks later. Thus for a time there are two copies of the state vector. The archive file should be kept sorted by DELIVERY-DATE within CUST-ID, though it is much more convenient for FN2 if it also supported direct access by key and more convenient yet for FN3 if it supported indexing of CUST-ID and DUE-DATE. The scheduler described below assumes that it does.

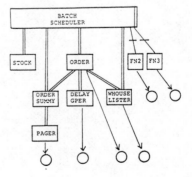

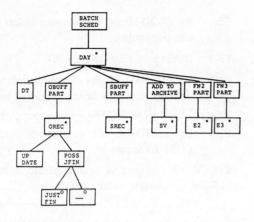

Comments on the Solutions

Questions 1, 14, 16, and 17 are mainly concerned with access requirements on the stored SVs and, therefore, with file and database design.

Questions 2 and 3 are about the replacement of direct access batch updating with standard serial accessing and collating.

Questions 4, 12, and 13 are about multiple processor implementations. Typical on-line environments supply one virtual processor per terminal.

Question 5 involves a different pattern of inversions that leads to two separate batch runs to update the ORDERs and run WHOUSE LISTER where previously there was one.

Questions 6 to 10 are about the dismemberment of various scheduler and function processes.

Questions 11 and 15 describe some different patterns of scheduling.

Question 18 is about a slightly more complicated implementation and is intended to give an idea of some particular issues that can arise in practice.

Chapter 4.4   Further Aspects of JSD

4.4.1 More Complicated Models

The following set of questions are about possible extensions and variations to the rather simple model of the Widget Warehouse Company chosen in Section 4.3.1.

Question 1 introduces three new actions and the new entity, CUSTOMER. PLACE, AMEND, and CANCEL are common actions of ORDER and CUSTOMER.

In a JSD realised model, common actions in different structures are not mutually synchronised. Because buffered data streams are used, either the CUST or the ORDER entities could run ahead of the other. This is justified by appealing to a methodological idea introduced, in passing, in Section 4.3.3. If two systems can be developed completely independently, then if they are developed as one, it should still be possible to reach the original independent implementations. Suppose X is a common action in the model structures A and B. We may imagine two independent systems, one containing A and the other containing B, separately specified and separately implemented. In the separate implementations, the action X in structure A is not synchronised with the action X in structure B. Therefore, a specification of a composite system should not demand that they are synchronised. Otherwise a perfectly reasonable implementation would contradict the specification.

Similar reasoning can be used to justify the use of buffered data streams to connect level-0 entities to level-1 entities and level-1 entities to function processes. Without buffering in the specification, we are cut off from some perfectly reasonable implementations.

Questions 2 and 6 concern details of the range of functions that particular models can or cannot support.

Question 3 removes the restriction that an ORDER should be for one product only. Note that this implies that the ORDER state vector will be larger and more complex.

Questions 4, 5, and 7 introduce more complications. The process type CUST/PROS introduced in the answer to Q7 is in addition to, and does not replace, the CUST process type introduced in the answer to Q1.

The term "marsupial" is sometimes used to describe an entity all of whose actions are common with another entity's. The marsupial entity expresses constraints on a subset of the other entity's actions. The marsupial structure cannot be contained inside the other structure. Like a marsupial animal, it jumps out of its mother's pouch and assumes a life of its own.

Widget Warehouse Company—Modelling Variations and Extensions

1. Extend the model by including the extra entity CUSTOMER and the three extra actions—SET CREDIT RATING, SUSPEND, and REINSTATE—all actions solely of CUSTOMER.

   SUSPEND: action of CUSTOMER. For reasons which are omb but are mainly to do with not paying bills, a customer may be suspended.

   Customers who are suspended may not place orders or amend orders by increasing the quantity. Only in special cases will a clerk allocate an order to a suspended customer.

   REINSTATE: action of CUSTOMER. A REINSTATEment reverses a suspension.

   SET CREDIT LIMIT: action of CUSTOMER. The credit limit is the limit on the value of orders which may be placed by a customer without special arrangement.

   A SET CREDIT LIMIT action must precede the PLACing of any orders. However, subsequent SET CREDIT LIMIT actions may occur at any time and have the effect of changing the credit limit.

   The special arrangements which allow a customer to exceed his limit are outside our model boundary. The structure of CUSTOMER will not differentiate between PLACEs and AMENDments which exceed the limit and those which do not.

   Draw a structure of this third entity, the CUSTOMER, and indicate what changes, if any, need to be made to the ORDER structure.

2. Describe some functions that could not be supported by the model if the DELAY action were omitted. Remember that an imposed function with access to the date could output a list of overdue, and by implication, delayed, orders.

Portions of this Chapter are excerpted from previously unpublished Michael Jackson Systems Limited (MJSL) internal documents with permission from MJSL.

3. Suppose that an order can be for many products but that it is characterised by a single delivery date and delivery address. Partial deliveries are still not allowed. An AMEND action can amend the quantities of several of the products. What change does this imply for the model?

4. Suppose that partial allocations and partial deliveries are allowed.

5. Roughly, what model would be required if we had to keep track of individual widgets, gadgets, and so on as if we were building a quality control–safety system, such as is required in the production of aircraft engines.

6. What further functions could the model support if ISSUE was also considered to be an action of ORDER?

7. At last the director of marketing has had his way. The new system is to include various facilities that will help monitor and organise the various marketing activities which are directed toward the Widget Warehouse Company's customers and prospective customers.

The following actions are to be included:

ASSIGN SALESMAN : Salesman x has been made responsible for this customer.

CONTACT NORMAL : A contact by the normal salesman for that customer. See below for attributes.

CONTACT OTHER : A contact by someone other than the normal salesman for that customer.

INFORMATION : The discovery of some item of information about a customer (presumably separately from a contact).

RECOMMENDED NEXT ACTION : A normal contact must and another contact may have a recommended next action as an attribute (see below). However, sometimes a salesman may want to amend an earlier recommendation by this stand-alone recommended next action.

Attributes of CONTACT NORMAL:

Name of contact;

Date;

Type of contact (phone, mail, visit, or meet, (as at conference));

Products of interest;

Recommended next action;

Date of recommended next action;

Name and job title of other people involved in buying decision ($\leqslant$ 4 of these);

Comment line.

The last two of these are optional.

Attributes of CONTACT OTHER:

are as those of CONTACT NORMAL, except that the last 4 attributes are optional and there is the additional attribute, name of WWC person making contact.

Extend the model and the initial model to include these actions.

Widget Warehouse Company—Modelling Variations and Extensions Solution

1.

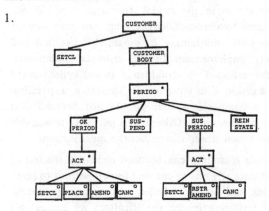

A ReSTRicted AMEND is an amend which does not increase the quantity of the order.

Both in this structure and in the ORDER structure, we might have made AMEND a selection of RSTR AMEND and INC QTY AMEND, changing the action list accordingly. Apart from this, no changes are necessary to the structure of ORDER. No new actions have been defined for ORDER, and no change has been made to the possible sequencing of the existing set of actions.

2. The most obvious functions that could not be supported are embedded functions associated with writes allocated to the DELAY component of the ORDER process. The simplest of these are apology notes to be sent when a DELAY happens or when a

DELAY happens and some other condition is also met.

Imposed functions could produce lists of overdue orders either regularly or on request, but such a specification would be different from one based on embedded outputs created when a DELAY occurred.

3. There is not necessarily any change to the model apart from extra attributes of the actions PLACE, AMEND, and possibly also ALLOCATE and DELIVER.

   As functions are added, the state vector of ORDER is likely to contain a table with one entry per product ordered. The size of the table is limited only by the maximum number of products in an order. There will be opportunities in the implementation phase for the dismemberment of this table.

4. There are two extra actions of ORDER and a marsupial of ORDER. The extra actions are PARTIAL ALLOCATE and PARTIAL DELIVER.

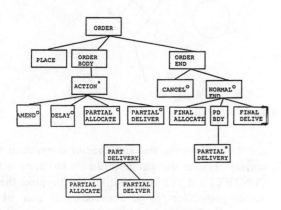

5. Actions would have to be defined that refer to individual widgets and gadgets. The identifier of an individual widget (and there would have to be such identifiers) would be an attribute of these actions. With RECEIVE, ISSUE, and WRITE-OFF redefined in this way, the following structure is appropriate, although almost certainly it ought only to be a fragment of a larger structure that contains actions describing what happens to a widget before and after it is in the warehouse.

6. Having ISSUE also as an action of ORDER of course allows more detailed functions on the state of orders. We will know not only that an order is not simply allocated but also that it has left the warehouse.

   More significantly, having ISSUE as part of the ORDER structure allows us to know how many orders are allocated but are not yet issued and so how much of the stock in the warehouse has already been allocated.

   There may need to be two types of ISSUE action: one associated with ORDERs, and one for other purposes.

   Having ISSUE as a common action of ORDER and STOCK is satisfying because this action represents the moment of transfer of the goods from the responsibility of the production director to that of the marketing director.

7.

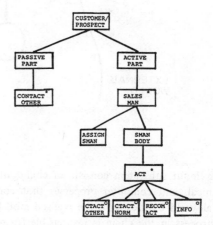

We assume that there are no constraints between the actions of a CUSTOMER as someone who places, amends, and cancels orders, is suspended and reinstated, etc. and a customer/prospect as the target of marketing activity.

The following can be added to the initial realised model:

4.4.2 Error Handling in the Initial Model Step

For many systems error-handling comprises the main part of the initial model step.

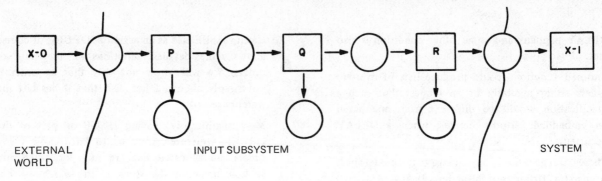

EXTERNAL WORLD   INPUT SUBSYSTEM   SYSTEM

Figure 4.4a

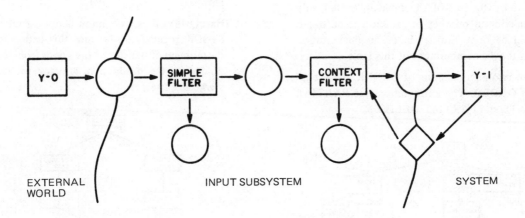

EXTERNAL WORLD   INPUT SUBSYSTEM   SYSTEM

Figure 4.4b

An input subsystem consists of chains of manual, mechanical, and computer processes that connect the external-world entities with the realised model entities. Each process in the chain is responsible for passing on input that is valid for the next. Each process produces diagnostics for its own erroneous input. The general arrangement is shown schematically in Figure 4.4a.

We classify input errors into three categories and introduce extra software processes into the chain to catch the first two of the categories.

The first category of errors is those that can be detected without reference to the state of the model by a process like SIMPLE FILTER in Figure 4.4b. An input is rejected because no action like the one it describes can ever happen.

The second category of errors is those that can be detected only by reference to the current state of the model. An input is rejected because if refers to an action that cannot happen now, given the preceding sequence of events, although it can happen under other circumstances.

Intuitively, the secondary category of errors can be detected by processes like CONTEXT FILTER in Fig-

ure 4.4b. However the state vector connection is not correct because we would need zero buffering between CONTEXT FILTER and Y-1. We must replace the state vector inspection by a conversational pair of data streams as in Figure 4.4c.

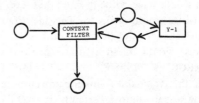

Figure 4.4c

Two arrangements are possible. In one, CONTEXT FILTER enquires of Y-1 if a certain record is acceptable. Y-1 has to be elaborated to answer these enquiries. The pattern of elaboration is the same as the elaboration of on-line JSP data structures for input errors (see Section 2.3.2). The second arrangement does not involve any structural elaboration of Y-1. A write operation is allocated in Y-1 immediately before each read specifying what records Y-1 is prepared to accept. By reading this record, the CONTEXT FILTER knows without specially asking whether a particular record is acceptable.

If an action is common to two or more model processes, the CONTEXT FILTER may check that the input is acceptable to both. In Figure 4.4d the CONTEXT FILTER checks that input records are acceptable to both CUST and ORDER processes and passes PLACE, SETCL, ALLOCATE, etc., records to one or both processes.

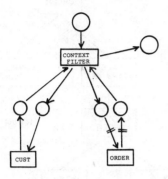

Figure 4.4d

Checking more than one model process is only possible if the update of a common action is synchronised. Otherwise, as in batch systems, checking can only be on one process, and errors detectable in the other process must be dealt with as category-three errors.

By definition, the model describes the sequences of actions that can happen. Therefore, it also implicitly defines the sequences of actions that are to be regarded as impossible. CONTEXT FILTER only passes on actions that form the initial part of an acceptable input stream. The design of a CONTEXT FILTER process can be deduced from the specification of the relevant part of the model. For a given state of the model only certain records may appear next on each input stream. Equivalently, for a given input record to be acceptable, the model must be in a certain subset of its states.

The third category of errors consists of errors that cannot be detected by processes like SIMPLE FILTER and CONTEXT FILTER. For example, the mistyping of an AMEND action in the Widget Warehouse system may still result in a record that is perfectly acceptable to ORDER. Redundancy can be introduced into the input to make these category-three errors less frequent, but they cannot be eliminated altogether. Relatively expensive procedures for dealing with them can be tolerated if their frequency is low enough.

The harsh fact is that category-three errors show that the model, as defined, cannot be realised exactly. Before stating the general approach to category-three errors, we consider the following examples that refer to the Widget Warehouse system with the CUSTOMER

entity and the three extra actions defined in Question 1 of the previous Section.

Suppose that a SUSPEND record is created that is correct in every way, except that it is for the wrong customer. One "solution" is to create an artificial REINSTATE action, artificial because it does not reflect a real reinstatement. This record is input, followed by the input for any actions that were wrongly rejected by the input subsystem because of the false SUSPEND. We may consider that this sequence of actions, while not accurately reflecting the real external world, is equivalent enough for the function of the system.

However, this may not be acceptable. The number of suspended periods may be held as a local variable and used by function processes for reports and for answers to on-line enquiries. As a result of the spurious SUSPEND and RESUME, this customer may be treated less favourably than he ought. If this is so, we must distinguish between two reinstate actions, between a normal REINSTATE and a REINSTATE AFTER ERROR. The structure of CUSTOMER must be modified accordingly. Strictly, we should perhaps differentiate also between a normal SUSPEND and a SUSPEND IN ERROR. The structure of the relevant part of CUSTOMER is shown in Figure 4.4e. This model is realisable at level-1, but only with backtracking. A SUSPEND and a SUSPEND IN ERROR action cannot be differentiated at data-collection time and given different record types.

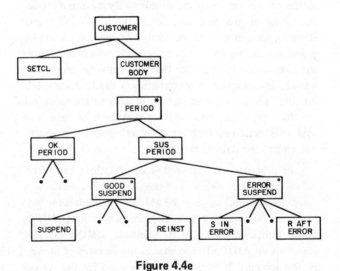

Figure 4.4e

The problem of category-three errors is not completely solved by creating new types of actions and elaborating the model. Suppose that in this example we have adopted the second solution and that a REINSTATE AFTER ERROR action is wrongly entered instead of a normal REINSTATE action. Are we to create a new

NORMAL REINSTATE REPLACING REINSTATE AFTER ERROR action? Perhaps, and under some set of circumstances this would be the right thing to do. Then we would have to consider the case of a NORMAL REINSTATE REPLACING REINSTATE AFTER ERROR action that is input to the wrong customer. Eventually, we have to stop defining new actions and rely on defining artificial sequences of existing actions that bring the model back to an acceptable state and whose functional effect is equivalent enough to what it would have been if no errors had been made. In this example, instead of defining a new action, we might enter an extra artificial SUSPEND and an extra artificial REINSTATE action to compensate for the erroneous REINSTATE AFTER ERROR.

The general approach to category-three errors is to define artificial sequences of actions for each possible false input, or series of false inputs. The artificial sequences must leave the model in a state equivalent enough to its state had there been no errors. The functional outputs of the artificial sequences of actions must be equivalent enough to the functional outputs had there been no errors. Where this is not possible, extra actions must be introduced into the model both to compensate directly for the errors and to be used in artificial sequences of actions.

At first, it may seem that this approach is hopelessly inelegant. However, it is no more than a recognition of the nature of the problem. By having a model consisting of processes that define the acceptable input streams, we can see that correcting category-three errors is like specifying an on-line program in which the operator can decide at any time that any previous input was wrong. The essential characteristics of the JSD approach are that the artificial sequences of actions are specified by the developers and users at system-build time and that only action records input to well-defined processes can amend the data of the system.

In practice artificial sequences of actions can often be defined quite simply. For the account processes in a financial system, we may be able to conclude that any error can be corrected by a single extra action, ADJUST, and a judicious choice of its attribute, AMOUNT. The effect of an ADJUST is to change the amount of money in the account. If an ADJUST is entered for the wrong account or with the wrong AMOUNT, more ADJUSTs will put things right.

In the Widget Warehouse system, we may be able to correct errors in ORDERs by introducing an artificial CANCEL and artificially creating new input for a new ORDER. When an ORDER is in a mess, we cancel it and start again with a new ORDER. There is no connection in the model between the artificially cancelled

ORDER and the new one. In this respect the model is not an exact reflection of the real world.

If this is not acceptable, we may differentiate between a normal cancel and an ARTIFICIAL CANCEL and use a structure like that in Figure 4.4f.

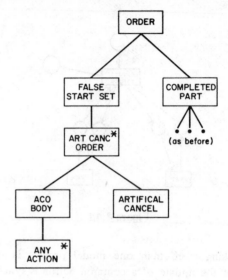

Figure 4.4f

The essential characteristic of "fault tolerant" software systems is that the extra actions and the extra artificial sequences of actions are generated by interactive functions rather than being generated externally, as is usually the case for data-processing systems.

4.4.3 The Interactive Function Step

The final exercise on the Widget Warehouse Company introduces an interactive function. Inputs for the actions ALLOCATE and DELAY are generated interactively within the system instead of externally by the clerk. Extra ALLOCATOR processes are introduced into the specification. They have a functional relationship with the ORDER and STOCK model processes, but they also generate some of the input for the model.

In the solution the process ORDER-1 is an exact reflection of ORDER-0, the relevant abstraction of the external-world actions. The important abstraction, the model of ORDER defined in step one of the method, is here called ORDER-2. Its structure is the same as that of ORDER in the previous versions.

Nothing would be different if the clerk could still make some of the more difficult decisions, except that some of the DELAY and ALLOCATE actions would come from the external world via ORDER-1.

Widget Warehouse Company—Interactive Function

The clerks have assured us that their decisions in allocating stock to orders are too complex and subtle to be organised into an algorithm which can be executed on a computer. However an investigation has shown that this is something of an exaggeration. Most of the decisions are quite routine, and the few which are not do not matter very much anyway.

It has therefore been decided to build the system so that it allocates and delays the orders. The algorithm is as follows: When a product is allocated, priority is given to orders which have already been delayed. Within both delayed and normal orders, those for the largest quantities are dealt with first. Orders are never partially filled; an order for which there is not enough stock is simply delayed. The same algorithm is used for all the products independently. Normally, an allocation is performed for each product each working day, but the clerks should be left the possibility of making an extra allocation for a particular product on request.

Draw an SSD and the structures of any new processes in the specification of this new system.

What, if anything, would be different if the clerks were still left to make some of the more difficult decisions themselves?

For the purposes of this exercise, assume that customer is not an entity in the model.

Widget Warehouse Company—Interactive Function Solution

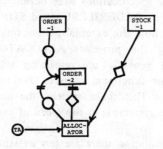

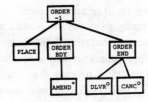

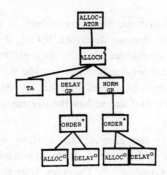

Note that there is one ALLOCATOR process per product.

The description of the algorithm is, of course, not complete. The structure shown implies that there is no extra priority given to orders which have been delayed a long time. A different structure for an ALLOCATOR which did have this rule would be:

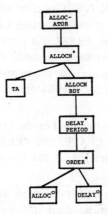

The orders in one DELAY PERIOD have all been delayed the same length of time. The NORMal GP in the previous structure is simply a special DELAY PERIOD.

This version of the Widget Warehouse system is an important paradigm. Many systems have entities that reflect the joint actions of an external agent and an agent internal to the organisation of which the system is a part. In this example the ORDER is the entity, the customer is the external agent, and either the clerk or the ALLOCATOR processes the agent internal to the organisation. In a banking system an ACCOUNT may be an entity; the customer, the external agent; and something within the bank, the internal agent that generates actions like adding interest or subtracting bank charges. In the simple telephone system described in Chapter 5.2, the TELEPHONE is an entity whose actions are generated by the telephone user and by either a telephone operator or the automatic switching system. In the system to control an elevator described below, there is a similar pattern. Automation is largely the replacement of agencies within the organisation but outside the system that are the source of model actions by interactive function processes that are within the organisation and within the system.

Now consider the Simple Lift System, which is described in the fifth section of the reprinted paper "Two Pairs of Examples ...". There are four actions in the model: ARRIVE(j) and LEAVE(j) are both actions of the entity LIFT; PRESS and RESET are actions of the entity BUTTON (also called LCBUT).

[In the reprinted paper, BUTTON-0 refers to the real button; BUTTON-1, to a process reflecting only real-world actions; and (unhelpfully) LCBUT is the name of the interesting abstraction, the one with both PRESS and RESET actions.]

The action ARRIVE(j) occurs when the LIFT arrives at the jth floor and the action LEAVE(j), when it leaves the jth floor. PRESS is a press of one of the buttons that the users use to summon the lift. RESET is an interactively generated action indicating that a group of service requests (PRESSes) are deemed to have been served.

Sensors on the buttons and on the lift shaft generate input for ARRIVE, LEAVE, and PRESS actions. RESET actions are generated by the interactive function LIFTCONTROL.

The model process LIFT-1 reflects what can happen to the lift, not what we want to happen. It includes such bizarre behaviour as oscillation between the first and second floors without reaching either. Effectively, it embodies the constraints imposed by the lift shaft. To express all the constraints, the local variable FLOOR-NO must be added to the structure of LIFT-1. FLOOR-NO must take only values 0, 1, 2, and 3 and must never change by more than 1.

The LIFTCONTROL process contains the algorithm by which the lift is to be controlled. Note that we do not assume that the lift will definitely go up just because the system outputs a message telling it to go up. Part of the function of LIFTCONTROL could be to output warnings if the actual behaviour differs from the expected behaviour. (See the discussion on the casuality of external actions in Section 4.2.3.)

In the algorithm described in the paper, the lift waits at the ground floor if there are no outstanding requests. ("Outstanding request" is, of course, defined in terms of the model: an outstanding request is a PRESS that has not yet been followed by a RESET.)

When there are requests, the lift moves as high as the highest request, stopping to service requests on the way, and then returns to the ground floor, stopping to service new requests on the way down.

The LIFTCONTROL process has embedded output from LIFT-1 and a state vector connection with the LCBUT processes. While the lift is moving, LIFTCONTROL is waiting for a record from LIFT-1 that comes when the LIFT ARRIVES at a floor. LIFTCONTROL then examines the state vectors of the relevant LCBUT processes to see whether it should stop, change direction, or just continue. When LIFTCONTROL stops at a floor, it sends a RESET record to the appropriate LCBUT. When the lift is waiting at the ground floor, there is a busy loop of state vector examinations of the LCBUT processes that ends when a button is PRESSed.

The functional outputs are to the motor, to go on and off and up and down, and to lamps that indicate for each button whether or not there is an outstanding request.

There is a comparison in the reprinted paper effectively between the Lift system and a version of the Widget Warehouse system in which the clerks are replaced by interactive ALLOCATOR processes. The two specifications are very similar. So is the JSD method of developing the specification. The ORDER/LCBUT processes are model processes whose input comes in part from the customers/lift users and in part from the interactive function processes ALLOCATOR/LIFTCONTROL. The ALLOCATOR/LIFTCONTROL allocates the resource STOCK/LIFT among the competing ORDER/LCBUT entities. The specifications were developed by defining the actions of ORDER/LCBUT and STOCK/LIFT, by establishing how the external actions may be detected, by defining the processes ALLOCATOR/LIFTCONTROL that generate the remaining actions, and by adding other functional outputs. Just as in the Car Rally/Golden Handshake system, the main difference between the systems is in the speed of execution of the processes.

In a simulation there are few externally generated actions; in a closed simulation there are none at all. JSD is directly applicable to simulation systems. The interactive function step is proportionately larger, and the initial model step small or non-existent.

We can easily turn the lift system into a simulation by, for example, generating PRESS actions by a suitable random-number generator and generating ARRIVE and LEAVE actions by a process that reads the embedded output from LIFTCONTROL and simulates the operation of the real LIFT-0 by imposing a time delay between the receipt of a motor control output and the subsequent generation of the ARRIVE and LEAVE actions.

A distinction is commonly made between "event-driven" and "time-sliced" simulations. Generalising, the interactive functions in an event-driven simulation get embedded output from the model that stimulates them to generate more actions, perhaps after examining other model state vectors. The interactive functions in a time-sliced simulation usually have only state vector connections with the model. They have an external stream of records, one for each slice of simulated time, that stimulate them to examine state vectors and generate actions. LIFTCONTROL follows the "event-driven" pattern because it has embedded output from LIFT-1. ALLOCATOR follows the "time-sliced" pattern. Allocations are performed when a record of TA is read.

4.4.4 State Vector Dismemberment

A state vector may be stored by dividing it into a number of parts and storing the parts separtely. This is called "state vector dismemberment".

For example, we may have an on-line function that examines only one variable of the state vectors of entities of type P. The on-line function may have to deal with a high volume of enquiries. There may be a very large number of instances of P. Each state vector of P may contain a large number of variables. In these circumstances the dismemberment of the state vectors of P is an attractive implementation possibility. The variable needed by the on-line function is stored separately from the rest of the state vector on a file that can be accessed more quickly and efficiently.

Speed of access is not the only reason for dismembering state vectors. Sometimes dismemberment can lead to more economical use of storage. Suppose that one of the actions of entity P has an attribute that has to be held as a local variable in the state vector. Suppose that the variable is a long character string and further, that over all the instances of P, it may only take a relatively small number of different values. The possible values or the currently-used values of the string may be stored separately and a pointer may be used in the rest of the state vector to indicate which value is the correct one.

The main reasons state vectors are dismembered is that they have grown large and complex, perhaps they are of variable length, and particular imposed functions require only parts of the whole.

Question 3 in Section 4.4.1 allows many products per ORDER. The ORDER state vector can be dismembered into $(n+1)$ parts where n is the number of products in the ORDER. N parts each hold the QTY and other information for one product. The other part holds the rest of the state vector. Techniques of data normalisation are appropriate in the implementation phase for choosing a good dismemberment.

The state vector is the history of an entity and is built up as functions are added. Some functions require very detailed and extensive historical information. For example, suppose we require a function that uses the CUSTOMER-as-PROSPECT model defined in Question 7 of Section 4.4.1 to produce, on request, a listing of the complete marketing history of a customer. The listing is to contain one line for each CONTACT, lines being grouped by the ASSIGNED salesman, each group being headed by information from the ASSIGN SALESMAN action.

The state vector of CUST/PROS must contain all the information that can appear in the listing. In these circumstances the state vector can be dismembered into a "current" part consisting of variables in constant use and an "archive" part consisting of variables that are never updated and are only required by the history function. Probably the archive part will itself be dismembered into many components, one for each CONTACT or ASSIGN. In the limiting case, all the input may have to be stored as part of the state vector.

4.4.5 System Maintenance

The total life cycle of a system is an iteration of model–function–implementation (m-f-i) developments. The early instances of the iteration may be prototypes. The development of a large system may be planned around a series of releases, each containing a larger proportion of the total system. Each release is an instance of m–f–i development. Later in a system's life, the specification changes normally referred to as system maintenance lead to more instances of the m–f–i iteration. The question repeatedly asked in these iterations is, "Because of the new situation, what changes or additions need to be made to the decisions in this step?"

(We are oversimplifying here. For example, work on successive releases may overlap. Within one release, work on a particular function may be going on in parallel with the development of model processes not used by this function. See also the discussion of decision independence in Section 4.5.4.)

There is also unintended iteration in development. When you realise that you have made a mistake, you repeat some of the work, though not a whole m-f-i cycle. JSD aims to reduce unintended iteration by making the consequences of each decision clearer. The independence of decision (see Section 4.5.4) also limits the amount of work that has to be repeated.

JSD specifications consist of large numbers of long-running processes. In JSD terms, a change in a system specification implies that processes must be amended partway through their execution. System maintenance is therefore to be distinguished from program maintenance, which involves changing a program between complete executions.

Moreover, in JSD, each program text is, in general, used by many processes, each of which has reached a different point in the text. We have to change the single text of many processes, each at a different point in its execution, so that they can all continue to execute according to the changed specification. This is the true nature of the system maintenance problem. In fact, changing programs partway through their execution is not as intractable as it sounds.

In JSD terms, the problem of system cutover or starting a new system is the problem of starting one program in the middle so that it takes over from where another partially executed program left off.

We examine two small examples, one a functional change and one a change to the model.

A simple example. Figure 4.4g shows many instances of the model processes, MOD, an embedded function process, EMBF, and an imposed function process, IMPF. Assume that there is only one instance each of EMBF and IMPF and that their structures are as shown in Figure 4.4h. IMPF is an iteration of enquiry; EMBF is an iteration of the periods defined by the rough-merged T stream. Assume that IMPF has no local variables that retain their values from enquiry to enquiry.

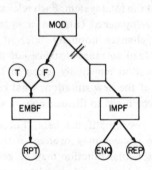

Figure 4.4g

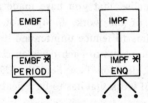

Figure 4.4h

A change to the specification of IMPF reduces to a problem of program maintenance: since communication with the model is by state vector inspection, the model is not affected; a new version of IMPF may replace the old version at any time IMPF has completely dealt with one enquiry and is at the end of the IMPF ENQ iteration.

Now consider a change to the specification of EMBF that does not affect the contents of the data stream F. Assume again that EMBF has no local variables that retain their values from one EMBF PERIOD to the next. Again the problem reduces to a problem in program maintenance. The new version of EMBF may be installed at any time the old version has consumed a T record, completely processed it, but has not yet read any F records from the next period.

Suppose now that the change involves different embedded output operations on F in the model processes, MOD. Doing this maintenance requires knowledge of the scheduling of the MOD processes. After the new version of the MOD processes is installed, a T record must be added to the rough-merged F streams before the amended model processes can write any new F records. This ensures that the change in the F records occurs on the PERIOD boundary. The new version of EMBF can be installed to deal with the periods containing the new F records.

These examples are easy because the function programs are structured as iterations and there is no memory from one iteration to the next.

Before considering the general case, we emphasise that most maintenance falls into one of the following easier categories:

(1) The change needs only extra function processes.

(2) The change can be accomplished by the replacement of function processes as described above.

(3) The only change to the model is the addition of extra model process types.

(4) The change can be accomplished by changing to a new version of a model process without any single instance requiring conversion. For example, in the Widget Warehouse system we may change the structure of an ORDER. However, because an ORDER is a relatively short-lived entity, the change may be that all new orders from a certain date are to be of the new type. The existing orders may continue under the old rules.

A harder example. In general, whereas program maintenance involves the replacement of part of the program text, system maintenance requires the extension of the process texts.

Suppose that a bank decides to change the rules that govern the repayment of loans of a certain type. Figure 4.4i is the top-level structure of the entity CUSTomer. A customer may have only one loan at a time. If one supposes that loans of the old type are allowed to run their course, according to the rules originally agreed, then Figure 4.4j is the structure of the new entity CUSTomer. The whole lifetime of a customer is described; that lifetime consists of zero of more OLD LOANS followed by zero of more NEW LOANS.

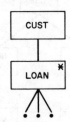

Figure 4.4i

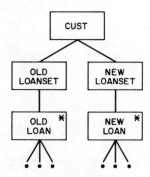

Figure 4.4j

The process text has been extended in a particularly simple way by the addition of the NEW LOANSET component as a high-level sequence. In outline the new version can be installed as follows (remember that one copy of the CUST text is used to implement many CUST processes):

At any time before the first NEW LOAN is started, replace the old CUST text by the new extended version. The new state vector is also a superset of the old. (If the text pointer has a different representation in the state vector of the new version, there may need to be an explicit mapping from the old representation to the new. The values of the text pointer in the old version map one-to-one onto the values in the OLDLOANSET part of the new version.) Now the new version is installed, but all

the instances of CUST are in the OLDLOANSET part of their structure. As they finish their old loans and take out new loans, more and more will move to the NEWLOANSET part of their structure. Eventually, all the customers will be in the NEWLOANSET, and the OLDLOANSET part of the text can be deleted.

There may be some local variables used only within OLD LOAN and some used only within NEW LOAN. The complete state vector contains both, but since any instance of customer needs only some of the complete state vector, there is the possibility of reducing the storage requirement during and after the changeover.

Suppose instead that customers with old loans are to be told that they are to be converted partway through their life to the new rules. A loan starts as an old loan but ends as a new loan. The structure for a CUSTomer in these circumstances is shown in Figure 4.4k. There is backtracking in this structure. What started out as an OLD LOAN sometimes turns out to be a HYBRID LOAN. Obviously this backtracking comes from the subject matter and is not an artifact of our approach. In the development of the complete CUST process (not just its structure), quits are placed in OLDLOANSET at precisely those points in a LOAN's life at which we wish to start applying the new rules. Instead of changing all the LOANs overnight (though this could be done by having quits everywhere in OLDLOANSET and entering special CHANGEOVER records to all the CUSTs), we may want a less radical changeover, for example changing each loan on its anniversary or when it has reached a certain point in its life. We may even have to wait for the customer's permission to make the changeover.

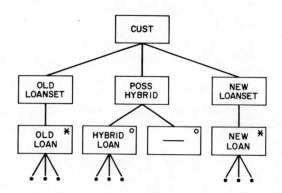

Figure 4.4k

The handling of the side-effects in the development of the extended CUST process is also a reflection of a real-world problem; it is a reflection of the decisions the bankers have made over the conversion of OLD LOANs to HYBRID LOANs.

The changeover strategy for this extended CUST process is exactly the same as that described above.

These simple but common cases involve the extension of the process by a simple sequence at the top level. A CUSTomer entity structure must include the OLD LOANs even though the customer is no longer allowed to start an OLD LOAN. Changes in process structures to meet changed specifications are always extensions. In describing their whole lifespan, we must not exclude the early parts. Branches can only be removed when no instances of the process need them any more.

The general pattern follows: install the extended structure at any time before the change is due to come into effect; gradually more and more instances of the processes will use the additional parts, causing some of the old parts (possibly) to fall into disuse; and the structure may be contracted by deleting old parts when no process instance can ever need them again.

Strictly, the function changes described in the simple example above are extensions of the type shown in Figure 4.41. However, because there is only one instance of EMBF (we supposed) and no local variables are retained between periods, and therefore none are retained between OLD PART and NEW PART, the contraction by removing the OLDPART could immediately follow the installation of the extended version. In effect, OLD-PART can be replaced immediately by NEWPART, provided the changeover is done at the correct time.

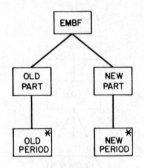

Figure 4.41

Chapter 4.5   Justifications of the JSD Approach

The following example (also discussed in Jackson [2]) is taken from Jackson [3].

"An organisation provides resources for use by the public. (It might be, for example, that the resource is a time-sharing system, or boats on a pleasure lake). Each session of use by a customer has a starting time and an ending time, which are recorded, in chronological order, on a magnetic tape file. Each record of the file contains the session-identifier, a type code ("S" for start and "E" for end) record, in that order, for each session in one day.

"It is desired to produce a report from the tape showing the total number of sessions of use and the average session time. Time for a session is computed as Te−Ts, where Te and Ts are the start and end times respectively for the session".

By considering the function of the program we arrive, with little difficulty, at the following text:

```
P: begin
        sessions: = 0;
        totaltime: = o;
        open tape;
        read tape;
        while not eof(tape)
            do
                if code = 'S'
                    then begin
                        sessions: = sessions + 1;
                        totaltime: = totaltime - Ts
                    end
                else   totaltime: = totaltime + Te
                fi
                read tape
            od
        print 'number of sessions = ', sessions;
        if sessions ≠   0
            then print 'average session time = ',
                (totaltime / sessions)
        fi
        close tape
    P: end
```

The example is a tiny information system about a pond where customers hire boats for sessions of boating. The function of the information system, at least initially, is simply to total the number of sessions of boating and to average the session time. The input to the system is a chronologically ordered stream of records, one for each start of a session and one for each end of a session. Each record has a session identifier, a type code ("S" for start and "E" for end), and the time. The solution presented is a perfectly structured program that exactly meets the functional requirement.

Unfortunately, the solution is almost completely unmaintainable. Quite reasonable changes to the specification cannot be made without completely rewriting the system. Three examples are: To print out the longest session time; to split the report into two parts, one for sessions ending in the morning and one for sessions ending in the afternoon; and to accommodate an input stream in which some records are missing.

Since maintainability is one of the most desirable qualities of a system, we may conclude that this solution to the Boating Pond problem is a bad one and ask what there is in the development approach that leads to such a bad solution.

The fundamental error is to think of systems as functions mapping inputs to outputs. Rather, we should think of systems more as simulations. The inputs (excluding functional inputs like enquiries) realise the simulation, which is the domain of the functions that produce the outputs.

We are given little information about how much of the world of the boating pond ought to be simulated. Certainly the START and END of sessions of boating must be included. Also, there must be some process to show that the START of one session must precede the END of that session. Figure 4.5a shows the minimum JSD model that can support functions about sessions

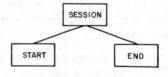

Figure 4.5a

of boating. The model we choose, whether it is this minimum model or one with a bigger set of actions, defines the domain of the function of the system. A coherent family of functions is defined and made explicit at an early stage of development. Maintenance within this family will be relatively easy. Maintenance that

Portions of this Chapter are excerpted from previously unpublished Michael Jackson Systems Limited (MJSL) internal documents with permission from MJSL.

demands extension or change to the model will be much more difficult.

When presented with the Boating Pond example, developers of practical systems will comment that in their functional specifications and requirements definitions they try to take a wider view of requirements, that they try to describe a range of functional requirements, and that they take care to include in their functional description material about the subject matter of the system. They are saying, in effect, that although the title of their document is "functional specification" or "requirements definition", they know they must include more than is implied by the title. They are intuitively doing something that JSD seeks to make explicit, formal, and separate in the modelling stage of development.

Much work in software engineering is based on the following (partial) software development life cycle: first, work on the requirements of the system, specifying these without prejudice to its internal structure; then work on the internal structure, choosing a structure that will make subsequent variations to the requirements easy to handle. The Boating Pond example suggests that this life cycle is wrong because:

(1) it suggests that attention should be focused first on the functional requirements and not on the subject matter of the system;

(2) it suggests that requirements ought to be specified without any internal structure;

(3) it implies that there is a way of choosing a good internal structure based only on a statement of requirements.

Each of these points is addressed in turn.

We have already suggested that focussing on requirements may lead to unmaintainable systems. Another argument for the precedence of model over a more direct statement of requirements is the need to give meaning to functions. In JSD the function of a system is expressed in terms of the model. Each field of the output and each noun, adjective and verb used to describe the output must be defined directly or indirectly in terms of the actions and their attributes.

To understand an isolated requirements definition or functional specification, a user has to be able to supply the connection with the subject matter of the system. What, for example, does the field on the report entitled "average session time" mean in the Boating Pond problem? The time of one session is the difference between the TIME attribute of the END action and the TIME attribute of the START action. The average session time is the average of these times for one day. A START action occurs when a customer hires a boat, pays a deposit, and is given a ticket as a receipt. A END action occurs when a customer brings the boat back. This connection must be in the user's mind whether it has been made formal or not. A user needs the connection to understand the specification of a system and to understand the outputs of a system. JSD makes the connection explicit. The action definitions are informal, but everything else is formally defined in terms of the actions.

Developers complain of users that "they don't know what they want". Users complain of developers that "they don't understand the business". The complaints are symptoms of a serious difficulty, not soluble simply by having the two sides spend more time together. An explicit modelling phase forces the developer to think about and understand the relevant part of the business. (Often it helps the user understand it better too.) Moreover the developer does not start by asking the difficult or impossible question, "What do you want the system to do?" Instead he asks the easier and less hostile question, "What is the system about?"

In deferring consideration of internal structure, developers follow the maxim, "Understand what the system has to do before thinking about how the system is going to do it". The requirements are identified with the "what" of the system, and the internal structure, with the "how". The JSD view is that the sequential structure of the model ought to be an integral part of the requirements definition. The fact that a session always STARTS before it ENDS is not an artifact of a solution to the Boating Pond problem. It ought to be fundamental to a statement of the problem. Identification of all internal structure with the "how", that is, with the implementation, is misleading and wrong.

There is plenty of negative evidence to support the third point. Despite considerable effort, there has been very little success in stating generally how to develop a good internal structure from a requirements definition. The Boating Pond problem suggests that the key lies in the model and not directly in a narrow functional definition of requirements.

The subject matter of programs and systems has a structure, usually a sequential structure, and this structure should be preserved in the structure of the software.

In Chapter 2.5 it was argued in the context of JSP that only the persistence of objects in the subject matter through a series of changed specifications gives the term "maintenance" any meaning.

In JSD the structure of the subject matter is preserved by starting the development with an explicit description of a model in terms of sequential processes and by using these processes as the basis of the specification. In this section we have argued that this modelling phase guarantees relatively easy maintenance within an explicitly defined range of functional statements. Further we have argued that an explicit model is also needed to give meaning to functional statements. We therefore expect the modelling phase to be valuable in promoting mutual understanding between developers and users.

In both JSP and JSD, modelling is part of a coherent development path. There is no discontinuity between modelling and the rest of the development.

4.5.2 Process Models, Not Data Models

In JSD we use sequential processes as a modelling tool. An alternative approach, to use data as the modelling tool, has been the focus of much attention, partly because it is closely associated with the use of database management systems. We prefer the use of processes to data for modelling because they are more natural, more generally applicable, less complicated and they avoid the largely self-inflicted data-integrity problem. These four reasons are considered in turn.

When a customer of a bank enquires about a mortgage, the branch manager will explain the mortgage roughly as follows: "When the mortgage agreement is signed, we will pay you the agreed sum. Each month, starting one month after the agreement is signed, you will repay a certain amount. Sometimes the interest rate will change, but we will always give you two months notice of this, and you will then have the option of changing the monthly payment or changing the period over which the repayment is made. If you default on your payments, ..."

He does not explain like this: "To understand a mortgage you have to understand sixteen data fields: the agreed sum of the mortgage, the current interest rate, the current monthly repayment, the amount still owed, the date by which the mortgage will be repaid, ..."

The first description is in terms of the events that make up the like of the mortgage and the time sequence in which they occur. The second is in terms of data. Of course, this is only one example; the reader is invited to think of others. Most people describe things in terms of events and the order in which they occur. Since our users think informally in terms of processes, it is natural to start a development by formalising this process-oriented view.

Process models unify the approach to the development of data-processing systems and what are variously called embedded systems, control systems, and real-time systems. In Chapter 4.4 we showed that one version of the Widget Warehouse system is very similar to a system for controlling the operation of an elevator (a lift). Not only are the final specifications very similar, so also are the various development steps used to reach the final specification. JSD applies to a very wide range of systems because of the wide applicability of sequential processes as a modelling tool. Data modelling techniques do not seem to be applicable to process-control problems like the elevator system.

Process models are less complicated than the equivalent data models for two main reasons. First, only attributes of actions are considered part of the JSD model. Other data items (the majority) are defined in terms of the actions and their attributes. Examples are "outstanding" and "stock-level" in the Widget Warehouse system. The two-valued data item "outstanding" is defined only in terms of sequences of actions, that is, in terms of the text pointer of the ORDER process. Data that, in JSD, is defined in terms of sequences of actions is awkward to handle in a data model because the latter describes only the states of entities and not their evolution.

The second reason data models are more complicated is that they include relationships that are deferred in JSD until the function steps. In the Widget Warehouse system, "customer-id" was made an attribute of the action PLACE. In the function step, a process was defined that for each enquiry accessed all the orders for a specified value of customer-id. The relationship between the orders with the same customer-id is defined in the function step. The relationship is not part of the JSD model.

If we wanted reports on orders placed by customers who own a Japanese automobile, we would include "nationality of customer's automobile" as an attribute of PLACE and expect a new relationship between orders to be defined by the access paths in the function processes. By defining arbitrary attributes of actions, we can add new function processes that define arbitrary new access paths. JSD models are simpler and more stable because the groupings defined by these access paths are not considered part of the model.

The data-integrity problem is the problem of ensuring that different data items are not given mutually inconsistent values. Consider the diagram in Figure 4.5b. The diagram describes a view of a CAR in a variation of the Car Rally problem. Cars that do not drive the correct course are called illegal cars and are given zero marks. Cars that keep driving after they have completed the course do not lose marks. They are assumed to be driving a lap of honour. This structure has a recognition difficulty in the top-level selection, but that is not our concern here.

The state vector of the process in Figure 4.5b contains the data that is equivalent to the data model. The contents of the state vector are not immediately obvious but can be deduced by examining the eighth figure of the reprinted paper. "Two Pairs of Examples ..." and observing that neither variation introduces any new local variables. The state vector consists of the text pointer, the MARK accumulator, the LASTTM variable that holds the last checkpoint time and the CAR-ID.

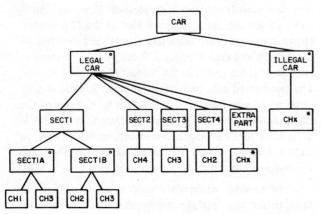

Figure 4.5b

Now imagine a suitable data model for a CAR in this small example. Thinking first about the data is the conventional approach; a designer starts by specifying the contents of the CAR master record. He might choose the following fields:

MARK, an accumulator;

LASTTM, the time at the last checkpoint;

CAR-ID,

LASTCHECKPOINT, the identity of the last checkpoint;

GOODFLAG, to store whether the car is still correctly on course;

FINISHEDYET, to store whether the car has correctly finished the course;

CH3YET, to store whether the car has reached checkpoint three for the first time.

The last four data items have respectively five, two, two, and two permissible values. Superficially, it may appear that together they have forty permissible values. In fact there are so-called "integrity constraints" between the variables that limit the permissible states to a fraction of these forty values. If FINISHEDYET is set, so must GOODFLAG. If FINISHEDYET is set, so must CH3YET. If LASTCHECKPOINT has value "3" CH3YET must be

set. Even in such a small example the set of integrity constraints is quite complicated and hard to specify completely.

These four variables are exactly equivalent to the text pointer in the state vector of the JSD process. There is no data-integrity problem in JSD because the possible evolution of the CAR process is described first and the extra data to calculate outputs added later. Using data models, the updating is quite separate from the model itself. The data describe the state of the entity, not its evolution.

Of course a data model is built up during the function steps as local variables are added to model processes. However data is not the preferred modelling tool; most of the data is defined after the JSD modelling phase: techniques of data normalisation are considered part of the implementation phase.

There is no contradiction between the preference for process models over data models and the emphasis in JSP on static considerations over dynamic. The arguments presented here are for the use of processes as a modelling tool. The argument in JSP is that, in designing and thinking about processes, we should concern ourselves first with their static properties.

4.5.3 Implementation By Transformation

The emphasis throughout JSP and JSD is to provide a pathway to solutions to software problems. The pathway through implementation is one of transformation of the specification and addition of extra implementation framework software.

This yields a very attractive answer to the question posed during a system acceptance test, "How can we be sure that the implemented system meets the specification?" Provided that the transformations used are known to preserve the specification, we only have to check that they have been carried out correctly.

The answer is of the same form as if we had asked, "How can we be sure that this object code is a correct implementation of this Pascal source program?" We rely on the correctness of the transformation between source and object code. Similarly, in JSD, we rely on the fact that inversion, state vector separation, program dismemberment, and the other transformations preserve the correctness of the specification.

If the transformation from source to object code has been mechanised by a compiler, our confidence in the implementation will be very high. The common JSD transformations can also be mechanised. Given software tools to do these transformations, most of the implementation step consists of the developer specifying the desired set of transformations and the machine carrying them out. For the foreseeable future, though, most transformations will have to be done by hand, and the system acceptance test will have to check that they have been done correctly.

Testing and mathematical proof are the two main alternatives to the problem of checking that an implementation meets a specification. The disadvantages of testing are well known, although we have had to learn to live with them. Mathematical proof has only been used and seems applicable to only small systems.

4.5.4 Decision Independence in JSD

The result of the Entity/Action and Entity Structure step in JSD is a model consisting of a set of disconnected sequential processes. The fact that they are disconnected confirms that the decisions described in each process are independent one from another.

For example, in the Widget Warehouse system, the decision that actions of STOCK are included is independent of the decision that actions of ORDER are included and also of the decision to exclude actions associated with widget manufacture. Decisions about STOCK actions are independent of the decision that AMEND, CANCEL, and DELIVER are among the selected ORDER actions and that AMEND can occur many times for one ORDER but only before either a CANCEL or an ALLOCATE.

There is almost total independence among the three steps that follow the entity/action and entity structure step. The information function step does not depend on the means of generating input to the model, whether by external data collection or by interactive function. It only depends on the fact that the model can be realised. Once the actions are divided between externally and internally generated actions, the initial model step is independent of the interactive function step. These three steps have been put in sequence for ease of presentation. In practice, their mutual independence allows them to overlap considerably.

There is also considerable independence of decisions within each of these three steps. Within the initial model step, error handling on data streams input to different model processes may be specified separately.

Different functions can be specified independently one from another; they are related only in that they have the same domain, that is, they are connected to the same model processes.

The model is the only connection between different functions and between the functions and the input subsystem. The elegance of a JSD specification is that the part containing all the interaction, the model, is defined first and is itself such a disconnected object.

TWO PAIRS OF EXAMPLES IN THE
JACKSON APPROACH TO SYSTEM DEVELOPMENT

J R Cameron

Michael Jackson Systems Ltd
21 Old Devonshire Rd
London SW12 9RD England

Abstract

The Jackson System Development method (JSD) develops formal system specifications
in a number of distinct steps. The specifications are written in terms of sequential processes; the early steps made a description or model of the relevant
external reality; the later steps add the functional requirement; the specifications are implemented in a series of mechanisable transformations. The method
is illustrated by two pairs of examples, each pair having rather similar
specifications, but different likely implementations.

1. INTRODUCTION

Conventional system development emphasises an
early definition of requirements, and the early
decomposition of a problem into subproblems. This
approach has at least the following disadvantages.

(1) The user is usually unable to state the
    system requirements.

(2) Demonstrating that an implementation meets
    the requirements is difficult.

(3) The decomposition into subproblems is
    usually based on machine oriented
    considerations.

(4) The decomposition is usually imprecisely
    formulated and is only made precise by
    further decomposition. This often comes
    too late to change a poor initial decision.

JSD aims to make improvements by rearranging the
order decisions are made in a development, and by
making the consequences of each decision more
explicit.

In particular, before system requirements are
directly addressed, there is a significant modelling phase in which an abstraction of the relevant
external world is agreed with the user. This

model is realised as a set of long running sequential processes (conceptually each having its own
dedicated processor). Note that neither of the 2
JSD uses of model - the abstraction in the external
world and the realisation of the abstraction as
computer processes - are equivalent to 'model' as
used by some other writers. Model is often used
to describe an abstraction of the system itself
for the purposes of development or of performance
evaluation.

The requirements or system function is then specified by constructing new long running sequential
processes, which access information through their
connections with the model processes.

The finished specification is formally stated, is
in principle directly compilable, but not into an
efficient system. The usual implementation phase
consists of:

(1) transformations of the texts of the model and
    function processes which make up the specif-
    ication

(2) construction of special purpose scheduling
    programs to run the specification processes.

Program inversion (ref 1,2) is the prototypical

example of a JSD transformation. (The transformation is from a process to a procedure by including a suspend and resume mechanism at each
relevant I/O operation.) The separation of state
vectors (the textpointer and local variables of a
process) to allow one text and many state vectors
to implement many identical processes is another.
These transformations can be mechanised.

Above all JSD decomposes the development in a way
other than merely by decomposing the system. In
this sense it can properly claim to be a method.

The main JSD phases are model, function and implementation. These phases are further subdivided
but these further divisions are not considered
in this paper, either in general or in the
solutions to the examples.

2. MAJOR JSD PHASES AND NOTATIONS

2.1 MODELLING

We are going to view the finished system as an
information system about the real world which is
described by the model.

The JSD model describes the evolution of the external entities of interest. The time varying
behaviour of entities is central to JSD. (Contrast
data models built out of data analysis, which do
not describe the evolution of entities, only their
permissible states.)

The model description covers the complete period
during which the entity is of interest. If a
mortgage lasts for 25 years, then the model of the
mortgage covers all 25 years. An aircraft in an
air traffic control system may be of interest for
3 hours; the model of the aircraft spans this
complete period.

JSD models are running models. At build time we
specify what can happen to an entity. As the
system runs, input from the external world tells
us what did happen, and the model is co-ordinated
with the reality.

A JSD model has no outputs, nor is it concerned
with system outputs. It merely records and
reflects - models - a set of interesting external
events.

Why modelling is so important.

(1) By including an explicit modelling phase we
    aim to avoid the mutual misunderstandings
    between user and designer which dog tradit-
    ional system development.

(2) The model is the user's world (part of it
    anyway) and that is a good place to start.
    Moreover users naturally describe things in
    terms of events, and the order they can
    happen, so it is reasonable to start by
    formalising his view of these processes.

(3) The model is indirectly equivalent to a
    range of functions and it is easier to
    specify this range than the particular
    outputs required.

(4) The model defines the terms needed to
    describe system requirements.

Modelling notations. A diagrammatic and an equivalent textual notation are both used to specify
the model processes and the later function
processes and scheduling programs.

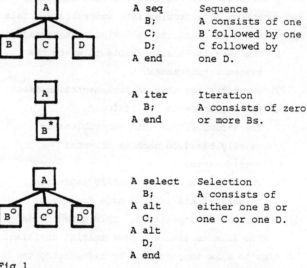

A seq	Sequence	
B;	A consists of one	
C;	B followed by one	
D;	C followed by	
A end	one D.	

A iter	Iteration
B;	A consists of zero
A end	or more Bs.

A select	Selection
B;	A consists of
A alt	either one B or
C;	one C or one D.
A alt	
D;	
A end	

Fig 1

There is also a textual posit ... quit construct
for problems requiring backtracking (ref 1,2).

In JSD an entity is an object or person who
performs or suffers a number of time ordered
actions (events). The model consists of 1 or more
diagrams; each diagram has an entity as the root
and the actions as leaves; together they describe
the real world time constraints on the actions.

2.2 FUNCTION

<u>Extra function notations.</u> Fig 2 illustrates the notations used in the system specification diagram which shows the connections between model and function processes.

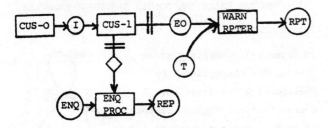

Fig 2

The rectangles are processes. The circles are data streams (unbounded FIFO queues). The diamonds are state vector connection: the process at the arrowhead may examine the state vector of the process to which it is connected.

In this example the model consisted of CUS-O, I and CUS-1. The suffix -O denotes the real world entity, the real CUStomer; the suffix -1 denotes the computer realisation of the same abstraction. The input I comes into the system to synchronise and coordinate the actions of CUS-1 with those of CUS-O.

The double bars denote relative multiplicity of processes: many CUS-1 for one ENQPROC; many CUS-1 for one WARNRPTER.

In this example ENQPROC and WARNRPTER were function processes. ENQPROC answered ad hoc enquiries about the CUStomer by examining the appropriate CUS-1's state. WARNRPTER produced periodic reports based on information written by I/O operations directly embedded in the model. The arrival of a record on the T data stream defines the end of a period. Note that both ENQPROC and WARN-RPTER are also long running processes: ENQPROC answers all the ENQuiries; WARNRPTER produces all the reports.

CUS-1 will lag behind CUS-O, perhaps only by a fraction of a second, perhaps considerably if it is scheduled unfavourably. The exact amount of lag is not part of the JSD specification.

Because the result of an enquiry to ENQPROC is based on the current state of CUS-1, not CUS-O, there is a looseness in the specification. The answer depends on how up to date is CUS-1. This looseness is a deliberate part of JSD.

The arrangement of the arrows from EO and T indicates that WARNRPTER consumes a single data stream. The implied merge process is not exactly specified. Again there is a deliberate looseness in the specification. Cumulatively WARNRPTER consumes all EO but the division into periods is to some extent arbitrary.

This looseness can be avoided in JSD specifications but the possibility of including a degree of indeterminacy allows a considerable simplification. Ad hoc enquiries about the balance of a bank account give out of date replies, out of date to an extent which is unclear. And noone minds if a cheque is missing from the bottom of a monthly statement, provided it appears at the top of the next.

In each of these cases the exact operation of a process B depends on the scheduling of a process A. In JSD this relationship is never reciprocal.

2.3 IMPLEMENTATION

How do we assure ourselves that an implementation meets a requirements specification? Traditionally by testing, though the disadvantages of testing are well known. Mathematical proof has possibilities, but they have not been realised. Moving from specification to implementation in a series of transformations is an attractive 3rd possibility. Each transformation can be proved correct in general; an implementor can choose any succession of the standard transformations and know that the implementation is correct. Since the main transformations can be mechanised, he may even be sure that they have been correctly carried out.

Of course this presupposes that we have a suitable specification language to start with. We assert here that the networks of long running processes outlined above are such a suitable language.

In fact, for DP systems at least, some element of

transformation is necessary in any approach which separates problem oriented issues from machine oriented issues. Systems are about large numbers of entities (10^3-10^8 processes) which perform actions over a long period (10^4 days) at infrequent intervals (10^{-1} per day). Systems are run in target environments which have few processors (maybe 1), which run for short periods (maybe less than 1 day) but which can handle many transactions. This mismatch between problem structure and target machine structure can only be bridged by some type of transformation.

Approaches based only on the successive refinement of a single system structure (top down design, structured analysis and design, stepwise refinement) must, whether it is admitted or not, be refining the machine oriented structure. They start by considering the implementation.

Implementation notations

Q has been inverted with respect to 2 of its data streams to become a subroutine of P. (n+1 lines imply inversion with respect to n data streams.)

Fig 3

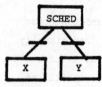

The components X and Y are invoked by SCHED (perhaps many times, order unspecified), but each runs to completion on each invocation.

Fig 4

When invoked, an inverted process partially executes. For our long running processes, partial execution on invocation is very much the norm. However as we near a final implementation, the notation in fig 4 allows the description of jobs, runs and procedures which do execute completely on invocation.

Subscripts on process names indicate that the process has been cut into pieces and we are referring to one of the parts.

Fig 5

Separate implementation of different parts of a

process - program dismemberment - is an important transformation, especially for function processes and scheduling processes.

Traditional DP symbols for e.g. tapes and disks are also sometimes used.

3. THE CAR RALLY AND GOLDEN HANDSHAKE EXAMPLES

3.1 THE CAR RALLY

In a car rally, drivers start from either checkpoint-1 or checkpoint-2 and drive the course in fig 6 without stopping. At each checkpoint there is a remote terminal. As each driver passes (or starts or finishes), an operator keys in the car-id;

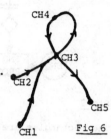

Fig 6

this causes a record to be sent to a single queue at a central computer; the record contains the car-id, the time and the checkpoint-id. A driver scores $A(t_1)+C(t_2)+D(t_3)+E(t_4)$ points or $B(t_1)+C(t_2)+D(t_3)+E(t_4)$ points (where t_j is the time taken for the jth section of the course and A,B,C,D,E are given functions) according to whether he started at CH-1 or CH-2. The program has to calculate each driver's total score and output it to a device which will display it on a scoreboard opposite the main grandstand. Assume all the drivers finish the course correctly.

3.2 THE GOLDEN HANDSHAKE SYSTEM

A company gives each employee a golden handshake when they retire; the amount depends on the length of time he or she has worked at the various jobs in the company. The career path of all employees is: start as office boy or messenger; promoted to clerk; promoted to manager; demoted to clerk (usually some other title); retires. When an employee starts, is promoted, demoted or retires, a record containing his employee-id, the date and a code discribing his new position (OB, ME, CL, MA, RE) is created and sent to the DP department. A program is required to compute the golden handshakes so that the cheques can be presented at the official retirement party. The golden handshake is $\$(A(t_1)+C(t_2)+D(t_3)+E(t_4))$ or $\$(B(t_1)+C(t_2)+D(t_3)+E(t_4))$ according to whether he started as an office boy or a messenger (where

t_j is the number of days spent in the jth company job and A,B,C,D,E are given functions). Assume that all employees follow this career path exactly.

3.3 COMPARISON OF THE TWO SYSTEMS

The specifications are identical in almost every respect. The career path of an employee is the same as the route of the rally. In each case the input is a merged serial stream of records each of which has 3 fields, the car-id/employee-id, the ch-id/job-code, and the time/date. The same calculation produces the output. Each problem even has a scheduling constraint - output must be produced quickly enough for the scoreboard/retirement party. The Golden Handshake system just runs more slowly. The comparison emphasises the abstraction of the time dimension in the long running processes used in JSD models and specifications. (In the GH system a single process may run for 40 years.)

3.4 MODELLING PHASE

A misleading point. JSD does not normally start from a description as detailed and precise as 3.1 and 3.2.

CAR is the only entity. The actions are to start and end the various sections of the course. For convenience in fig 7 the actions are identified by the appropriate checkpoint-ids.

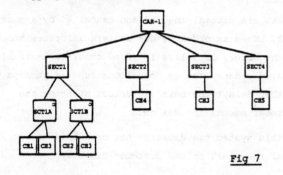

Fig 7

The decisions made at this stage are precise; no later steps are needed to remove ambiguity.

The implications are also clear. From here we may only develop systems which supply information about cars driving the sections of this course in this way. The model supports a defined range of functions; we have not yet considered which ones we

actually want.

Decisions about the abstraction of the user's world are here made in considerable detail, ideally by the user with some help from someone familiar with the formal diagrammatic language. Traditionally many of these decisions are made very late in the programming phase by whoever finally builds the 'update' program.

3.5 FUNCTION PHASE

Reporting on the car's total mark can be done by direct embedding in the CAR-1 processes. Unusually, no extra process is needed.

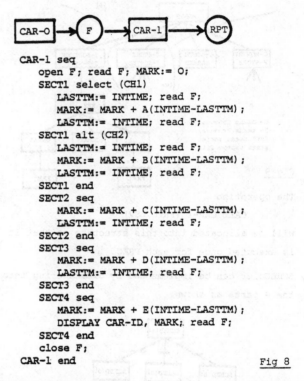

```
CAR-1 seq
    open F; read F; MARK:= O;
    SECT1 select (CH1)
        LASTTM:= INTIME; read F;
        MARK:= MARK + A(INTIME-LASTTM);
        LASTTM:= INTIME; read F;
    SECT1 alt (CH2)
        LASTTM:= INTIME; read F;
        MARK:= MARK + B(INTIME-LASTTM);
        LASTTM:= INTIME; read F;
    SECT1 end
    SECT2 seq
        MARK:= MARK + C(INTIME-LASTTM);
        LASTTM:= INTIME; read F;
    SECT2 end
    SECT3 seq
        MARK:= MARK + D(INTIME-LASTTM);
        LASTTM:= INTIME; read F;
    SECT3 end
    SECT4 seq
        MARK:= MARK + E(INTIME-LASTTM);
        DISPLAY CAR-ID, MARK; read F;
    SECT4 end
    close F;
CAR-1 end
```
Fig 8

There are as many instances of CAR-1 as there are cars in the rally.

3.6 IMPLEMENTATION

Almost all implementations of this system will start with 2 basic transformations.

(1) Invert CAR-1 with respect to its input F.
(2) Separate the state vectors of the CAR-1 processes.

For an on-line implementation the operation

    CALL CAR-1 (FREC, SV)

must be executed as soon as an FREC is available.

The operation will probably be part of a module (along with the SV accessing) under the control of a teleprocessing monitor.

We concentrate here on a batch implementation with monthly update, with the state vectors stored on a serially accessible medium. (Unless the cars are very slow this had better be the Golden Handshake system.) We design a special purpose SCHEDuler to consume the merged input stream of all the Fs and marker records which show the month ends.

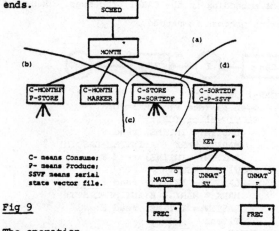

C- means Consume;
P- means Produce;
SSVF means serial
state vector file.

Fig 9

The operation

        CALL CAR-1 (FREC, SV)

will be allocated into this structure so that it is executed once for each FREC.

SCHEDuler can be implemented by dismembering into the 4 parts as shown.

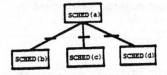

Fig 10

SCHED(a) will almost certainly be implemented by operator instructions: 'each month run SCHED(b) until the month marker (2nd Thursday of month) and then run the SORT ...'.

SCHED(b) could be operator instructions - 'keep input cards on this tray' - or a data entry program. SCHED(c) is a standard SORT. SCHED(d), the only part which invokes the specified processes, is the monthly job which runs the system.

Notice that the SCHEDuler contains a significant

portion of the finished system, including the SORT, but also that schedulers follow rather standard patterns.

The finished system consists of a monthly job and a combination of software and operator instructions to prepare the input. The code in the monthly job comes partly from the scheduler (the upper level collate), partly from the model (the structure of the inverted subroutine), and partly from the function (the embedded operations).

4.   TWO ORDER PROCESSING SYSTEMS

4.1 MODEL OF VERSION (1)

In a simple order processing system ORDER and STOCK ITEM were chosen as entities; PLACE, AMEND, DELAY, ALLOCATE and CANCEL were the actions of an ORDER; INTRODUCE, ISSUE, RECEIVE and WRITE OFF were the actions of STOCK ITEM.

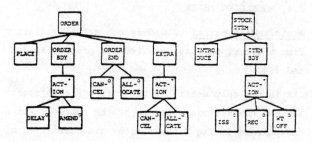

Fig 11

Orders are placed, amended and cancelled by a customer. When an order is due a clerk allocates stock to the order, or delays it if no stock is available. Delayed orders come up for allocation (or perhaps another delay) the next day unless meantime the customer amends the due date.

In this system the decision has been made not to model the clerk or the customer directly.

The EXTRA part in an ORDER's life is included because the clerk and the customer are not well enough coordinated to prevent a CANCEL after an ALLOCATE or vice versa.

This model could support functions such as: ad hoc enquiries about particular orders, or about stock levels; apology notes to customers whose orders have been delayed; warnings about low stock levels; periodic reports about outstanding orders analysed relative to the current stock level; lists of all-ocated orders from which picking lists can be made etc.

4.2 AUTOMATION OF ORDER ALLOCATION

In this version 2 of the system we replace the clerk by a computer process which will delay and allocate orders. The model is reduced; less happens in the world external to the system. Fig 12 shows the structure of ORDER without the actions DELAY and ALLOCATE.

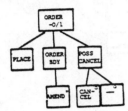

Fig 12

In the function phase, 2 new processes must be added, ALLOCATOR which is the direct replacement of the clerk, and ORDER-2 which is a functionally oriented view of an order and which may well have the same structure as the modelled ORDER in version 1.

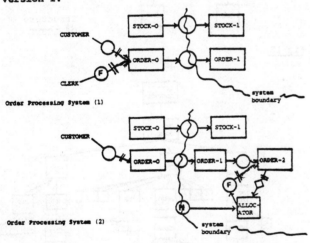

Order Processing System (1)

Order Processing System (2)

Fig 13

Fig 13 shows the system specification diagrams for the realised model in version 1, for the realised model + allocator function in version 2, both with an informal indication of what is happening outside the system boundary. The records on F, supplied by the clerk in version 1, are supplied

by the ALLOCATOR in version 2 (though possibly by following a different algorithm). ALLOCATOR is of course a long running process; it performs all the allocations in the system's life; arrival of a record on H triggers one round of allocation.

This type of function is called an interactive function in JSD. Interactive functions are closely connected with automation. They are specified before other types of function, immediately after the modelling phase. Since the extent of the required automation is often not clear at the outset, the subphase dealing with interactive functions gives an opportunity to reconsider what will happen externally in the real world, and perhaps as a result to redefine the model of that external real world.

Neither of these systems are developed further here.

5. A SIMPLE LIFT SYSTEM

N.B. An elevator in the USA is a lift in England.

5.1 MODELLING PHASE

Our system must control a lift which operates in a building with 4 floors (0(=ground), 1, 2 and 3). At first we assume there are only 4 request buttons all inside the lift. Pressing button j means a user wants to go to floor j. Later we will add 6 request buttons - up buttons on floors 0,1,2 and down buttons on floors 1,2,3.

The model turns out to have 2 entities: LIFT with actions ARRIVE FLOOR(j) and LEAVE FLOOR(j), and BUTTON with action be PRESSed.

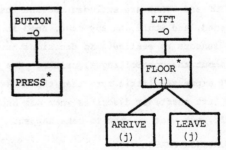

Fig 14

(Fig 14 assumes the lift starts between floors.)
The system specification diagram of the realised model (fig 15) implies that a record can be input to BUTTON-1 when the real BUTTON-0 is PRESSed.

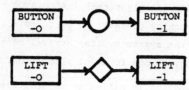

Fig 15

The connection LIFT-O to LIFT-1 is via sensors on
each floor. Sensor(j) sets a value 1 (directly
accessible by our system) if the lift is within 6"
of its home position at floor j and sets a value O
otherwise. The sensors do not generate records.
They must be examined by LIFT-1 (actually continually) on LIFT-1's initiative - hence the state
connection between LIFT-O and LIFT-1 in fig 15.

LIFT-1 therefore needs a more elaborate structure
than LIFT-O, simply to realise in a computer
process the same actions.

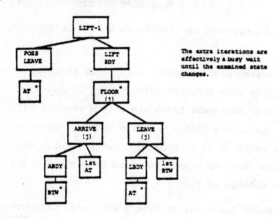

The extra iterations are
effectively a busy wait
until the examined state
changes.

Fig 16

The model of LIFT contains very little. Actions
like STOP and START are excluded because they are
not needed, and would, in any case, need an extra
set of sensors to realise. No decisions have been
taken about the controlling algorithm. The model
of LIFT expresses little more than the constraints
of the lift shaft; it describes what can happen to
the lift, not what we want to make happen.

5.2 FUNCTION PHASE

In the specification below, the lift only waits at
the ground floor; when it moves, it goes all the
way to the top, stopping to service requests on
the way, and then back down, also servicing
requests on the way. The lamp is switched on when

there is an outstanding request - defined as a
PRESS received since LIFTCONTROL last told the
lift to stop at that floor.

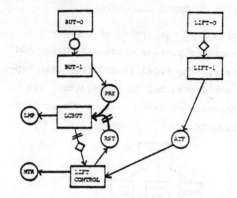

System
Specification
Diagram

Fig 17

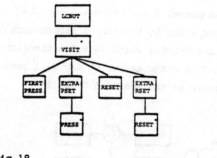

Structure
Of LCBUT

Fig 18

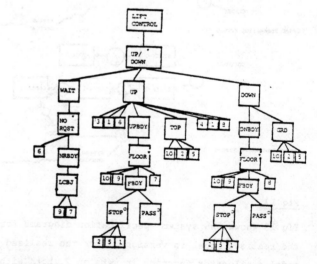

1. MOTOR:= ON
2. MOTOR:= OFF
3. POLARITY:= UP
4. POLARITY:= DOWN
5. write RST(K)
6. K:= 1
7. K:= K+1
8. K:= K-1
9. get SV of LCBUT(K)
10. read ATF

Structure of
LIFTCONTROL
With Operations
Allocated

Fig 19

```
LIFTCONTROL iter
   UPDOWN seq
      WAIT iter
         NORQST seq
            K:= 1;
            NRBDY iter while (K LE 3)
               get SV of LCBUT(K)
         WAIT quit (LCBUT(K) is PRESSed)
            K:= K+1;
            NRBDY end
         NORQST end
      WAIT end
      UP seq
         POLARITY:= UP;
         MOTOR:= ON;
         K:= 1;
         UPBDY iter while (K LE 2)
            FLOOR seq
               read ATF;
               get SV of LCBUT(K)
               FBDY select (LCBUT(K) IS PRESSed)
                  MOTOR:= OFF;
                  write RST(K);
                  MOTOR:= ON;
               FBDY alt (LCBUT(K) NOT PRESSed)
               FBDY end
               K:= K+1;
            FLOOR end
         UPBDY end
         TOP seq
            read ATF; MOTOR:= OFF; write RST(K);
         TOP end
      UP end
      DOWN seq
         POLARITY:= DOWN; MOTOR:= ON; K:= K+1;
         DNBDY iter while (K GE 1)
            FLOOR seq
               read ATF;
               get SV of LCBUT (K);
               FBDY select (LCBUT(K) is PRESSed)
                  MOTOR:= OFF; write RST(K); MOTOR:= ON;
               FBDY alt (LCBUT(K) NOT PRESSed)
               FBDY end
               K:= K-1;
            FLOOR end
         DNBDY end
         GRD seq
            read ATF; MOTOR:= OFF; write RST(K);
         GRD end
      DOWN end
   UPDOWN end
LIFTCONTROL end
```
                                    Complete
                                    Structure
                                    Text of
                                    LIFTCONTROL

Fig 20

LIFT-1 outputs an ATF record when it arrives at a
floor. When travelling LIFTCONTROL is usually
hung up waiting to read the next ATF record. When
waiting at floor 0; LIFTCONTROL continually
examines the SVs of LCBUT(j) for j=1,2,3.

To complete the specification: write the text of
BUT-1 and LIFT-1 with their embedded output oper-
ations; write the text of LCBUT with the embedded
SWITCH ON and SWITCH OFF operations.

A different algorithm. To change the service
algorithm, simply replace LIFTCONTROL. We may,
for example, want the lift only to travel up as
far as the highest request, and down as far as the
lowest, returning to wait at floor 0 when there are
no outstanding requests at all.

Ten buttons, 3 up buttons, 3 down buttons, 4 in the
lift itself. Remarkably few changes are needed.
LIFT-0 and LIFT-1 are unchanged. BUT-0, BUT-1 and
LCBUT are also unchanged except of course now there
are 10 of them. (Think about this; the buttons
have different meanings, as the original 4 did, one
from another, but they are still only PRESSed and
in LCBUT RESET.) The only real change is that the
conditions in LIFTCONTROL are much more complex.

Implementation. A full implementation is not developed here. We only remark that BUT-1 only copies
its input to output; that there are 6 other processes in the original version; that a simple implementation on one microprocessor can be based on a
round robin scheduler.

5.3 COMPARISON OF LIFT SYSTEM AND ORDER PROCESSING
    SYSTEM(2)

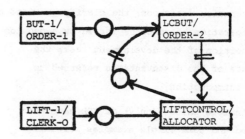

Fig 21

The patterns of processes in the system specification diagrams for these 2 systems are identical.
(Of course the internal structures and texts do
differ.)

LIFTCONTROL is an allocator of the single resource,
the lift, between the competing claims of the outstanding request. LIFTCONTROL can be regarded as
the replacement of the manual lift operator in the
same way that the ALLOCATOR replaced the clerk,
but in the lift problem, there was no ambiguity
about what external world had to be modelled.

The near identity of these problems throughout the
modelling and function phases is a sign of our
success at separating specification from implementation. Many approaches to system development,
(particularly those based on successive

decompositions of the system function, as has already been suggested) have specification decisions and implementation decisions hopelessly entangled. The design question is posed: 'how to decompose the system?'. But often the design question is not much more than: 'knowing as little as I do know about the problem, what implementation decision now is least likely to prove embarrassing later?'.

6. SUMMING UP

The order of decision making in JSD differs considerably from that of the traditional approach. Many traditional requirements decisions belong in the JSD function phase; many traditional design decisions belong in JSD implementation; many JSD detailed modelling decisions are made very late by a programmer.

The method promises considerable advantages: better communication with the user; deferral of implementation decisions; the clarity provided by that separation of concerns forced by a genuine decomposition of the development task; the avoidance of the disadvantages referred to in the introduction.

The principle phases (only) of JSD have been outlined and some simple examples partially developed to illustrate and motivate them.

The method has important implications in a number of other areas not explored here. For example:-
System maintenance using JSD. The model is more robust than the functional requirement; this is another important reason for basing the development on an agreed model. System maintenance is viewed in JSD as the modification of processes part way through their execution.
Project organisation. The analyst/programmer division is meaningless in JSD. Instead there is a distinction between user oriented people who work closely with the user developing specifications and machine oriented people who transform processes, write special purpose schedulers, organise SV access paths on databases etc.

Background. JSD has developed out of JSP, a programming method. JSP is described in ref (1), (2). The development can be traced in chapter 11 of (1) and in (3).

Acknowledgements. Many of the ideas presented here are due to Michael Jackson. Our numerous discussions have meant that even ideas I think are mine are actually partly his.
Richard Beck of STL Ltd gave me the Lift problem.

References

(1) Jackson M A; Principles of Program Design; Academic Press, 1975.

(2) JSP: A Practical Method of Program Design; Leif Ingevaldsson; Chartwell Bratt, London 1979. Also in Swedish, Studentlitteratur.

(3) Information Systems: Modelling, Sequencing and Transformations; M A Jackson; in Proceedings of the 3rd International Conference on Software Engineering; ACM/IEEE.

PART FIVE

JSD CASE STUDIES

Chapter 5.1　The IFIP Conference System

The problem definition for this system was developed by IFIP Working Group 8.1. They invited submissions on the problem from the data-processing community in order to make a comparative review of information systems design methodologies.

The reprinted JSD solution was not submitted as part of the IFIP WG8.1 exercise. About a year after the IFIP review, the European JSP Users Group organised a similar exercise to compare system design methods that were compatible with JSP. The European JSP Users Group is an independent body, which held its first meeting in 1974. They decided to use the same problem as had been used in the IFIP study. Participants submitted some material, had a meeting with a subcommittee who pretended to be users, and then submitted their final system documentation. There is no guarantee that the answers the subcommittee gave are consistent with what actually happens at IFIP conferences or with a system IFIP conference organisers would really want, or with the equivalent answers given during the IFIP WG8.1 study.

The material reprinted here is in three parts: the original problem statement; the short initial submission; and the rather longer final submission.

The following are some extra comments on the final submission.

INVITE was considered to be an output of the system, not an action. The action NOMINate happens when the committee decides that some extra individual should be invited, someone who, presumably, is not in any of the relevant groups and who has not submitted a paper. When the functions are added, INVITE records are output as a result of NOMINates (among other reasons), provided that person has not already received an invitation. A slightly different specification would have INVITE as an action that can be generated both internally and externally.

The entities POTDEL and PAPER refer to one conference only. The time sequencings of actions of the same individual at two conferences, or referring to one paper submitted to different conferences, are deliberately left outside the model boundary. In the case of PAPER, there would be some difficulty in realising a model that connected the same PAPER actions at different conferences. Even now, people give the same paper repeatedly at different conferences, using different titles.

The vet programs in this solution are the filter programs of Section 4.4.2. To vet is to check for errors.

Errors that cannot be caught by the vet programs are handled in a standard way. An extra managerial CANCEL action ends one instance of the relevant process when it is discovered that some previous input was wrong. Correct input is created for a new instance of the process. This is rough-and-ready, but it is probably quite adequate, given that redundancy in the definition of input data allows the vet programs to catch a large proportion of the errors.

Neither the vet programs nor the function programs have been fully specified. The design of the vet programs is partially implied by the definition of the model, but it also depends on formatting and other details of data collection. Only the outline structure of the function processes is given. To complete the functional specification, operations must be listed and allocated for each function, and structure text must be written.

Most of the functions are defined very directly in terms of time sequences of actions (promised but not yet submitted, accepted but not yet registered, etc.). This problem shows very clearly the centrality of the time dimension in data-processing systems.

The problem is also a good example of the definition of functions in terms of the model. The technical documentation on the model and the functions is very concise.

Of the three implementations briefly discussed, the most plausible is the distributed batch implementation.

IFIP Conference Problem

Problem Definition

1. Background

An IFIP Working Conference is an international conference intended to bring together experts from all IFIP countries to discuss some technical topic of specific interest to one or more IFIP Working Groups. The usual procedure, and that to be considered for the present purposes, is an invited conference which is not open to everyone. For such conferences it is something of a problem to ensure that members of the involved IFIP Working Group(s) and Technical Committee(s) are invited even if they do not come. Furthermore, it is important to ensure that sufficient people attend the conference so that the financial break-even point is reached without exceeding the maximum dictated by the facilities available.

IFIP Policy on Working Conferences suggest the appointment of a Programme Committee to deal with the technical content of the conference and an Organising Committee to handle financial matters, local arrangements, and invitations and/or publicity. These committees clearly need to work together closely and have a need for common information and to keep their recorded information consistent and up to date.

2. Information system to be designed

The information system which is to be designed is that necessary to support the activities of both a Programme Committee and an Organising Committee involved in arranging an IFIP Working Conference. The involvement of the two committees is seen as analogous to two organisational entities within a corporate structure using some common information.

The following activities of the committees should be supported.

Programme Committee:

1. Preparing a list to whom the call for papers is to be sent.
2. Registering the letters of intent received in response to the call.
3. Registering the contributed papers on receipt.
4. Distributing the papers among those undertaking the refereeing.

5. Collecting the referees' reports and selecting the papers for inclusion in the programme.
6. Grouping selected papers into sessions for presentation and selecting chairman for each session.

Organising Committee:

1. Preparing a list of people to invite to the conference.
2. Issuing priority invitations to National Representatives, Working Group members and members of associated working groups.
3. Ensuring all authors of each selected paper receive an invitation.
4. Ensuring authors of rejected papers receive an invitation.
5. Avoiding sending duplicate invitations to any individual.
6. Registering acceptance of invitations.
7. Generating final list of attendees.

3. Boundaries of system

It should be noted that budgeting and financial aspects of the Organising Committee's work, meeting plans of both committees, hotel accommodation for attendees and the matter of preparing camera ready copy of the proceedings have been omitted from this exercise, although a submission may include some or all of these extra aspects if the authors feel so motivated.

IFIP Problem. Initial Submission

I have done some preliminary work on the system and I would like some feedback before continuing.

1. The clear implication of the first paragraph of section 2 is that this system is to support one Organising Committee and one Technical Committee in arranging one IFIP Conference, not to support many such committees arranging many such conferences. I would like you to confirm that this is so.

Of course the same system can be run several times to support several conferences, but there would in this case be no connection between the different instances of the system. For example, any items such as lists of national representatives, working group members etc. would not be global to the many instances of the system; they would have to be set up separately for each instance.

You may feel that a stand alone system for one conference would not be very useful and that you would prefer a single system to handle many conferences. If so, please say so.

In what follows I have assumed a one conference system. The work would need extension rather than large scale amendment if you chose a multi conference system.

2. Preliminary lists of entities and actions. Preliminary entity structures.

Entities	Actions
PAPER	PROMISE : someone replies to say they intend to submit a paper
	SUBMIT:
	SENDREF: paper is sent to a referee
	RETREF: paper returned from the referee
	REJECT:
	ACCEPT:
	SESSDEF: paper is allocated to a session
POTential DELegate	LIST: The committee lists the potential delegate because he is one of a group who must be invited e.g. national rep, working group member.
	REGISTER:
	ATTEND:

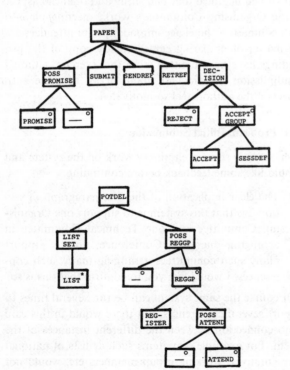

3. Comments on this model.

a. The implications of accepting a model are many and detailed. Normally I would want to go over them face to face with the user. For the purposes of this exercise, I have to assume that you have a certain knowledge of JSD, and understand the more obvious implications of the diagrams.

b. I have chosen to make a small, simple model consisting of only two entities. This is just about the smallest model which is consistent with the given application description.

Referee, Organising Committee, Technical Committee were among the candidate entities which have been (provisionally) rejected. Broadly, the system should be regarded as an information system about the behaviour or evolution of the chosen entities. This model could support functions such as:-

print list of submitted papers

print list of referees who have been sent papers (assuming referee is an attribute of the action SENDREF, which is reasonable)

print list of referees who have been sent papers but have not returned all of them.

The exclusion of the referee as an entity does not mean that no functions may refer to the referees. Here referee is an attribute of one of the actions of PAPER. If POTential DELegates are LISTed because they are referees, then referee is a possible attribute of LIST. But we may not have a function such as:-

print list of referees who have been sent papers after they have resigned from the approved panel.

Other entities were (provisionally) rejected because

– interesting actions for extra entities were not apparent,

– the functions referred to in the application description can be supported by this small model,

– for the purposes of this exercise, it seems appropriate to develop a small prototype system first, and then consider extensions, rather than start with something bigger.

If you understand the implications of rejecting entities other than these 2, then please comment on whether this is acceptable. If you do not sufficiently understand the implications, then we must talk before you can comment.

c. Within the structure of PAPER:-

– there is no action for selecting a referee.

– RETREF is a separate action from ACCEPT and REJECT because the referees decision may not be final. The technical committee makes the decision some time after RETREF, I assume.

- The diagram assumes that each paper only has one referee. If there were several referees, there would need to be a marsupial structure to describe the sequence SENDREF and RETREF for each referee.

- We assume that defining the session a paper is to appear in is an interesting action.

In the structure of POTDEL:–

- A potential delegate may be LISTed for several different reasons. (For one POTDEL, LIST can occur several times with different attributes.)

- We assume that the committees perform these LIST actions. (Were we building a multi conference system, we might have WORKING GROUP and NATIONAL REP as entities whose SVs contained the current names of members and specified lists could be produced by entering appropriate parameters. But this doesn't seem worthwhile for a one conference system.)

- We assume that REGISTER is a registration which is acceptable to us and not a rogue who is trying to come to the conference uninvited. We are regarding ROGUE REGISTRATION as outside the model boundary. This raises some questions of error handling which will be addressed later. (Essentially we have to set up error vetting programs which prevent such invalid actions reaching the model process; if this is not possible we cannot continue to regard this action as omb.)

4. Issuing invitations is a function of the system. It can be embedded in a level-2 POTDEL process, and this will ensure that no-one gets more than one invitation.

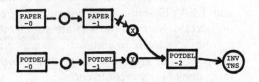

There is one record on X for each SUBMIT (or for each ACCEPT and REJECT, if we want to delay sending the invitation) and one record on Y for each LIST.

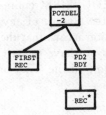

An invitation is only written for the first record; the others are ignored.

5. Examples of other functions which can be supported

- Lists on request of accepted papers
  of authors of accepted papers
  of authors who have submitted more than 1 paper
  of promised papers not yet submitted
  of papers not yet returned from referees
  of papers not yet allocated sessions
  of sessions with the sublist of papers in each session
  of registered delegates
  of all invitees
  of attendees
  of people who registered but who were not listed
  of authors of accepted papers who have not registered

- producing invitations as above

- any function whose information content can be expressed in terms of the defined model, including attributes.

As soon as the earlier questions on the model are sorted out, you will need to give guidance on the functions you would like.

IFIP Problem. Final Submission

Modelling Phase

Technical Documentation

1. Entity/Action List

Entities	Actions	
PAPER	PROMISE:	Someone writes in, presumably having seen the call for papers saying that they intend to submit a paper
	SUBMIT:	To send in a paper for inclusion at the conference.
	SENDREF:	The paper is sent to a referee.
	RETREF:	The paper is returned from the referee.
	REJECT:	The technical committee rejects the paper.
	ACCEPT:	The technical committee accepts the paper for the conference.
	SESSDEF:	The paper is allocated to a session.
POTential DELegate	NOMINate:	The committee nominates the individual, so that he will be invited to the conference. Presumably, though through error not always, he is not in any of the groups who are automatically invited.
	REGISTER:	The POTential DELegate sends in the official registration form for the conference.
	ATTEND:	He attends the conference.
GROUP MEMber	JOIN:	The GROUP MEMber joins a group (e.g. national committee, working group etc) whose members are invited as of right to some conferences.
	LEAVE:	The GROUP MEMber leaves the group.

2. Entity Structures

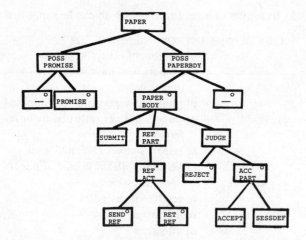

As the paper can be sent to more than one referee, we need the marsupial entity, PAPER/REF.

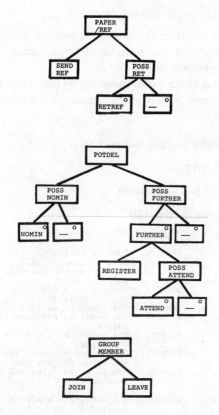

3. Model Realisation (without errors)

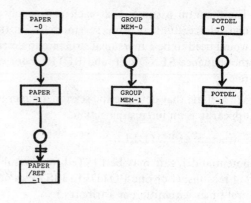

User Commentary (abbreviated) on steps so far.

1. There are a number of changes in this model, both in the definition of the model boundary and in accuracy of the description of events within the boundary, when compared with the version in the preliminary notes.

   - There may be more than one referee for a paper. A referee does not always return papers sent to him before a judgement has to be made. If he returns a paper after a judgment, his opinion is ignored; this LATE RETREF is omb (outside model boundary—it is not modelled; if it is entered into the system we will rely on error vetting programs to prevent it being passed into any level-1 process).

     Having many referees per paper forces the introduction of the new entity structure to describe the time constraint between SENDREF and RETREF.

   - A promised paper is not always submitted.

   - The LIST action has been replaced by the more restrictive NOMINate action and also by the JOIN and LEAVE action. The committee now need only NOMINate people who are not members of a group which has an automatic invitation as well as specify the groups who are to get automatic invitations for their conference.

2. Note that a NOMINate after a REGISTER is not permitted. This LATE NOMINate is omb in the same way that LATE RETREF is omb.

3. We have a multi conference system in that the lifetime of the GROUPMEM entities is longer (presumably) than the lifetime of any one conference, and their inclusion means that the committee of a conference does not have to start from scratch in working out who to invite. They only need to work

out which groups to invite. However both the entities PAPER and POTDEL refer to one conference only. A PAPER can be submitted only once. If a PAPER is rejected at one conference and submitted for another, our model sees this as two separate papers; the connection between the two papers is omb. Similarly if someone registers for two different conferences, he will be two different POTDELs.

Of course, we could have included the parent entities, SINGLE PAPER and CONFERENCE GOER. Our PAPER and POTDEL entities would be marsupials of these. However for the functions we have in mind, there is no need for this extra complication. Here we are following the general principle that, unless a parent has actions which are not also actions of the marsupial, then include only the marsupial in the model, until this is shown to be inadequate.

This principle has also been followed in keeping only GROUP MEMber but excluding both the GROUP itself and the INDIVIDUAL who may belong to several groups.

4. We assume that each paper has only one author, or that if there are several authors, then one will be designated and to the system he will appear as the sole author. At the discretion of the committee, additional authors of accepted papers may be nominated and consequently be sent invitations.

Modelling Phase (cont)—Error Handling

Technical Documentation (excluding process structures)

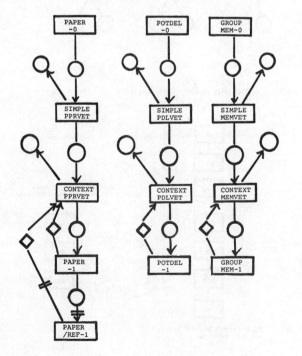

The SIMPLE xxxVET programs detect, diagnose and reject records which have errors, the errors being detectable without reference to the current state of the model.

The CONTEXT xxxVET programs detect, diagnose and reject records with errors which are only detectable by referring to the current state of the model.

Note that CONTEXT PPRVET examines the SV of both PAPER-1 and PAPER/REF-1. Thus, for example a RETREF is only passed if PAPER-1 has been submitted but not yet rejected or accepted and if the appropriate PAPER/REF-1 has been sent to this referee.

Other examples of errors trapped by CONTEXT PPRVET:

- Anything other than a PROMISE or SUBMIT first.
- After the PROMISE, if there is one, anything other than a SUBMIT.
- After the SUBMIT, anything other than a SEND-REF, RETREF (though this may be rejected by a later criterion referring to PAPER/REF-1), ACCEPT or REJECT.
- etc.

There must be zero buffering between CONTEXT xxxVET and the corresponding level-1 process. There must also be zero buffering between PAPER-1 and PAPER/REF-1.

So far this has been standard JSD error handling for errors defined as such by the model. Now we consider errors which cannot be detected immediately by vetting programs such as the above—records which are spurious but which describe actions which according to the current state of the model could have happened.

For any given case, there are two possible approaches: either define an artificial sequence of actions which will bring the model to an equivalent enough state; or first add some new managerial corrective actions to the model (both action lists and entity structures) and then define the sequence of actions which will cover the error by bringing the model to an equivalent enough state.

For GROUP MEMber, the first approach is adequate. If a JOIN has been wrongly entered, simply enter an artificial LEAVE; and similarly add a JOIN if there has been a spurious LEAVE. (There may need to be more to it than this. We may need to distinguish between real and artificial actions so that conference committees can be warned that they have invited someone they shouldn't have or not invited someone they should. But here we assume that this is unnecessry.)

For POTDEL we add a CANCEL action to the action list. CANCEL means there have been errors in the model of this POTDEL, and we are starting again with a new version of POTDEL. The new structure is:–

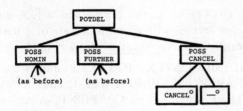

When a POTDEL is CANCELled, the correct sequence of records must be made up and entered into the new version of POTDEL.

For PAPER we may do the same.

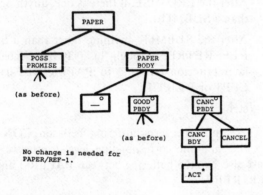

No change is needed for PAPER/REF-1.

In both cases there is no connection in the model between the cancelled entity and its replacement. If this is not adequate, we would make the structure of PAPER-BDY an iteration of CANCPBDY followed by a GOOD-PBDY. However we would then also have to make CANCEL an action of PAPER/REF which would similarly become an iteration of CANC PART followed by a GOOD PART.

The reason these rather crude additions are good enough is principally because the entities do not last longer than the conference. The side effects of partially (and wrongly) executed GOOD PARTs before the quit and not very serious. If, for example, we were building a personnel system for a company, we would be likely to need more subtle corrective actions than a simple CANCEL and reinput.

Function Phase

Required Functions

1. On request, a list and the number of papers which have been promised but not yet submitted.

2. On request, a list of referees who have not yet returned all the papers they were sent. For each referee, list the papers concerned.

3. On request, a list and the number of delegates who have registered.

4. On request, a list of authors with papers which have been accepted, but who have not yet registered for the conference.

5. Output invitations to anyone who has been nominated, to any author who has submitted a paper and to any member of a specified group (the names of these groups to be input). But make sure that no individual receives more than one invitation.

6. On request, a list of papers which have been accepted but not yet given sessions.

7. On request, a list of people who have been invited but who have not registered.

8. Output the list of names of members of specified groups, so that the committee can send out a call for papers to these individuals.

This list is meant to be an interesting selection of functions, rather than an exhaustive list of the committees' actual requirements.

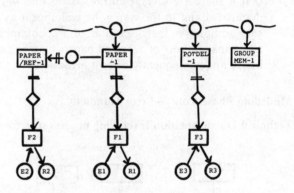

Outline function process structures.

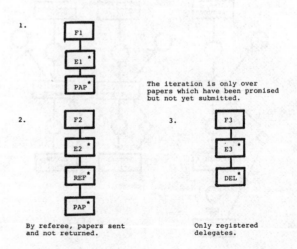

The iteration is only over papers which have been promised but not yet submitted.

By referee, papers sent and not returned.

Only registered delegates.

222

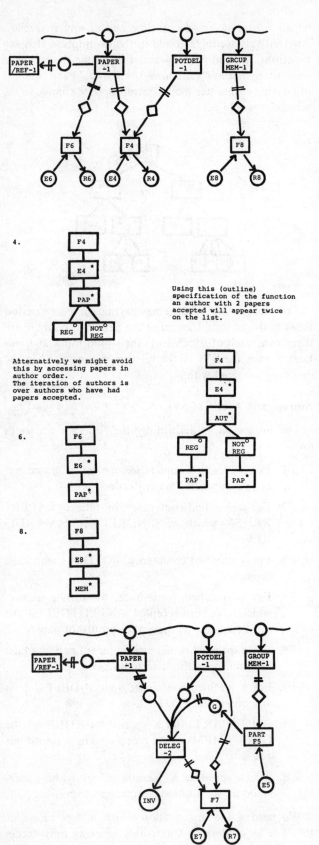

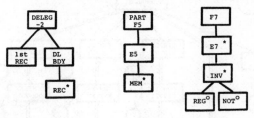

to F8 in that it examines the SVs of GROUPMEM; however its output goes direct to DELEG-2. DELEG-2 outputs the invitations, making sure that each person only receives one.

F7 is completely independent of function 5. It produces output by comparing the SVs of POTDEL-1 and DELEG—2. Notice that F7 gives the correct output whatever the buffering between POTDEL-1 and DELEG-2.

Implementation.

Preliminary Comments

1. The multiplicity of the processes in the specification is as follows:– One PAPER for each paper submitted at any conference (same paper at two conferences means two PAPER processes). Similarly one POTDEL per potential delegate per conference. One PAPER/REF per paper per referee. One GROUPMEM per member per group. One each of F1, F2, F3, F4, F6, F7 per conference. Exactly one F8 and PARTF5 overall. One DELEG-2 for each POTDEL-1.

2. We will consider briefly 3 implementations: a centralized batch system; a distributed batch system in which each conference centre runs the processes relevant to it and a centralised system runs the remainder and finally distributed partly on-line system. Note that the distributed implementation is easy and attractive because the Fj function processes for a given conference only need to examine the SVs of processes which are concerned with that conference.

3. None of the functions seem to be likely on-line functions. Most outputs are probably needed before each meeting of the relevant committee. We have added an on-line option not because it seems particularly plausible, but to show in outline how it would be done.

4. There are 3 major sets of issues in implementation: the transformation of the specified processes; the scheduling of the (many) processes on the (few) processors; and the storage and access of the state vectors.

5. The treatment of implementation here is even more sketchy (relatively) than the treatment of the earlier

E5 contains the names of the groups whose members are to be given automatic invitations. PARTF5 is similar

223

steps. Moreover, a greater knowledge of JSD is probably also needed. Remember though, that implementation is not a matter which concerns the user and the notations used here and the documentation ought never to be shown to him.

Centralised batch system.

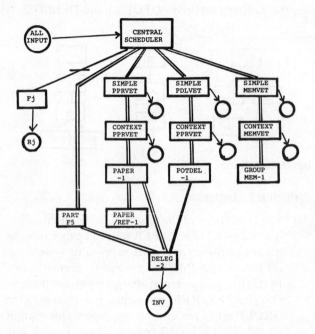

This System Implementation Diagram (SID) show the transformations which are to be applied to the specified processes. All processes except the Fj (where j = 1, 2, 3, 4, 6, 7, 8) are inverted with respect to their possibly rough merged input. Thus PAPER/REF-1 is a subroutine of PAPER-1, which is a subroutine of CONTEXT PPRVET, which is a subroutine of SIMPLE PPRVET, which is a subroutine of the scheduler. The Fj have been dismembered into components which deal with one enquiry.

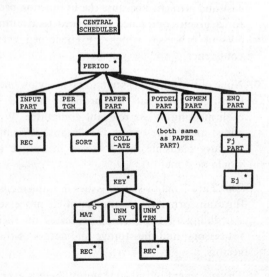

Here we continue assuming that the Ej are requests

which can come in at any time and at any frequency. Alternatively we might build in the assumption that say functions 1, 2 and 6 were wanted each time the technical committee met and functions 3, 4, 5 and 7 each time the organising committee met. The appropriate change to the scheduler would be:–

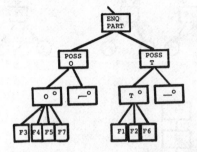

This scheduling scheme means that in every period input is stored until the end of the period; then there are three runs each of which sorts the stored input and collates it with the SVs of the relevant processes; then the enquiries are dealt with.

Storage and Access of SVs.

The access paths defined by the function processes are:–

F1: For a specified conference, papers promised but not yet submitted (in any order).

F2: For a specified conference, by referee, PAPER/REF SVs which are SENDREF but not yet RETREF.

F3: For a specified conference, POTDELs who have registered

F4: For a specified conference, by author, papers which have been accepted. Also POTDELs in the same sequence as the author groups of papers.

F6: For a specified conference, accepted papers which have not been allocated to a session.

F7: For a specified conference, invited DELEG-2s in any order, and POTDEL-1s in the same order.

F8: and F5PART: For a specified GROUP all the GROUPMEMs of the group who have joined but not left.

N.B. 'For a specified X', should of course be understood as 'for a random sequence of specified Xs'.

We need a file organisation which allows access of PAPER by conference (preferably allowing only access of promised but not yet submitted, and only accepted but not yet SESSDEFed) and also by author within conference. We need access of PAPER/REF by referee within conference for F2 and by paper for updating. We need access to POTDEL by conference (preferably only accessing registered POTDELs) and directly by POTDEL-id. We need access to GROUPMEMs by group. This is not a hard problem in file or database design. If we realise these paths directly, there is no need to elaborate the function processes. If we do not realise the paths exactly—e.g. by accessing all PAPERs of a specified conference (simple indexed sequential access)—then the function process must be elaborated—e.g. by adding a selection to select out the unwanted SVs.

Distributed Implementation

We assume one processor for each conference which will run the PAPER, POTDEL, PAPER/REF processes of that conference, their associated vet programs, and the function processes. We also assume a central processor which will run the GROUPMEM processes, their associated vet processes, and F8 and F5PART.

The conference processors do not need to communicate with each other at all. They do communicate with the central processor in that the output from F5PART is sent by some medium (post?) and input to the relevant conference processor.

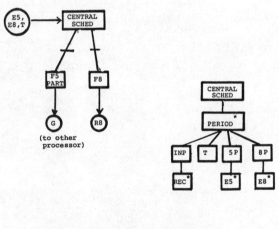

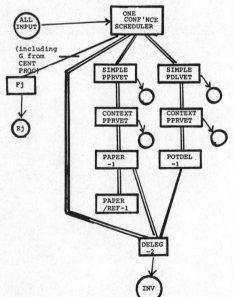

Comparing this with the equivalent to a centralised implementation: the GROUPMEM processes are excluded; F8 is excluded from the Fj; the scheduler calls DELEG-2 directly with the G records which have been passed across from the central processor.

Similar simple changes are all that are required to change the diagram on page 18 into a scheduler structure for this distributed ONE CONF'CE SCHEDULER.

Storage and Access

The GROUPMEM SVs will be held centrally; the SVs of all the other processes will be held on the appropriate conference processor. The access problems are identical except that keying on conference is (obviously) no longer necessary for the distributed implementation.

On-line implementation

The system implementation diagram showing the inversions and dismemberments of the specified processes is the same for an on-line scheduling as for the batch schedulings which we have considered. The scheduler structure is:-

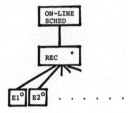

For a realistic implementation using a TP monitor, this scheduler would be dismembered into components for each record type and the dismembered component fitted into a framework which includes the code necessary for the interface with the TP monitor.

For the distributed implementation, there would be 9 such components, one each for an input to the PAPER and the POTDEL sets of processes, one for a G record from the central processor, and one each for F1, F2, F3, F4, F6 and F7.

The component for a G record would only contain the DELEG-2 process. The component for the POTDEL processes would contain SIMPLE PDLVET, CONTEXT PDLVET, POTDEL-1 and DELEG-2.

The storage and access problem in the on-line case is much the same as for the batch case, except that, in general, response time constraints force us to implement access paths more or less directly. There is not the time to access large numbers of unwanted records and select them out in the function process. The file organisation must support our access paths directly or nearly directly.

Chapter 5.2 The Toy Telephone Problem

5.2.1 Simple Telephone Service

To make a local phone call, a telephone user lifts the handset, waits for the "dial" tone, and dials the appropriate number of digits. If the call cannot be connected because the other party is already on the phone, the user will hear the "busy" tone. He must then replace the handset before he can make or receive another call. If the call is connected he hears a "ringing" tone that continues until either the other party answers the phone or the original party gets tired and hangs up.

Either party may finish the call by replacing the handset. The party still on the line will hear a "line-dead" tone, and he must also replace the handset before he can make or receive another call.

The system to be developed must supply a telephone service to the users by interfacing with the user phones and with an existing piece of software and hardware called the Network. The system may send the following messages to the Network:

> Get
> Conn (tiepoint, telephone)
> Remove (tiepoint, telephone)
> Put (tiepoint).

Get is a request to the Network for a tiepoint, which is a resource of the Network. Conn connects a telephone to a tiepoint. Remove removes a telephone from a tiepoint. Put returns the tiepoint to the Network.

Network sends a Reply message to any process that sends it a Get message. The Reply is either a tiepoint number or a "no tiepoints available" message. One tiepoint is needed to make a local call. If no tiepoints are available, the system must send a "system busy" tone to the user's telephone instead of the normal "dial" tone. The sequence of messages

> Get
> Reply (tie-no)
> Conn (tie-no, tel-X)
> Conn (tie-no, tel-Y)

has the effect of setting up a talking connection between telephone X and telephone Y. The sequence of messages

> Remove (tie-no, tel-X)
> Remove (tie-no, tel-Y)
> Put (tie-no)

ends the talking connection and returns the tiepoint to the network.

It may not be strictly necessary to send Remove messages for all the connected telephones before sending the Put message. For the moment assume it is.

Use this system description to build a specification in the following stages.

(1) Make an appropriate model describing the subject matter of this system. Include both user actions that come from level-0 and system actions that must be interactively generated.

Most of the tones that are output to the telephone user are direct embedded outputs from the model. They are good clues toward identifying appropriate system actions.

In this problem, the separation of user actions from the types of input messages is important. Do not hesitate to name two different actions where appropriate, for example ANSWER PHONE and START OWN CALL, even though there is only one type of input message, in this case LIFT HANDSET.

(2) Generate the system actions, adding interactive function processes where necessary. These extra processes have a functional relationship with the model and interact with it by supplying some of the model's input.

The relationship of the interactive functions to the Network is similar to their relationship with the telephone model. The Network, or at least the part of it with which this system has to interface, is a model of some hardware resources. The interactive functions also generate some of the actions for the Network's model.

(3) Add the following functions to the specification:

(a) Output the various tones that are sent to the telephone user.

(b) Produce bills for the telephone users. The bills should be produced periodically or on request, and should detail the calls that are included in the bill.

(c) For subsequent use by a statistics program, output every fifteen minutes a message containing totals of the number of telephones in use and the number of these that are in the middle of a call. Also output a message containing the total number of calls in progress and, of these, the number that have not yet achieved a talking connection.

Portions of this Chapter are excerpted from previously unpublished Michael Jackson Systems Limited (MJSL) internal documents with permission from MJSL.

Simple Telephone Service — Solution

Action List

STARTOWNCALL The user lifts the handset to make a call.

DIALDIGIT The user dials a digit (or presses a button).

CANCELOWN The user replaces the handset before a talking connection is established.

ANSWERPHONE The user answers the phone, that is, he lifts the handset when it is ringing.

ENDCALL The user replaces the handset to end a call.

CLEAR The user replaces the handset after the call has ended or when the call cannot be made because the system or the other phone is busy.

The above actions are level-0 actions; they originate outside the system. The following are system actions that have to be interactively generated.

TIEPOINTOK The Network allocates a tiepoint.

NOTIEPOINT The Network cannot allocate a tiepoint.

CONNECT A connection has been made with the requested phone.

FAILTOCONNECT A connection has not been made with the requested phone (presumably because it is busy).

OTHERANSWERS The called party answers his phone.

OTHERENDSCALL The other party ends the call.

STARTRINGING The start of a request to answer the phone. (As a result of this action, the phone should start ringing.)

ENDRINGING The end of a request to answer the phone. (The phone should stop ringing.)

Entity List

TELEPHONE

TELEPHONE CALL (of which a synonym is CALL)

All the above actions are actions of the entity TELEPHONE. The following are actions of TELEPHONE CALL.

START OWN CALL
DIAL DIGIT
CANCEL OWN
ANSWER PHONE
END CALL
TIE POINT OK
NO TIEPOINT
CONNECT
FAIL TO CONNECT

The structures for TELEPHONE and for CALL are shown in Figures 5.2a and 5.2b. In Figure 5.2a we distinguish between an outgoing call and an incoming call right through to the end of the call. An alternative structure would only maintain this distinction in a successful call until a talking connection is established.

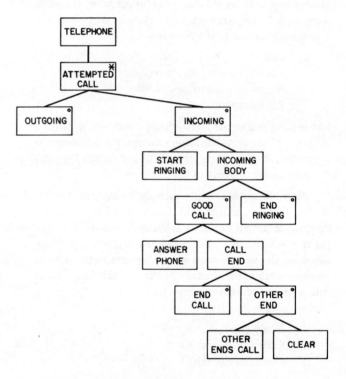

Figure 5.2a

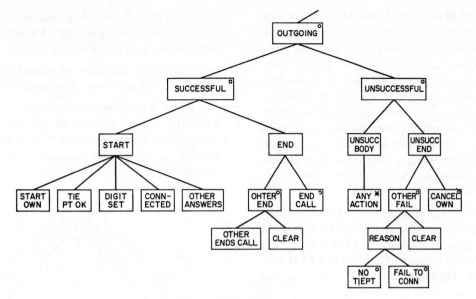

Figure 5.2a (continued)

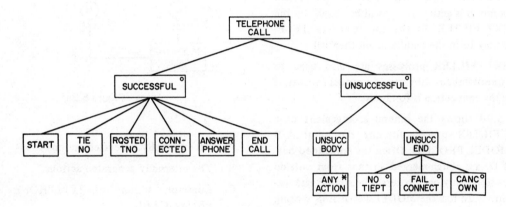

Figure 5.2b

Generating System Actions. All the actions of TELEPHONE CALL are also actions of TELEPHONE. We have to decide whether to replicate inputs for the common actions before passing them to TELEPHONE and CALL or to allow one of these process types to pass them on to the other. We choose to have the TELE-PHONE processes write records for the common actions to the CALL processes. (The other way around is bad because it introduces a rough-merge between the common actions and the other actions on the input to TELE-PHONE. Replicating the input is difficult or impossible because the external input lacks a CALL identifier. The TELEPHONE processes can supply the CALL identi-fiers.) The initial SSD is shown in Figure 5.2c. Over its lifetime, each TELEPHONE writes to many CALL proc-esses; each CALL process is written to by two TELE-PHONE processes.

Figure 5.2c

229

Both the TELEPHONE and the CALL processes are augmented by CONTEXT FILTER processes that protect the TELEPHONE and CALL processes from input records that do not make sense in their current state. They are exactly equivalent to the CONTEXT FILTER processes discussed in Section 4.4.2 that stop spurious input reaching model processes. In this problem they mainly filter out records that have become superfluous because another record has reached the process first, and consequently the process is no longer in a suitable state. These circumstances are commonly called "race conditions". Examples are as follows:

(1) If two people hang up a call almost simultaneously, both TELEPHONEs have an END CALL action and both will write a record to TELEPHONE CALL. Only the first is accepted. The CONTEXT FILTER in front of TELEPHONE CALL filters out the second.

(2) A user may dial a number and hang up (CANCEL OWN) before the system can generate either a CONNECT or a FAIL TO CONNECT action. The system will generate this action, but it will be caught by the CONTEXT FILTER. By the time it arrives, TELEPHONE may be in the middle of another call.

(3) CONTEXT FILTER processes are also used to answer queries about the state of a model process, if state vector connection is too loose.

Figure 5.2d shows the general arrangement of a CONTEXT FILTER process filtering the input A/B stream for MODEL PROCESS. Often the embedded outputs, C and D, are rough-merged so that from outside there appears to be only one process. The simple arrangement in Figure 5.2d has the MODEL PROCESS writing records on the E stream telling the CONTEXT FILTER

which type of F records it will accept. A "write E" operation is placed in MODEL PROCESS immediately before each "read F" operation.

To simplify the SSDs, we often leave out the CONTEXT FILTER processes. Their presence is implied.

Figure 5.2e shows an SSD with an ACTION GENERATOR process to generate the eight system action types. There is one ACTION GENERATOR per CALL process. To explain the diagram, we describe each data stream in turn.

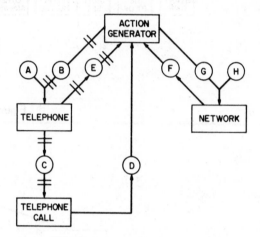

Figure 5.2e

A   All externally generated actions.

B   The internally generated actions.

C   Common actions of TELEPHONE and TELEPHONE CALL.

D   The stimuli that cause the ACTION GENERATOR to generate something.

E   The ACTION GENERATOR sends a START RINGING request to the called TELEPHONE. The reply on E, either OK (from the TELEPHONE process itself) or NOT OK (from the CONTEXT FILTER), determines whether the ACTION GENERATOR sends a CONNECT or a FAIL TO CONNECT to the originating phone.

F   The Reply messages that the Network gives to Get messages.

G   The Get, Conn, Remove, and Put messages. The ACTION GENERATOR is also a generator for the Network. Its relationship with the TELEPHONE processes is identical to its relationship with the Network.

For simple telephone service, the ACTION GENERATOR has the same structure as the CALL PROCESS.

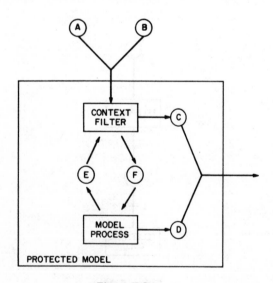

Figure 5.2d

A STARTRINGING action is generated when a complete set of digits has been dialed in the first telephone. A CONNECT action is also generated if the second telephone is available. ("Available" is defined in the obvious way in terms of the actions.) If the second TELEPHONE is not available, a FAIL TO CONNECT is generated.

The TIE POINT OK or NO TIEPOINT actions are generated in exactly the same way, except that communication is with the Network rather than with the second TELEPHONE process. The equivalent of the START RINGING action is the GET, which asks for a tiepoint and reserves it if possible.

The OTHER ENDS CALL action is generated when the END CALL happens. If a TELEPHONE process receives an OTHER ENDS CALL when it has already performed its own END CALL (and is perhaps in the middle of a new call), the OTHER ENDS CALL will be absorbed harmlessly by its FILTER. If the TELEPHONE process has not already performed its own END CALL, the message will be accepted by the filter.

The OTHER ANSWERS action is generated for the originating TELEPHONE when the called TELEPHONE has an ANSWER PHONE action.

The END RINGING action is generated when a CANCEL OWN action comes after a CONNECT action.

Noninteractive Functions. The SSD for the three noninteractive functions is shown in Figure 5.2f. The embedded outputs for billing are allocated in the TELEPHONE process to the OTHER ANSWERS action and to either the END CALL or the OTHER ENDS CALL actions. The input to BILL FN could also have been taken from the CALL processes.

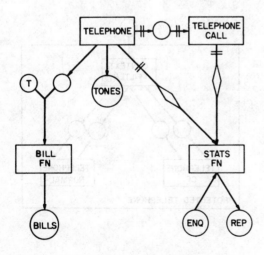

Figure 5.2f

5.2.2 Call Forwarding

The call forwarding feature allows a user to specify a number to which his incoming calls are to be forwarded. The feature may be specified in several ways. The following are two:

(1) Call forwarding may be set up only when the phone is not being used for a call. To set up call forwarding, the user lifts the handset, presses the special CF button, dials the digits, and replaces the handset. Subsequently, but again only when the phone is not being used for anything else, he may cancel the call forwarding by lifting the handset, pressing the same CF button, and replacing the handset.

(2) Alternatively, call forwarding may be specified and cancelled at any time, even in the middle of a call. The user sets call forwarding up by pressing a CFSETUP button and dialing the digits. To end call forwarding, he presses a CFCANCEL button.

There are many other possible specifications. For example, call forwarding may only be set up when the phone is not being used, but it may be cancelled at any time. Setting up call forwarding may start a call. A successful set-up may require that this call is a successful call or at least that the number is a good number.

Probably there ought to be some user output associated with call forwarding. There might be a light that is put on when calls are being forwarded and off otherwise. The light could also be made to flash while call forwarding is being set up.

The specification may include a run-time check to make sure that there is no call forwarding loop or perhaps that the length of a call forwarding chain does not exceed some limit. This check could also be done when the call forwarding is set up, and the set up could be rejected if it would establish a loop.

Call Forwarding—Solution

Extra Actions

SPECCF	The user presses a button to indicate that he is going to set up call forwarding.
CANCCF	The user presses a button to cancel call forwarding.

If there is to be a check at set-up time on call forwarding loops, there will also be two system generated actions.

ACCEPTCF	The call forwarding is accepted.
REJECT	The call forwarding is rejected.

All the new actions are actions of TELEPHONE only.

The two given specifications represent two extremes. In the first, there are strong constraints between call

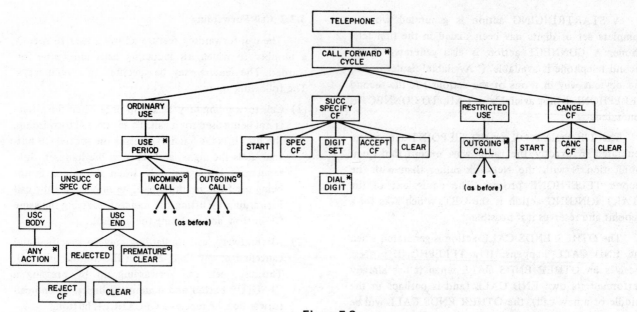

Figure 5.2g

forwarding actions and the other TELEPHONE actions. In the second, there are almost no constraints at all.

For the first, the single TELEPHONE structure in Figure 5.2g is sufficient to describe all the constraints on the actions. Between a successful specification of call forwarding and the subsequent cancel, the telephone may be used only for outgoing calls. There may be any number of unsuccessful attempts to set up call forwarding within the period of ordinary use.

For the second specification, two structures are needed to express the time constraints on the TELE-PHONE actions. One is Figure 5.2a, the same structure as for simple telephone service. The other is shown in Figure 5.2h. This new structure describes the constraints

on the new call forwarding actions and their relationship with the START RINGING action, the only action common to the two structures. A START RINGING action can only happen when there is no call forwarding and when the phone is not in the middle of a call. The two structures must be taken together to understand the constraints on this common action.

There is a single CONTEXT FILTER for these two TELEPHONE structures. The arrangement is shown in Figure 5.2i. The CONTEXT FILTER must know which actions belong to which processes. An input for an action common to several structures must be acceptable to all of them, otherwise it will be rejected by the CON-TEXT FILTER.

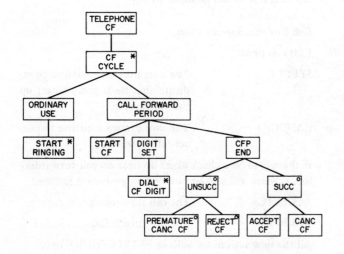

Figure 5.2h

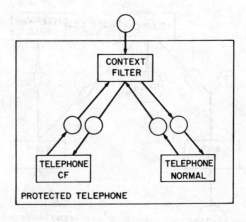

Figure 5.2i

232

The two extremes, strong constraints or nearly complete freedom, make the simplest specifications. The strong constraints can be expressed in a single structure. Lack of constraints leads to many structures (in this example, two) with very few common actions.

Figures 5.2j and 5.2k show a more complicated specification. Call forwarding may only be set up when the phone is not in use, but it may be cancelled at any time. CF CANCEL is the only action in the TELEPHONE CF structure not also in the TELEPHONE NORMAL structure. The common actions are the START RINGING action and all the actions that set up call forwarding.

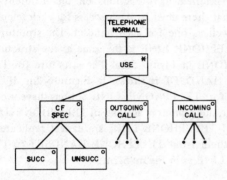

Figure 5.2j

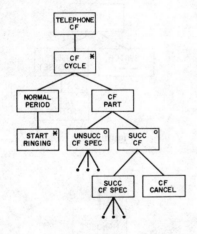

Figure 5.2k

We have already come across many instances of several different actions being detected by the same input record type. STARTOWNCALL and ANSWERPHONE are both generated by lifting the handset; CANCOWN, ENDCALL, and CLEAR are all generated by replacing the handset. So far, though, any structure that had one of a set of actions detected by the same input records has had them all. The CONTEXT FILTER could tell by the input record types where to send it (as well as whether to send it).

In this last specification, there could be only one CF button. When call forwarding has already been set up, pressing the CF button means a CF CANCEL, an action of only TELEPHONE CF. At other times, pressing the CF button means a SPEC CF, an action of both structures. The CONTEXT FILTER has to sort this out. To do so, it needs the following information:*

The actions that are represented by each input record type.

The processes that each action must be sent to.

At each instant, the action types each process is prepared to accept next.

With this information, the CONTEXT FILTER can decide which action a given input is representing and send it to the appropriate processes. For example, a press CF button input can be either a SPEC CF or a CANC CF. The CONTEXT FILTER will pass it on to both processes only if both can accept a SPEC CF; it will pass it on only to TELEPHONE CF if that process is waiting for a CANC CF; otherwise the record will be rejected.

The CONTEXT FILTERs are still simple programs that deal with each record in isolation.

Figure 5.2l shows an extra CF ACTION GENERATOR in the SSD for this system. This new process generates ACCEPT CF and REJECT CF actions on the X data

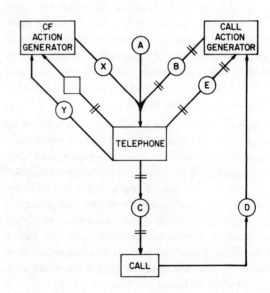

Figure 5.2l

---

*This approach is due to Pamela Zave.

233

stream. It checks for a call forwarding loop by examining the state vectors of the TELEPHONE processes. This extra action generator would be omitted if we dispensed with the check at set-up time.

The rest of the SSD is the same as for simple telephone service. The TELEPHONE process in the SSD is to be understood as the complete, protected telephone. It will look like Figure 5.2i if we are dealing with the second of the specifications.

The structure of the CALL ACTION GENERATOR is now a little more complicated. Between the stimulus from a CALL process to send a START RINGING action and the output of a CONNECT or a FAIL TO CONNECT, there may be an iteration over call forwarded TELEPHONEs. The CALL ACTION GENERATOR may also have a run-time check on call forwarding loops. The reply on E to a START RINGING action may be "OK", "busy", or "calls forwarded to X". The latter two replies come from the CONTEXT FILTER; the first, from the (NORMAL) TELEPHONE process.

5.2.3 Several Lines Per Telephone

Suppose that a number of handsets are each connected to a set of lines. Each line corresponds to one telephone number. On each telephone handset there is a switch that can be put into any one of n positions. The position of the switch defines the line to which the handset is connected.

Switching from line A to line B simply suspends activity by this handset on line A. Subsequent handset input is interpreted as belonging to line B. A user must switch back to position A to resume activity on line A. Only this handset's activity is suspended on line A when the switch is not at position A. The other party may end a call that was left in the middle; another party may attempt to start a call into this line.

A separate light is associated with each position of the switch. The light should be made to flash when there is an incoming call on that line. The inputs that were previously generated by lifting and replacing the handset are now generated by special logon and logoff buttons. (This is a slight simplification over the real situation. There, a switch away from a line is equivalent to replacing the handset if no other handset is on the line; a switch to a line is equivalent to lifting the handset if no one else is on that line; and the switch has other positions to put a call on hold.)

The sequence of operations

Switch to A,
Logon,
Dial number,

Switch to B,
Logon, and
Dial number,

has the effect of starting calls on both line A and line B.

Several Lines Per Telephone—Solution

There is one extra action.

SWITCH   A user switches from one position to another.

In this simple version of the problem, SWITCH is an action of TELEPHONE HANDSET only.

The interleaving of actions on the different lines means that there must be one process for each telephone line as well as one for each handset. The structure for the TELEPHONE LINE is the same as the structure of TELEPHONE in Figure 5.2a. The structure for TELEPHONE HANDSET is shown in Figure 5.2m. If input records for TELEPHONE LINE actions have no line identifier, the common actions of TELEPHONE HANDSET and TELEPHONE LINE are easiest replicated by passing them from TELEPHONE HANDSET to TELEPHONE LINE as in Figure 5.2n.

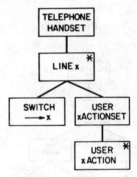

Figure 5.2m

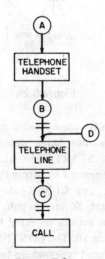

Figure 5.2n

The only extra complication in the generation of the system actions is over the choice of a line for incoming calls and the generation of a FAIL TO CONNECT message if no line is available. A telephone number is specified by the caller, but he may be connected to any of the lines. The exact line number has to be included in any Conn messages. Subsequent system-generated input must also be directed to the correct TELEPHONE LINE process.

If line numbers are assigned cyclically, the generation of START RINGING actions and CONNECT/FAIL TO CONNECT actions is done by two processes, one LINE SELECTOR process per telephone and one ACTION GENERATOR per call. The arrangement is shown in Figure 5.2o.

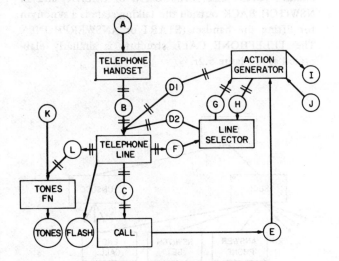

Figure 5.2o

The output that causes the lights to flash is embedded directly in the TELEPHONE LINE processes. Every handset has a set of flashing lights. However, each handset should only hear the tones that belong to the line it is currently switched to. By outputting the tones on the data streams, L, and the switch commands on the data stream, K, the TONES FN processes (one per handset) can send the correct tone output to each handset. This version of the problem is particularly simple because SWITCH is only an action of TELEPHONE HANDSET.

In the realistic case, a SWITCH from A to B is equivalent to a logoff on line A, if this was the last handset on line A, and to a logon on line B if no handset is already on line B. (In some systems, the SWITCH away from A is a separate action from the SWITCH to B.) Therefore we must distinguish four types of SWITCH action:

SWITCH A TO B (A LAST, B FIRST)
SWITCH A TO B (A LAST, B NOT FIRST)

SWITCH A TO B (A NOT LAST, B FIRST)
SWITCH A TO B (A NOT LAST, B NOT FIRST)

(LAST and FIRST actions are easily detected because they open and close circuits.)

All four of these actions are actions of TELEPHONE HANDSET: two of them are also actions of TELEPHONE LINE A and two of them are actions of TELEPHONE LINE B. The TELEPHONE HANDSET process passes the relevant actions on to the TELEPHONE LINE processes. If it passes them on as logon and logoff messages (with which they are exactly synonymous), there need be no change to the TELEPHONE LINE process at all.

The problem is still simple because there is no change to either the LINE structure or the CALL structure.

5.2.4 Call Hold and Call Waiting

The call hold feature allows a user to suspend a call, make another call, and transfer back to the original call. The feature is different from the *n* lines case because there is only one line and one tiepoint. When a user puts a call on hold to make another call, his telephone is removed from the tiepoint and is connected to another. When he transfers back to the original call, he is reconnected to the original tiepoint.

The call waiting feature is based on the same idea. When the phone is in use, an incoming call is not rejected. Instead, a light flashes on the handset (or the user hears a special tone). This tells him there is a call waiting. If he puts his current call on hold, he can transfer to take the incoming call, and subsequently transfer back.

Usually, at most two calls may be simultaneously active in this way, but two is not a necessary limit. If two is the limit, a single button may be used for both the call hold and the call waiting features to transfer back and forth between the notional lines.

Call Hold and Call Waiting—Solution

From the user's point of view there is little difference between the notional lines of this feature and the real lines of the previous feature. A necessary difference is that the switch action (called NSWITCH to distinguish it) must also be an action of CALL. Switching away from a line affects a call because, unlike the previous case, the telephone is disconnected from the tiepoint.

We also choose to interpret an NSWITCH away from notional line X as a replacement of the handset if the call on notional line X is not in a talking state. Thus if a user lifts the handset, dials a number, and presses the hold button to take an incoming call before a talking connection is set up, the first call is ended. We choose to regard the several notional lines as equivalent. In the above circumstances, the first notional line is now free, and the call waiting light may come on if there is another incoming call. Incoming calls are only rejected if all the notional lines are being used.

There are four different types of NSWITCH action. If X has a talking connection, NSWITCH from X means a temporary disconnect; if not, it means the same as a handset replacement. If Y has a talking state, NSWITCH to Y means a reconnect; if not, it means the same as lifting the handset. The four actions are:

NSWITCH X TO Y
    (X TALKING STATE, Y NOT TALKING)
NSWITCH X TO Y
    (X TALKING STATE, Y TALKING STATE)
NSWITCH X TO Y
    (X NOT TALKING, Y NOT TALKING)
NSWITCH X TO Y
    (X NOT TALKING, Y TALKING STATE)

There are still three entity types in the model, one for the handset, one for each notional line, and one for the telephone call. The TELEPHONE HANDSET structure is shown in Figure 5.2p. The TELEPHONE NLINE structure is the same as Figure 5.2a except that between the START and END of a SUCCESSFUL OUTGOING CALL and between the ANSWERPHONE and END of an INCOMING CALL (i.e. while the phone is in a talking state) there can be an iteration of SWITCH AWAY and SWITCH BACK. The fragment of amended structure

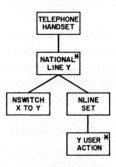

Figure 5.2p

for the OUTGOING CALL is shown in Figure 5.2q. The TELEPHONE NLINE structure must also be amended in a trivial way to show that an NSWITCH AWAY action outside the talking state is a synonym for replacing the

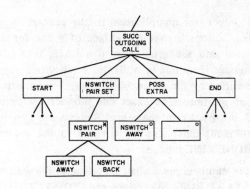

Figure 5.2q

handset (ENDCALL, CANCOWN, or CLEAR) and an NSWITCH BACK outside the talking state is a synonym for lifting the handset (START or ANSWERPHONE). The TELEPHONE CALL structure is similarly elaborated as in Figure 5.2r.

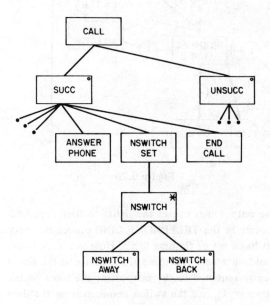

Figure 5.2r

A variation in the specification would be to end a call that everyone had switched away from. Only a small change to the TELEPHONE CALL structure is needed to show that a FINAL SWITCH AWAY is enough to end the call.

The SSD and the generation of the system-generated actions is the same as for previous versions. (There are no new system-generated actions.) See Figure 5.2o.

5.2.5 Trunk Calls

We could consider the trunk lines and their protocols as fixed and therefore part of the subject matter of the specification. The model would have one process per trunk line in each local office; there would be either a variation in the structure of CALL or an alternative structure for a distinct process type TRUNK CALL. This view is not very different from the conventional one.

More ambitiously, the trunk lines and their protocols can be viewed as part of a distributed implementation of a specification not very different from one with only local calls. Such a specification is explored in this section and its implementation considered in the next.

Suppose that local telephone numbers are all three-digit numbers but that no local number begins with a "0". Suppose that there are nine local exchanges. To make a trunk call to a number in another exchange, five digits must be dialed. The trunk number is of the form "0xabc", where "x" is the number of the desired exchange and "abc" is the local number within the exchange.

To set up a talking connection on a trunk call, the following messages must be sent to Network.

> Get (exch1)
> > to get a tiepoint in exchange one
> Reply (tieno1)
> Conn (tieno1, telX)
> Get Trunk (exch1, exch2)
> Reply (trunkno)
> Conn (tieno1, trunk no)
> Get (exch2)
> Reply (tieno2)
> Conn (tieno2, trunkno)
> Conn (tieno2, telY)

Three resources are needed, a tiepoint in each exchange and a trunk-line between the exchanges. In each exchange the telephone and the trunk-line are connected to the tiepoint, and this establishes the talking connection.

The sequence of the various Get and Conn messages is not nearly so tightly constrained as the above instance implies. A Get for a tiepoint must precede any Conn message for that tiepoint. A Get Trunk must precede the connection of that trunk-line to either tiepoint. At the end of a call, appropriate Remove messages must be sent, followed by Put messages that return the resources to the Network.

There are different possible rules for the generation of the system actions and for the output of the Network messages. For example,

(1) Get a tiepoint in the local exchange as soon as the caller lifts the handset, and get a tiepoint in the other local exchange as soon as a trunk number is dialed. However, wait until you know the desired number is not busy before sending a Get Trunk message. At the end of a call, return the trunk to the network as soon as possible.

This arrangement is sensible if the trunk-line is the most valuable resource. However, it implies either that the phone may start ringing and have to be stopped because a trunk-line is not available or that the model of TELEPHONE must be elaborated to allow the reservation of a phone before the ringing starts. It also implies that there is some means of communicating with the other TELEPHONE process without using the trunk.

(2) Send Get and Conn messages so that the connection is built outward from the first phone.

> Get (exch1)
> Conn (tieno1, telX)
> Get Trunk (exch1, exch2)
> Conn (tieno1, trunkno)
> Get (exch2)
> Conn (tieno2, trunkno)
> Conn (tieno2, telY)

This arrangement is necessary if a distributed implementation is planned, in which the trunk-line is also used for the implementation of the data streams between the two TELEPHONE processes. The Get Trunk message must precede the message to the second TELEPHONE querying whether it is busy.

(3) This second set of rules may be combined with a change in the trunk calls part of the TELEPHONE model. The CONNECT/FAIL TO CONNECT action is left out. Instead a talking connection is set up as soon as the trunk number is dialed. This means that the "ringing" tone or the "busy" tone is not output by the originating TELEPHONE process. The first user will hear over the talking connection either the called telephone ringing or a "busy" tone generated somewhere in the second exchange.

This reduces the number of system actions in TELEPHONE and, particularly, the number generated in the originating telephone as a result of actions in the remote telephone. The OTHER ANSWERS and the OTHER ENDS CALL actions are still included; they are necessary for billing.

This reduction in the specification is made for implementation reasons that make it desirable to limit the data sent from the second TELEPHONE to the first.

Trunk Calls — Solutions

There are no new user-generated actions except for the new pattern of digits that make up a trunk number. Each of the three sets of rules for the generation of system actions is considered in turn.

Rule (1)

There is no change to the TELEPHONE structure, except a selection between the two types of dialed numbers. In the process TELEPHONE CALL, there must be two extra components in the SUCC CALL sequence, corresponding to successful replies from the Network to the messages requesting a trunk line and the second tiepoint. There are similar extra reasons for an unsuccessful call. The structure is similar to Figure 5.2s with some components of the sequence rearranged.

This specification is very similar to the specification for simple telephone service. So it should be, for the service appears very similar to the user, and the extra actions generated for the Network are not very complicated.

Trunk calls appear to be very different, because they are normally given a very different implementation. Simplifying, the usual implementation is to have one computer in each exchange. All the processes involved in a local call are scheduled on the same processor. For a trunk call, the two TELEPHONE processes are scheduled on different processors. The TRUNK CALL process is scheduled on one or both of the processors, depending on our implementation choice.

Scheduling the same process on different processors is quite common. In JSD terms, when many terminals can update the same data, one process is being scheduled on many virtual processors. The locking and unlocking facilities of the database ensure that the process may not be scheduled simultaneously on two processors and that one processor picks up where the previous one left off.

Implementation is discussed further in the next section. A distributed implementation of this specification

is not possible unless there is some means of communication between the processors other than the trunk line.

Rule (2)

Same TELEPHONE as above, and a TRUNK CALL process with the same components in a different sequence. The structure of this TRUNK CALL is shown in Figure 5.2s.

Rule (3)

The CONNECT and FAIL TO CONNECT actions are removed from the trunk part of the TELEPHONE structure. This means that the trunk/local selection must appear at a high level in the OUTGOING part of the structure.

Without a CONNECT action, the calling TELEPHONE relies on the talking connection to hear the telephone ringing at the other end. Without a FAIL TO CONNECT action, the "busy" tone must also come over the talking connection. When the ACTION GENERATOR finds that its START RINGING action has been rejected, instead of generating a FAIL TO CONNECT action, it generates a CONN message to the Network to attach a standard busy-tone generator to the tiepoint in the second exchange. The originating telephone hears this instead of the remote telephone.

5.2.6 Implementation

In this section we discuss a single-processor implementation and a one-processor-per-local-exchange implementation for trunk calls.

We consider the implementation of the SSD in Figure 5.2e. The main issue is the scheduling of the processes in this specification. We shall include the scheduling of Network, even though we have not considered its specification. This SSD excludes the processes in Figure 5.2f, but it contains the most difficult part of the scheduling problem because it contains the loop of data streams C, D, and B.

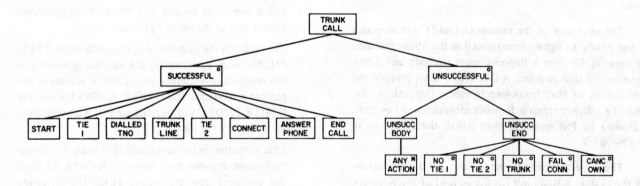

Figure 5.2s

238

Figure 5.2t shows a general-purpose scheduler. All of the processes have been inverted with respect to all their data streams. For example, TELEPHONE is inverted with respect to three streams, A & B, C, and E. (Remember that rough-merged input streams appear as one stream.) When a process is inverted with respect to several data streams, it returns to the invoking level when it reaches any I/O operation on any of the data streams. It also informs the invoking level of the reason for its return. The invoking level is responsible for meeting this I/O request, though not necessarily immediately.

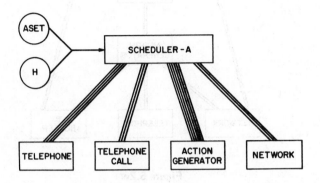

Figure 5.2t

The scheduler in Figure 5.2t is therefore aware of what I/O operations each of the processes under its control wishes to execute. It has internal buffering available (not shown in the diagram, but understood) for the data streams B, C, D, E, F, and G. According to its scheduling algorithm (as yet completely unspecified), it chooses a process whose request it can meet and invokes it.

The disadvantage of this scheme is that it is liable to be inefficient. Every record on each of B, C, D, E, F, and G passes through SCHEDULER-A. A process has to be scheduled both to write each record and to read each record. The implementation is made more efficient by localising scheduling decisions in processes other than the SCHEDULER. These local scheduling decisions are fixed by a different pattern of inversions.

Figure 5.2u is a step in this direction. Instead of returning to the SCHEDULER with a C record, and letting it decide when to invoke the TELEPHONE CALL process, TELEPHONE invokes TELEPHONE CALL directly. Similarly, TELEPHONE CALL does not have to return to the SCHEDULER to write a D record; it writes the D record directly into the external D BUFFER. TELEPHONE CALL therefore only ever returns to its invoking level when it wants to read a C record; there is no danger of it being invoked with a C record it is not ready for.

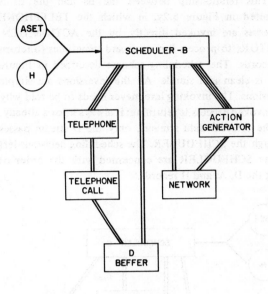

Figure 5.2u

The D BUFFER is external to the SCHEDULER in that it may be accessed without going through the SCHEDULER. The SCHEDULER does access the D BUFFER to remove records and subsequently passes them to the ACTION GENERATOR.

A feature of the specification not visible in Figure 5.2e is exploited in the inversion pattern between the ACTION GENERATOR and the NETWORK. An F record is a reply to a particular type of G record. F records are never produced under any other circumstances. Two I/O operations in Network can therefore be implemented by a single invocation. Instead of being invoked to process a G record and being invoked separately to return an F record, Network can be invoked once to process a G record and return an F record. This is acceptable to ACTION GENERATOR, because reading an F record is exactly the next thing it wants to do. (If this wasn't the case, a little piece of scheduler text would have to be clumsily inserted into ACTION GENERATOR to put the F record into a buffer.)

Network is now cast in the familiar form of a subroutine invoked by the SCHEDULER with H records and by the ACTION GENERATOR with G records, to some of which it returns a reply.

There is a similar relationship between the B records and the E records that pass between the SCHEDULER and the TELEPHONE process. An E record is the reply to certain types of B record. The interface between the SCHEDULER and TELEPHONE processes could be simplified.

239

This relationship between the Bs and the Es is exploited in Figure 5.2v, in which the TELEPHONE processes are invoked directly by the ACTION GENERATORs to process B records and sometimes to return E records. The scheduling scheme described in Figure 5.2v is clean and simple. All the inversions are simple inversions. The invoking level never needs to be told why the invoked process is returning; it always knows already. Of the internal data streams, only the D stream passes through the SCHEDULER. The scheduling decisions left in the SCHEDULER are concerned with the order of using the D, A, and H records.

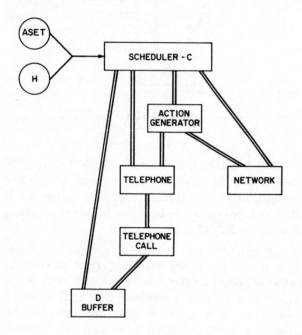

Figure 5.2v

Figure 5.2w shows another distribution of local scheduling decisions. The idea is that for each input A record, as much of the system as possible should be run before returning to the SCHEDULER. ACTION GENERATOR is called directly from TELEPHONE CALL with D records. We could have chosen to have ACTION GENERATOR put all its B records into the B BUFFER. Instead we exploit another particular feature of this specification. Some of the B records (START RINGING, OTHER ANSWERS, OTHER ENDS CALL) do not result in C records being sent from TELEPHONE to TELEPHONE CALL. We have chosen to let ACTION GENERATOR invoke the appropriate TELEPHONE process directly to process these records. ACTION GENERATOR invokes a different instance of TELEPHONE from the one above it in the invoking hierarchy. Only B records of other than these three types are written to the B BUFFER.

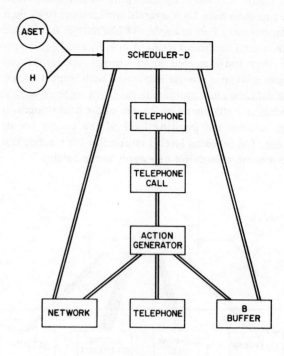

Figure 5.2w

TELEPHONE CALL cannot be invoked at the bottom of this hierarchy because only one instance of TELEPHONE CALL is involved, and that instance is effectively stuck in the middle of a "write D" operation (coded as a call to ACTION GENERATOR) and is not ready to be invoked by any other record.

Trunk calls. We now consider the distributed implementation of trunk calls, with one (or more) processor(s) in each local exchange. Some processes, for example the TELEPHONE processes, are executed in only one exchange. Others, like TELEPHONE CALL, may be partially executed by two processors, one in each exchange.

There is nothing unusual about this. In on-line data-processing systems, single processes are executed from different terminals on different virtual processors. The locking and unlocking facilities of the file or database system ensure that the two processors cannot execute simultaneously and that one will take over where the other left off. (This is discussed in Section 4.3.4.)

Alternatively, TELEPHONE CALL processes may be executed, say, in the local exchange of the originating telephone. Inputs to the process from the other local exchange and outputs from the process back are passed over a communication link.

Figure 5.2x shows two schedulers, one in each local exchange. Each is similar to the scheduler described by Figure 5.2t. Relevant B, C, D, and E records are passed

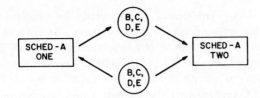

Figure 5.2x

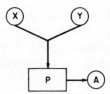

Figure 5.2z

between the two schedulers. Figure 5.2y shows a more efficient scheme, in which many scheduling decisions are fixed locally, and fewer records are passed between the two schedulers.

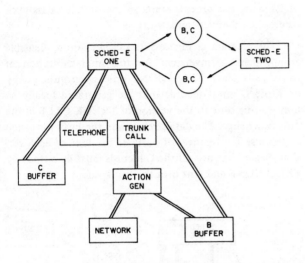

Figure 5.2y

The trouble is that this is not realistic. In practice there is very restricted means of communication between the local exchanges. Often the trunk lines themselves are the only means of communication, and the information that can pass along the trunk lines in either direction is severely limited.

In these circumstances processes like TELEPHONE CALL have to be dismembered and partially executed in each local exchange. The approach is not yet completely worked out and is presented here only in outline. It is similar, though not identical, to that described for certain on-line problems in Chapter 2.4.

The idea is to run two copies of the same process in each exchange, deleting from each those parts of the text that are not needed in that exchange.

Our aim is to execute a process like P in Figure 5.2z that has input X from one exchange and input Y from the other. First we create two copies of P, one in each exchange, that each pass copies of their local input on to

the other. In Figure 5.2aa X' is a copy of the X input; Y' is a copy of the Y input. The difficulty is that there is no guarantee that the merging of X and Y' will result in the same data stream as the merging of X' and Y. The extent and implications of their divergence must be analysed. The processes P1 and P2 must be elaborated so that inconsistencies caused by different mergings are no longer significant. If this cannot be done, then this form of implementation is not possible. Assuming it can, then the single process is implemented twice, once in each local exchange. Almost certainly, there will be parts of each process that can be deleted, because all the outputs are not required in both exchanges. This usually leads to a reduction in the number of records that have to be sent on the X' and Y' streams.

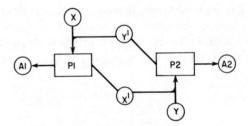

Figure 5.2aa

Consider, for example, Figure 5.2ab, a model of the use of the TRUNK LINE that must be somewhere in the Network part of the system (though not in the call processing part we have specified). This model implies that a

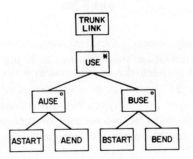

Figure 5.2ab

party in either exchange can originate a CALL on a TRUNK LINE. An AUSE is a use by local exchange A; a BUSE is a use by local exchange B. The AUSE and the BUSE are generated by the ACTION GENERATOR of a TRUNK CALL.

If there is another communication link between the exchanges, this process can easily be executed in one or other of the exchanges. However, if the trunk line is the only means of communication between the exchanges and can only be used after a USE record, there is a problem over race conditions. Both exchanges may try to start using the trunk line. The ASTART and the BSTART records clearly do not commute. The first START ought to be successful, and the second one ought to be rejected by the TRUNK LINE filter program. In fact, both sides think they have the trunk line.

If we can detect this situation (called GLARE), we can generate an extra CANCEL record when it occurs. The structure of TRUNK LINE is elaborated to the structure in Figure 5.2ac. Different mergings of START records do not matter. The second START is now not rejected by the FILTER program. The execution of the process in Figure 5.2ac is not materially affected by the exact rough-merging of the A and B inputs. Duplicate copies of the process in Figure 5.2ac may be implemented in each exchange. However, we do not need or want complete duplicates. The process in exchange A may be reduced by the removal of the B inputs; the process in exchange B may be reduced by the removal of the A inputs.

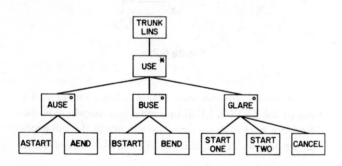

Figure 5.2ac

This may appear a very long-winded route to the final implementation. However, the case of limited communication between the two processors is very specialised. There are bound to be a number of steps in an implementation in this specialised environment if the specification is to be independent of the number of processors and the means of communication between them.

No elaboration of the existing TRUNK CALL process is necessary, essentially because the structure of

TRUNK CALL already accommodates the rough-merging of the actions from the two exchanges. The order of two ENDS CALL actions is not significant. A CANCOWN followed by an ANSWERPHONE has an equivalent effect to an ANSWERPHONE followed by an END CALL (as replacing the handset would be interpreted). Therefore the TRUNK CALL can be implemented as two processes, one in each exchange. Various parts of the text of each version can be deleted: for example, the parts dealing with the tiepoint in the other exchange. Other optimisations are possible: for example, instead of receiving the first five inputs in the structure of Figure 5.2s, the version in the second exchange may receive the state vector of the other version after it has processed the first four inputs. Instead of starting at the beginning of its text, the process starts in the middle of its text, where the other version left off.

The diagram in Figure 5.2ad shows a more plausible arrangement of inversions for this implementation of trunk calls. Each TELEPHONE process outputs a copy of those C input records that are generated locally so they can be sent to the version of TRUNK CALL in the other exchange. The data streams and the buffer is called C' because the removal of parts of the text of each version means that not all the C records must be output by TELEPHONE and sent over the trunk line.

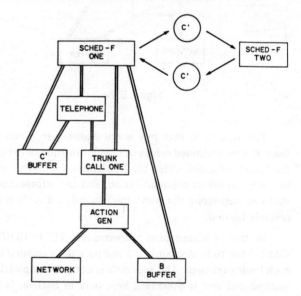

Figure 5.2ad

This transformation to implement the trunk call process in two parts, one in each local exchange, is the same transformation that is needed for an implementation of local calls using one microprocessor per telephone. You can see this by imagining that telephones can only be used to make trunk calls and further imagining that there is only one telephone in each local exchange.

5.2.7 Some Further Points

This chapter has dealt with only a simple version of the problem of call processing. Many aspects of simple telephone service have been left out, for example: there is often a time delay between replacing the handset and the end of the call so that an incoming call can be taken in another room; there are time-outs on digit dialing; the handset does not have to be replaced between outgoing calls; and other resources are needed to make a telephone call, for example, tone generators and digit analysers.

Only a few of the useful features that could be added to the specification of a telephone service have been considered.

We have not considered at all the processes that model the hardware resources; we simply assumed an easy interface with Network.

We have not considered the audit processes that are a crucial part of a fault-tolerant system like an automatic switching system.

We only note the following two points.

(1) If extra resources are needed to make a phone call, there will be a more complicated interface between ACTION GENERATOR and the Network, but there will not necessarily be any change in the interface between ACTION GENERATOR and TELEPHONE. (The only actions of TELEPHONE that depend on Network are TIEPOINTOK and NOTIEPOINT. If the several resources are all required together at the beginning of a call attempt, these actions can be renamed RESOURCESOK and NOT ENOUGH RESOURCES. In this case there is no change to the TELEPHONE model or to the interface with ACTION GENERATOR.)

(2) Audit programs are interactive function processes that generate input for extra corrective actions, usually actions that prematurely terminate calls. They compensate for category-three errors in the way described in Section 4.4.2.

All the data in a JSD specification are local variables of processes in the specification. Data can only be changed by executing the processes to which it belongs. The JSD approach to the difficult category-three errors is to elaborate the processes so that they include extra corrective actions and to define artificial sequences of actions that bring the model back to an acceptable state. Once defined, corrective actions are treated in the same way as any other actions. The audit programs that generate most of them (and the other actions in the artificial sequences) are perfectly ordinary interactive function processes. Often they have only state vector connection with the model. Some of the corrective actions, particularly those that have an extreme effect, may still be generated externally.

PART SIX

MANAGEMENT
AND HUMAN FACTORS

Chapter 6.1   Management and Human Factors

The methods described in the first five parts of this book change the way software developers do their work. Our experience with JSP, and more recently with JSD, suggests that there are human and managerial problems associated with such change. Most of the problems are intrinsic to any change in the software development approach and are not specifically associated with JSP or JSD. They are not insuperable, but they can significantly reduce the benefits of the new approach.

This chapter is fairly superficial, not much more than an acknowledgement that the management of change can be difficult. The nature of the problem is briefly discussed and a number of miscellaneous suggestions are made to help avoid some of the pitfalls. Section 6.1.3 summarises some specific points arising out of JSD. Section 6.1.4 addresses a phenomenon that will be familiar to anyone who has tried to change working practices in software development shops: people say the new approach is excellent in general but, unfortunately, it doesn't apply to them.

6.1.1 Attitudes and Perceptions

In management what people perceive is often more important than what is true. Consider the case of a programmer who believes that structured programming "deskills" programming and that his managers are interested in it for this reason. He believes that in the middle term they want to pay programmers less and be less vulnerable to programmer shortages. If he expects to remain a programmer, he will almost certainly tend to oppose, either actively or passively, the introduction of structured programming. If he is involved in a pilot project, he will have every incentive to show that structured programming is not better than his more "skillful" methods.

Now suppose that the method under discussion is JSP and that the programmer attends a course. As a result of the course, his own perceptions change. He thinks that JSP increases the net skill-level in programming. He may even think that JSP makes programming a more professional activity. However, nothing in the course changes his perceptions of his manager's attitudes, and these perceptions may be completely accurate. His position is now much more complicated. Certainly he is unlikely to be publicly enthusiastic about JSP unless he is senior enough or

technically self-confident enough to try to persuade management that they are mistaken.

The reason for the widespread belief in the "deskilling" myth has to do with marketing. A salesman or a marketing organisation will naturally project their product as fitting their customers' perceived need. If the managers want to buy a product that reduces the skill level in programming, then the salesmen will tend to present structured programming as that product. If the customers don't want a product that is difficult to learn, the marketing people will tend to leave out some of the harder technical ideas. Even Dijkstra's "Notes on Structured Programming" can be turned into salesman's patter, given time.

The reasons an organisation may want to adopt better methods of software development are fairly obvious. The following are some reasons why an individual within the organisation may not welcome the change.

(1) To be positive towards change, a designer, analyst, or programmer must, at some level of consciousness, be dissatisfied with the current approach. Many people are very content with what they do now.

(2) Someone may belong to what they perceive as an elite group that does things in the best possible way. They will only accept change that originates from within this group.

(3) Many programmers are only comfortable within a rather narrow environment, solving a narrow range of problems. Over several years and with some difficulty they have learned a number of coding tricks and a few special-purpose techniques. They are not interested in a method that is more general and more powerful because they don't imagine moving outside their narrow environment. Much more significantly, they may be frightened by the prospect of using a method that forces them to abandon the tricks and techniques so painstakingly acquired, the very tricks and techniques that they perceive as the basis of their competence.

(4) A manager may be interested in methods more as a defence against his upper management than out of genuine belief that they have something to offer. He is quite prepared to set down a formal guideline, and to have the standards manual in his office to show visitors how things are done in his department, but he isn't prepared to do much else. A list of

special cases that are exempt from the guideline builds up, a list that, on close examination, includes virtually everything that is done.

(5) People may fear that the introduction of new methods will mean that they lose effective seniority over new recruits.

(6) People fear that they will not be able to learn how to do things in new ways or that the skills needed to master the new techniques will not be the same as those needed for the old.

(7) A programmer may enjoy being the only one in the department who understands the software he produces.

(8) An analyst may have escaped from the precision of programming and may not welcome the introduction of more formal specification techniques.

(9) People may perceive the introduction of "method" as an attack on the way they do things and may defend their position.

(10) People may think that new methods may not deskill but that they are nevertheless less fun to use and take some of the creativity away from the job.

(11) A technical manager may have moved away from technical work. He may not welcome new methods, for which he will be responsible, but which he has little inclination to learn.

In any individual, any one of these beliefs and tendencies is only one aspect of a much more complicated attitude to change. The person responsible for trying out and introducing new methods must aim to deal sensitively with negative attitudes. Someone else's fears will not go away just because you can see that they are groundless.

People will not remain negative towards change if they can see that the change is in general sensible and if they can see that their position in the new environment will not be worse than it was in the old.

The following are some problems that can arise in an organisation when a new method is adopted.

(1) The more experienced people hang back from using the new method. Having most to lose from a public failure, they have a tendency to let someone else do it first. This can create tension between the more recent recruits and the experienced people. The recruits may pick up the method more quickly because they don't have to unlearn another approach. They may be enthusiastic because they want to get started with the very latest thing. The more enthusiastic they become, the more cagey the experienced programmers will become and the more worried they will become that they are going to be

overtaken. The very people who should be leading the endeavour will try to hold it back.

(2) An organisation may use only a limited part of the method. This is not necessarily bad. They may consciously decide that they want to use only a subset. Often, though, the reasons for excluding some techniques are less well worked out. In the case of JSP, companies often leave out inversion and backtracking. They say that they do not seem to have problems that need these techniques. In fact, their programmers did not understand the techniques on their first course well enough to become comfortable with them. There was no subsequent support to help them build confidence and to show them how the techniques applied to their own problems. The techniques were never used, and management was told that they do not apply in their environment. The examples in Chapter 2.3 and the case studies in Part Three show that backtracking and inversion are essential techniques for a wide range of problems.

The root cause of this situation is a false assumption by management that a course is all that is needed to install a method. Unfortunately, a method is not like a software package or a language. A course is the start of the learning curve for a method, not the end. Only by using it in their own work can people become really comfortable. The learning curve for JSP takes, on average, three or four medium-sized programs.

Despite these comments, there are benefits to even the partial use of a good method. The perfect should not become the enemy of the good. Some experienced JSP programmers have said that they are glad no one looked too critically at their first JSP programs because they now realise that they were only partially using the method. They were happy with what they had done and thought it was an improvement. Gradually, they moved toward a more complete acceptance and an even bigger improvement.

(3) There may be insufficient support at a technical level. Most people are willing to give something new a chance only if they know they have someone to turn to for help. Under normal pressure to finish a job, they will not persevere on their own with unfamiliar techniques.

(4) There may be insufficient support from the management. Management may misjudge the nature of the change and underestimate and therefore not anticipate the problems that can arise. The management of a department can encourage an atmosphere conducive to the introduction of methods. Someone

whose natural instinct is to hang back will react very differently if he thinks that the new method really is the coming thing than if he thinks that it is just another temporary management whim. Different levels of management need to be involved. A project leader is no more likely to risk his reputation on a new method than is a programmer. He will need the blessing, the support, and sometimes shielding from the management above him.

6.1.2 Some Dos and Don'ts

Try to schedule courses on the detailed application of a method just before the students will have an opportunity to use it. If the gap is too long, they will forget and be less enthusiastic.

Make sure that people who interface with the group using the new method are given any necessary training. For JSP, technical managers and analysts benefit from a one- or two-day overview course. For JSD, users can be given a half-day appreciation of the new pattern of a JSD project.

Set up an internal support function, even if at the beginning the technical expertise has to come from outside. You might say something like, "Use this method; if you have trouble, go to Joe or Sally". Joe and Sally may themselves be able to help, they may bring in someone from outside, or they may agree that the method need not be used. At least, though, they will know what is going on. With JSP, people have sometimes found out some months later that the method was abandoned in some area. The reason that is given was not made public at the time because the people involved were only lukewarm about using the method anyway.

Try to create a nucleus of success and build out from that. Forget any idea of a big changeover. A department of ten people can move to JSP in a relatively short time because everyone can learn at the same time. A department of fifty people will take around eighteen months to change, and even then many old non-JSP systems will still be around needing small scale maintenance. A larger organisation will take several years.

Change should be organised on a project by project basis. Try to start with the people who are most enthusiastic. Try also to make sure that the existing technical leaders within the department are also leaders for the new methods. Consider sending some of them on courses ahead of the others to give them a chance to familiarise themselves with the new methods so they can advise and support the others later.

Programmers are often hostile towards any change that increases the amount of documentation. For JSP, a rigid standard enforcing the accurate upkeep of the program structure diagram is better than a standard that also includes data structures and operations lists but which is ignored or which causes resentment to be directed at the whole method.

Excessive neatness in documentation is also disastrous. People will not take the time to redraw a large diagram neatly, nor will they destroy a work of art by making changes on the existing diagram. Use scissors, paste, and a photocopier to maintain diagrams if more sophisticated tools are not available.

Investigate the possibility of using software tools to support the method. Software support is valuable for a number of reasons. It may help the developer with clerical aspects of the job and automate such techniques as program inversion. In an unobtrusive way, a good tool can partially enforce the use of a method. Perhaps most significantly, a tool can sugar the methodology pill. A graphics package for JSP diagrams may be no more than a convenient way of inputting designs. It may even encourage programmers to rush to a terminal in the way they used to rush to the coding sheet. However, people like to use terminals. A graphics package may make the difference between enthusiasm and neutrality, between people using the method and not bothering. Whether we like it or not, cosmetics are sometimes at least as important as substance.

If someone has taken an entrenched position and doesn't want to use the new approach, don't force him. Look for a more favourable opportunity either with different people or at a different time.

6.1.3 Some Specific JSD Points

The JSD life cycle differs in some important respects from the traditional life cycle. At the highest level, the JSD life cycle is first model, then function, then implementation. (We ignore, for the moment, the fact that the true life cycle, including possible prototyping and subsequent maintenance, is an iteration of this sequence of three.) Approximately, the equivalent traditional life cycle is requirements first, next design, and then programming.

The difference in life cycles is an expression of different orderings of decisions. Many traditional requirements decisions are taken in the JSD function phase. Most traditional design decisions are, in JSD terms, implementation decisions: for example, the decision to have daily, weekly, and quarterly batch jobs; the decision to have an indexed sequential file; or the decision to have a particular database design. Some JSD modelling decisions are traditionally taken very late in the programming phase. JSD model processes end up as update routines. Traditionally a programmer works out the remaining details of these updating routines, details that in JSD are fixed in the first phase of the whole development.

These technical differences affect the management of projects. The nature of the major checkpoints changes. The nature of the documents produced at each of the major checkpoints changes. Once JSD becomes established in an organisation, the skills required at different stages of the project also change.

Each of the six steps in JSD defines a checkpoint at its end. The discussion on decision independence in Section 4.5.4 shows that steps two, three, and four can be done largely in parallel.

Throughout the development, the decisions made are precise and are therefore expressed in a formal language. In general, users are not familiar or comfortable with formal languages, so the technical documentation can never be the same as the user documentation. Technical JSD documentation is described in Chapter 4.2. The user documentation must explain the technical documentation and the consequences of the decisions it describes.

The exact nature of the user documentation depends on the user. Many users are happy to learn to read (but not to write) structure diagrams. This helps because structure diagrams are the only notation used in the modelling phase, and the agreement on a suitable model requires the most intense user involvement. User documentation has to contain some detailed explanation of the implications of accepting a diagram. If the user cannot read the diagrams, he will need a complete description of them in natural language. No other JSD notations need be explained to a user. Informal descriptions are normally adequate for the function phase. The user need not be involved in the implementation phase at all.

JSD encourages a different division of skills from the traditional analyst/programmer division. In the modelling phase, the developers need excellent communication skills, knowledge of and interest in the users and their business, fluency in the use of structure diagrams, and an understanding of the role of the model in the subsequent development. In the function phase, the developers mainly need traditional programming skills. In the implementation phase, the developers need a knowledge of and an interest in computers, database systems, JCL, and the myriad other technical aspects of the target environment. Here fits the computer buff who is really not interested in users but who loves playing with the machine.

Not the least of the advantages of JSD is this more coherent division of labour.

6.1.4 JSP Doesn't Apply To Me

The not-applying-to-me syndrome is here discussed in the context of JSP, but it is certainly more general than this. Of course people often don't give the real reason they don't want to do something and it may be worth asking if they have any other reasons before jumping in with answers.

The following are some comments on some instances of the syndrome.

JSP is fine for small problems, but not for larger, practical problems. Through limitations of time, courses often use only small examples to illustrate the steps and techniques of the method. A characteristic of the examples is taken to delimit the range of applicability. To refute the point, there is no alternative but to tackle larger problems such as the two case studies in Part Three. Of course, if by "larger, practical problems" the speaker means system development problems for which the specification is not clear, then he is right. Some other techniques, such as are in JSD, will be needed.

JSP doesn't apply to on-line problems. See Chapters 2.3 and 3.2. The reason for this misconception is a combination of not understanding that the data streams relevant to JSP are the whole series of inputs and outputs to and from the terminal; not understanding the role of program inversion in those environments that need it; and not understanding that the job distinction between the analyst, who dismembers the conversation, and the programmer, who deals with single message pairs, leads to a premature and destructive decomposition of the program. If the analyst is doing part of the programming, JSP covers part of the analyst's job too.

JSP is good for complicated problems, but I only ever write small programs. This is true to the extent that the investment in learning a method has to be set against its subsequent use. The objection is sometimes combined with the on-line point above. If the analyst is prematurely cutting a programming problem into bits, then programming one bit will appear a small problem. Programs that deal with complicated conversations are not small.

JSP does not apply to programming for small computers. This is ridiculous. Probably it originates with the belief that the results of using a method in programming are bound to be inefficient. People say that they can't use structured programming on a project because the implementation constraints look as though they might be tight. The fallacy is connected with the memory, for many only a folk memory, of the introduction of high-level languages. An assembler programmer could program more efficiently. Similarly, program generators like report writers and on-line development tools sometimes produce less efficient programs. Progress has become identified with implementation inefficiency.

This is a fallacy because optimisation is still possible after the four steps of JSP. A correct program should be developed first and then, if necessary, made more efficient. Some possible optimisation techniques are discussed in Jackson [1]. The dismemberment technique discussed in Chapter 2.4 is probably the same technique that is needed to split up a program into a number of overlaid parts.

JSP does not apply to mathematical programming. This statement needs qualification, not refutation. See Section 2.5.3.

JSP does not apply to low-level software. See the short paper on designing a microcode module, "Structured Programming techniques in interrupt-driven routines", reprinted at the end of Part Three.

JSP is a technique that may help very bad programmers reach an acceptable standard, but it has nothing to offer a good programmer like me. You have to judge for yourself in the context of examples like those discussed in Part Three. People will not be interested in this, or any other method of software develop-

ment, unless, at some level of consciousness, they are dissatisfied with the way they do things now.

JSP is a technique that can only help very clever programmers, but it has nothing to offer an average programmer like me. Experience has shown that JSP can be taught to average and worse-than-average programmers. In the end, though, you have to decide for yourself whether JSP is helping you solve your programming problems.

JSP doesn't apply to me because very little of my programming deals with physical data sets. See Section 2.2.4. A data stream is a more general object than a physical dataset.

The databases I work with have fixed or nearly fixed data structures. I therefore haven't the freedom to keep changing data structures to meet slight changes in application program specifications that are demanded by JSP. See Section 2.2.4. The term "data structure" is used in a number of different senses. The JSP sense is not the same as the database sense. Approximately, a database data structure is a pathway through the data that allows the accessing of certain data streams. A JSP data structure is a view of the data in a data stream as seen from the application program, not the database.

References

This reference list contains only articles and books referred to in the text. The reader who would like to investigate other approaches is referred to two other tutorial texts in this series and to their extensive bibliographies: "A Tutorial on Software Design", edited by Freeman and Wasserman, and "Tutorial: Software Design Strategies", edited by Bergland and Gordon.

Gries [1], Jackson [3], and an earlier version of Bergland [1] are also reprinted in this latter tutorial text.

Bergland [1]

"A Guided Tour of Program Design Methodologies"

Computer, Vol. 14, No. 10, October 1981

Dijkstra [1]

A Discipline of Programming

Prentice Hall 1976

Gries [1]

On Structured Programming

Programming Methodology 1978 pages 31-52

Ingevaldsson [1]

JSP: A Practical Method of Program Design
Chartwell-Bratt, Old Orchard, Bickley Road, Kent BR1 2NE, England
(Originally published in Swedish by Studentlitteratur (1977))

Jackson [1]

Principles of Program Design

Academic Press, London (1975)

Jackson [2]

System Development

Prentice Hall, Englewood Cliffs, NJ (1982)

Jackson [3]

Information Systems: Modelling, Sequencing and Transformations

Third International Conference on Software Engineering, 1978

Glossary

Access path. The ordered set of state vectors accessed through a state vector connection by a function process. See Section 4.1.5.

Data stream. An infinitely buffered First-In-First-Out queue. Data streams are one of the two allowed means of process communication in JSD specifications. See Section 4.1.2. See also Section 2.2.4 for a discussion of data streams in JSP.

Dismemberment. A transformation in which the text or state vector of a process is broken into a number of parts for convenient and efficient execution. See Section 4.1.3.

Embedded function. A function process whose only connection with the model is by data stream. See Section 4.3.3.

Imposed function. A function process whose only connection with the model is by state vector inspection. See Section 4.3.3.

JSP. An acronym for Jackson Structured Programming, the subject of Parts Two and Three of the book. See Section 1.1.1.

JSD. An acronym for Jackson System Development, the subject of Parts Four and Five of the book. See Section 1.1.1.

Level-0. The part of the world external to the system that is in the subject matter of the system. See Section 4.2.2.

Level-1. The direct model of the level-0 abstraction. See Section 4.2.2.

Level-2. A further model of the level-1 model, for the purposes of specifying particular functions. See Section 4.3.3.

Marsupial entity. An entity that emerges from the structure of another entity, especially where several interleaved instances exist of the marsupial entity within one instance of the other. See Section 4.4.1.

Model boundary. A conceptual boundary dividing entities and actions included in the model abstraction from those excluded. See Section 4.2.1.

MJSL. An acronym for Michael Jackson Systems Limited, the British software company for which Michael Jackson and the author work. Most of the reprints in this book are extracts from MJSL course material.

Rough merge. A merge of two or more data streams according to the order in which the records become available for reading. See Section 4.1.2.

SID. System Implementation Diagram. A diagram used to describe transformations of processes in the implementation step. Notations for SIDs are described in Section 4.1.3.

SSD. System Specification Diagram. A diagram used to describe interprocess communication in JSD specifications. See Section 4.1.2.

State vector. The local variables of a process, including the process text pointer. See Section 4.1.2.

SV inspection. One of the two allowed means of process communication in JSD, in which one process examines the state vector of another. See Section 4.1.2.

The Author

John Cameron has an M.A. degree in mathematics (Cambridge University, 1973) and Part III in mathematics (Cambridge University, 1975). From 1975 to 1977 he worked for Scicon, a British software company, mainly on simulations of communication networks. Since 1977 he has worked with Michael Jackson at Michael Jackson Systems Limited developing, teaching, consulting in, and (peripherally) building software tools to support the methods described in this book.